Ending Hunger:
An Idea Whose Time Has Come

The Hunger Project

PRAEGER SPECIAL STUDIES • PRAEGER SCIENTIFIC

New York • Philadelphia • Eastbourne, UK
Toronto • Hong Kong • Tokyo • Sydney

Library of Congress Cataloging in Publication Data
Main entry under title:

Ending hunger.

Bibliography: p.
Includes index.
1. Food relief.   2. Hunger Project.
3. Hunger.   I. Hunger Project.
HV696.F6E53 1985   363.8'8   85-6469
ISBN 0-03-005549-0

Published in 1985 by Praeger Publishers
CBS Educational and Professional Publishing, a division of CBS Inc.
521 Fifth Avenue, New York, NY 10175, USA

Printed and bound in Italy by Amilcare Pizzi S.p.A.
Design: Massimo Vignelli and Jim Stockton

Praeger Publishers International Offices
Orders from outside the United States
should be sent to the appropriate address
listed below. Orders from areas not
listed below should be placed through
CBS International Publishing
383 Madison Avenue
New York, NY 10175 USA.

Australia, New Zealand
Holt Saunders, Pty, Ltd., 9 Waltham St.,
Artarmon, N. S. W. 2064, Sydney, Australia

Canada
Holt, Rinehart & Winston of Canada,
55 Horner Ave., Toronto, Ontario,
Canada M8Z 4X6

Europe, the Middle East, & Africa
Holt Saunders, Ltd., 1 St. Anne's Road,
Eastbourne, East Sussex, England BN21 3UN

Japan
Holt Saunders, Ltd., Ichibancho Central
Building, 22-1 Ichibancho, 3rd Floor,
Chiyodaku, Tokyo, Japan

Hong Kong, Southeast Asia
Holt Saunders Asia, Ltd., 10 Fl,
Intercontinental Plaza, 94 Granville Road,
Tsim Sha Tsui East, Kowloon, Hong Kong

Manuscript submissions should be sent to the
Editorial Director, Praeger Publishers,
521 Fifth Avenue, New York, NY 10175 USA

The Hunger Project Edition

Contents

Ending Hunger:
An Idea Whose Time Has Come

**Ending Hunger:
An Idea Whose Time Has Come**

Ending Hunger: The Time to Begin Is Now

World hunger is not "news"—it is the norm.

Given that we live in a kind of "media age," what we pay attention to often depends on what is prominent in the media at the moment.

An apartment-house fire, an airplane crash, a murder in our city—these are the items of interest that make up our daily news diet. As discrete events, relevant largely only to the current moment, they come and go in our lives with little real impact. They speak to no enduring concern.

And then there are the really important matters of our time, underlying issues that rarely make it to the news because there are no "events"—in the news sense—connected with them. To our personal and planetary loss, these issues do not often emerge from the background to enter our daily concerns.

We do not see, therefore, how their existence—not as events, but as processes—tangibly affects and shapes life for us on the planet. We rarely make any connection between what we call "our lives" and these underlying processes.

The persistence of world hunger is one of those issues that permeates the background of life. With the exception of the occasional news-making event—typically, a famine in which the human disaster is so acute that it cannot be ignored—hunger lives as a process, a persistence, a chronic condition. People die day in, day out; and because this is the norm, it is not "news."

For those of us who are adequately fed and for whom food is a commonplace of daily life, hunger—if it is thought of at all—is something "out there"; something tragic, horrible, awful; something we wish did not exist. It is not, however, something we keep front and center as one of our primary and fundamental concerns.

Imagine our concern—and the attention of the world's media—were an earthquake to strike San Francisco, killing 35,000 people in a single day.

Imagine our concern were a virus to descend on London, killing 18 children a minute without stop, week after week after week.

Imagine our concern were nuclear weapons to explode in the capitals of the world's major industrial countries, killing 13 million people and maiming and injuring a billion more in the surrounding countryside.

35,000 people die each day from hunger. These are precisely the figures of human devastation resulting from hunger: 1 billion of us chronically undernourished; 13–18 million of us dead a year; 35,000 of us a day; 24 of us (18 of whom are children) a minute. Yet because we view hunger in the background of life, this terrible toll does not enter our headlines, nor, for most of us, our concerns.

For most of us. But not for all.

Today, even as you read, an unprecedented outpouring of public sentiment, concern, and commitment is gathering. Quietly and without fanfare, individuals throughout the planet are declaring their personal commitment to a world without hunger. One by one by one, as *individuals,* not as a part of a movement, men and women in North and South America, Europe, Asia, Africa, and elsewhere are looking into their lives and their world, and choosing to include hunger as one of their life concerns and personal commitments.

They do so on their own, without direction from government, without prodding from the media, without any particular encouragement from their leaders.

They come from every country, worship in every faith, speak in every language. They live in the world's richest countries and in the poorest; some work on the cutting edge of computer technology, and others farm their tribal lands with the same methods as did their grandfather's grandfathers.

What unites them all is their common stand, a commitment, a declaration for the end of the persistence of hunger and starvation by the end of this century. Out of their stand, they are taking a leadership role in the emergence of a worldwide, grass-roots commitment that is unique to our time.

This growing expression of commitment goes largely unreported and unnoticed in the media age. No matter. These are the people the late Buckminster Fuller called "little individuals," men and women who may be unknown to history but who nonetheless are boldly determined to direct the world in which they live.

Looking out at their world, they ask themselves the question, "What will I do to cause the end of hunger?" Their answers, multiplied a millionfold, arrived at newly and authentically each day, are literally speeding up the process of history by ensuring that the end of hunger is an act of creation rather than an event that occurs through the inevitable passage of time.

The commitment to end hunger is speeding up the process of history.

This book is a product of the demand on the part of thousands upon thousands of these individuals for potent, powerful, accessible information about world hunger, its persistence, and its end. They are not experts; they have not studied the issues of development, food production, and population growth in depth. Yet they know that in order to increase their own ability to create the end of hunger, they need to be aware of the essential information and the important thinking taking place on these issues.

They are demanding a new kind of information—information that empowers their stand and enables them to be more effective in expressing their commitment; information that is accessible, comprehensive, and up to date; information that makes available both facts and points of view, and distinguishes between the two; information for people who have a job to do in the world and want the tools to get that job done.

Ending Hunger: An Idea Whose Time Has Come was created to fulfill that demand. It is intended as a tribute to those men and women for whom hunger is a personal and daily concern—not because they themselves are hungry, but because they themselves are committed.

This book is intended also for all individuals who are willing to be responsible for the state of their planet; who want their life to have made a real difference; who have a vision of a world that works and the commitment to realize their vision.

In other words, this book has been written for you.

3

About This Book

This is a sourcebook and road map to the issue of hunger.

Ending Hunger: An Idea Whose Time Has Come will give you access to the essential facts, data, and information about world hunger. Culled by our researchers from thousands of articles, books, treatises, speeches, and reports, the material in the following pages forms a kind of sourcebook and road map to what otherwise might seem a confusing and even overwhelming subject. We know of no more comprehensive review of the subject than the book you are holding in your hands.

The first section of the book provides an overview of the basic facts of world hunger—the kind of who, what, where, and when information about which the community of experts generally agrees.

Following this overview is an exploration of a diversity of approaches, points of view, and perspectives about five major issues—population, food, foreign aid, national security, and the New International Economic Order—that are at the center of the international debate about ending hunger.

The third section of the book reviews the little-known but substantial, even dramatic, progress the world has achieved and is achieving in ending the persistence of hunger.

The appendices offer a wealth of useful material—key terms, recommended reading, how to contact hunger organizations—that will support you in your continuing education and participation with ending hunger. The appendices also include a brief description of The Hunger Project.

Within the following pages, you will find the answers to basic questions about hunger such as: What is hunger? Where are hunger and starvation located in the world? How widespread is the persistence of hunger? What is it like to be hungry, day in, day out? What is already working to end hunger, and where? The book will also be a reference sourcebook for answering other questions you may have, or for helping you formulate questions you may not have thought of.

There is no one right way to read this book.

There is no one right way to read this book. You may want to begin at the beginning and read it cover to cover. Or you may prefer to explore the first section and the third section to get a basic grounding in the essential facts of world hunger and the progress being achieved in ending it. Or you may wish to review a single issue that interests you—population, for example.

As you familiarize yourself with this book, you will come to know the broad range of thinking being done today about hunger and how to end it. You will meet scores of experts who represent the major schools of thought about the important issues that are interconnected with world hunger. You will learn the basic facts about subjects such as population growth, food production, and foreign aid; simultaneously, you will discover what prominent experts, scientists, and government leaders have to say about these subjects and how they relate to the persistence of hunger.

If we have succeeded, not only will you gain a firm foundation of information, but you will also be able to create for yourself:

A way of interacting with hunger and other global issues that can lead to the resolution, rather than the persistence, of the problem;

A method of sorting through often confusing and contradictory information, which you can use to better understand other global issues as well;

An ability to hold and reconcile divergent viewpoints so that their differences mutually support and reinforce, rather than obstruct, your arriving at a solution;

The principles for action by which intention and vision can be turned into reality.

In the final analysis, this book is not about hunger but about *ending* hunger. As such, it is about an opportunity.

Opportunity is not a word we generally associate with a condition that takes the lives of 35,000 of us each day. Yet perhaps it is hunger, more than any of our other concerns or interests, that provides humanity with its greatest opportunity in these last years of the twentieth century.

Given the facts and figures of hunger, we have demonstrated to ourselves that we know how to end it. The opportunity, therefore, is to achieve that which is achievable; to make a difference with one of the fundamental global issues that underlies our existence.

The opportunity is to achieve that which is achievable—the end of hunger by the end of the century.

We have an opportunity to transcend the differences of nations and religions and ideologies by working together to address the most fundamental need of all—the need for food.

We have an opportunity to learn and grow by achieving the end of hunger, and by so doing to begin developing the skill, experience, knowledge, and self-confidence to tackle other formidable global issues.

We have an opportunity to make our lives matter, to recognize our own personal power and responsibility for our planet, to perceive what needs to be done and do it.

The time to begin is now.

Basic Facts about World Hunger

What Is Hunger?

Hunger: a strong desire for food; the weakness, debilitation, or pain caused by a prolonged lack of food; starvation.[1]

Hunger: 1a: a craving or urgent need for food or a specific nutrient; b: an uneasy sensation occasioned by the lack of food; c: a weakened condition brought about by prolonged lack of food; 2: a strong desire.[2]

All of us have been "hungry" at some time or other. This usually means simply that we have an appetite. But the hunger experienced by hundreds of millions of people on our planet is not an appetite that comes and goes; it is a consuming, debilitating, minute-by-minute, day-after-day experience. Hunger—the persistent, chronic, relentless condition—keeps people from working productively and thinking clearly. It decreases their resistance to disease. It can be intensely painful. Prolonged hunger can result in permanent damage to body and mind. And, ultimately, if hunger goes on long enough, it kills.

Kamala Markandaya, the Indian writer, evokes the horror and pain of hunger in personal terms:

There is a gnawing and a pain as if your very vitals were being devoured.

For hunger is a curious thing: at first it is with you all the time, waking and sleeping and in your dreams, and your belly cries out insistently, and there is a gnawing and a pain as if your very vitals were being devoured, and you must stop it at any cost, and you buy a moment's respite even while you know and fear the sequel. Then the pain is no longer sharp but dull, and this too is with you always, so that you think of food many times a day and each time a terrible sickness assails you, and because you know this you try to avoid the thought, but you cannot, it is with you. Then that too is gone, all pain, all desire, only a great emptiness is left, like the sky, like a well in drought, and it is now that the strength drains from your limbs, and you try to rise and find you cannot, or to swallow water and your throat is powerless, and both the swallow and the effort of retaining the liquid tax you to the uttermost.[3]

In the following excerpt from Loretta Schwartz-Nobel's book, *Starving in the Shadow of Plenty,* a woman from Boston describes the obsessive quality of a life in which one's total energy must go toward getting enough food simply to stay alive.

I've had no income and I've paid no rent for many months. My landlord let me stay. He felt sorry for me because I had no money. The Friday before Christmas he gave me ten dollars. For days I had had nothing but water. I knew I needed food; I tried to go out but I was too weak to walk to the store. I felt as if I were dying. I saw the mailman and told him I thought I was starving. He brought me food and then he made some phone calls and that's when they began delivering these lunches. But I had already lost so much weight that five meals a week are not enough to keep me going.

*I just pray to God I can survive. I keep praying I can have the will to save some
of my food so I can divide it up and make it last. It's hard to save because I
am so hungry that I want to eat it right away. On Friday, I held over two peas from
the lunch. I ate one pea on Saturday morning. Then I got into bed with the taste
of food in my mouth and I waited as long as I could. Later on in the day I ate
the other pea.*

*Today I saved the container that the mashed potatoes were in and tonight, before
bed, I'll lick the sides of the container.*

*When there are bones I keep them. I know this is going to be hard for you to believe
and I am almost ashamed to tell you, but these days I boil the bones till they're soft
and then I eat them. Today there were no bones.[4]*

This intensely dehumanizing and debilitating hunger is experienced by one out
of every five people on the planet.[5]

The facts are staggering:

More than one billion people are chronically hungry.[6]

Every year 13 to 18 million people die as a result of hunger and starvation.[7]

Every 24 hours, 35,000 human beings die as a result of hunger and starvation—
24 every minute, 18 of whom are children under five years of age.[8]

No other disaster compares to the devastation of hunger:

More people have died from hunger in the past two years than were killed in
World War I and World War II combined.[9]

The number of people who die every two days of hunger and starvation is
equivalent to the number who were killed instantly by the Hiroshima bomb.[10]

The worst earthquake in modern history—in China in 1976—killed 242,000
people. Hunger kills that many people every seven days.[11]

The Great Hunger Belt

Most of the hungry people in the world live in the countries that appear shaded
in green on the map in Figure BF. 2. The shaded region—stretching from
Southeast Asia, through the Indian subcontinent and the Middle East, and
throughout the continent of Africa and the equatorial region of Latin America—
is the "Great Hunger Belt."

The shaded countries are those in which hunger exists as a basic, society-wide
issue.[12] They form a remarkably diverse grouping. Many are tropical, others
are not. Many are former colonies, others are not. Some are capitalist; some are
socialist. Most are poor, but some have very high per capita gross national
products (GNPs).

A full 50 percent of the world's hungry people live in just five countries—India,
Bangladesh, Nigeria, Pakistan, and Indonesia. If hunger were eliminated in
India alone, as much as one-third of the world's hunger would be ended.[13]

*More people have died from hunger
in the past two years than were killed
in World War I and World War II
combined.*

**FIGURE BF.1. THE HUNGER CYCLE—
THE HUMAN COST**

Birth to six
months: Protection
from breast milk,
but mothers
sometimes are
overworked and
undernourished

Six months to two
years: Poverty and
lack of parental
knowledge can
mean inadequate
solid foods and
unhygienic living
environment

Adult: Poor diet
and heavy work-
load for pregnant
mothers; one baby
in six is born
underweight

Age three: Listless
child does not
demand stimula-
tion needed for
development

Teenager to adult:
Low-paid job, or
lack of strength;
cannot obtain
adequate diet

Age six: Lack
of energy and
poor school
performance

Source: UNICEF News 113 (1982): 9.

FIGURE BF.2. NATIONS OF THE WORLD IN WHICH HUNGER PERSISTS AS A BASIC, SOCIETY-WIDE ISSUE

The most widely accepted standard of measurement of the existence of hunger is the infant mortality rate (IMR). Hunger exists as a chronic, society-wide condition when the IMR of a nation is greater than 50—that is, when more than 50 children per 1,000 die in the first year of their lives.

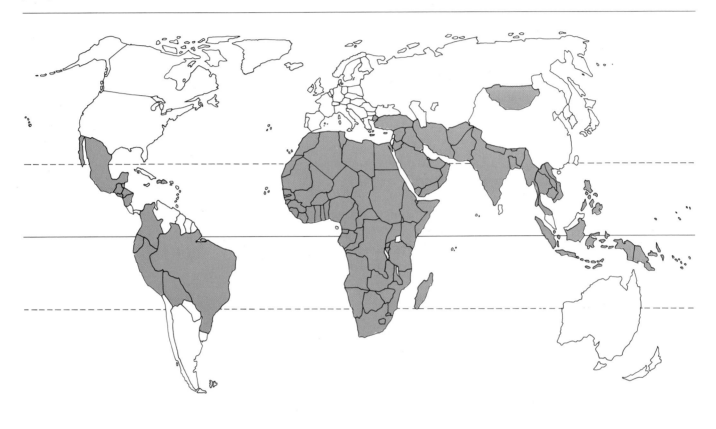

Source: The Hunger Project, *The Ending Hunger Briefing Workbook* (San Francisco: The Hunger Project, 1984).

Types of Hunger

Most people think of hunger as something "out there"—distant, vague, and undefined. Yet it takes distinct forms, each with different causes, effects, and treatments. Dr. Jean Mayer, an internationally recognized expert on nutrition and the president of Tufts University, explains the various kinds and degrees of hunger:

Malnutrition may come about in several ways. A person may not get enough food, which is undernutrition. A diet may lack one essential nutrient or more, giving rise to deficiency diseases such as pellagra, scurvy, rickets, goiter, or the blindness that is caused by vitamin A deficiency. There may be a condition or an illness, either genetic or environmental, that prevents the digestion of food or absorption of nutrients, which is secondary malnutrition. Finally, a person may be taking in too many calories or consuming an excess of one or more components of an otherwise-reasonable diet. Malnutrition in this sense of overnutrition is a disease of affluent people in both the rich and the poor nations.

In areas where food supply is limited the first three causes of malnutrition are often found in combination. In children, a chronic deficiency of calories causes listlessness, muscle wastage, and failure to grow. In adults it leads to a loss of weight and a reduced inclination toward and capacity for productive activity. Undernourished people of all ages are more vulnerable to infection and other illness, and recover more slowly and with much greater difficulty. One of every four children in the developing world will die before the age of five of diseases related to malnutrition.[14]

Hunger is an invisible killer, silently exacting its toll on humanity—particularly on infants and children, the most vulnerable of its victims. For this reason, James P. Grant, executive director of UNICEF, speaking in 1980, called hunger the "silent emergency":

Some 15 million small children die each year.... They die very quietly; one hears very little about them; they come from the world's poorest families, who themselves are the weakest and most powerless members of those powerless families.... Just last month ... there was this terrible earthquake in Algeria where 12,000 people died [that] made the front page of every paper, yet some 35,000 small children died that same day needlessly from the silent emergency—almost triple that, but it did not make the headlines.[15]

What is this "normal" hunger, not part of an outright famine, that accounts for the vast majority of the 13 to 18 million deaths from hunger and hunger-related diseases each year?[16]

Chronic Undernutrition

The most basic and widespread manifestation of hunger today—and the least recognized—is chronic undernutrition.[17] To suffer hunger in the form of chronic undernutrition means that over a long period of time an individual consumes fewer calories and less protein than the body needs. Ultimately, the person is too weakened to resist diseases, work productively, or think clearly. Yet because the condition is chronic, it is often unobserved, undramatic, and continuous. In fact, the lethargy and ill health that result from undernutrition often seem the normal state of life in areas where hunger persists.

Hunger takes distinct forms, with different causes, effects, and treatments.

Some 15 million small children die each year.... They die very quietly.

9

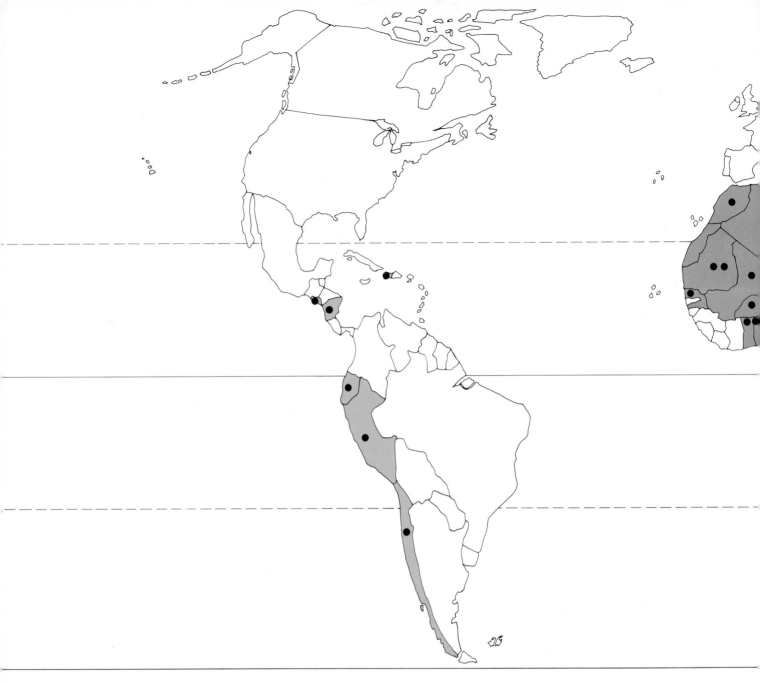

Famines make news because they are not the <u>normal</u> condition. But they account for no more than a small fraction of the hunger-related deaths in the world.

FIGURE BF.3. MAJOR FAMINES BETWEEN 1876 AND 1975

■ AFRICA
Algeria: 1962
Angola: 1971–1974
Burundi: 1972
Central African Republic: 1971–1974
Chad: 1971–1974
Dahomey (Benin): 1971–1974
Egypt: 1974
Ethiopia: 1973–1975
Ghana: 1971–1974
Mali: 1971–1974
Mauritania: 1960, 1971–1974
Morocco: 1960
Mozambique: 1971–1974
Nigeria/Biafra: 1967–1970
Nigeria: 1971–1974
Niger: 1971–1974
Republic of Congo (Zaire): 1960–1961
Rwanda/Urundi: 1943

Sahel: 1968–1973
Senegal: 1971–1974
Sudan: 1973
Togo: 1971–1974
Tunisia: 1958
Upper Volta (Burkina Faso): 1971–1974
■ LATIN AMERICA
Chile: 1960
Ecuador: 1949
El Salvador: 1951
Haiti: 1954
Nicaragua: 1972
Peru: 1970
■ EUROPE
Greece: 1942–1943
Holland: 1944–1945
Poland: 1941–1942
■ USSR
1921–1922, 1932–1934, 1947

■ MIDDLE EAST
Iran: 1962
Iraq: 1954
Syria: 1969
Syria/Palestine: 1945–1949
■ ASIA
Afghanistan: 1971–1972
Bangladesh: 1970–1975
Bengal: 1943–1944, 1950–1955
Cambodia (Kampuchea): 1970, 1975
China: 1876–1879, 1892–1894, 1920–1921,
1928–1929, 1945–1949
India: 1876–1878, 1896–1897, 1899–1900, 1965–1967
Japan: 1945
Korea: 1950–1957, 1959
Pakistan: 1950–1956, 1960, 1971–1973
Philippines: 1972
Taiwan: 1959
Viet Nam: 1946, 1954, 1961, 1964, 1968, 1975

Source: Medard Gabel, *Ho-Ping: Food for Everyone* (Garden City, NY: Doubleday, Anchor Books, 1979), 32.

Chronic undernutrition has particularly severe effects in children. Diseases that a healthy, well-nourished body would quickly throw off—such as measles, diphtheria, diarrhea, and respiratory problems—often mean death for children whose bodies are malnourished. In fact, many children who are thought to have died from diseases such as these were actually victims of undernutrition.

Malnutrition

Malnutrition may not cause death, but it can cripple, maim, and deform.

Another "invisible" form that hunger can take is malnutrition, a condition that occurs when an individual's diet has a relative deficiency or excess of specific nutrients vital to good health. Malnutrition may not cause death, but it can cripple, maim, and deform.

Lack of vitamin C can lead to scurvy, loss of teeth, and an inability to fight infection. Lack of iron can produce anemia and loss of energy. Lack of iodine can produce physical crippling and even mental retardation. Lack of vitamin A can cause blindness; 250,000 children become blind every year as a result of this insufficiency.[18] Nutritional anemias are found in developing countries among 20 to 25 percent of children, 20 to 40 percent of women, and up to 10 percent of adult males.[19] In Latin America and the Caribbean, studies indicate that malnutrition is the primary cause of or major contributing factor in 60 percent of the deaths of children under the age of five.[20]

Goiter, generally attributed to an inadequate intake of iodine, affects at least 200 million people in the world. According to the World Bank, "Available evidence suggests that iodine deficiency can stunt physical and mental development, and reduce energy and motivation. In communities that have an exceptionally high incidence of goiter, 4 percent or more of the children may be deaf-mutes or cretins."[21]

Malabsorptive Hunger

Malabsorptive hunger, a condition that often occurs along with undernutrition and malnutrition, means that the body is incapable of absorbing nutrients from the food that has been eaten. This type of hunger is often due to parasites in the intestinal tract or to severe protein deficiency. Studies show that people can lose up to 20 percent and occasionally more of the nutritional value of their food in this way.[22]

Malabsorptive hunger is common where water is contaminated and where there is an absence of medical care.

Seasonal Hunger

Seasonal hunger occurs annually before each harvest.

In some parts of the world, seasonal hunger occurs annually before each harvest, when the food from the last harvest runs out. Until the new crop comes in, people may be hungry for weeks or even months at a time. As a result of this seasonal hunger, people often enter a harvest season too weak to cope with its heavy physical-work demand.

Where seasonal hunger is prevalent, it is viewed as a "natural" part of the annual cycle. In these regions hunger is part of the culture, and words describing hunger are part of the everyday language:

12

In the language of the Iteso people of Eastern Uganda, as in many African languages, each month of the year is given a descriptive name. August—the month after the millet harvest is "the month of the big stomachs"; but, in poignant contrast, the pre-harvest month of May, when the granaries are empty, is "the month when the children wait for food."

All over the vast savannah areas of Africa, where the main staple foods are cereals and legumes, the lives of millions of people are conditioned to the rhythm of the rains, the harvest, and the pre-harvest "hungry months" when grain is scarce and often full of weevils, and when they must look to the perennially-available but low-protein cassava for their major source of food.

It is in these hungry months, when the millet crop is growing and ripening, oh how slowly, under the brazen sun that the spectre of malnutrition stalks the land. It is in these months that many children, weakened by malnourishment, can die of illnesses which would hardly affect normal children. Growing children are always the first to be affected, and are the most seriously affected by food scarcity. It is, perhaps, not by chance, that the month of May is called "the month when the children wait for food."[23]

The month of May is called "the month when the children wait for food."

Famine

Famine is as old as recorded history. In recent years, major devastating famines have struck Bangladesh, Kampuchea (formerly Cambodia), and the eastern region of Nigeria (which temporarily seceded as Biafra). Since the beginning of the 1980s, famine has gripped much of sub-Saharan Africa.

Famine is a widespread lack of access to food that occurs when drought, flood, or war disrupts the availability of food in a society of chronically undernourished people. Famine occurs in countries that do not have the institutional capacity to compensate for bad weather or political disruption. Although some countries—in, for instance, Western Europe and North America—may experience floods, heat waves, or droughts, these disasters do not result in famine, because the social system can absorb them.

During a famine, food may actually be present within the stricken area, but large segments of the population may not have access to it. Food may be so high-priced that only the wealthy can afford to buy it. Or delivery and distribution systems may break down, causing food to pile up on docks or in warehouses and thus not reach those who need it. In some cases, food from the stricken country has even been exported to neighboring countries.

Because of its acute and terrible nature, famine and the resultant starvation have a particularly disruptive impact on a society. In the 1840s, a serious famine struck Ireland. A survivor of the Irish potato famine later wrote:

It didn't matter who was related to you, your friend was whoever would give you a bite to put in your mouth. Sport and pastimes disappeared. Poetry, music and dancing stopped. They lost and forgot them all and when the times improved in other respects, these things never returned as they had been. The famine killed everything.[24]

Because famine is the most visible and dramatic manifestation of hunger, it is not surprising that it has received greater media attention than have the other types of hunger. Famine makes news precisely because it is not the *normal*

In children, chronic protein-energy malnutrition causes listlessness, muscle wastage, and failure to grow. If chronic deficiencies are severe, the damage may be permanent.

FIGURE BF.4. THE EFFECT OF PROTEIN-ENERGY MALNUTRITION ON GROWTH

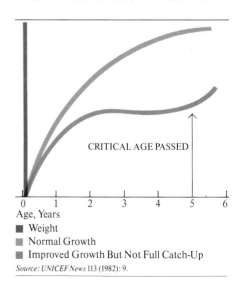

CRITICAL AGE PASSED

Age, Years
■ Weight
■ Normal Growth
■ Improved Growth But Not Full Catch-Up
Source: UNICEF News 113 (1982): 9.

condition. Yet it accounts for no more than a small fraction of the hunger-related deaths. The overwhelming majority of hunger-related deaths are caused by "normal hunger" (undernutrition, malnutrition, and malabsorptive hunger). These often go unnoticed and unreported.

Who Are the Hungry?

About 40 percent of the world's hungry are children; most of the rest are women.

Behind the grim statistics, the clinical definitions, and the maps are *people*. They are men, women, and children, with hopes and dreams, loves and hates, strengths and weaknesses, who find themselves caught in the circumstances of hunger. They are African refugees, Peruvian peasants, beggars in the streets of Calcutta, barrio dwellers in Mexico City, subsistence farmers in Indonesia, women who tend herds of livestock in Kenya. About 40 percent of the world's hungry are children; most of the rest are women.[25]

The majority of hungry people live and work in rural areas. Many are landless laborers or tenant farmers who do not own their land. If they do, their land is a small plot, and they lack access to the credit and technical support needed to make the land productive. There are also a large number of hungry people living in sprawling urban slums, ghettos, and shanty towns.

Although the circumstances in which they live are as varied as the many cultures of the human race, the hungry have one thing in common—they live in *poverty*. Here is how the Brandt Commission describes this condition:

Few people in the North have any detailed conception of the extent of poverty in the Third World or of the forms that it takes. Many hundreds of millions of people in the poorer countries are preoccupied solely with survival and elementary needs. For them work is frequently not available or, when it is, pay is very low and conditions often barely tolerable. Homes are constructed of impermanent materials and have neither piped water nor sanitation. Electricity is a luxury. Health services are thinly spread and in rural areas only rarely within walking distance.... Permanent insecurity is the condition of the poor. There are no public systems of social security in the event of unemployment, sickness or death of a wage-earner in the family. Flood, drought or disease affecting people or livestock can destroy livelihoods without hope of compensation....

It is a condition of life so limited as to be, in the words of the President of the World Bank, "below any rational definition of human decency."[26]

Hungry people most often are illiterate, unhealthy, and without political power. They give birth to more children than do other people, and their children die at a much higher rate. Their life expectancy is considerably shorter than that of individuals in the developed world.

Hungry people are remarkably self-reliant, productive, and skilled at surviving.

Yet, their circumstances notwithstanding, hungry people are far from helpless victims. The image of a hungry person holding out an empty rice bowl is hardly the normal situation—hungry people are remarkably self-reliant, productive, and skilled at surviving. And they are doing the lion's share of the work to end hunger. Above all else, the one billion hungry are those who most want hunger to end.

If, say some observers, all the activities taking place in the world to end hunger and poverty could really be measured, the finding would be that the poor and hungry themselves are doing nearly all of the work. Despite circumstances

Per Capita GNP	
$500	
$5,500	

Deaths per 1,000 Live Births	
120	
20	

Grams of Protein per Day per Person	
54	
97	

Number of People per Doctor	
3,490	
680	

Life Expectancy in Years	
52	
71	

Literacy	
43%	
97%	

▢ Less Developed Country
◼ Developed Country

Source: U.S. Presidential Commission on World Hunger, *Overcoming World Hunger: The Challenge Ahead*, abridged version (Washington, DC: U.S. Government Printing Office, June 1980), 4.

that have looked hopeless, since World War II hundreds of millions of people have not only survived but indeed have risen above these circumstances and ended hunger in their lives.

Pran Chopra, a prominent Indian journalist, says:

The poor are a productive asset that has been thrown out of business by the inequities heaped upon [them]....They have been deprived of their productive capacity and the means of production....

Once this injustice is ended.... the poor will have their production to contribute, not just the spectacle of their poverty.

The poor are therefore a challenge to everyone's economic and social ingenuity, to everyone's power to do what each country and every person can do to reverse this injustice until it ends.[27]

These are some of the basic, agreed-upon facts of world hunger.

By the year 2000, the persistence of hunger can be eradicated from every nation on earth.

The most important fact of all, however, is not that people are dying from hunger, but that people are dying unnecessarily. As we shall see later in this book, the world's community of experts agrees that by the year 2000, the persistence of hunger can be eradicated from every nation on earth. No one need die from hunger.

In study after study, prestigious international commissions have come to one conclusion: Humanity now possesses the resources, technology, and know-how to end hunger.

The Brandt Commission, composed of leaders from seventeen rich and poor countries, conducted a two-year study. A major conclusion reflected wide consensus within the expert community:

Mankind has never before had such ample technical and financial resources for coping with hunger and poverty. The immense task can be tackled once the necessary collective will is mobilized. What is necessary can be done, and must be done.[28]

NOTES

1 *American Heritage Dictionary of the English Language,* 1981, s.v. "hunger."

2 *Webster's Ninth New Collegiate Dictionary,* 1984, s.v. "hunger."

3 Kamala Markandaya, *Nectar in a Sieve,* 2nd American ed. (New York: John Day Company, 1955), 121–22.

4 Loretta Schwartz-Nobel, *Starving in the Shadow of Plenty* (New York: G. P. Putnam's Sons, 1981), 35–36.

5 Estimates of the number of chronically hungry people in the world range from as low as 300 million to 2½ billion, depending upon how an adequate diet is defined. This discussion estimates that approximately 1 billion of the world's 4.7 billion people are chronically undernourished—a figure that has been used by the World Food Council. Statistics are from *1983 World Population Data Sheet* (Washington, DC: Population Reference Bureau, 1983); United Nations, World Food Council, *Food Strategies: Overcoming Hunger Country by Country* (DESI.E76), May 1980; and Philip Nobile and John Deedy, eds., *The Complete Ecology Fact Book* (Garden City, NY: Doubleday/Anchor Books, 1972), 272.

6 Ibid.

7   Roy L. Prosterman, *The Decline in Hunger-Related Deaths,* The Hunger Project Papers, no. 1, ed. Beverly Tangri (San Francisco: The Hunger Project, May 1984): 9.

8   Ibid., ii.

9   *World Book Encyclopedia,* 1983, s.v. "World War I" and "World War II."

10 *Encyclopedia Americana,* 1982, s.v. "Hiroshima."

11 The earthquake referred to occurred July 28, 1976, in Tangshan, China. *Information Please Almanac 1983,* 37th ed. (New York: A&W Publishers, 1982), 660.

12 We define countries in which hunger exists as a basic, society-wide issue as those with an infant mortality rate (IMR) above 50 per 1,000 live births.

    Achievement of an IMR of 50 as a minimum goal for meeting basic needs has been cited by the Third United Nations Development Decade, UNICEF, the World Health Organization, and the RIO study (*Reshaping the International Order: A Report to the Club of Rome,* coordinated by Jan Tinbergen). (See note 25.)

13 These estimates are based on the common correlation between a high rate of infant mortality and the prevalence of hunger and malnutrition in a society.

14 U.S., Congress, House, Committee on Agriculture, *World Hunger Situation,* prepared statement by Dr. Jean Mayer, 97th Cong., 1st sess., 23 July 1981, 386.

15 Canada, *Parliamentary Papers* (Commons), no. 25, "Proceedings and Evidence of the Special Committee on North-South Relations," 32nd Parliament, 1st sess., 18 November 1980, 25:6.

16 Chronic malnutrition accounts for far more deaths than does famine. Except for China's massive famine of 1960–1961, which may have taken over 8 million lives, no famine in modern times has accounted for more than a tenth of the deaths that result each year from all forms of malnutrition. The other single largest famine in recent years, the Biafran famine of 1968–1969, resulted in an estimated 1 million deaths. Since that time, the number of deaths caused by famine has steadily declined, largely because of the distribution of food aid from developed countries. Worldwatch Institute estimates, in Lester Brown, *State of the World 1984* (New York: W. W. Norton, 1984), 188.

17 U.S. Presidential Commission on World Hunger, *Overcoming World Hunger: The Challenge Ahead* (Washington, DC: U.S. Government Printing Office, March 1980), 16.

18 United Nations, World Health Organization, *Strategies for the Prevention of Blindness in National Programmes: A Primary Health Care Approach,* 1984, 48.

19 United Nations, Food and Agriculture Organization, *The Fourth World Food Survey,* FAO Statistics Series, no. 11 (1977): 48.

20 Roy L. Prosterman, *The Decline in Hunger-Related Deaths,* 3.

21 World Bank, *World Development Report 1980* (New York: Oxford University Press, 1980), 60.

22 John Field, School of Nutrition, Tufts University, Medford, MA, telephone communication with The Hunger Project, San Francisco, 23 July 1984.

23 Jim McDowell, "The Month When the Children Wait for Food," *UNICEF News* 85, no. 3 (1975): 27–28.

24 Roger J. McHugh, "The Famine in Irish Oral Tradition," *The Great Famine: Studies in Irish History, 1845–52,* eds. R. Dudley Edwards and T. Desmond Williams (New York: New York University Press, 1957), 434–35.

25 Jan Tinbergen et al., *Reshaping the International Order: A Report to the Club of Rome* (New York: E. P. Dutton & Co., 1976), 28.

26 Independent Commission on International Development Issues, *North-South: A Program for Survival* (Cambridge, MA: MIT Press, 1980), 49–50.

27 Pran Chopra, "The Poor Are Not a Burden," *A Shift in the Wind,* no. 11 (October 1981): 4.

28 Independent Commission, *North-South: A Program for Survival,* 16.

Introduction to the Issues

We turn from basic facts about hunger to a more controversial arena.

We now turn from the basic, agreed-upon facts of world hunger to a more controversial arena, one that can be summed up by these questions:

What are the causes of hunger?

Why does hunger persist?

What are the solutions and ways to end hunger?

Clearly, there is no one right answer to any of these questions. Given the scope and importance of an intractable and persistent problem such as world hunger, there are many perspectives and approaches to the problem as well as many vigorously argued views and interpretations about how to end it.

In the following pages, we will hear from the proponents of many of these perspectives on and approaches to hunger. The world's foremost agricultural experts, development theoreticians and practitioners, political leaders, and scientists, as well as Third World farmers, peasant leaders, and entrepreneurs, will share with us, in their own words, their perspectives about the causes of and solutions to hunger.

The individuals quoted in these chapters have been selected not only because of their knowledge, expertise, and stature within their field, but also because they represent important schools of thought. Taken as a whole, the many dozens of men and women cited in the text articulate the full range of the diversity of thinking and opinion on the important issues surrounding hunger. Obviously, the excerpts included in this book do not and cannot reveal the full breadth of their individual scholarship, knowledge, and viewpoint.

No matter what perspective or approach to viewing hunger they have adopted, these important voices uniformly believe that hunger does not exist in isolation. To talk of hunger—and the end of hunger—is to talk of poverty, population growth, the international economy, development, employment, agriculture, energy resources, and much, much more. In seeking the elimination of hunger, we are immediately confronted by a myriad of global forces—economic, social, ideological, political, philosophical, cultural, even psychological—that hold hunger in place.

Five major issues are examined.

In the next section of this book we take up five major issues surrounding the persistence of hunger. They are:

Population

Food

Foreign Aid

National Security

The New International Economic Order

Obviously, these are not the only pertinent issues. A comprehensive listing might also include chapters on the international debt crisis, political power and oppression, land reform, the role of women in Third World countries, literacy and education, employment opportunities, sanitation and health care, environmental degradation, and many others.

We have chosen to explore the five issues listed because they have been part of the international debate long enough to be surrounded by a body of accepted facts as well as a wide range of viewpoints. Were you to attend an international conference on development, these issues would figure prominently in the discussion.

While they are of real importance and even urgency in the world, we are not suggesting that these issues necessarily need to be resolved before hunger can end. Indeed, hunger has already ended as a basic issue in scores of nations—sometimes with massive foreign aid, sometimes without; sometimes accompanied by large-scale programs designed to lower the birth rate, at other times with little emphasis on population planning.

In organizing the five issue chapters, we have sought to distinguish clearly between (1) the generally agreed-upon facts at the heart of an issue and (2) the points of view, interpretations, opinions, and approaches that could be pursued, given those facts. While it may seem self-evident that such a distinction is crucial in order to effectively carry out any research or examination, often what appears to be the complexity and overwhelming nature of the subject of hunger results from a failure to clarify this distinction.

We have sought to distinguish clearly between agreed-upon facts and points of view.

Each issue chapter begins with a statement of some of the basic facts and background about which people of all viewpoints and perspectives widely agree. The chapter on population, for example, provides data on the size of the world's population, how it has changed over time, the geographical distribution of population, and how birth and death rates differ in different parts of the world.

Next is a review of the major points of view about which policies and actions need to be pursued in order to end hunger. Rather than synthesize this thinking for you, we have provided a forum in which the leading proponents of these policies and actions can speak directly, in their own words.

For example, in the issue area of foreign aid, one school of thought holds that foreign aid has been effective in the past and is needed to promote development and end hunger. Citing different evidence and representing another perspective, a second school of thought finds that foreign-aid programs have made no difference or have been an impediment to development and thus to ending hunger.

Occasionally, these powerfully articulated and forcefully argued approaches may seem adversarial, even mutually exclusive. Yet precisely because they provide a full range of thinking, viewpoints, alternatives, and options, they can clarify and illuminate what will make a difference in ending hunger.

Our intention in the following pages is not only to provide a sound base of information about these issues, but also to offer a framework or context for examining, holding, and thinking about them. That context is one in which, within the overall commitment to the end of hunger, all points of view and interpretations—even those that appear to be in disagreement—can be seen to contribute to the resolution of this problem.

All points of view can contribute to ending hunger.

What you are about to read, then, consciously and purposefully embraces many positions and points of view about the issues surrounding the persistence of hunger. It is not just one more point of view; it is an attempt to create a forum in which all ideas can be heard, illuminated, clarified, and understood.

At the same time, it is not in the forum of ideas that a persistent, intractable problem such as hunger and starvation will be resolved. Such a forum may help articulate the various options and approaches that can be pursued, but it is insufficient for resolving the problem, and even for identifying which solution or pathway will ultimately take us to the end of hunger.

It is from committed action that the end of hunger will come.

It is from committed action that this resolution will come.

While no current position or path will take us to the end, any one of the solutions or pathways that we can currently envision will get us to the place where we can see the path to the end. As the world moves along the various pathways toward the end of hunger, entirely new ideas, approaches, and policy recommendations will emerge and yet-unimagined pathways will open up to us.

We are not in danger of taking the wrong path—we are in danger of not taking any path at all. It is always safer and more comfortable to wait until we are certain before we move. However, waiting for the "right" answer is almost invariably a prescription for doing nothing at all, while getting on a path—even if it is mistaken—generates enough motion to give us information about which path is more effective.

The truth is that taking informed action on all available paths is what you do when you are seriously committed to finding the answer to any problem. If our child is ill and the first thing we try doesn't work, we don't just give up or keep trying only that solution—we visit other doctors, consult with specialists, read more child-care books, buy additional medicines, seek advice from our friends. And we don't stop until the problem is resolved.

Another danger is so believing in our chosen path that we exclude other paths, options, and approaches. Of course, resolving any problem depends on some people being dedicated to a single answer. By strongly holding to their viewpoint, they contribute something that would otherwise be missing.

Most of us, however, can be most effective if we listen to all other perspectives, if we sufficiently inform ourselves about the other alternatives, and if we support other individuals on the paths they have chosen for themselves.

We can teach ourselves to select paths of action that will ultimately end hunger.

Our dilemma: to be on a path with sufficient intentionality to move along it, but to be sufficiently aware of what's outside the path to be able to correct the errors in our chosen path. By moving down our chosen path with blinders off, we have the opportunity to teach ourselves how to select the path that will ultimately open up the way to the end of hunger.

The challenge, then, is not primarily to create new technological breakthroughs or more productive agricultural techniques—the world's experts agree that there is no technical, financial, or physical constraint on our ability to end hunger. Never before has the world had at its command such ample resources for coping with the problem.

The real challenge is: Are we, as a world community, prepared to move along whatever paths are available to us now, in a way that produces a breakthrough that will achieve the end of hunger? Are we willing to bring forth a new kind of commitment that will ensure that what can be done shall be done?

This is the opportunity before us as a world community—an opportunity that, if seized, will put us on the pathway to the end of hunger by the end of the century.

Population

It is a common assumption that the issue of hunger is largely a question of the relationship of people to food: To put it in its simplest terms, is there enough food on the planet to feed the people who exist?

In this chapter, we will get underneath this generalization to explore the complex of factors—biological, ecological, economic, moral, and political—which shape the many perspectives on the population issue.

The chapter begins with a presentation of the basic information and background on population about which there is general agreement. The *Basic Facts* section begins with data on population growth and distribution. Three important facts stand out in this discussion: (1) current population growth rates are an unprecedented phenomenon in human history; (2) approximately 50 percent more people will be on the planet by the year 2000 than there were in 1975; and (3) for the first time in recent history, population growth rates have begun to decline.

The *Basic Facts* section concludes with a review of the growing trend throughout the world in support of population-planning programs.

Do high population growth rates contribute to hunger or will more people help to solve the problem?

Turning from the agreed-upon facts, we then explore two schools of thought on the population issue. Within each broad school of thought, we will hear from a number of proponents of various points of view and approaches to the subject of population.

The first school of thought holds that population densities and growth rates in the Third World are contributing to hunger and poverty. Thomas Robert Malthus, Paul Ehrlich, Garrett Hardin, and others believe that population growth limits economic development and may even threaten the survival of the human race. While Ehrlich and others strongly advocate population planning, Hardin focuses more on the problems modern technologies can create by lowering death rates below "natural" levels. Further, we present Third World women speaking out in favor of limiting family size through population planning.

An alternative school of thought holds that population growth is not at the root of hunger and therefore need not be a major focus in the work of ending hunger. Julian Simon's views receive major emphasis. In *The Ultimate Resource*, Simon's widely publicized book, he argues that ending hunger and poverty will occur as a result of larger, not smaller, populations, and as a result of more, not fewer, people. Simon believes that most population-planning programs are immoral. Others feel that population planning is not necessary, because population growth does not contribute to hunger—there are more than enough food and other resources to meet the needs of the current and future world-populations. Denis Goulet and Michael Hudson, Roy Prosterman, and others offer yet another perspective: The real focus of our efforts should be not on population planning but on creating a more equitable economic system so that the poor and hungry can attain self-sufficiency. We will also hear several other points of view: that having many children is an economic necessity in a Third World family; that population planning is largely a smokescreen for neocolonialism and repression by rich nations against the poor; and that the very issue of population planning is immoral and dehumanizing and thus cannot be the foundation of a more equitable and just world order.

Basic Facts

Population Growth and Distribution

Population Densities. In 1983, approximately 4.7 billion people lived on the earth—92 million more than in 1982.[1] This population increase was roughly equal to the combined total populations of Costa Rica, Australia, the United Kingdom, Iraq, and Israel; or to ten times the population of the New York metropolitan area; or to ten times the population of the city of Calcutta.[2]

Table P.1 presents the percentage of the world's population in each of ten major regions. One way to use the information in this table is to imagine that there are only 100 people living in the world. The numbers in the table show how many of these 100 people would live in the different regions, if they were distributed as the current population is.

Population densities differ widely in different parts of the world. For instance, Europe, one of the most prosperous regions in the world, has a relatively high population density. Africa, a continent with severe poverty and hunger problems, has a relatively low population density. Whether the population densities of the present era are desirable is a matter of debate. But what is certain is that current densities and growth rates are a unique phenomenon in human history.

Current population densities and growth rates are unique in history.

Obviously, we can't determine exact figures about early human populations. However, authorities have suggested that 2 million years before the birth of Christ, this "very rare food-gathering biped" numbered around 100,000.[3] By 10,000 B.C.—about the time agriculture was invented—there were about 5–10 million people in the world—about as many as the present population of New York, or London, or Cairo, or Mexico City.[4] By 3000 B.C.—the time of the first dynasty in Egypt—the population may have risen to 100 million. And at the time of the birth of Christ, the world's population was probably about 250 million.[5]

It was around 1750—coincident with the Industrial Revolution—that world population began to expand rapidly. At that time, it was probably a little less than 750 million (about the same as the combined populations of India and Sri Lanka today).[6] About 1800 we reached our first billion; by 1930, the figure was 2 billion. Only thirty years later—in 1960—we reached the third billion; only fifteen years after that—in 1975—came the fourth billion.[7] (See Table P.2.) Until very recently,

TABLE P.1. POPULATION DISTRIBUTION IN TEN MAJOR REGIONS OF THE WORLD

Region	Percentage of the World's Population
East Asia	26
Middle South Asia	22
Africa	11
Europe	10
Latin America	8
Southeast Asia	8
North America	6
USSR	6
Southwest Asia	2
Oceania	1

Source: Derived from Population Reference Bureau, *1983 World Population Data Sheet* (Washington, DC: Population Reference Bureau, 1983).

FIGURE P.1. POPULATION DENSITY OF THE
WORLD'S NATIONS

POPULATION PER SQUARE KILOMETER
- Over 250
- 125–250
- 25–124
- 4–24
- 0–3

Source: Derived from United Nations, Department of International Economic and Social Affairs, *Demographic Yearbook 1982* (ST/ESA/STAT/SER.R/12), 1984, 134–40.

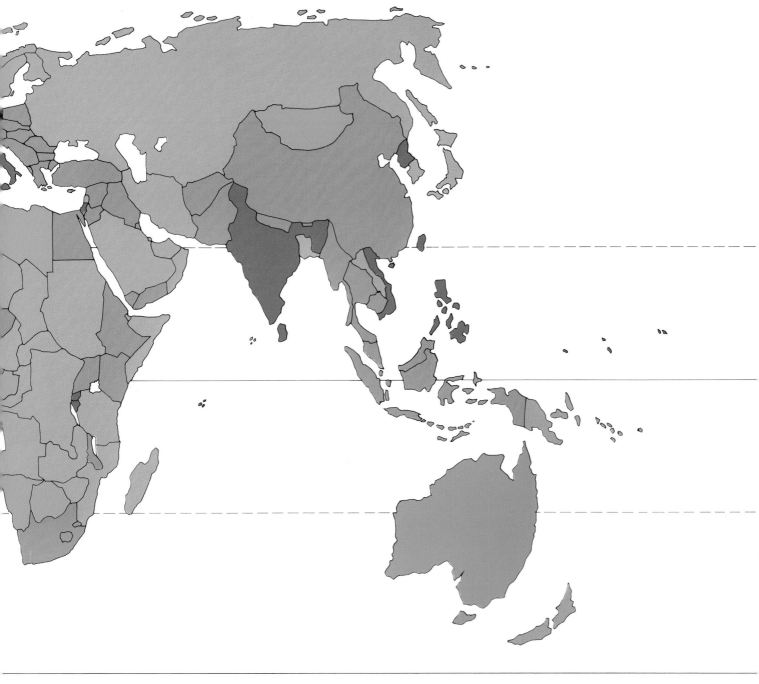

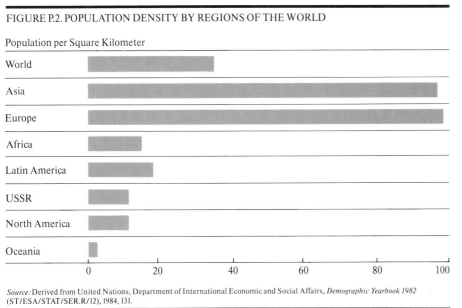

FIGURE P.2. POPULATION DENSITY BY REGIONS OF THE WORLD

Current population densities are an unprecedented phenomenon in human history.

Population per Square Kilometer

World	
Asia	
Europe	
Africa	
Latin America	
USSR	
North America	
Oceania	

0   20   40   60   80   100

Source: Derived from United Nations, Department of International Economic and Social Affairs, *Demographic Yearbook 1982* (ST/ESA/STAT/SER.R/12), 1984, 131.

the *rate* of population growth had been increasing as well. Starting from less than 1 percent per year in 1800, it reached almost 2 percent by the mid-1960s. After that, it began to decline slightly and has continued to do so.[8]

TABLE P.2. WORLD POPULATION GROWTH: 1800–1983

Year	Number of People	Time Taken to Reach
1800	1.0 BILLION	2–5 MILLION YEARS
1930	2.0 BILLION	APPROXIMATELY 130 YEARS
1960	3.0 BILLION	30 YEARS
1975	4.0 BILLION	15 YEARS
1983	4.7 BILLION	8 YEARS

Source: Derived from Jean van der Tak, Carl Haub, and Elaine Murphy, "Our Population Predicament: A New Look," *Population Bulletin* 34, no. 5 (December 1979): 4; and Population Reference Bureau, *1983 World Population Data Sheet* (Washington, DC: Population Reference Bureau, 1983).

Countries with high growth rates tend to be poor and countries with low growth rates tend to be rich, but this is not always true.

Table P.3 lists the five nations that have the highest population growth rates, and the five that have the lowest. Although countries with high growth rates tend to be poor and countries with low growth rates tend to be rich, this is not always the case. Saudi Arabia, one of the world's richest countries, has an annual population growth rate of 3.1 percent. China is poor—its GNP per capita is only $304 (U.S.)—yet its population growth rate is only 1.5 percent per year.[9] Population growth rates for all the countries in the world are pictured in Figure P.5.

Population growth rates vary widely in different nations and in different parts of the world. Before looking at these differences, however, we need to clarify our terms: Because hunger and poverty are significant national issues in many of the developing nations, we will sometimes refer to these nations as a group—normally by the term "Third World," occasionally by the term "developing" nations.

TABLE P.3. POPULATION GROWTH RATES OF THE WORLD'S NATIONS
WORLD'S FASTEST-GROWING NATIONS
(WITH POPULATIONS OF 8 MILLION OR MORE)

Nation	Annual Growth Rate (Percentage)	1983 Population
Kenya	4.1	18.6 MILLION
Syria	3.8	9.7 MILLION
Zimbabwe	3.4	8.4 MILLION
Iraq	3.4	14.5 MILLION
Nigeria	3.3	84.2 MILLION

WORLD'S SLOWEST-GROWING NATIONS
(WITH POPULATIONS OF 10 MILLION OR MORE)

Nation	Annual Growth Rate (Percentage)	1983 Population
West Germany	−0.2	61.5 MILLION
Hungary	0.0	10.7 MILLION
East Germany	0.0	16.7 MILLION
Italy	0.1	56.3 MILLION
United Kingdom	0.1	56.0 MILLION

Source: Population Reference Bureau, *1983 World Population Data Sheet* (Washington, DC: Population Reference Bureau, 1983).

The concept and significance of the Third World is discussed in Michael Todaro's *Economic Development in the Third World:*

The 141 African, Asian, and Latin American member countries of the United Nations often collectively refer to themselves as the Third World. They do this primarily to distinguish themselves from the economically advanced capitalist (First World) and socialist (Second World) countries. Although the precise origin of the term Third World is obscure, it has become widely accepted and utilized by economically poor nations themselves, especially in their negotiations with economically rich nations on critical international controversies relating to trade, aid, energy, natural resource depletion, and dwindling world food supplies. While it is unfortunate that numbers such as First, Second, and Third occasionally bear the regrettable connotation of superiority and inferiority when used in reference to different groups of nations, the fact remains that the term Third World is widely used among developing nations primarily in an effort to generate and represent a new sense of common identity and a growing unity of purpose.[10]

Demographic Transition Theory. Population grows when birth rates exceed death rates. Death rates have been falling, due to better nutrition, vaccinations, sanitation, and a variety of other factors; however, they are still high in the poorest regions, especially Africa. Birth rates, too, are falling nearly everywhere.[11]

Every population that has become industrialized has had decreases in death rates, later followed by decreases in birth rates. This pattern is called the *demographic transition.*[12] Figure P.11 offers the example of two countries, Sweden and Mexico, at different stages of the transition. Sweden's period of rapid population growth occurred during the nineteenth century. By 1930, its population growth had dropped close to replacement levels. By 1983, the growth rate was reported as 0.0 percent.[13] Mexico, on the other hand, is still in a stage of explosive population growth. Death rates began to drop rapidly in the 1930s, but birth rates did not begin to fall until the 1970s.

In general, high population growth rates seem to be associated with high infant mortality rates (IMR), and vice versa: The higher the IMR, the higher the growth rate. Countries with an IMR greater than 50 per thousand live births have an average population growth rate of 2.7 percent. Nations with an IMR of 50 or fewer per thousand live births have an average growth rate of 1.2 percent.[14]

Population Age Structure by Sex. The population age structure by sex—that is, the percentage of population of each sex in different age categories (or cohorts)—is often used to look at questions related to age and sex distribution.[15] If, for example, we want to predict future growth trends and population levels, it helps if we know about age structure. Differing age structures also constitute one source of social and economic differences among nations.

The age structure of a nation's or region's population often is represented by a population pyramid diagram. Figure P.3 shows a population pyramid for the United States. The horizontal bars represent successive age groups. The youngest group ("Under 5" in the example) is at the bottom, while the oldest group ("85+") is at the top. The bars are divided vertically between males and females—females are on the right, males are on the left. The length of each bar, measured on the percent scale at the bottom of the pyramid, indicates the percentage of the total population in that particular category. For example, in 1976 about 3.5 percent of the U.S. population consisted of girls under 5 years of age, and about the same percentage of women were in the 30–34 age bracket.

FIGURE P.3. POPULATION PYRAMID OF THE UNITED STATES ON JANUARY 1, 1976

Age	Year of Birth
85+	BEFORE 1891
80–84	1891–1895
75–79	1896–1900
70–74	1901–1905
65–69	1906–1910
60–64	1911–1915
55–59	1916–1920
50–54	1921–1925
45–49	1926–1930
40–44	1931–1935
35–39	1936–1940
30–34	1941–1945
25–29	1946–1950
20–24	1951–1955
15–19	1956–1960
10–14	1961–1965
5– 9	1966–1970
Under 5	1971–1975

5   0   5
Percent of Population

■ Male
■ Female

Source: Arthur Haupt and Thomas T. Kane, *The Population Reference Bureau's Population Handbook* (Washington, DC: Population Reference Bureau, 1978), 12.

Knowing about population age structure helps to predict future growth trends and population levels.

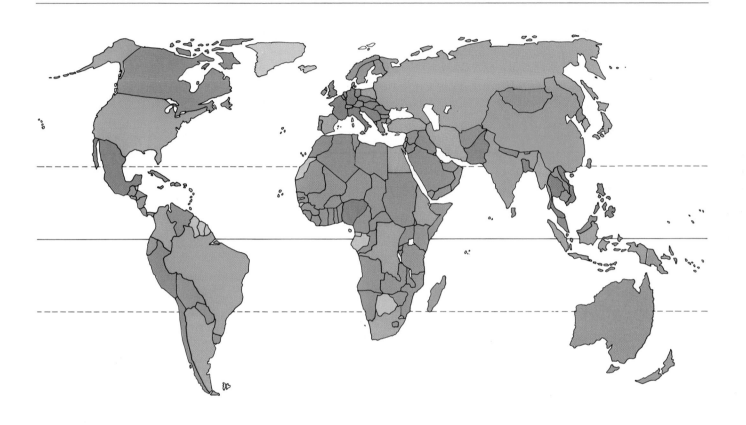

Size of Population
- ■ Over 500 Million
- ■ 100 to 500 Million
- ■ 50 to 100 Million
- ■ 25 to 50 Million
- ■ 10 to 25 Million
- ■ 1 to 10 Million
- ■ Under 1 Million

Source: Population Reference Bureau, *1983 World Population Data Sheet* (Washington, DC: Population Reference Bureau, 1983).

FIGURE P.5. POPULATION GROWTH RATES

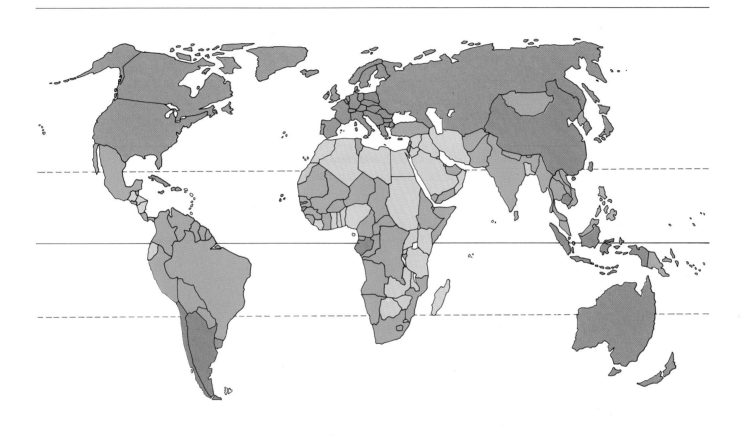

Annual Rate of Population Growth (Percentage)
- 3.0 or Over
- 2.0–2.9
- 1.0–1.9
- Less than 1.0
- Data not available

Source: Population Reference Bureau, *1983 World Population Data Sheet* (Washington, DC: Population Reference Bureau, 1983).

FIGURE P.6. STAGES IN A TYPICAL
DEMOGRAPHIC TRANSITION

■ Male
■ Female

Expansive
Pakistan

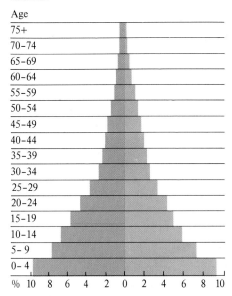

Stationary
Sweden

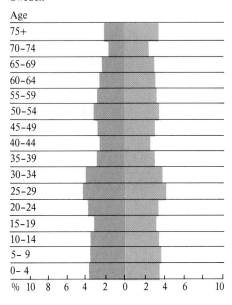

Source: U.S., Department of State, "World Population: The
Silent Explosion," *Department of State Bulletin,* Department of
State Publication 8956, October 1978, 6.

Rapidly growing populations have very different population age structures from those that grow slowly. A rapidly growing population (identified by a broad base of the population pyramid) has an *expansive* structure (see Figure P.6). It indicates a high ratio of children to adults. A low-growth population (identified by a narrow base) has a *stationary* structure. It has roughly equal numbers of people in all age ranges.

These two types of population-age structures correspond to two stages in a typical demographic transition. Expansive typifies the beginning of the transition, when birth rates are high and death rates are starting to come down; stationary typifies the end of the transition, when birth rates are just about at replacement level (see Figure P.6). Pakistan's expansive age structure is typical of Third World nations; Sweden's stationary age structure is typical of developed nations.

Projecting Growth Trends. Although projecting future population levels and growth trends is a risky business, projections often are made. Figure P.12 and Table P.4 depict two projections. Both show the same general trends, although the projection in Figure P.12 is somewhat higher. Speculative though predicting may be, further population growth is almost inevitable because of the age structure of the population and because birth rates still exceed death rates. Barring major catastrophe, it appears that about 50 percent more people will be on the planet in the year 2000 than there were in 1975—that is, 6.1 billion instead of 4 billion.

While global population will continue to increase in the foreseeable future, in recent years the growth *rate* has decreased. In 1970, the world population growth rate was just under 2 percent per year. Had this continued unchanged, the world's population would have doubled in thirty-five years.[16] By 1983, the population growth rate fell to about 1.8 percent per year; if this rate holds steady, the world's population will double in approximately thirty-nine years. The change in the annual growth rate means that in 1983 alone, about 9.4 million fewer people than anticipated joined the earth's population.[17] The United Nations now predicts that the population growth rate will drop to an annual rate of about 1.5 percent by the year 2000, and to 1 percent by the year 2025 (see Table P.4).

Population-Planning Programs

Most population-planning programs provide educational and clinical services that help families choose, easily and cheaply, how many children to have and when to have them. Family-planning technologies differ greatly from culture to culture. Among the items included are sex education, various types of contraception, information on the rhythm method, sterilization, vasectomy, and abortion. Historically, population-planning programs have steered clear of trying to convince or coerce families to have fewer children. Some countries, however—China, for example—now strongly pressure people to limit family size.[18]

National attitudes about the value of population growth and the acceptability of family planning have changed markedly over the past twenty years. In 1983, more than 80 percent of the 109 nations responding to a United Nations survey reported that they now provide access to family-planning services.[19]

Of the Third World population, about 80 percent now live in countries that consider their fertility rates too high and would like them reduced; only 3 percent live in countries that consider their fertility rates too low; and the remaining 17 percent live in countries that are satisfied with their fertility rates.[20]

TABLE P.4. POPULATION PROJECTIONS TO THE YEAR 2025

Year	World		More Developed Regions[a]		Less Developed Regions[b]	
	Population (Millions)	Rate of Increase (Percentage)[c]	Population (Millions)	Rate of Increase (Percentage)[c]	Population (Millions)	Rate of Increase (Percentage)[c]
1950	2,525	—	832	—	1,693	—
1955	2,757	1.76	887	1.28	1,870	1.99
1960	3,037	1.94	945	1.27	2,092	2.25
1965	3,354	1.99	1,003	1.19	2,351	2.33
1970	3,695	1.94	1,047	0.87	2,648	2.38
1975	4,067	1.91	1,092	0.84	2,975	2.32
1980	4,432	1.72	1,131	0.71	3,301	2.08
1985	4,826	1.70	1,170	0.68	3,656	2.04
1990	5,242	1.65	1,206	0.61	4,036	1.98
1995	5,677	1.60	1,242	0.58	4,435	1.89
2000	6,119	1.50	1,272	0.48	4,847	1.77
2005	6,558	1.39	1,298	0.40	5,261	1.64
2010	6,988	1.27	1,321	0.35	5,667	1.49
2015	7,407	1.17	1,342	0.31	6,066	1.36
2020	7,813	1.07	1,360	0.27	6,453	1.24
2025	8,195	0.96	1,377	0.24	6,818	1.10

(a) "More developed regions" include Europe, North America, Australia, Japan, New Zealand, and the USSR.
(b) "Less developed regions" include Africa, Asia, Latin America, and Oceania, excluding Australia, Japan, and New Zealand.
(c) Average annual rate of increase for each five-year period since the preceding date.

Source: United Nations, Department of International Economic and Social Affairs, *World Population Prospects as Assessed in 1980,* Population Studies, no. 78 (ST/ESA/SER.A/78), 1981, 5.

FIGURE P.7. THREE PERSPECTIVES ON POPULATION GROWTH

The three graphs on the right look different and provide different perspectives; however, they all are based on the same facts. The top graph shows an enormous population explosion, beginning sometime after 1750. It points upward at the year 2000, with no apparent limit. The middle graph indicates that these recent dramatic increases have been produced by relatively small, though accelerating, growth rates. Although the line for the growth rate points upward, it shows a recent dip; therefore it is not so dramatically threatening. The bottom graph shows the growth of population from the eve of the agricultural age, when it was somewhat less than 10 million. The first rise in the curve indicates that population expanded gradually toward the limit acceptable to a hunting and gathering society. The second burst of growth began with the adoption of farming and animal husbandry. The third burst of population growth was triggered by the industrial age. On a logarithmic scale, this last burst appears no more rapid or unusual than earlier growth spurts.

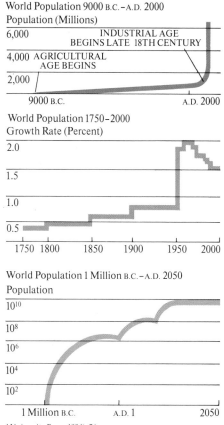

World Population 9000 B.C. – A.D. 2000
Population (Millions)

World Population 1750–2000
Growth Rate (Percent)

World Population 1 Million B.C. – A.D. 2050
Population

Source: World Bank, *World Development Report 1984* (New York: Oxford University Press, 1984), 76.

Timing of Each Additional Billion
of World Population

Approximate Years

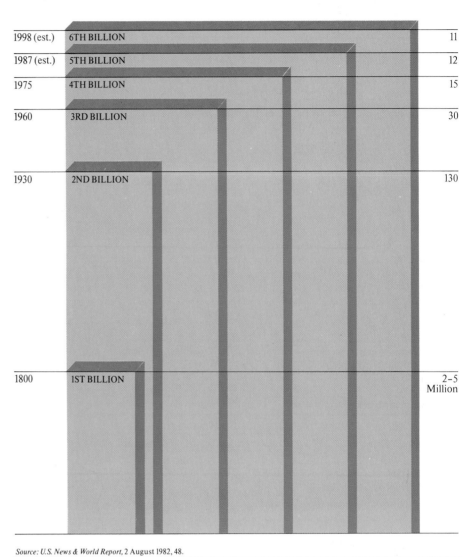

1998 (est.)	6TH BILLION	11
1987 (est.)	5TH BILLION	12
1975	4TH BILLION	15
1960	3RD BILLION	30
1930	2ND BILLION	130
1800	1ST BILLION	2–5 Million

This chart shows how additional billions of people are being added to the world's population in successively shorter periods of time.

Source: U.S. News & World Report, 2 August 1982, 48.

FIGURE P.9. WORLD POPULATION GROWTH THROUGH HISTORY

Billions of People

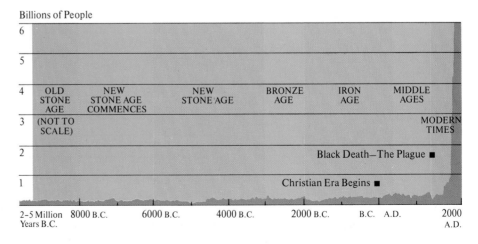

This chart presents a different view of population growth in history and in modern times.

Source: Jean van der Tak, Carl Haub, and Elaine Murphy, "Our Population Predicament: A New Look," *Population Bulletin* 34, no. 5 (December 1979): 2.

FIGURE P.10. WORLD POPULATION GROWTH (1950–1983)

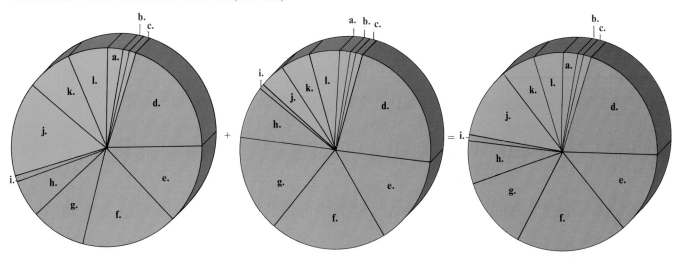

1950 POPULATION—2.5 BILLION
a. Japan 3.3%
b. Australia and New Zealand 0.4%
c. Other Oceania 0.1%
d. China 21.6%
e. India 14.6%
f. Other Asia 15.6%
g. Africa 8.8%
h. Other Latin America 5.6%
i. Temperate South America 1.0%
j. Europe 15.5%
k. USSR 7.1%
l. North America 6.5%

GROWTH 1950–1983—2.18 BILLION
a. Japan 1.6%
b. Australia and New Zealand 0.4%
c. Other Oceania 0.1%
d. China 23.4%
e. India 16.5%
f. Other Asia 21.3%
g. Africa 13.4%
h. Other Latin America 9.4%
i. Temperate South America 0.9%
j. Europe 4.4%
k. USSR 4.2%
l. North America 4.3%

1983 POPULATION—4.7 BILLION
a. Japan 2.5%
b. Australia and New Zealand 0.4%
c. Other Oceania 0.1%
d. China 22.4%
e. India 15.5%
f. Other Asia 18.3%
g. Africa 10.9%
h. Other Latin America 7.3%
i. Temperate South America 0.9%
j. Europe 10.4%
k. USSR 5.8%
l. North America 5.5%

▨ More Developed Countries
▨ Less Developed Countries

Source: U.S., Department of Commerce, Bureau of the Census, *World Population 1983: Recent Demographic Estimates for the Countries and Regions of the World* (Washington, DC: U.S. Government Printing Office, December 1983), 35.

FIGURE P.11. POPULATION INCREASE: BIRTH RATES AND DEATH RATES IN MEXICO AND SWEDEN

Sweden has completed the demographic transition: Its population growth is at replacement levels. Mexico is still in a stage of explosive population growth.

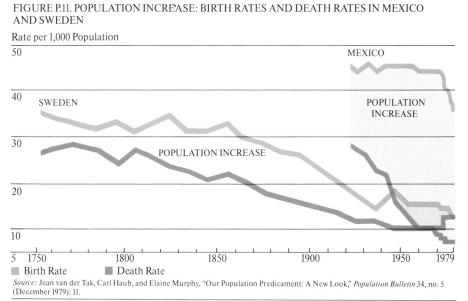

Rate per 1,000 Population

▨ Birth Rate   ▨ Death Rate

Source: Jean van der Tak, Carl Haub, and Elaine Murphy, "Our Population Predicament: A New Look," *Population Bulletin* 34, no. 5 (December 1979): 11.

FIGURE P.12. POPULATION PROJECTIONS TO THE YEAR 2000 (U.S. DEPARTMENT OF STATE)

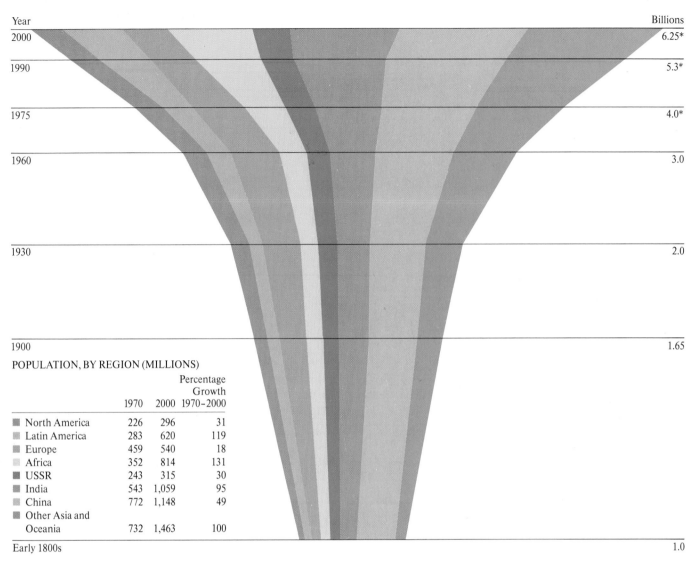

Year		Billions
2000		6.25*
1990		5.3*
1975		4.0*
1960		3.0
1930		2.0
1900		1.65

POPULATION, BY REGION (MILLIONS)

	1970	2000	Percentage Growth 1970–2000
North America	226	296	31
Latin America	283	620	119
Europe	459	540	18
Africa	352	814	131
USSR	243	315	30
India	543	1,059	95
China	772	1,148	49
Other Asia and Oceania	732	1,463	100

Early 1800s		1.0

* UN medium projection variant.

Source: U.S., Department of State, "World Population: The Silent Explosion," *Department of State Bulletin,* Department of State Publication 8956, October 1978, 5.

This chart projects population growth rates for eight regions of the world. Of these, Asia, Africa, and Latin America are projected as the significant growth areas. (Estimates of growth rates have declined somewhat since 1978, when the chart was prepared.)

FIGURE P.13. PROJECTED POPULATION GROWTH OF MAJOR CITIES

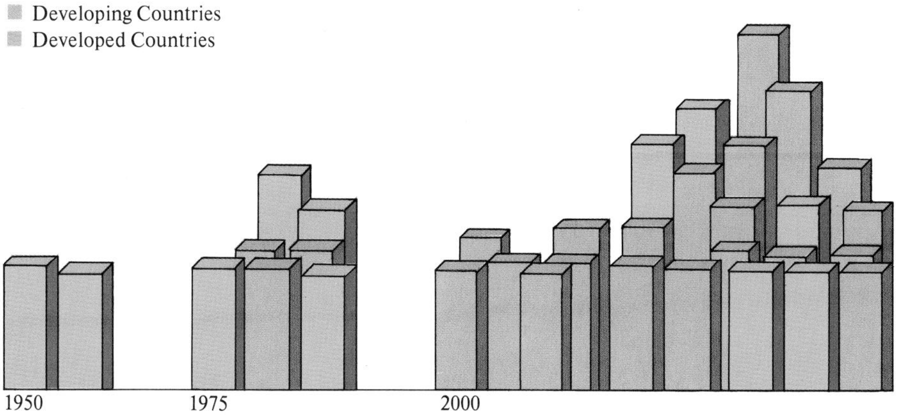

▓ Developing Countries
▓ Developed Countries

This chart shows the growth of major cities in 1950 and 1975, and projected to the year 2000. In 2000, the UN estimates, there will be 25 urban areas with a population of more than 10 million. Most of these areas will be in the Third World.

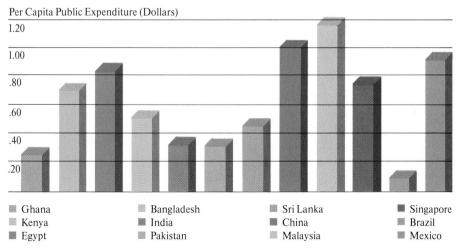

1950   1975   2000

1950 (Millions)
New York, Northeast New Jersey 12.2
London 10.4

1975 (Millions)
New York, Northeast New Jersey 19.8
Tokyo, Yokohama 17.7
Mexico City 11.9
Shanghai 11.6
Los Angeles, Long Beach 10.8
São Paulo 10.7
London 10.4

2000 (Millions)
Mexico City 31.0
São Paulo 25.8
Tokyo, Yokohama 24.2
New York, Northeast New Jersey 22.8
Shanghai 22.7
Peking 19.9
Rio de Janeiro 19.0
Greater Bombay 17.1
Calcutta 16.7
Jakarta 16.6
Seoul 14.2
Los Angeles, Long Beach 14.2
Cairo, Giza, Imbaba 13.1
Madras 12.9
Manila 12.3
Greater Buenos Aires 12.1
Bangkok, Thonburi 11.9
Karachi 11.8
Delhi 11.7
Bogotá 11.7
Paris 11.3
Tehran 11.3
Istanbul 11.2
Baghdad 11.1
Osaka, Kobe 11.1

Source: World Bank, *World Development Report 1984* (New York: Oxford University Press, 1984), 68.

FIGURE P.14. PUBLIC EXPENDITURES ON POPULATION-PLANNING PROGRAMS FOR SELECTED COUNTRIES (1980)

Per Capita Public Expenditure (Dollars)

1.20
1.00
.80
.60
.40
.20

▓ Ghana   ▓ Bangladesh   ▓ Sri Lanka   ▓ Singapore
▓ Kenya   ▓ India   ▓ China   ▓ Brazil
▓ Egypt   ▓ Pakistan   ▓ Malaysia   ▓ Mexico

Source: World Bank, *World Development Report 1984* (New York: Oxford University Press, 1984), 149.

The growth of nongovernmental family-planning organizations also reflects this change in attitudes. For example, overall income of the International Planned Parenthood Federation increased from $60,000 in 1962 to $19.3 million in 1971, and to $52.7 million in 1984.[21]

Third World countries spend between $6 and $100 (in U.S. dollars) per user each year on family planning. The average program involves both the public and private sectors; provides access to a variety of family-planning technologies, including voluntary sterilization; and supports demographic data-collection. If such programs were to reach 80 percent of all reproductive-age couples in the world (excluding China), their total cost would be about $4.5 billion annually—$7.4 billion by the year 2000, when the population will be larger. By contrast, in 1980 only $1 billion in funding was actually committed to population- and family-planning programs in developing countries (excluding China). Of this total, $450 million came from the developing countries themselves, $100 million from private voluntary organizations, and $450 million through aid from governments of developed nations.[22]

Schools of Thought on Population

Is population planning moral? Do Third World population densities and growth rates require governmental action?

The population debate focuses mostly on the Third World, although population planning is an issue in most nations. One issue is the efficacy and morality of population-planning programs. Another is whether Third World population densities and growth rates constitute a problem requiring governmental action.

Proponents of population planning believe that uncontrolled population growth rates and high population densities are major causes of hunger and poverty. In their view, the reason that Third World nations are not developing is that they can barely keep up with their burgeoning populations. Thus, although these nations are achieving some high levels of growth in terms of the economy and food production, such achievements are not leading to improvements in human well-being. Advocates of population planning also see high population densities as a threat to the environment, and even to the survival of the human race. Finally, proponents believe that Third World people, especially women, want information and technology to help them limit their families, and that failing to provide this information and technology amounts to denying them freedom of choice.

Most opponents of population planning begin with the principle that where population planning involves population control, it is morally wrong. People are a valuable resource, not a liability, they believe. Population growth rates will stabilize naturally (as they did in the West), once there is sufficient food and people are less poor. Personal reproduction decisions are the individual couple's business and nobody else's, especially not the government's. Many opponents believe that one widely practiced technology for limiting births—abortion—is actually murder. While opponents of population planning do not deny that problems of starvation, poverty, and environmental degradation exist, they reject the idea that population growth has caused these problems or that population-planning programs will help solve them.

School of Thought: Population Densities and Growth Rates in the Third World Are Contributing to Hunger and Poverty

The first school of thought— that hunger and poverty are encouraged by population densities and growth rates in the Third World— is supported by three points of view. First, in Third World nations, food production and economic growth cannot keep up with the needs of the rapidly growing populations; this population growth holds back the success of economic development. Second, population growth threatens the survival of the human race. Finally, poor Third World people, especially women, desire fewer children; they need information and family-planning technologies to limit the size of their families.

Point of View Number 1

Food Production Cannot Keep Up with Population Growth

Thomas Robert Malthus, an English clergyman who lived in the eighteenth century during the first decades of rapid population growth, was an early proponent of this viewpoint. The conditions of English urban industrial life in this period were becoming a topic of increasing political and literary interest. Young Malthus, it is said, "used to argue at breakfast against his father's perfectionist view that the human race was getting ever better."[23] Malthus's enduring classic, *An Essay on the Principle of Population*, was first published in 1798. This is his basic argument:

I think I may fairly make two postulata.

First, That food is necessary to the existence of man.

Second, That the passion between the sexes is necessary and will remain nearly in its present state....

Assuming then, my postulata as granted, I say that the power of population is indefinitely greater than the power in the earth to produce subsistence for man.

Population, when unchecked, increases in a geometrical ratio. Subsistence increases only in an arithmetical ratio. A slight acquaintance with numbers will shew the immensity of the first power in comparison of the second....

This implies a strong and constantly operating check on population from the difficulty of subsistence. This difficulty must fall some where and must necessarily be severely felt by a large portion of mankind....

The period when the number of men surpass their means of subsistence has long since arrived.

If the proportion between the natural increase of population and food which I have given be in any degree near the truth, it will appear... that the period when the number of men surpass their means of subsistence has long since arrived, and that this necessary oscillation, this constantly subsisting cause of periodical misery, has existed ever since we have had any histories of mankind, does exist at present, and will for ever continue to exist, unless some decided change takes place in the physical constitution of our nature.[24]

Paul Ehrlich, a Stanford University biology professor, is a widely read contemporary advocate of population control. His book, *The Population Bomb*, published in 1968, went through eleven printings in little more than a year. This book combines hard scientific data with passionate advocacy for population control. Ehrlich candidly admits his intention to raise public consciousness and concern about the population problem. He describes his experience of understanding the population explosion for the first time:

I came to understand it emotionally one stinking hot night in Delhi a few years ago. My wife and daughter and I were returning to our hotel in an ancient taxi. The seats were hopping with fleas. The only functional gear was third. As we crawled through the city, we entered a crowded slum area. The temperature was well over 100, and the air was a haze of dust and smoke. The streets seemed alive with people. People eating, people washing, people sleeping. People visiting, arguing, and screaming. People thrusting their hands through the taxi window, begging. People defecating and urinating. People clinging to buses. People herding animals. People, people, people, people. [25]

The late C. P. Snow, distinguished British author and physicist, also believed that population growth must be curbed:

Millions of people…are going to starve to death before our eyes.

Many millions of people in the poor countries are going to starve to death before our eyes…we shall see them doing so upon our television sets.…

The major catastrophe will happen before the end of the century. We shall, in the rich countries, be surrounded by a sea of famine, involving hundreds of millions of human beings.…

The increase of population all over the rich world may get a little less. In the poor world it won't, except in one or two pockets. Despite local successes, as in India, the food-population collision will duly occur. The attempts to prevent it, or meliorate it, will be too feeble. Famine will take charge in many countries. It may become, by the end of the period, endemic famine. There will be suffering and desperation on a scale as yet unknown. [26]

David and Marcia Pimentel, a husband-and-wife team, highlight two themes that underlie the assumptions of almost every population-planning advocate: First, resources are, ultimately, limited. The human population must divide a finite stock of resources; more people means less for each person. And second, there is something called "quality of life," [27] which should take precedence over most other values. (*Critics* of population planning order these values differently. They see quality of life as less important than the right to human life and, in some cases, than the right of individuals to make their own reproductive decisions.) The Pimentels write:

Man…has allowed his numbers to increase…beyond the capacity of his biological environment.

One is tempted to ask who is responsible for the shortages in food supplies.… Man can not escape the answer that he, himself, has allowed his numbers to increase up to and even beyond the capacity of his biological environment to provide adequate supplies of needed resources.

The best calculation is that if there were only about 1000 million humans on earth, all could enjoy a relatively high quality [of] life. With the present world population above 4000 million world food and energy resources even now are being stretched to cover needs. How then can we expect that the same pool of resources will be able to provide amply for the more than 6000 million humans expected by 2000 A.D.? Perhaps we should abandon hope for a high quality life? Or perhaps we can acknowledge the problem now and begin to try to solve it. [28]

Lester Pearson, former Canadian prime minister, wrote a pathbreaking report, *Partners in Development*, which was released in 1969. He pointed to the problems of population growth by making some simple calculations of a growing population's needs. Many leaders in the field of development echo his views, pointing out the disproportionate population increases in countries where development needs are greatest. Pearson writes: "No other phenomenon casts a darker shadow over the prospects for international development than the staggering growth of population."[29]

Since the Pearson report was written, nearly a billion people have been added to the population.[30]

Pearson and other proponents of population control are concerned that the increase in people who must be fed, clothed, educated, and employed will constantly undercut progress in all kinds of human endeavors. They point to Mexico: Every 50 minutes the government builds a new classroom; but the needs of the children who would benefit from these classrooms cannot be met, because 240 children are born during the same time period.[31] Just to keep even with population increases, India each day would have to build 1,000 new classrooms, 1,000 hospital wards, and 10,000 new houses.[32] At current rates of population growth, according to one study, "most developing countries will have to double their economic output... [by the year 2000] just to stay even with population growth, let alone trying to improve living conditions."[33]

U Thant, former secretary general of the United Nations, expressed the viewpoint that population growth hinders economic development:

There is ever-increasing realization that too rapid population growth constitutes a major obstacle to education and the promotion of the welfare of the young in general, the attainment of adequate standards of health, the chance of earning a decent living, and in many cases even the availability of food at subsistence level. We must conclude from the demographic projections that the task of providing opportunities for the world's as yet unborn children and developing their talents and their capabilities to the full appears in a number of countries well-nigh insuperable, unless action is taken to moderate the population growth rate.[34]

Point of View Number 2

Curbing Population Is Necessary for the Survival of the Human Race

Another point of view among those who regard population growth as the root of hunger is expressed here by Paul Ehrlich and colleagues. They insist that if we do not limit population, we are headed for a global catastrophe:

The nature of exponential growth is such that limits can be approached with surprising suddenness. The likelihood of overshooting such a limit, with catastrophic results, is made even greater by (a) the momentum of human population growth, (b) by the delays between cause and effect in many environmental systems, and (c) by the fact that some kinds of damage are irreversible by the time they are visible....

The momentum of human population growth has two origins. First, attitudes toward childbearing have deep biological and cultural roots, and therefore resist change. Second, today's population is heavily weighted with young people....This means there are far more young people who will soon be reproducing—adding to the population—than there are old people who will soon be dying—subtracting from it. Thus, even if... every pair of parents in the world henceforth had only enough children to replace themselves, the imbalance between young and old would cause the population to grow for another 50 to 70 years before leveling off....

Time lags between the initiation of environmental insults and the appearance of the consequent effects further compound the predicament, because they postpone recognition of the need for any corrective action at all. Such environmental time lags come about in a variety of ways, depending both on the ability of some pollutants to persist in dangerous forms for long periods and on the ways in which such pollutants move, accumulate in and damage biological systems....

Thus the momentum of growth, the delays between causes and effects, and the irreversibility of many kinds of damage combine to make overshooting some natural limit a likely outcome of mankind's present course. Indeed, one cannot be sure that we have not already overshot; the practices that support today's world population at the present level of affluence may be unsustainable in the long term, or already may have done enormous irreversible damage that has yet to manifest itself. As zoologists are well aware, animal populations often overshoot the carrying capacity of their environment—a phenomenon invariably followed by a population crash.[35]

We cannot continue to be "our brother's keeper" if the consequence is survival for no one.

Most advocates of population control who see unlimited growth as dangerous focus on methods for lowering the birth rate. But that is not the only option; another alternative is *not to lower death rates*. According to biologist and systems theorist Garrett Hardin, we cannot continue to be "our brother's keeper" if the consequence is survival for *no one*. He suggests that disease and starvation must be allowed, as in the past, to perform their natural role in limiting population:

If we divide the world crudely into rich nations and poor nations, two thirds of them are desperately poor, and only one third comparatively rich, with the United States the wealthiest of all. Metaphorically each rich nation can be seen as a lifeboat full of comparatively rich people. In the ocean outside each lifeboat swim the poor of the world, who would like to get in, or at least share some of the wealth. What should the lifeboat passengers do?

First, we must recognize the limited capacity of any lifeboat....

So here we sit, say 50 people in our lifeboat. To be generous, let us assume it has room for 10 more, making a total capacity of 60. Suppose the 50 of us in the lifeboat see 100 others swimming in the water outside, begging for admission to our boat or for handouts. We have several options: we may be tempted to live by the Christian ideal of being "our brother's keeper," or by the Marxist ideal of "to each according to his needs." Since the needs of all in the water are the same, and since they can all be seen as "our brothers," we could take them all into our boat, making a total of 150 in a boat designed for 60. The boat swamps, everyone drowns. Complete justice, complete catastrophe....

The harsh ethics of the lifeboat become even harsher when we consider the reproductive differences between the rich nations and the poor nations. The people inside the lifeboats are doubling in numbers every 87 years; those swimming around outside are doubling, on the average, every 35 years, more than twice as fast as the rich. And since the world's resources are dwindling, the difference in prosperity between the rich and the poor can only increase....

For the foreseeable future, our survival demands that we govern our actions by the ethics of a lifeboat, harsh though they may be.[36]

Point of View Number 3

Poor People Want Fewer Children and Need Information on How to Make That Possible

The third and final group of population-limitation advocates whose views are presented are poor people, especially women from the Third World.

40

A woman from Kenya talks about the problem of raising many children:

It is difficult to have many children these days. Before, there was plenty of land. Families that had many children could simply dig and farm as far as they needed; but now, if you have seven sons, how will you divide up the land?[37]

A woman in Villagran, Mexico, speaks of her life:

We were very poor when I was a child. We were six children, and my father didn't earn much. That is why I want just two or three children. I don't want my children to grow up like me—without an education. I feel very ashamed and bad about not having any education. I want my children to go to school and learn many, many things. I don't want them to live by the rumors of the street. I want them to learn for themselves. I want them to be independent and proud of themselves.[38]

And another from Sri Lanka says:

I had nine children, but I lost the ninth just a year ago. The eighth child is three years old. I have five sons and three daughters. I never went to school. I was just twelve when I was married. I had not seen my husband before. My marriage was arranged by my parents. I had my first child at the age of thirteen.

When I was a small child, I was quite all right, since my mother had only three children. But now I find life extremely difficult because I have such a large family. That's the main reason. If people have more than three children, they find it difficult to manage....

Many have very large families, and we are lodged in these bungalow rooms. There is hardly any space. There are too many people, and one room is not enough for a large family. We now have to ask the superintendent for another room, and it will be more expensive for us. If we weren't so many, the problem wouldn't arise.[39]

A Calcutta woman makes this statement:

I think about it like this. There is a water shortage here. With the water I have, I cannot bathe the children I have. Rationed food is getting less, and the price of everything is rising. In a country like ours I can't afford to have children. That is why I want the pill.[40]

Some have seen improvement, such as this Tunisian woman:

Before, women were unhappy. They were always in poor health, nursing the children, having children, always weak. Now women are flourishing. They can take advantage of all that is offered. They can have family planning and be in good health. They are clean and healthy and have freedom....

That's all we talk about—family planning, women's freedom. We talk about all the subjects that concern women. In my day, because we were not educated, we lived like beasts. We didn't know anything. It is obvious that we were always bypassed by men.

Now women can go to buy things by themselves; they have the choice to come and go. Their husbands can't forbid it any more. It is much better. But still there are problems for all the women of the world anyway. Not just Tunisian women. All women are reaching out to learn, to go out, to listen. Not only us. All the women of the world.[41]

If you have seven sons, how will you divide up the land?

In a country like ours I can't afford to have children. That is why I want the pill.

What these women express is confirmed statistically in an article on family planning by James W. Brackett, R. T. Ravenholt, and John C. Chao:

It is often heard that poor, uneducated, rural women will not want to limit their fertility until they have experienced better education; employment opportunities outside the home, particularly outside agriculture; and so on. To evaluate this assertion we looked at data on desire for additional children in relation to various sociodemographic characteristics of the women surveyed.

A large proportion of the women interviewed stated that they wanted no more children.

The World Fertility Survey asked currently married women who believed they and their husbands were physically capable of having another child whether they wanted to have any more children.... A large proportion of the women interviewed stated that they wanted no more children—from 72 percent in South Korea to 30 percent in Nepal....

For all ten countries a majority of women with four children—in fact, in most a substantial majority—wanted no more children.

In South Korea, 66 percent of the women with two children wanted no more; in Colombia and Sri Lanka around 50 percent; and in Thailand 46 percent....

Notwithstanding the broad differences in geography, culture, religion, race, and level of socioeconomic development among the ten countries studied, the WFS found that a large proportion of women in every country do not want any more children. Moreover, the desire not to have any additional children was strong among rural, poor, and uneducated women....

Most importantly the findings ... show that a large proportion of married women of reproductive age in these poor countries do not want any more children and that there is a huge unmet demand for fertility control services. Until this existing demand is much more fully met, it is critical that adequate resources—both within these countries and from donor agencies—be allocated to support service programs. [42]

School of Thought: Population Growth Is Not the Problem

Now we come to those who do not think population growth is a problem and who oppose population control. Proponents of this school of thought offer various points of view: (1) Population growth is, if anything, a blessing to humanity; (2) Plenty of food is available, and this will continue for the foreseeable future; (3) Hunger and poverty are caused by the consumption patterns of the rich; (4) Hunger and poverty result from structural imbalances in the society, so the focus should be on these imbalances rather than on population control; (5) People in the Third World want more children, and no one but themselves should dictate in this matter; (6) Population planning is an attempt by rich nations—some of them former colonial powers—to keep poor nations subservient; and finally (7) Population-planning programs are immoral.

Point of View Number 1

Population Growth Is Good for Humanity

Julian Simon, professor of economics and business administration at the University of Illinois, wrote *The Ultimate Resource*, which has brought an anti-Malthusian view to the public's attention. His work has prodded vigorous debates about the question, is population growth a problem? Simon explains how confronting the empirical data brought him to his view:

FIGURE P.15. A BENEFIT OF POPULATION GROWTH, ACCORDING TO JULIAN SIMON

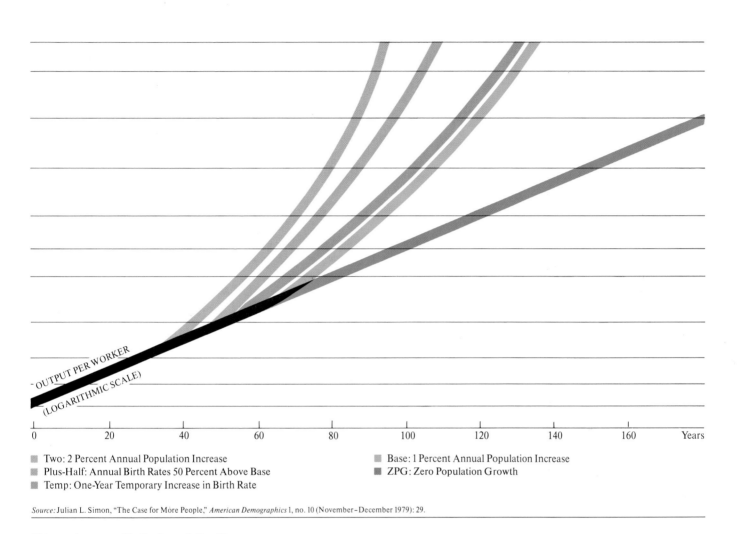

- OUTPUT PER WORKER
(LOGARITHMIC SCALE)

0   20   40   60   80   100   120   140   160   Years

■ Two: 2 Percent Annual Population Increase
■ Plus-Half: Annual Birth Rates 50 Percent Above Base
■ Temp: One-Year Temporary Increase in Birth Rate

■ Base: 1 Percent Annual Population Increase
■ ZPG: Zero Population Growth

Source: Julian L. Simon, "The Case for More People," *American Demographics* 1, no. 10 (November–December 1979): 29.

*This graph, prepared by Professor Julian Simon
and based on a computer simulation model,
shows that output per worker would be higher
for a growing population in the long run.*

When I began to work on population studies, I assumed that the accepted view was sound. I aimed to help the world contain its "exploding" population, which I believed to be one of the two main threats to mankind (war being the other). But my reading and research led me into confusion. Though the standard economic theory of population (which has hardly changed since Malthus) asserts that a higher population growth implies a lower standard of living, the available empirical data do not support that theory.[43]

Simon's argument, based on a mathematical model built from his empirical data, is the proposition that *more people mean more knowledge:*

Why is the standard of living so much higher in the United States or Sweden than in India or Mali? And why is our standard of living so much higher now than it was 200 years ago? The all-important difference is that there is a much greater stock of technological know-how available, and people are educated to learn and use that knowledge. The knowledge and the schooling are intertwined; in India today, unlike the United States 200 years ago, the knowledge is available in books in the library, but without schooling and productive social organization the knowledge cannot be adapted to local needs and put to work.

The stock of industrial capital is also intertwined with the stock of knowledge and education; the value of much of our capital such as computers and jet airplanes consists largely of the new knowledge that is built into them. And without educated workers, these chunks of capital could not be operated and would be worthless.

The amount of improvement depends in large measure on the number of people available.

Because improvements—their invention and their adoption—come from people, it seems reasonable to assume that the amount of improvement depends in large measure on the number of people available.[44]

In answer to the question of scarce resources, a major concern of the Malthusians, Simon responds:

There is no persuasive reason to believe that the relatively larger use of natural resources that would occur with a larger population would have any special deleterious effects upon the economy in the future....

Sound appraisal of the impact of additional people upon the "scarcity" (cost) of a natural resource must take into account the feedback from increased demand to the discovery of new deposits, new ways of extracting the resource, and new substitutes for the resource. And we must take into account the relationship between demand now and supply in various future years, rather than consider only the effect on supply now of greater or lesser demand now. And the more people, the more minds there are to discover new deposits and increase productivity, with raw materials as with all other goods, all else equal.

This point of view is not limited to economists. A technologist writing on minerals put it this way: "In effect, technology keeps creating new resources." So the major constraint upon the human capacity to enjoy unlimited minerals, energy, and other raw materials at acceptable prices is knowledge. And the source of knowledge is the human mind. Ultimately, then, the key constraint is human imagination acting together with educated skills. This is why an increase of human beings, along with causing an additional consumption of resources, constitutes a crucial addition to the stock of natural resources.[45]

Additional children, adds Simon, do not drain resources—in fact, they increase them.

44

Population growth can be an asset, suggest the editors of *The Wall Street Journal* in reporting how Mahathir Mohamad, the Malaysian prime minister, promotes population growth. Mohamad announced a policy to encourage Malaysia's 14.8 million people to increase the country's population to 70 million by the year 2000. Discussing this recommendation, the *Journal* says:

People, even poor people, are assets.

Mr. Mahathir's aim—a big domestic market for Malaysian goods—must be particularly galling to population-control enthusiasts. But anyone reading the U.S. economists of the 1950s, who based what proved to be accurate predictions of strong economic growth on a projected population expansion, would not scoff. And there is something refreshing about his rejection of those dire limits-to-growth arguments that the poor are poor because there are so many of them. People, even poor people, are assets—at least when they're given enough incentives to work or to plant or otherwise to contribute to the economy. Mr. Mahathir has debunked two decades of developmental economics orthodoxy.[46]

Economists Peter Bauer and Basil Yamey agree that population growth is not a problem. Like Simon, they believe that an increased population growth rate denotes an improved standard of living:

The so-called population explosion is the result of a sharp fall in mortality, unaccompanied by a corresponding decline in birthrate. It is usually deplored, because of the resulting decline in per capita income. Yet what it means is that people and their children live longer, and therefore it represents a manifest and pronounced improvement in the standard of living of those who have survived and whose children live longer. This improvement is omitted from the conventional national income statistics which ignore improved health, longer life expectation, and the survival of children as positive components of income and living standards.

Per capita income, as conventionally measured, is in no way a surrogate for economic well-being. If it were, then an increase in the death rate of the poor in a country would have to be regarded as an economic improvement. Paradoxically, the birth of a calf shows up in these statistics as an improvement, because it is registered as an increase in total—and hence also in per capita—income, while the birth of a child shows up as a deterioration, because, by itself, it causes a fall in per capita income.[47]

Point of View Number 2

There Is Already Enough Food for Everyone, and More Can Be Grown

Proponents of this point of view cite food-production data to prove that population control should be de-emphasized. Professor Jerrie DeHoogh and his colleagues did a research project at a major agricultural university in the Netherlands. The object was to determine which factors would affect the maximum amount of food the world could, theoretically, produce. Although the authors recognize that world food shortages persist and must be addressed, they note:

There are many technological methods by which food production in the world can be increased. On the basis of a detailed inventory of soil characteristics, rainfall, temperature and sunshine, ... [it is] calculated that—depending on natural restrictions to the growth of agricultural crops—the earth is capable of producing 25 times the present amount of food. A great deal of agriculturally-suitable land is not yet used; but above all, production per hectare could be considerably increased. According to these data, there ought to be sufficient food both now and in the future; the world food supply is thus not primarily threatened by the finiteness of the earth.[48]

45

John Maddox, editor of *Nature* magazine, points to increases in food production:

Food production in the world is now increasing much faster than the population....

There are several ways in which food production may continue to increase so as to better the pace of growth of population....

Bringing cultivable land under the plough should be enough to support 7,500 million people, but this is plainly an underestimate of what might be done.[49]

The earth is rich enough to support billions of additional people.

The late Herman Kahn, founder of the Hudson Institute, argued that we don't have to do anything about the birth rate, because the earth is rich enough to support billions of people. He writes, with William Brown and Leon Martel, in *The Next 200 Years:*

Because large sections of the world, especially in the developing areas, appear crowded and on the verge of famine, most observers seem to feel that the gap between food demand and food supply must inevitably grow. But we argue that, as a direct consequence of available resources and improving technology, a more reasonable projection would be in the direction of an eventual abundance of food....

The prospect for an abundant supply of food for future generations is not in any reasonable sense limited by existing physical resources. The world is likely to be much better fed 100 years from now than it is today....

The task ahead looks difficult, but it may seem less so looking back from the year 2176. From that vantage point, 20th-century concerns about food may appear merely as a temporary detour of imagined and real troubles on the road to success—troubles that were largely self-imposed. The motivation now exists for increasing per capita food production and providing security against severe annual fluctuations in output. The resources, the technology and the capital all appear to be adequate now and improving steadily.[50]

Point of View Number 3

If the People of Rich Nations Consumed Less Food, the People in Poorer Nations Would Not Go Hungry

Advocates of this view feel that it holds true for energy and mineral resources as well as for food. Table P.5 shows the major differences in food, energy, and commodities consumption in four nations. According to this table, an individual in the United States consumes substantially more food, and more than sixty times as much energy, as an individual in India. Proponents of this point of view feel that some specialists and leaders in the developed nations focus too much on the "population problem" and not enough on their own "consumption patterns."

Sartaj Aziz, assistant president for the economic and planning department of the International Fund for Agricultural Development (IFAD), was a leader in the planning and direction of the 1974 World Food Conference. He favors paying more attention to consumption patterns in rich countries:

It is clear that as long as the available food supply is distributed according to commercial demand rather than nutritional needs, the over-consumption in the rich countries will be an important cause of hunger and malnutrition in years of food shortages. Today about 30 percent of the world population in the rich countries uses about two-thirds of the world grains supply.... Per capita consumption

46

of grain in the rich countries is three times that in the developing countries. The total quantity of grain fed to livestock... is more than the quantity consumed by human beings in India and China taken together.[51]

René Dumont, a French agricultural and economic planner, has written for decades on the issues connected with hunger. He was the director of research at the National Institute of Agronomy in Paris when his *Utopia or Else...* was published in 1973.

Pets consume enough to give 12 million Asiatic children a decent diet.

According to Robert Lattés: "In 1967, industrial production of dogfoods represented roughly the same sum per dog as the <u>average</u> income in India." Which means a good deal more than the income of a <u>poor</u> Indian. Writing in <u>Le Monde</u> (22 August 1972), Gérard Chalencon tells us that 1 French household in 3 has a dog and at least 1 in 4 a cat, the highest figures in Europe. The consumption of petfood (or at least of food intended for pets) rose from 14 million tins in 1961 to 280 million in 1970. In all pets consume 2 million metric tons of food, or enough to give 12 million Asiatic children a decent diet, since petfood, catfood in particular, has a high protein content. I realize that it's nice to have a pet about the house, but should we put pets before children? If the world population figures were lower, if all children were well fed I shouldn't mind so much seeing pets being looked after better than Vietnamese children.[52]

TABLE P.5. A COMPARISON OF FOUR NATIONS' CONSUMPTION

	U.S.	USSR	Mexico	India
FOOD Calories per person per day[a]	3,658.0	3,372.0	2,791.0	1,880.0
ENERGY Kilograms of coal equivalent per person per year[b]	11,681.0	5,793.0	1,535.0	194.0
COMMODITIES Kilograms per person per year[c] STEEL	549.0	554.0	103.0	14.0
COTTON	6.7	7.4	2.6	2.0
GASOLINE	1,346.0	280.0	140.0	2.0
Kilograms of paper per 1,000 persons per year[c] PAPER	45,315.0	4,621.0	5,337.0	749.0

Source: (a) World Bank, *World Development Report 1983* (New York: Oxford University Press, 1983), 194–95.
(b) World Bank, *World Development Report 1982* (New York: Oxford University Press, 1982), 122–23.
(c) George Thomas Kurian, *The Book of World Rankings* (New York: Facts On File, 1979), 263–69.

Point of View Number 4

Hunger and Poverty Result from Imbalances in the Social and Economic Structure; Population Control Is Not the Issue

Another widely held perspective is that the key to ending hunger lies in redistribution of land, income, and/or political power rather than population-control programs. Those who hold this view see starvation as the result of inequity and oppression, not of population growth.

Denis Goulet and Michael Hudson's *The Myth of Aid* expresses this view:

Population control without fundamental social reform does nothing in itself to tackle the related underlying causes of poverty. Its result can therefore only be an intensification of the vicious circle of economic poverty and social backwardness.[53]

If the poor became better off, they wouldn't rely on having a lot of children to support them.

Roy Prosterman is a law professor and eminent authority in the field of development, specializing in land reform. His feeling is that if the poor became better off, they wouldn't rely on having a lot of children to support them.

Given the high rates of infant mortality and death rates of young children, parents in developing countries must have large families to assure that children will survive to be able to help support the family and the parents in illness or old age.

With higher food production and lower infant mortality rates, parents see that more of their children will survive, so "insurance births" taper off and the birth rates drops substantially....

In ending hunger and malnutrition, we prevent births as well as deaths....While family planning information and techniques are an important part of overall health care, the <u>real</u> answer to overpopulation is not population control, but rather creating self-sufficiency for impoverished parents.[54]

Pierre Pradervand had worked in the development field for more than eight years and was attached to the International Development Research Centre, Ottawa, Canada, when he wrote "The Malthusian Man." In this article, he takes the position that family planning should be tied to social justice and development rather than to a campaign for social control:

As someone with wide international experience in the field of population problems, I do not hesitate to write that the population problem, as traditionally defined, is the greatest red-herring in the field of world development. By stressing population in such an isolated, simplistic manner, neo-Malthusian thinking might have lost the world twenty precious years in solving its number one problem—poverty. If twenty years ago, India had undertaken massive structural changes, a real land reform programme, and distributed services and resources more equally among its people instead of trying to persuade illiterate women to adopt the rhythm method by bribing them with coloured beads, it would probably not now be sterilizing people at the rate of 63,000 in two weeks (a goal achieved not long ago in a much-publicised family planning festival). Nor would it have to admit that millions of its people are worse off than they were fifteen years ago (as was shown recently by the Dandekar study on poverty in India). At the root of India's population problem is not 'copulation' but an alliance of national and Western vested interests which is opposed to radical change.[55]

Mary Alice Caliendo, a specialist in nutrition and development, provides additional empirical data to support her proposition that population control is not a separate issue but must be linked to development. Her 1979 study, *Nutrition and the World Food Crisis*, describes a pattern that suggests a relationship between the decrease in infant mortality rates and the decrease in birth rates— a pattern that shows up in Taiwan, Korea, Sri Lanka, British Guiana, and Mauritius:

With decreased child mortality only half as many additional births were desired.

Many studies have demonstrated relationships among desired family size, child mortality, and family planning acceptance. In Hong Kong, Bernard demonstrated that approximately double the percentage of mothers who had three or four pregnancies but had lost a child wanted more children, as compared with women who had not lost a child. Cunningham demonstrated in Nigeria that with decreased child mortality only half as many additional births were desired....

In developing countries, the number of children needed to ensure that one or two reach adulthood is often high. May and Heer report the results of a computer simulation study which indicated that with current infant and adult mortality rates in India, a couple must have 6.3 children to ensure a 95 percent chance of one son living until the father's sixty-fifth birthday.

It is clear that if family planning programs are to succeed, people must want to have fewer children. And if this is to happen, certain preconditions must be met. These include a reduction in the economic attractiveness of children and an end to the need for parents to plan on many live births to assure long-term survival of one or two male offspring. These preconditions imply an improvement in the overall quality of human life for the poor with special emphasis on improvements in education, health care, nutrition, and socioeconomic security.[56]

Point of View Number 5

Poor People Want More Children, Not Fewer

While proponents of birth control claim that poor people in the Third World want fewer children, some opponents of population control say that the poor do not want to have fewer children at all.

Mahmood Mamdani's 1972 book on the implementation of population-control programs in India, *The Myth of Population Control,* focuses on the Khanna region in the Punjab. Mamdani supports his position with extensive field work and interviews. His message is simple: People will not limit their families unless it pays to do so.

The farmers with small holdings…stand only a few steps away from material ruin. The land they hold is <u>already</u> small; their total concern is with making ends meet in the present, with reducing their costs of production as much as possible. Given a very small income, to have to hire even one farm hand can mean disaster. If such a farmer is merely to survive, he must rely on his family for the necessary labor power. If he is to think of any advancement, which every farmer in such a precarious position does, he must add to his family labor force and thus augment his resources.…With a large enough family—especially with one spaced close together—a few children could be spared to live away from the family land, thus accumulating some savings and perhaps buying more land, land which could be worked with the manpower available within the family itself.…

A son or daughter can bring grass and water for the cattle before going to school.

The farmer's children can be of considerable assistance, even while they are young. A son or daughter can bring grass and water for the cattle before going to school at eight in the morning, can help in the field in the afternoon if necessary, and can graze the cattle in the evening. In fact, primary responsibility for the cattle can be left to the children and the adult's load lightened a little.

If a farmer's wife has no young children, it would mean intolerable hardship. She would then have to walk to the fields to deliver two meals and one tea every day. The walk over and back, the wait while everybody eats—so the utensils can be taken back, washed, and cleaned for the next meal—can take as much as four hours.[57]

An Indian farmer explains his need for sons:

I have no machinery.…Just look around: no one without sons or brothers to help him farms his land. The more sons you have, the less labor you need to hire and the more savings you can have. If I have enough, maybe we will buy some more land.[58]

Estela Jaramillo, a Colombian expecting her twelfth child in 1970, describes another practical reason for having a big family:

49

The more children I have, the more security I will have in my old age. There isn't much money in these parts, but the children are a hope to me that I will be cared for when I am no longer able to work. [59]

Point of View Number 6

Population Control Is a Tool of Racism and Repression

Some people are against population control because it seems to be a device of rich nations for keeping the poor of the world subservient.

Julian Bond, the American civil rights leader, expresses one fear in a 1970 speech:

Without the proper perspective <u>The Population Bomb</u> becomes a theoretical hammer in the hands of the angry, frightened and powerful racists, as well as over the heads of black people, as the justification for genocide. [60]

Maaza Bekele, former head of Ethiopian social services, believes that Western planners—who have little empathy for those whose lives they would alter—want to impose upon Africa a development experience that differs greatly from that of the West. Many Third World leaders share this view.

The prophets of doom contend that both the structure and the consequent potential size of the African population…is a threat to general world prosperity and a deterrent to economic development in African countries….

This [is a] one-dimensional approach….

In Africa we cannot afford to look upon our growing population as a problem. We have to face up to the challenge of engaging our young, expectant peoples in the struggle to achieve the most rapid development possible….

It seems almost sinister that there is so much money available to <u>control</u> life and hardly any to <u>promote</u> it.

It also seems unrealistic to expect that poverty-stricken, hard-working African mothers—many close to death before the age of 35—can be expected to limit the number of their children when only 1 out of 3 or 4 survive. The onus is on the "controllers" to demonstrate to these women that 3 out of 4 of their children <u>will</u> survive. They cannot run the risk that their major creative contribution to humanity (given that the rest of their existence is almost pure drudgery), will be denied them. In each woman is the grain of hope that life for her offspring will be better than hers.

Procreation and the loving, tender rearing of children is one of society's most important goals.

Besides, in African society, procreation and the loving, tender rearing of children is one of society's most important goals. Children are not a burden, they are an asset in the average farm family. [61]

These opponents of population control claim that the implementation of population control programs is where Western specialists often reveal their true attitudes toward the people they are supposed to be helping. Such programs are undertaken with little regard for the human rights or physical well-being of the women and children affected. Here is an excerpt from a report against the contraceptive drug, Depo-Provera:

Depo-Provera is a contraceptive injection. It is given to thousands of women all over the Third World.

50

Yet it is not considered safe enough for general use in Britain or the United States of America. Why are there such double standards?

The Campaign Against Depo-Provera's booklet gives detailed evidence of the drug's abuse by governments, drug companies and the international family planning agencies.

The booklet sets out the grim health hazards of the injection—risks of cancer, danger to the children of women taking the drug, alarming side-effects. Women who receive the drug can suffer from heavy and unpredictable menstrual bleeding, rapid weight gain, headaches, depression, hair loss.

Monkeys given Depo-Provera developed cancer of the womb, beagle dogs developed cancerous breast tumours, and these animal experiments suggest that the drug interferes with the body's natural mechanisms for fighting all kinds of infection. Yet all this evidence has been largely ignored or dismissed, and the injection is given to healthy women with the aim of controlling population growth. [62]

Many Third World leaders also resent how development specialists "meddle" in the area of population. Brazilian diplomat Miguel Ozorio Almeida has argued that people should be free to choose for themselves. What right, he questioned, have experts from developed nations to impose their values on such personal choices? In an interview with Dom Moraes, author of *A Matter of People*, he explains:

So far as family planning is concerned, we have never had an explicit policy.... The Brazilian citizen is free to choose what he wishes for himself and his family. We have emphasized it.

But what we resent is this. Certain organizations and countries tell us that people should not have children unless future generations are assured a good life. What about the Eskimos in the Arctic? Are we to say to them that the conditions in which they live are terrible, therefore they must not have children and their people must die out? Can you ethically make such assertions? What logically follows is that the Swedes, say, have a right to live and we haven't.

Moraes recounts that Miguel Ozorio Almeida then picked up a book in English, and read from it:

"One of the great problems the world faces today is population." This is [a quote] from a textbook, please note. It is brainwashing of the worst type. There are other sentences about the evils of population....This kind of thing is what we resent. [63]

Samir Amin, an Egyptian economist, points out that outsiders may be particularly prone to generalizing falsely from one region to another. He argues, for instance, that Africa is not overpopulated, but rather depopulated. Africans do not welcome population-reducing advice from the societies they hold responsible for the depopulation. Amin says:

People actively don't want family planning in Africa. And growth in terms of population has to equal economic growth....

There's a difference between a national attitude and the attitude of a family. There's also a difference between the attitude of a nation and the attitude of an international body like the United Nations. When the Portuguese came to the Congo for the slave trade, they estimated there were a million people there.

Many Third World leaders resent how development specialists "meddle" in the area of population.

Three hundred years later, they estimated that there was a population of about 300,000. Black nations think of oppression on many levels, both past and present. If the whites ask black nations to reduce their population now, what are the blacks to think?[64]

Point of View Number 7

Population Control Is Immoral

Advocates of this viewpoint focus on intrinsic questions of morality about population-planning methods: What *are* the values we want to maximize on the planet? On what understanding of men and women as human beings are such values founded? These issues concern those who question the morality of population control.

Julian Simon raises all these questions:

The value that I personally wish to use as a criterion for decisions about population growth is one that I think a great many other people also subscribe to, as they will find if they inspect their beliefs closely. In utilitarian terms it is "the greatest good for the greatest number." That is, my judgment about the welfare of a community depends both *on the average income per person and on the number of people who partake of that standard of living....*

If life is good and worth supporting, why not encourage more births?

This criterion seems to be consistent with our other values— our abhorrence of killing, and our desire to prevent disease and early death. And why not? Why should we feel so strongly that murder is bad, and that children in war-torn countries should be saved, and then not want to bring more people into the world? If life is good and worth supporting, why does preventing murder make sense, but not encouraging births? I understand well that a death causes grief to the living— but I am sure that your abhorrence of killing would also extend to the extermination of a whole group at once, under which conditions there would be no one to suffer grief. So, what are the differences between the murder of an adult, the infanticide of another's child, and the coercion of someone else not to have a child? The main difference between murder and forcing someone not to bear children is that murder threatens our own *persons, and unregulated murder would rip up the fabric of our society— good reasons indeed to be against murder. But we also condemn murder on the moral ground that murder denies life to someone else— and in this sense it seems to me that there is no difference between murder, abortion, contraception, and abstinence from sex. I am not* equating *abortion or contraception to murder, and I am* not *branding as immoral all who do not have as many children as are biologically possible. Nor do I want to impose my own values, which come to these conclusions, upon you. Rather, I just wish us to get clear on the meaning of the moral distinctions we make.*[65]

The Roman Catholic Church has been, and remains today, one of the staunchest opponents of most population-control methods. During the 1960s, the Church's doctrine regarding abortion and especially contraception was examined rigorously by both individual Catholics and members of the hierarchy. Here, Pope Paul VI reaffirms the Church's traditional position:

And now We wish to speak to the rulers of nations. To you most of all is committed the responsibility of safeguarding the common good....The family is the primary unit in the state; do not tolerate any legislation which would introduce into the family those practices which are opposed to the natural law of God. For there are other ways by which a government can and should solve the population problem— that is to say by enacting laws which will assist families and by educating the people wisely so that the moral law and the freedom of the citizens are both safeguarded.

We are fully aware of the difficulties confronting the public authorities in this matter, especially in the developing countries. In fact, We had in mind the justifiable anxieties which weigh upon them when We published Our encyclical letter Populorum Progressio. But now We join Our voice to that of Our predecessor John XXIII of venerable memory, and We make Our own his words: "No statement of the problem and no solution to it is acceptable which does violence to man's essential dignity; those who propose such solutions base them on an utterly materialistic conception of man himself and his life. The only possible solution to this question is one which envisages the social and economic progress both of individuals and of the whole of human society, and which respects and promotes true human values."[66]

Mother Teresa won the Nobel prize for her work in the slums of Calcutta, India. After years of living and working with the poor in India, she reluctantly accepted the need for some form of birth control (the rhythm method) for the Indian people, although she remains adamantly opposed to contraception. She asks:

Why are people so worried about world population? There is plenty of land in India for people to live on. It is so rich a country. Why are people worried?…

Children should be a joy and a pleasure.[67]

Why are people so worried about world population?…Children should be a joy and a pleasure.

Conclusion

This chapter has presented the wide range of thinking about the relationship of the issue of population to the persistence of hunger. Our intention has been to provide a forum in which all of these ideas could be illuminated.

Are population growth rates and high population densities major causes of hunger and poverty? Will population-planning programs reduce hunger and promote economic development? Since a large number of national programs are based on the belief that the answer to these questions is yes, it is certain that the coming years will provide us with a continuing opportunity to explore the relationship of population and population planning to the end of hunger.

The question of whether to limit population, and if so, how best to do it, is a profoundly controversial one. The very question raises both points of fact and scientific data as well as points of morality and values.

In the midst of these varying ideas about what should be done, it is worth restating that the vigorously held views on the issue of population are contributing something that would otherwise be missing in the global effort to eradicate hunger.

These many and differing approaches are providing the kind of momentum and new information about what works and doesn't work that will allow us to reach the place where we can see the most effective pathways to the end of hunger.

Differing approaches about population allow us to see the most effective pathways to the end of hunger.

As such, these many dimensions of looking at the issue of population—though obviously presenting distinct points of view about the issue—share an underlying commonality when viewed from the perspective of the goal of ending hunger by the end of the century.

NOTES

1 Population Reference Bureau, *1982 World Population Data Sheet;* and *1983 World Population Data Sheet* (Washington, DC: Population Reference Bureau, 1982 and 1983).

2 Population Reference Bureau, *1983 World Population Data Sheet;* and *Information Please Almanac 1983,* 37th ed. (New York: A&W Publishers, 1982), s.v. "World Statistics" and "U.S. Statistics."

3 Hugh Thomas, *A History of the World* (New York: Harper & Row, 1979), 49.

4 Ibid.; and *Information Please Almanac 1983,* s.v. "World Statistics."

5 Thomas, *History of the World,* 49.

6 Ibid.; and Population Reference Bureau, *1983 World Population Data Sheet.*

7 Jean van der Tak, Carl Haub, and Elaine Murphy, "Our Population Predicament: A New Look," *Population Bulletin* 34, no. 5 (Washington, DC: Population Reference Bureau, December 1979): 4.

8 Shirley Foster Hartley, *Population: Quantity vs. Quality* (Englewood Cliffs, NJ: Prentice-Hall, 1972), 4; and United Nations, Fund for Population Activities, *The State of the World Population 1982,* by Rafael M. Salas, n.p. A revised figure of 2.06 percent for the period between 1965 and 1970 has been published by the Population Division of the United Nations in *World Population Prospects, Estimates and Projections as Assessed in 1982*, in 1985.

9 Population Reference Bureau, *1983 World Population Data Sheet.*

10 Michael P. Todaro, *Economic Development in the Third World,* 2nd ed. (New York: Longman, 1981), xxxii–xxxiii.

11 van der Tak, Haub, and Murphy, "Our Population Predicament," 4.

12 Ibid., 10–12.

13 Population Reference Bureau, *1983 World Population Data Sheet.*

14 Derived from Population Reference Bureau, *1983 World Population Data Sheet.* The Population Data Sheet "lists all geopolitical entities with a population larger than 150,000 and all members of the United Nations." For five countries, no infant mortality rates were reported. These countries were not included in the average.

15 This discussion of population age structures is based on the work of William Petersen, *Population,* 2nd ed. (New York: Macmillan, 1970), 76–77, 86–88.

16 Shirley Foster Hartley, *Population: Quantity vs. Quality,* 4.

17 Population Reference Bureau, *1983 World Population Data Sheet.*

18 van der Tak, Haub, and Murphy, "Our Population Predicament," 42–43.

19 United Nations, Population Division of the Department of International Economic and Social Affairs, *Report on the Fifth Population Inquiry among Governments* (ESA/P/WP/83), 11 January 1984, 51.

20 United Nations, Fund for Population Activities, *The State of the World Population 1982.*

21 International Planned Parenthood Federation, London, correspondence to The Hunger Project, San Francisco, 21 January 1983; updated by IPPF 1984. This measure would be somewhat less if the 1971 and 1984 figures were adjusted for inflation.

22 U.S., Congress, *World Population and Fertility Planning Technologies: The Next 20 Years* (Washington, DC: Office of Technology Assessment, February 1982), 13, 15, 16.

23 Paul A. Samuelson, *Economics,* 11th ed. (New York: McGraw-Hill, 1980), 27.

24 Thomas Robert Malthus, *An Essay on the Principle of Population,* ed. Philip Appleman (New York: W. W. Norton, 1976), 19, 20, 59–60.

25 Paul R. Ehrlich, *The Population Bomb,* rev. (New York: Ballantine, 1968), 1.

26 C. P. Snow, *The State of Siege* (New York: Charles Scribner's Sons, 1969), 25, 30, 39–40.

27   Paul F. McCleary and J. Philip Wogaman, *Quality of Life in a Global Society* (New York: Friendship Press, 1978), 25.

28   David and Marcia Pimentel, *Food, Energy and Society* (London: Edward Arnold, 1979), 142–43.

29   Commission on International Development, *Partners in Development,* chaired by Lester Pearson (New York: Praeger, 1969), 55.

30   Population Reference Bureau, *1983 World Population Data Sheet;* and United Nations, Department of International Economic and Social Affairs, *World Population Prospects as Assessed in 1980* (ST/ESA/SER. A/78), 1981, 5.

31   Cynthia P. Green, *People: An Endangered Species?* rev. (Washington, DC: National Wildlife Federation, 1980), 6.

32   Fr. Arthur McCormack, "Plenary IV—Population, Social Change and Development," *Since Bucharest—and the Future* (Washington, DC: World Population Society, 1976), 117.

33   Green, *People: An Endangered Species?* 7.

34   United Nations, Secretariat, *Text of Statement by Secretary-General, U Thant, at Opening of Orientation Course for Population Programme Officers* (Press Release SG/SM/1055, SOC/3624), 14 January 1969, n.p.

35   Paul R. Ehrlich, Anne H. Ehrlich, and John P. Holdren, *Human Ecology* (San Francisco: W. H. Freeman, 1973), 10, 11–12.

36   Garrett Hardin, "Lifeboat Ethics: The Case Against Helping the Poor," *Psychology Today,* September 1974, 38–40, 41, 126.

37   Perdita Huston, *Third World Women Speak Out* (New York: Praeger, 1979), 74.

38   Ibid., 83.

39   Ibid., 67, 68.

40   Dom Moraes, *A Matter of People* (New York: Praeger, 1974), 43.

41   Huston, *Third World Women,* 60, 61.

42   James W. Brackett, R. T. Ravenholt, and John C. Chao, "The Role of Family Planning in Recent Rapid Fertility Declines in Developing Countries," *Studies in Family Planning* 9, no. 12 (December 1978): 315, 322.

43   Julian L. Simon, *The Ultimate Resource* (Princeton, NJ: Princeton University Press, 1981), 9.

44   ———, "The Case for More People," *American Demographics* 1, no. 10 (November–December 1979): 26, 28.

45   ———, *The Ultimate Resource,* 221–22.

46   "Review & Outlook," *The Wall Street Journal* (Western ed.), 13 April 1984, 26.

47   Peter T. Bauer and Basil S. Yamey, "The Third World and the West: An Economic Perspective," *The Third World: Premises of U.S. Policy,* ed. W. Scott Thompson (San Francisco: Institute for Contemporary Studies, 1978), 107.

48   Jerrie DeHoogh et al., "Food for a Growing World Population," *Technological Forecasting and Social Change* 10, no. 1 (1977): 31.

49   John Maddox, *The Doomsday Syndrome* (New York: McGraw-Hill, 1972), 82, 83.

50   Herman Kahn, William Brown, and Leon Martel, *The Next 200 Years: A Scenario for America and the World* (New York: William Morrow, 1976), 106, 111–12.

51   Sartaj Aziz, "The World Food Situation—Today and in the Year 2000," *Proceedings: The World Food Conference of 1976* (Ames, IA: Iowa State University Press, 1977), 23.

52   René Dumont, *Utopia or Else...,* trans. Vivienne Menkes (New York: Universe Books, 1975), 51.

53   Denis Goulet and Michael Hudson, *The Myth of Aid* (New York: IDOC North America, 1971), 129.

54 Roy L. Prosterman, "More Food, Fewer Children," *A Shift in the Wind,* no. 3 (November 1978): 10.

55 Pierre Pradervand, "The Malthusian Man," *New Internationalist,* no. 15 (May 1974): 13.

56 Mary Alice Caliendo, *Nutrition and the World Food Crisis* (New York: Macmillan, 1979), 198, 199–200.

57 Mahmood Mamdani, *The Myth of Population Control: Family, Caste, and Class in an Indian Village* (New York: Monthly Review Press, 1972), 76, 99.

58 Ibid., 78.

59 James Nelson Goodsell, "A Continent Resists Birth Curbs," *The Christian Science Monitor,* 29 December 1970, 1.

60 "Family Size and the Black American," *Population Bulletin* 30, no. 4 (Washington, DC: Population Reference Bureau, 1975): 11.

61 Maaza Bekele, "False Prophets of Doom," *Unesco Courier,* July–August 1974, 43, 44–45.

62 Mario de Cautin, "Native Americans' Struggle for Survival," *IFDA Dossier,* no. 28 (March–April 1982): 83.

63 Moraes, *A Matter of People,* 191.

64 Ibid., 127–28.

65 Simon, *The Ultimate Resource,* 338–39, 339–40.

66 Pope Paul VI, "The Encyclical Letter 'Humanae Vitae,'" *The Pope Speaks* 13, no. 4 (Winter 1969): 341–42.

67 Moraes, *A Matter of People,* 41.

In 1983, 4.7 billion people lived on the earth—92 million more than the year before. This increase roughly equals the combined total populations of Costa Rica, Australia, the United Kingdom, Iraq, and Israel, or ten times the population of Calcutta or the New York metropolitan area. Historically, this increase has occurred quite rapidly. Around 1750, the time of the Industrial Revolution, there were fewer than 750 million people. By 1975, there were 4 billion. Whether the population densities of the present era are desirable is a matter of debate. But what is certain is that current densities and growth rates are a unique phenomenon in human history. Photos: Crowds shown in the following countries. Right: *Viet Nam* (Wally McNamee/Woodfin Camp & Assoc.); next two-page spread: *India* (© Dilip Mehta/Contact); following two-page spread: *China* (P. J. Griffiths/ Magnum Photos).

We explore two schools of thought on the population issue. One holds that population densities and growth rates in the Third World are contributing to hunger and poverty. An alternative school of thought holds that population growth is not at the root of hunger and therefore need not be a major focus of the work of ending hunger. Among the questions raised by these divergent schools of thought are: Do poor people in the Third World want more family-planning assistance? Do more people constitute a drain on the world's resources, or enhance them? Are population-control programs a crime against the human race, or essential to its survival? Left: *An African family* (J. P. Laffont/ Sygma); this page: *A Texas family* (Wally McNamee/Woodfin Camp & Assoc.). *Traditionally, families have been the backbone, the mainstay of human society. The Roman Catholic Church expresses a strong, family-centered view in the Encyclical Letter,*

<u>Humanae Vitae</u>: *"The family is the primary unit in the state; do not tolerate any legislation which would introduce into the family those practices which are opposed to the natural law of God."* Photos: Families in different regions of the world. Next page, left to right, top row: *Alaska* (Chuck O'Rear/Woodfin Camp & Assoc.); *Southern U.S.* (© David Burnett/ Contact); *Peru* (© Gianfranco Gorgoni/Contact); left to right, middle row: *Philippines* (Christopher Morris/Black Star); *Amazon region* (J. R. Holland/Black Star); *Somalia* (Wernher Krutein/Photovault); *Philippines* (Owen Franken/Sygma); *Malaysia* (© Rick Smolan/Contact); *Uganda* (C. Steele-Perkins/Magnum Photos); next two-page spread, left to right, bottom row: *Iran* (Anthony Howarth/Woodfin Camp & Assoc.); *Mexico* (Marc & Evelyne Bernheim/ Woodfin Camp & Assoc.); *U.S.* (Charles Harbutt/Archive).

Advocates and opponents of population planning share a deep concern for the future of the world's children. Former UN Secretary-General U Thant speaks for the advocates: "Too rapid population growth constitutes a major obstacle to education and the promotion of the welfare of the young in general.... The task of providing opportunities for the world's as yet unborn children...appears in a number of countries well-nigh insuperable, unless action is taken to moderate the population growth rate." Overleaf two-page spread: *Children and llamas, Peru* (J. P. Laffont/Sygma); left: *Boy breaking ground, New Delhi, India* (J. P. Laffont/ Sygma); this page: *Brother and sister, Bogotá, Colombia* (J. P. Laffont/Sygma); next two-page spread: *Girls pumping water, Africa* (Wernher Krutein/Photovault).

Advocates of population planning cite the concern of Third World mothers for the future of their children. A woman in Villagran, Mexico, looks at her children's future in the light of her own life: "We were very poor when I was a child. We were six children, and my father didn't earn much. That is why I want just two or three children. I don't want my children to grow up like me—without an education.... I want my children to go to school and learn many, many things. I don't want them to live by the rumors of the street. I want them to learn for themselves. I want them to be independent and proud of themselves." Left: *Mother and child in Thailand* (© David Burnett/Contact); below: *Woman studying IUD, India* (Paolo Koch/ Photo Researchers).

*The World Fertility Survey asked currently
married women who believed that they and
their husbands were physically capable of
having another child whether they wanted to
have any more children. A large proportion of
the women interviewed stated that they wanted
no more children—from 72 percent in South
Korea to 30 percent in Nepal.* Left: *Pregnant
woman and her child, Mexico* (David Alan
Harvey/ Woodfin Camp & Assoc.); below:
African women at a child-care clinic (Wernher
Krutein/ Photovault).

Some Third World mothers and fathers want large families. A Colombian woman, expecting her twelfth child, explains it this way: "The more children I have, the more security I will have in my old age. There isn't much money in these parts, but the children are a hope to me that I will be cared for when I am no longer able to work." Above: *Mothers and children, Somalia* (Mike Yamashita/Woodfin Camp & Assoc. and Kevin Fleming/Woodfin Camp & Assoc.); right: *Mothers and children, India* (© Rick Smolan/Contact).

Opponents of population planning do not view the birth of a child as a decline in standard of living. Rather, as economists Peter Bauer and Basil Yamey suggest, what is meant by the so-called population explosion "is that people and their children live longer, and therefore it represents a manifest and pronounced improvement in the standard of living of those who have survived and whose children live longer." Overleaf two-page spread: *A young girl, Jodhpur, India* (Robert Frerck/Woodfin Camp & Assoc.); left: *Young girl, U.S.* (Wernher Krutein/ Photovault); above: *Young girl, Mexico* (David Alan Harvey/Woodfin Camp & Assoc.); next two-page spread: *Young boy, Guatemala* (© Alon Reininger/Contact).

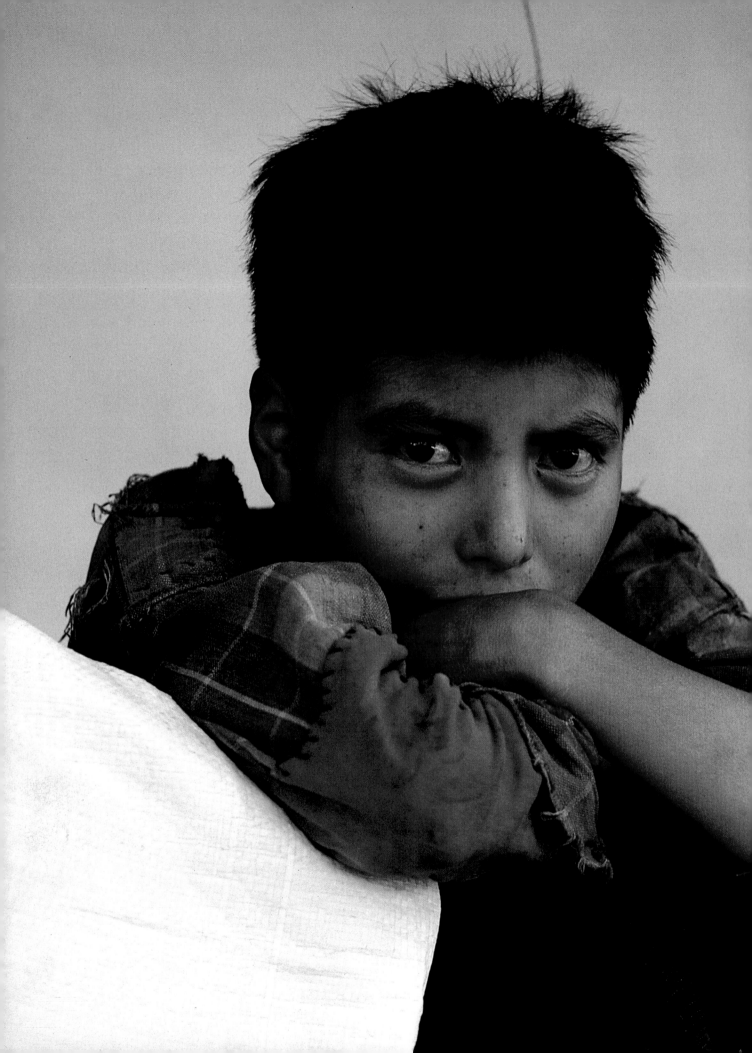

*Expanding populations in the Third World pose
a moral dilemma for some population-growth
critics, such as Garrett Hardin: "Metaphorically each rich nation can be seen as a lifeboat
full of comparatively rich people. In the ocean
outside each lifeboat swim the poor of the
world, who would like to get in, or at least share
some of the wealth.... We have several options:
we may be tempted to live by the Christian ideal
of being 'our brother's keeper,' or by the Marxist
ideal of 'to each according to his needs.' Since
the needs of all in the water are the same, and
since they can all be seen as 'our brothers,' we
could take them all into our boat, making a
total of 150 in a boat designed for 60. The boat
swamps, everyone drowns. Complete justice,
complete catastrophe."* Left: *Elderly Druze,
Israel* (Fred Mayer/Woodfin Camp &
Assoc.); above: *Grandfather and grand-
son, Pakistan* (© Jim Sheldon/Contact).

Many Third World leaders view development specialists' involvement in family planning as "meddling," rather than as helping. Population control is not a social good, according to this viewpoint, but a tool of racism and repression. Ethiopian social planner Maaza Bekele asserts that "In Africa we cannot afford to look upon our growing population as a problem. We have to face up to the challenge of engaging our young, expectant peoples in the struggle to achieve the most rapid development possible.... It seems almost sinister that there is so much money available to <u>control</u> life and hardly any to <u>promote</u> it. It also seems unrealistic to expect that poverty-stricken, hard-working African mothers—many close to death before the age of 35—can be expected to limit the number of their children when only 1 out of 3 or 4 survive.... [These women] cannot run the risk that their major creative contribution to humanity (given that the rest of their existence

is almost pure drudgery), will be denied them. In each woman is the grain of hope that life for her offspring will be better than hers." Photos of women from various Third World countries. This page: *Ethiopia* (Liz Major); opposite, top row, left to right: *Guatemala* (Alon Reininger/Contact for Woodfin Camp & Assoc.); *Somalia* (Mike Yamashita/Woodfin Camp & Assoc.); *Thailand* (© David Burnett/Contact); middle row, left to right: *Sri Lanka* (Thomas Hopker/Woodfin Camp & Assoc.); *Caribbean Islands* (Mike Yamashita/Woodfin Camp & Assoc.); *Ghana* (I. Berry/Magnum Photos); bottom row, left to right: *India* (Robert Frerck/Woodfin Camp & Assoc.); *Syria* (Robert Azzi/Woodfin Camp & Assoc.); *Niger* (Marc & Evelyne Bernheim/Woodfin Camp & Assoc.).

According to a recent study of Third World
women, "There is a large unmet demand for
fertility control services." A Tunisian woman
agrees: "Now women...can have family planning and be in good health.... All women are
reaching out to learn, to go out, to listen." Left:
A "one-child family" in Peking (Owen Fran-
ken/Sygma); above: A birth-control class in
Calcutta (M. Silverstone/Magnum Photos).

The "population problem," from two perspectives: (1) C. P. Snow warns that "Many millions of people in the poor countries are going to starve to death before our eyes ... we shall see them doing so upon our television sets."
(2) Mother Teresa asks: "Why are people so worried about world population? There is plenty of land in India for people to live on. It is so rich a country.... Children should be a joy and a pleasure." Above and left: *Mother Teresa and children* (Francolon/Gamma-Liaison and J. P. Laffont/Sygma); next two-page spread: *Hospital in the Philippines, newborn nursery* (© David Burnett/Contact).

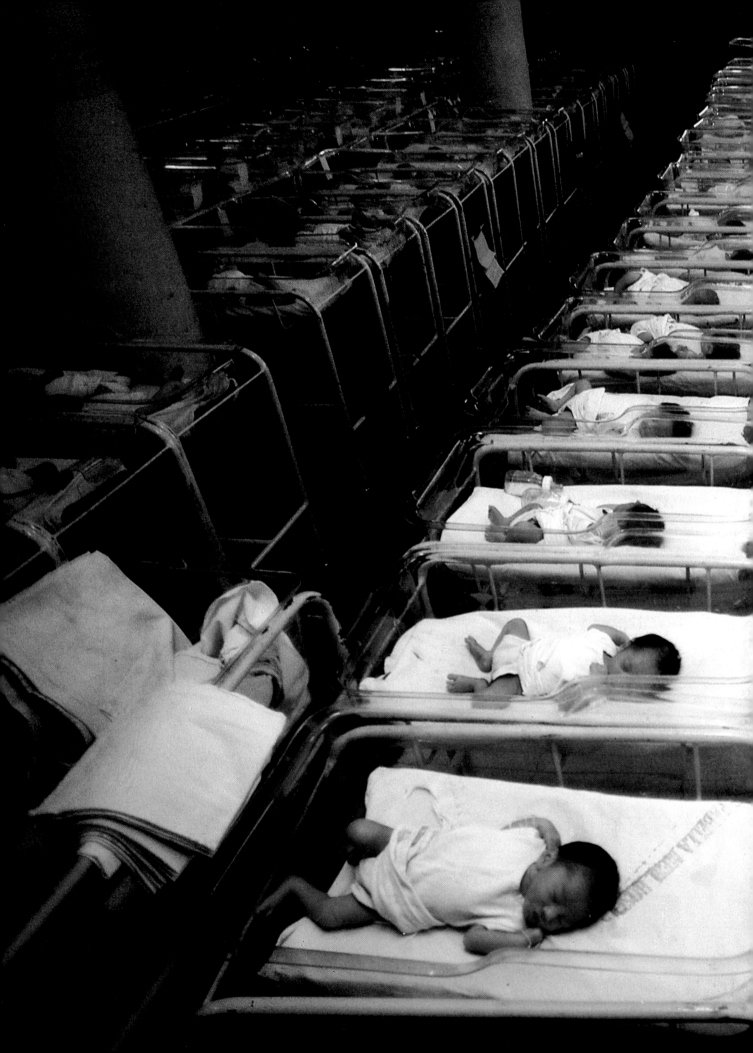

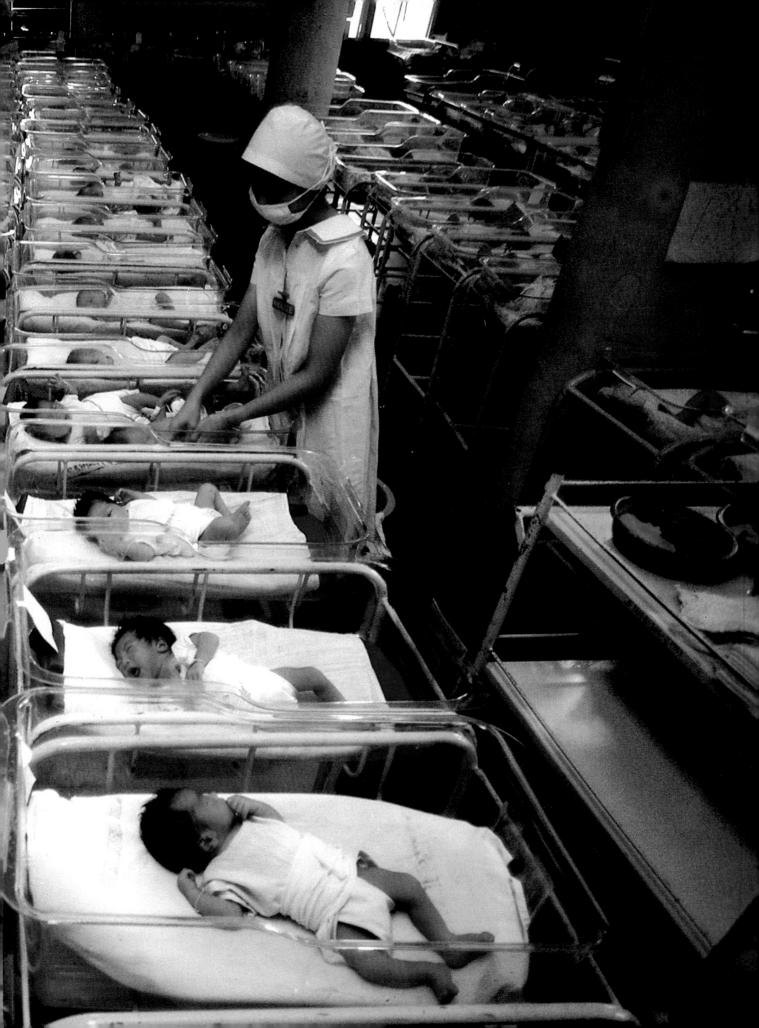

Food

Food availability is at the very heart of ending hunger.

Hunger exists when there is not enough food for the people who need it. This situation arises either because of problems in adequately producing or distributing the food, or because people cannot afford to buy the food that is available.

This chapter explores the issue of food availability—an issue that, for many analysts and observers, is at the very heart of the effort to end hunger.

Because food availability is such a major focus for those concerned with ending hunger, we will give it more attention than the other issues.

In this chapter we examine three distinct aspects of the issue—*Food Production, Food Storage and Security,* and *Distribution.*

Food Production

This section focuses on the actual growing of food and, in particular, on the question of how much more food can be grown.

In *Basic Facts on Food Production* we present background information on the total amount of food currently produced and basic technologies of food production. We also focus on the availability of key factors that contribute to food production—land, water, energy, and fertilizer.

Several important facts and projections stand out:

Enough grain was produced in 1982 to provide each man, woman, and child on the planet with about two loaves of bread each day.

In the United States (which has the most mechanized agricultural system in the world), only 3 percent of the national energy budget goes to food production.

A projection reported in *Scientific American* indicates that all of the available water on the planet may be in use by the year 2000.

The section concludes with a discussion of the controversial "Green Revolution," which, beginning in the 1960s, introduced newly developed high-yielding varieties of grain to several Third World nations.

What is the most effective way to increase food production? To explore this question, we examine two major schools of thought. The first holds that modern technologies are an effective path to the end of hunger. This position is supported by several experts and policy makers in the field of agriculture—including, most importantly, Nobel Laureate Norman Borlaug, the "father of the Green Revolution." The points of view presented emphasize that modern technologies can produce more food, contribute to beneficial social and political changes, and be used in ways that are sustainable and ecologically sound.

An alternative school of thought agrees that more food needs to be produced, but not by the modern agricultural techniques now in use. Representatives of this school include Robert Rodale, a proponent of organic agriculture from the United States; Asit Biswas, an Indian agricultural specialist; and Pierre Spitz, director for Asia of the Food Systems and Society research project at the United Nations Research Institute for Social Development in Geneva. They argue that high-technology agriculture is not sustainable even in the United States, and that proponents of the Green Revolution have ignored its adverse ecological and social consequences. Only organic agricultural methods will be sustainable in the long run; these methods can efficiently produce all the food needed to end hunger.

Food Storage and Security

Because food is needed every day but harvested only at infrequent times each year, effective food storage systems are critical to any program to end hunger.

This section begins by reviewing the basic facts of how the present system works and the history of attempts to modify it. Historically, grain has been the principal food stored to ensure food security, and this is true today as well. But the present system by which grain is bought, sold, and stored is subject to severe fluctuations when major producers (such as the United States and the USSR) have bad harvests. This happened to the USSR in 1972–1974, and again in 1979: Prices increased worldwide, and the people in many Third World nations suffered. Such price increases have led to periodic proposals for an international system of reserves. None of these proposals has been implemented, however, and many nations object to them strongly.

On the issue of food storage and security, major schools of thought focus on the question, "Should an international food reserve system be established?" One approach holds that establishing a large-scale internationally coordinated grain-reserve system is a necessary step in ending world hunger. Advocates of this position include the Carter Commission on World Hunger and Sartaj Aziz, former deputy secretary general of the World Food Conference. They argue that an international reserve system would provide effective famine relief, and would benefit farmers in both developed and Third World nations by stabilizing world markets.

The alternative perspective holds that establishing a large-scale internationally coordinated grain reserve is not desirable. A diverse group of specialists appear in support of this view, including author-activist Susan George, United States Senator Robert Dole, representatives of the Food and Agriculture Organization (FAO), and the American Farm Bureau Federation. They believe that an international system would be ineffective and would reduce incentives for more effective local and national programs. Some feel that the present "free market" system is likely to produce the best results over the long run.

Distribution

This section presents three schools of thought. The first holds that for hunger to end, the efficiency of the food system must be improved. Here we cite economists specializing in the fields of agriculture and development who argue that we must understand the food system as a whole, provide incentives to producers and distributors, and limit government intervention.

The second school of thought, although also concerned with incentives and the efficient functioning of the food system, focuses specifically on the question of land

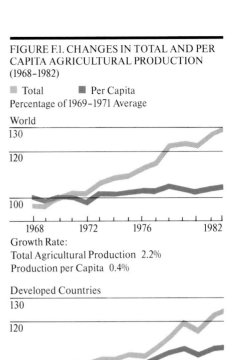

FIGURE F.1. CHANGES IN TOTAL AND PER CAPITA AGRICULTURAL PRODUCTION (1968–1982)

Total   Per Capita

Percentage of 1969–1971 Average

World

Growth Rate:
Total Agricultural Production 2.2%
Production per Capita 0.4%

Developed Countries

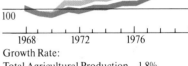

Growth Rate:
Total Agricultural Production   1.8%
Production per Capita   1.0%

Developing Countries

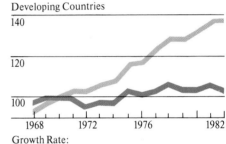

Growth Rate:
Total Agricultural Production 3.0%
Production per Capita 0.5%

Centrally Planned Countries

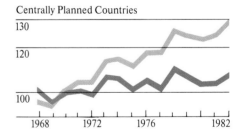

Growth Rate:
Total Agricultural Production   2.0%
Production per Capita 0.7%

Source: U.S., Department of Agriculture, *1983 Handbook of Agricultural Charts,* Agriculture Handbook, no. 619 (Washington, DC: U.S. Government Printing Office, December 1983), 65.

Both total agricultural production and per-capita agricultural production have been increasing steadily in most regions of the world. But the increase in per-capita production in developing countries has been less than in developed or centrally planned countries. In some African countries, per-capita production has actually declined.

reform. Land reform, say these experts, is an effective and necessary way to end hunger. This subsection presents the views of Roy Prosterman, a leading advocate and activist for land reform, as well as those of the World Bank and of Sterling Wortman and Ralph Cummings, Jr. These proponents believe that land reform is a proven solution, and that case studies support this point of view.

The final school of thought holds that in order to end hunger, inequitable power structures must become more equitable. Three leading advocates of this position— Susan George, Frances Moore Lappé, and Joseph Collins—argue that achieving the end of hunger requires a transfer of power from the rich to the poor and from the powerful to the powerless. Fundamentally changing social and economic structures would contribute to problems beginning to be solved. Without such changes, no other solutions will be effective.

Basic Facts on Food Production

The subject of food production raises certain basic questions:

How much food is there?

How is food produced?

How much more food can be grown?

How Much Food Is There?

In 1982, the total recorded food production in the world was 3,764 million metric tons. Of that food, about half by weight was grain. This means 1,675 million metric tons—an almost unimaginable amount of food.[1] The grain alone would be enough to fill a 1-foot-diameter tube that encircled the earth 742 times. And this amount of grain is produced on this planet *in just one year.*

The food currently raised would more than adequately feed 6.1 billion people.

If all the food produced on the earth each year were divided equally among all the people of the earth, every person would receive about 2.3 kilograms (five pounds) of food per day—more than three times the minimum amount needed to support life. The grain alone would provide everyone with the equivalent of two loaves of bread a day. The food *currently* raised each year is more than enough to adequately feed the 6.1 billion people anticipated by the year 2000.[2]

World food production has been increasing steadily for decades. From 1950 to 1980, annual world food production actually doubled—it grew at an average annual rate of about 2.6 percent, which was well ahead of the roughly 2 percent per year population growth rate. Over the past thirty years, the world's per capita food production has increased by about 25 percent.[3]

However, increases in food production have not occurred evenly throughout the world. From 1950 to 1980, per capita production increased 47 percent in the developed countries, but only 15 percent in the developing countries.[4] In sub-Saharan Africa, per capita food production has actually declined during the past two decades.[5]

During the late 1970s, in the poorer countries the *rate of increase* of food production rose somewhat, while in the richer countries it slowed down.[6] However, agricultural *yields* in developing countries are still notably lower.

96

FIGURE F.2. TRENDS IN TOTAL AND PER CAPITA FOOD PRODUCTION, FOR SELECTED COUNTRIES AND REGIONS

(The numbers in the graphs are indices. 1969-71 = 100.)

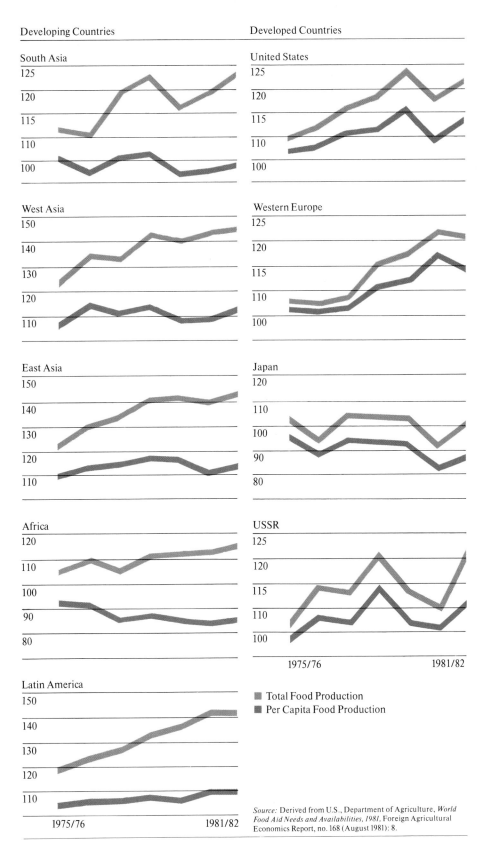

Developing Countries

South Asia

West Asia

East Asia

Africa

Latin America

1975/76   1981/82

Developed Countries

United States

Western Europe

Japan

USSR

1975/76   1981/82

■ Total Food Production
■ Per Capita Food Production

Source: Derived from U.S., Department of Agriculture, *World Food Aid Needs and Availabilities, 1981,* Foreign Agricultural Economics Report, no. 168 (August 1981): 8.

A more detailed regional breakdown of total and per-capita food production shows major problem areas. All the developing regions (on the left side) have increased their food production significantly. Nevertheless, they are having problems keeping pace with their rapidly growing populations.

This map shows, for different countries of the world, the percentage of total output (goods and services) produced by the agricultural sector. In the Third World, a much greater proportion of economic activity and resources must be devoted to the growing of food.

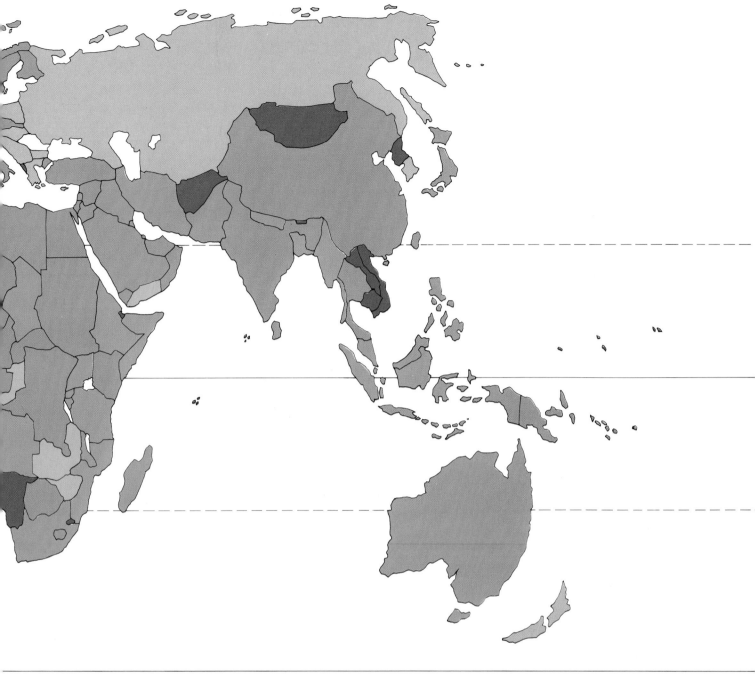

FIGURE F.3. HOW MUCH OF A NATION'S ECONOMY IS DEVOTED TO AGRICULTURE?

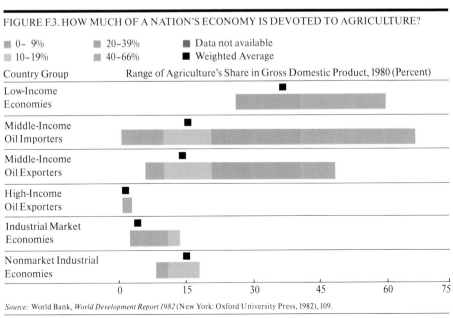

| | 0– 9% | | 20–39% | ■ | Data not available |
| | 10–19% | | 40–66% | ■ | Weighted Average |

Country Group	Range of Agriculture's Share in Gross Domestic Product, 1980 (Percent)
Low-Income Economies	
Middle-Income Oil Importers	
Middle-Income Oil Exporters	
High-Income Oil Exporters	
Industrial Market Economies	
Nonmarket Industrial Economies	

0   15   30   45   60   75

Source: World Bank, *World Development Report 1982* (New York: Oxford University Press, 1982), 109.

How Is Food Produced?

Food comes from plants, and is formed from the carbon dioxide in the air and from the water and nutrients in the soil. Plants use the sun's energy to combine chemically those basic ingredients into sugars, starches, proteins, and fats. Most of the food that humans eat comes directly from plants; the rest comes from animals that eat plants, or animals that eat animals that eat plants. Since from four to ten pounds of grain are needed to produce one pound of meat, eating meat from a grain-fed animal is equivalent to eating four to ten times that amount of grain.[7]

Animals do not necessarily compete with humans for food. Although cows, horses, sheep, and goats are often given grain supplements, they can live totally on forage that is not edible by people. Poultry and pigs are the main domestic animals that compete with humans for grains.

Although nature produces food, in the form of animals and wild plants, without any help from humans, the process is slow and uneven. Therefore, societies have intervened in natural processes to increase food production. Thousands of diverse technologies produce a variety of foods in different parts of the world. Agricultural technologies range from traditional labor-intensive modes to modern technologies, which usually are capital- and fuel-intensive.

Societies usually develop agricultural methods that fit their own particular resource endowments and cultural preferences. Some of these methods differ markedly from the highly capital- and energy-intensive agricultural practices common in the United States. In Taiwan and Japan, for example, land is limited, and the yield per unit of land is very high. Those countries get high yields by means of labor-intensive methods of production, high fertilizer use, and relatively little mechanization. By contrast, New Zealand, which has a small population and plenty of land, produces high yields per agricultural worker but relatively low yields per unit of land. European countries, which have limited amounts of both land and labor, obtain relatively high yields from both. However, most developing countries do not produce efficiently with either their labor or their land resources.[8]

How Much More Food Could Be Grown?

Considering how much we know about the earth's resources, we should find it easy to predict what could be produced in the future. However, we are dealing with a prediction, not with a clear and agreed-upon statement of what is so now; thus we are immediately confronted by the varying assessments and analyses of a range of experts. In other words, in seeking out the answer to the question, "How much more food could be grown?" we must enter the arena of points of view and differing perspectives. This is a departure from the organizational structure of the *Basic Facts* sections in the rest of this book; you will encounter in this section a number of clearly identified viewpoints regarding the potential for increasing food production in the years ahead.

Land. How much land is available for growing food? Of the more than 13 billion hectares of land in the world, the total amount of potentially cultivable land on earth is generally agreed to be about 3.2 billion hectares—only about 1.4 billion of which are now being cultivated. Thus, apparently, the area upon which food can be grown could be more than doubled.[9] However, other factors can make the planet's stock of agricultural land seem either scarce or abundant, depending on one's point of view. Here are just a few examples.

Major food crops of the world. Top row: *Corn* (John Blaustein/Woodfin Camp & Assoc.); *Rice* (Hans Hoefer/Woodfin Camp & Assoc.); second row: *Soybeans* (Dan Guravich/Photo Researchers); *Cassava* (Russ Kinne/Photo Researchers); third row: *Wheat* (Jim Pickerell/Black Star); *Milo-sorghum* (John Blaustein/Woodfin Camp & Assoc.); fourth row: *Millet* (Tom McHugh/Photo Researchers); *Plantain* (Andy Levin/Black Star).

FIGURE F.4. THE FOOD-PRODUCTION PROCESS

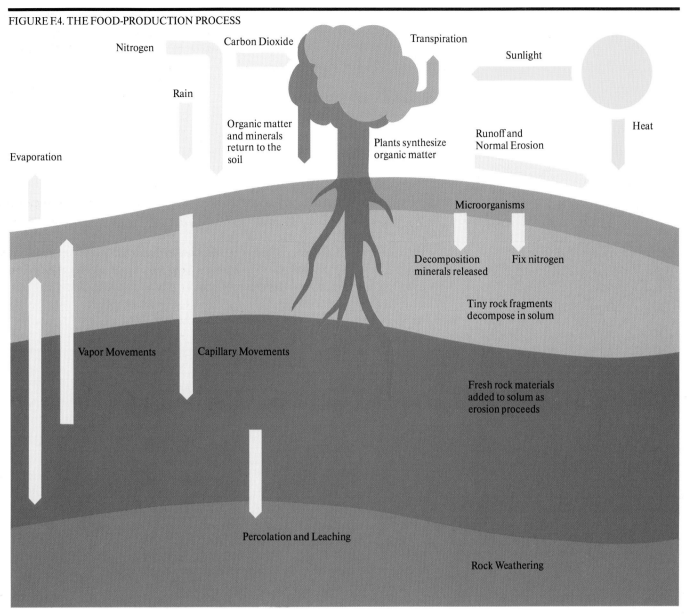

Source: Charles E. Kellogg, *Agricultural Development: Soil, Food, People, Work* (Madison, WI: Soil Science Society of America, 1975), 4.

FIGURE F.5. THE WORLD'S MAIN FOOD CROPS (1979)

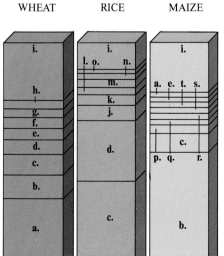

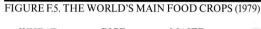

WHEAT   RICE   MAIZE

Wheat:
441 Million
Metric Tons
- **a.** USSR 27%
- **b.** U.S. 11%
- **c.** China 10%
- **d.** India 7%
- **e.** France 5%
- **f.** Canada 5%
- **g.** Australia 4%
- **h.** Turkey 4%
- **i.** Other 27%

Rice:
376 Million
Metric Tons
- **c.** China 35%
- **d.** India 29%
- **j.** Indonesia 7%
- **k.** Bangladesh 5%
- **l.** Thailand 4%
- **m.** Japan 4%
- **n.** Burma 3%
- **o.** Viet Nam 2%
- **i.** Other 18%

Maize:
363 Million
Metric Tons
- **b.** U.S. 49%
- **c.** China 9%
- **p.** Brazil 4%
- **q.** Romania 3%
- **r.** S. Africa 3%
- **s.** Argentina 3%
- **t.** Mexico 2.5%
- **e.** France 2.5%
- **a.** USSR 2%
- **i.** Other 22%

Source: *UNICEF News* 113 (1982): 8.

Food comes from plants: It is formed from the carbon dioxide in the air and from the water and nutrients in the soil. Plants use the sun's energy to chemically combine these basic ingredients into sugars, starches, proteins, and fats.

Three main cereal crops provide the basic food for most of the world, whether directly consumed or converted into meat and dairy products.

The richest, most accessible, and easiest land to farm is already in production. Development costs to clear, irrigate, drain, or provide access to new lands run to thousands of dollars per hectare, and those lands may never be as productive as the prime land we now use.

Much arable land is not included in the aggregate count, including: land in home gardens and suburban back yards; the private plots of collective farmers in the Eastern Bloc; city parks; and community gardens. Abundant food could be, and sometimes is, grown in all these places. In Holland, even the median strips of highways and the earthen tops of dams are used for grazing animals.

Arable land is lost continuously, irreversibly, and in enormous quantities to erosion, construction, and urbanization.

Human care, attention, labor, and energy can make deserts bloom.

New technologies are constantly being developed that permit the production of food on land previously believed uncultivable. For example, soil can be created where it did not previously exist by means of composting, fertilizing, green-manuring, and many other techniques. Human care and attention, combined with labor and energy, can make deserts bloom.

TABLE F.1. WORLD LAND-USE PATTERNS (1966–1980)

Land Use	1966	1980	1966	1980
	(Million Hectares)		(Percentage)	
Cropland	1,381	1,452	10.6	11.1
Permanent Pastures	3,122	3,117	23.9	23.8
Forests and Woodlands	4,236	4,093	32.4	31.3
Other Land	4,336	4,413	33.1	33.8
TOTAL	13,075	13,075	100.0	100.0

Source: U.S., Department of Agriculture, *World Agriculture: Outlook and Situation Report* (Washington, DC: U.S. Government Printing Office, June 1984), 26.

Technologies that permit nonerosion-producing farming are *far* less expensive than technologies that restore land once it is eroded.

The following quotations on the subject of erosion show how judgments about the extent and seriousness of the problem can significantly affect estimates of potentially arable land and its food-producing capability. Erosion could be a potentially serious problem—but is it?

Economist Julian Simon and social historian Robert Katz argue that there is enough food-producing land. In fact, says Simon, the amount of potentially arable land is actually increasing. He writes:

The potential for creating new land has increased as knowledge, machinery, and power sources have improved. At one time, most of Europe could not be planted, because the soils were "too heavy." When a plow that could farm the heavy soil was invented, much of Europe suddenly became arable in the eyes of the people who lived there. Most of Ireland and New England were once too hilly and stony for farming, but with effort the stones were removed and the land became "suitable for crops".... In the twentieth century, bulldozers and dynamite have cleared out stumps that kept land from being plowed. And in the future, cheap transportation and desalination may transform what are now deserts into arable lands. The definition of "arable" changes as technology develops and the demand for land rises. Hence

FIGURE F.6. TOTAL LAND PER CONTINENT, COMPARED WITH CULTIVABLE LAND (1981)

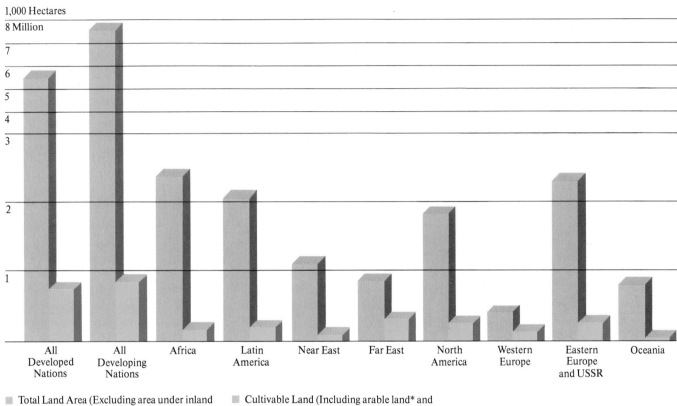

1,000 Hectares

Total Land Area (Excluding area under inland water bodies)

Cultivable Land (Including arable land* and land under permanent crops**)

*Includes land under temporary crops, temporary meadows for mowing or pasture, land under market and kitchen gardens, and land temporarily fallow or lying idle.

**Excludes land under trees grown for wood or timber.

Source: United Nations. Food and Agriculture Organization, *1982 FAO Production Yearbook* 36, FAO Statistics Series, no. 47 (Rome: FAO. 1983). 55, 56.

FIGURE F.7. WORLD LAND-USE CHANGES (1966–1980)

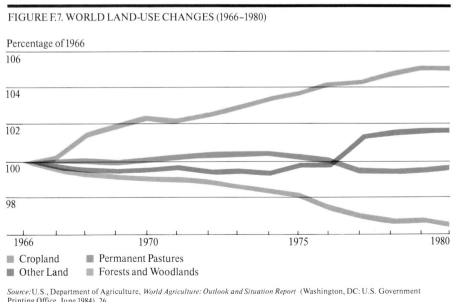

Percentage of 1966

■ Cropland   ■ Permanent Pastures
■ Other Land ■ Forests and Woodlands

World land use data for 1966–1980 (left) show that cropland expanded primarily at the expense of forests and woodlands, and, to a lesser extent, permanent pastures.

Source: U.S., Department of Agriculture, *World Agriculture: Outlook and Situation Report* (Washington, DC: U.S. Government Printing Office, June 1984), 26.

any calculation of "arable" land should be seen for what it is—a rough estimate without permanent force.[10]

Katz agrees:

Who…would not now, in view of the hysteria, be surprised to learn, or relearn, as the case may be, that the urban areas of the United States occupy only 1 percent of the entire land surface of the country? That all the cursed freeways, highways, turnpikes, cloverleafs, backroads, and service roads; all the airports big and small, and the 200,000 miles of railroad tracks take up but another 1 percent, or a fraction more? That the growth of our forests, which along with pastureland cover considerably more than half of America's land area, exceeds the total amount of annual tree removal by 60 percent?…

Ruined land can be reclaimed, water tables raised (or lowered). We can make rain. Soil erosion is preventable….

To the many admonitions that our planet's resourcefulness is waning fast, there is much one can oppose.[11]

A more pessimistic view is represented by conservationist M. Rupert Cutler, United States assistant secretary of agriculture for natural resources and environment in the late 1970s. He states:

Every day in the United States, four square miles of the nation's prime farmland are shifted to uses other than agriculture. Visualize a strip of land a half-mile wide stretching from New York to California. That's a million acres—the amount of prime farmland irreversibly lost to agriculture every year through urban sprawl.

Florida, producer of half the world's grapefruit and one-fourth of the world's oranges, will lose all of its unique and prime lands in less than 20 years if the current conversion rate continues. New Hampshire and Rhode Island also are destined to lose all of their prime agricultural land….

If conversion continues at the 1967–1977 rate, grave losses are foreseen in other states. West Virginia will lose 73 percent of its prime farmland in less than a generation; Connecticut, 70 percent; Massachusetts, 51 percent; Maryland and New Mexico, 44 percent; Vermont, 43 percent; Utah, 35 percent; Virginia, 24 percent; Washington, 23 percent; and Pennsylvania, 21 percent. New York and California, both top agricultural producers, will lose 16 and 15 percent, respectively, and New Jersey, 9 percent.[12]

In a similar vein, the report of the UN Conference on Desertification warns of an increase in arid land:

More than one third of the earth's land area is arid. Much of it has become desert since the dawn of civilization, and many vulnerable areas are even now being turned into desert. This process has intensified in recent decades, and threatens the future of 628 million people, or that 14 per cent of the world's population who live in the drylands; of this number, between 50 and 78 million people are affected directly by decreases in productivity associated with current desertification processes. In the past half century, on the southern edge of the Sahara alone, as much as 650,000 square kilometres of once productive land has become desert.[13]

The urban areas of the United States occupy only 1 percent of the entire land surface.

West Virginia will lose 73 percent of its prime farmland in less than a generation.

104

Water flows through the earth's atmosphere, oceans, rivers, and soils in a closed cycle, with little gain or loss. But only a small fraction of the water on the planet is available for human use.

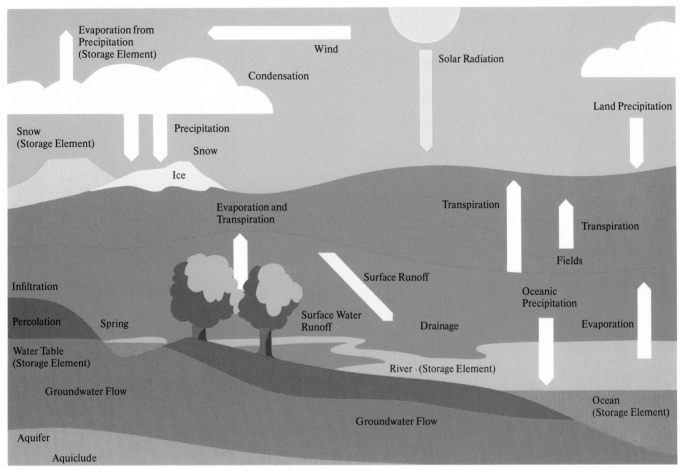

Source: David Crabbe and Simon Lawson, *The World Food Book* (London: Kogan Page, Ltd., 1981), 94.

FIGURE F.9. ENERGY NEEDED TO PRODUCE AND DELIVER A 1 KG. LOAF OF BREAD

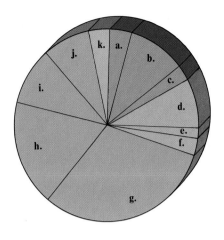

■ Growing Wheat 19.4%
a. Tractors, etc. 5.3%
b. Fertilizers 11.1%
c. Drying, Spraying 3.0%

■ Milling Wheat 12.9%
d. Direct Fuel and Power 7.4%
e. Other 2.1%
f. Packaging (1.3%) Transport (2.0%) 3.3%

■ Confection 64.3%
g. Direct Fuel and Power 30.2%
h. Other Items 17.3%
i. Packaging 9.0%
j. Transport 7.8%

■ Retail Stores 3.4%
k. Retail Stores 3.4%

Source: United Nations, Food and Agriculture Organization, *Energy for World Agriculture*, FAO Agriculture Series, no. 7 (1979): 75.

This chart shows the percentage breakdown of the energy required to produce a 1-kilogram loaf of white bread and deliver it to a retail store in the United Kingdom.

Water. Each year, the continents receive about 110,000 cubic kilometers (km³) of fresh water in the form of precipitation. Of this, 70,000 km³ are lost to evaporation, leaving a net influx of 40,000 km³ of water on the ground each year.

What happens to it?

About 14,000 km³ could reasonably be made available for human use in the form of stable runoff. The remaining 26,000 km³ are lost through floods, or are held in the soil or in swamps. Roughly 5,000 km³ of the stable runoff flow in sparsely inhabited regions, leaving 9,000 km³ available. This might be called the potentially usable world water-resource, from which all needs will have to be met for some years to come. In 1980, roughly 4,000 km³ were used for all human purposes. Of that amount, about 1,500 km³ were lost to pollution. Roughly 3,000 km³ of the potentially usable water were unexploited in 1980.[14]

All of the available fresh water in the world will be in use shortly after the year 2000, if present trends continue, according to projections by Robert Ambroggi that appeared in *Scientific American* in 1980.[15] Some parts of the world are already severely short of water and are drawing from underground pools at a rate faster than the water can be replenished.[16]

Energy. Energy, both human and mechanized, constitutes a third major factor in the production of food. Questions that concern many people who work in agriculture include: How much is needed? How can it be obtained? How can it be used most effectively?

Different agricultural technologies require vastly different amounts and types of energy. For instance, traditional dryland Asian rice culture uses about one calorie of energy (in the form of human labor) to produce about twenty calories of rice. Modern U.S. corn production requires about one calorie (mostly in the forms of tractor fuel, fertilizer, and heat for drying), to produce each calorie of corn. At the high extreme, feedlot beef production and modern deep-sea fishing require from ten to twenty calories of energy to yield one calorie of food. Thus, most modern, high-technology modes of food production depend heavily on the availability of energy (see Figure F.9).[17]

A low percentage—about 3.5 percent—of the world's total commercial energy is devoted to agriculture.[18] Even in the United States, which has one of the most mechanized agriculture systems, only about 3 percent of the nation's energy budget goes directly to food production. However, the percentage of total U.S. energy devoted to food swells to about 13 percent if processing and transport of food are included.[19]

The large increases in petroleum prices during the 1970s greatly affected the cost of raising food, as well as the accessibility of agricultural aids (such as fertilizers and tractors) to the world's farmers. Again, depending on one's point of view, the situation can be viewed as either dire and threatening or as potentially manageable. Here are assessments by two concerned experts.

David Pimentel, a biologist and energy specialist, and his colleagues warn:

While one may not doubt the sincerity of the U.S. effort to share its agricultural technology so that the rest of the world can live and eat as it does, one must be realistic about the resources available to accomplish this mission. In the United States we are currently using an equivalent of 80 gallons of gasoline to produce an acre of corn. With fuel shortages and high prices to come, we wonder if many

106

FIGURE F.10. ENERGY USE FOR AGRICULTURE IN DEVELOPING COUNTRIES (CURRENT AND PROJECTED)

Regional Totals in Million Tons Oil Equivalent

Different regions reveal different patterns of commercial energy use for food production. For example, fertilizer is used more heavily in the Far East, tractors more in Latin America.

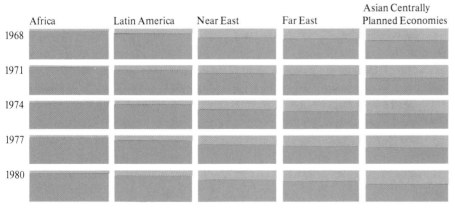

	1980	2000
Africa	1.9	12.1
a.	48%	50%
b.	9%	4%
c.	7%	2%
d.	36%	44%
Latin America	12.4	48.7
a.	45%	58%
b.	3%	2%
c.	4%	1%
d.	48%	39%
Near East	6.1	20.6
a.	36%	41%
b.	2%	2%
c.	19%	8%
d.	43%	49%
Far East	16.4	93.1
a.	15%	25%
b.	3%	5%
c.	19%	1%
d.	63%	69%

a. Farm Machinery   **c.** Irrigation
b. Pesticides   **d.** Fertilizers

Source: United Nations, Food and Agriculture Organization, *World Food Report 1983* (Rome: FAO, 1983), 54.

FIGURE F.11. THE GROWING TREND IN IRRIGATION

Land Area Irrigated as a Proportion of Total Arable Land, by Region, 1968–1980

	Africa	Latin America	Near East	Far East	Asian Centrally Planned Economies
1968					
1971					
1974					
1977					
1980					

■ Total Arable Land Area
■ Percentage Irrigated

Source: United Nations, Food and Agriculture Organization, *World Food Report 1983* (Rome: FAO, 1983), 54.

developing nations will be able to afford the technology of U.S. agriculture....

While no one knows for certain what changes will have to be made, we can be sure that when conventional energy resources become scarce and expensive, the impact on agriculture as an industry and a way of life will be significant.[20]

And agricultural economist Vernon W. Ruttan writes:

There is now something approaching a consensus that the real price of energy embodied in agricultural inputs will rise in the future. Even those who resist this perspective do not expect real energy prices to decline over the next several decades. What will be the direction of technical effort induced by the changing input-input and input-product price relationships? My reading of the literature and sampling of scientific opinion suggest that we do not know. The closest analogy to the present situation in American agricultural history was the period between 1900 and 1925. With the closing of the frontier, productivity growth declined. The new sources of productivity growth, chemical and biological technology, did not begin to emerge for several decades. My guess is that it will be at least another decade before the direction of technical change induced by the rising real price of energy becomes clear.[21]

Necessary nutrients are steadily removed from the soil as plants absorb them.

Fertilizer. Fertilizer, like land, water, and energy, makes food grow. Increasing the production of food depends on this factor as well. If plants were made only of carbon, hydrogen, and oxygen, they would need only water and air to make them grow and a little sand to hold them up. But they also are made of nitrogen, phosphorus, potassium, and dozens of other elements, all of which must be drawn from the soil in soluble form. These necessary nutrients, however, are steadily removed from the soil as plants absorb them. And once the plants are harvested, this removal is permanent. Although some nutrients are restored naturally through the slow decay of rocks and soil particles, most of them must be carefully renewed by farmers each year in the form of fertilizers.

There are two types of fertilizers: organic and inorganic. Organic fertilizers, primarily crop residues and manures, are used most often in traditional agriculture. Modern agriculture relies primarily on *inorganic* fertilizers. In 1982, the world used about 115 million metric tons of these chemically manufactured fertilizers, an increase from the 80 to 90 million metric tons used in the 1970s.[22] The increase of food production throughout the world is due in large part to the wider use of fertilizer. Developed countries use more fertilizer and produce more food per capita; underdeveloped countries use less fertilizer and produce less food per capita.

Inorganic and organic fertilizers differ in some important ways. Because organic fertilizers are natural, they require little processing and are relatively inexpensive. But because they are bulky, they cannot be stored or moved long distances. Inorganic fertilizers often are more convenient. However, producing such fertilizers requires significant capital investment for building and equipping factories, as well as large amounts of fossil fuel for production. Nitrogen fertilizer is made using natural gas or coal; phosphate fertilizer comes from natural phosphate rock decomposed with acid and heat; potassium fertilizer comes from potash mines. In developing countries, fertilizer accounts for 70 percent of the energy used in agriculture, while in developed countries, the figure is 40 percent. Nitrogen fertilizer, for example, consumes over 80 percent of all the energy used in manufacturing fertilizers.[23]

Fertilizer Use per Capita (Figures in Hundred Grams)

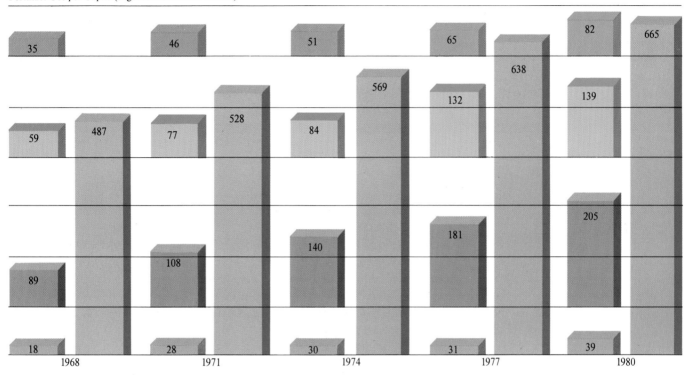

Far East
Near East
Latin America
Africa
All Developed Economies

Source: United Nations, Food and Agriculture Organization, *World Food Report 1983* (Rome: FAO, 1983), 54.

Chemical fertilizer costs have responded immediately and severely to rising energy costs. How this will finally affect agricultural production and food prices, experts are not yet sure.

The Brandt Commission report, *North-South: A Program for Survival,* was developed by an international group of world leaders and chaired by former German Chancellor and Nobel Laureate Willy Brandt. The report asks the question:

What will happen to agricultural production as supplies of oil become scarcer and so rise in price?... At the moment there should be no clear danger of a worldwide shortage of fertilizers, nor is there yet an urgent need to introduce plant varieties less dependent on chemicals. Modern high-yielding plants are efficient converters of nitrogen into food.... Fertilizers take only about 2–3 percent of current oil production, and there should be no serious volume deficiency over the next 15–20 years, especially if conservation of energy allows more oil to go into petrochemical production.[24]

S. H. Wittwer presents another view in *Science* magazine:

Thirty to 40 percent of the increased agricultural productivity in the United States in recent years is directly attributable to increased fertilizer usage. For developing nations it may be 50 percent. A fourfold increase in the cost of imported oil has precipitated a threefold jump in the price of nitrogen fertilizer. Increased food and feed prices are partially compensating for the additional cost of fertilizer. Recent shortages of fertilizer, arising from a rapidly rising demand, ...have intensified difficulties of expanding crop production, especially in developing countries. Existing food shortages will be compounded since there is neither oil nor fertilizer.[25]

The Green Revolution

Basic resources can be used to grow more food more efficiently, as scientists have discovered through study and experimentation. The "Green Revolution" is the successful introduction of newly developed high-yielding varieties of grain (wheat, rice, and others) in Third World nations. This has become one of the most widely implemented methods for increasing production. Mexico provided the site for the basic research, and successful programs were first initiated there and in India. In 1970, Norman Borlaug received the Nobel peace prize for his work in breeding the first high-yielding wheat varieties and, with the sponsorship of the Rockefeller Foundation, he actively encouraged their widespread adoption.

In 1966 Borlaug wrote a memorandum to Pakistan's secretary of agriculture, which conveys his vision and the excitement of the early years of the Green Revolution:

Sir...One year ago we predicted that Pakistan could increase its wheat production by fifty percent in five years, and by 100 percent in eight to ten years. Six months ago...we made the more optimistic forecast that wheat production could be doubled in five years. We now repeat that forecast...

On our recent tour of West Pakistan some officers said to us: "You must be out of your mind to predict that the wheat crop can double in five years. There has been no such change in our lifetime." Others said..."Pakistan cultivators are illiterate. They are slow to change."

What will happen to agricultural production as supplies of oil become scarcer and so rise in price?

The "Green Revolution" is the successful introduction of high-yielding varieties of grain in Third World nations.

We were not surprised by these comments. We heard the same comments in Mexico ten years ago…We repeat this story not to praise Mexico, but to reassure the doubters among your agricultural officers. West Pakistan now has all the advantages which Mexico had, and more. You have the same latitude, the same irrigation, the same progressive farmers, and many of the same crops. You have saved years of research by the importation of dwarf wheat seeds.…

This is a revolution. [26]

By now, the term "Green Revolution" refers to almost any package of modern agricultural technologies introduced into the Third World. New seeds constitute the foundation of the Green Revolution. The seeds require careful management, plus relatively high and regular amounts of fertilizers, pesticides, and water. Mechanization, large tracts of land, and great amounts of capital are not inherently required in the Green Revolution technology. However, those with the advantages of tractors, land, and capital adopted the new seeds first and benefited from them most.

TABLE F.2. CHANGES IN AREA, PRODUCTION, AND YIELD AFTER INTRODUCING NEW RICE VARIETIES IN PUNJAB, INDIA

Year	Area Planted to Rice (Thousand Hectares)	Production of Milled Rice (Thousand Tons)	Yield (Tons/Hectares)
1950	120	107	0.79
1955	149	107	0.72
1960	227	220	1.10
1965	292	292	1.00
1966	285	338	1.20
1967	314	415	1.30
1968	345	470	1.40
1969	350	535	1.50
1970	390	688	1.80
1971	450	920	2.00
1972	476	955	2.00
1973	498	1,140	2.10
1974	570	1,181	2.10
1975	566	1,445	2.60

Source: Sterling Wortman and Ralph W. Cummings, Jr., *To Feed This World: The Challenge and the Strategy* (Baltimore, MD: Johns Hopkins University Press, 1978), 391.

This has created controversy. On the one hand, proponents of the Green Revolution point to amazing increases in actual grain yields over vast areas of the world. On the other, skeptics see the system as a cause of social upheavals in peasant cultures. In their view, not only has it failed to improve the lot of the poor, but it also has caused ecological problems.

The Green Revolution's proponents point to increases in yields. Critics point to ecological and social problems.

We shall hear from both sides of this debate as we present the schools of thought about the role of modern agricultural technologies in ending hunger.

Schools of Thought on Food Production

What is the best method of increasing food production? Some people recommend the Green Revolution technologies and the use of American agriculture as a model. Others advocate organic "appropriate technologies."

School of Thought: Modern Technologies Are an Effective Path to the End of Hunger

The first school of thought—that modern technologies provide an effective way of ending hunger—is represented by several points of view: modern technology is the best method of food production; science and technology offer particular advantages to agricultural modernization; new technologies can promote positive social and political change; and technology can have a beneficial effect on the environment.

Point of View Number 1

Modern Technology Provides the Best Way to Grow More Food for Underdeveloped Countries

One of the first major policy statements to declare a government's support of development through the introduction of modern agricultural technologies was United States President Harry S. Truman's 1949 "Point Four" address:

More than half the people of the world are living in conditions approaching misery. Their food is inadequate. They are victims of disease. Their economic life is primitive and stagnant. Their poverty is a handicap and a threat both to them and to more prosperous areas....

I believe that we should make available to peace-loving peoples the benefits of our store of technical knowledge in order to help them realize their aspirations for a better life....

Greater production is the key to prosperity and peace. And the key to greater production is a wider and more vigorous application of modern scientific and technical knowledge.[27]

Two examples of the Green Revolution from India follow. Both illustrate the effects of successful Green Revolution programs at the local level. They support the view that, in general, the best way to grow more food is through modern technologies.

Modern techniques helped a young Indian farmer.

This report on a young Indian farmer shows how modern techniques helped him, although the results were not immediate:

Shri K. N. Deb Goswami (age 34) is a small farmer having only 3 acres of cultivable land in the central Brahmaputra valley district of Nowgong, in the State of Assam of North Eastern India.... Like many of his compatriots, Deb Goswami has been trying hard to produce more out of his land and his problems were many and difficult. His land is on an elevation and the soil is composed of a sandy loam with a rather low moisture-retentive capacity. It required some leveling.... His main crop is paddy [rice]. He had heard about HYV [high-yielding varieties] fertilizers and pesticides sometime in 1970...but used them infrequently. His reaction to these inputs and techniques was mixed....

Around 1973...he took a loan from a bank and installed a shallow tubewell on his land with a lot of enthusiasm. He started growing HYV paddy and wheat, using fertilizer, and obtained an average yield of 2 metric tons per hectare of paddy and 1.95 metric tons per hectare of wheat. Much to his dismay, he was losing money. By 1976, he had been able to repay only three of the seven instalments due to the

112

bank and he was worried. The fact is that his agricultural practices were poor. He did...little weeding, and still less of water management. His plant population was thin and quite often infested with pests.

The agricultural extension service was reorganized in Nowgong...[in] 1976....The VEW [Village Extension Worker]...selected Deb Goswami as a contact farmer and talked to his group a number of times...about major crops and, in general, about what extension is and can do. Deb Goswami...accepted the advice of the VEW and adopted line sowing on all 3 acres; he grew seedlings for his entire land in raised seedbeds, and provided for sufficient spacing and plant population. He also gave top dressing of fertilizers...supplemented by farmyard manure, and took care to remove weeds.... He has now learnt to use pesticides, can talk about the plant diseases in English terms, and mention the cures too. He has come to possess the basic technical knowledge of agriculture....

He has come to possess the basic technical knowledge of agriculture.

From a shaky farmer he has become a potential extension leader. Beaming with smiles he stated confidently that he would get about 4 metric tons to 5 metric tons per hectare of paddy in the current Kharif [season].[28]

Modern technologies also changed the life of another Indian farmer:

Jaghit Singh was a living embodiment of what the prosperity of the "green revolution" has meant to those who can lay their hands on 100 acres of good Punjab earth. He was...the epitome of the young progressive Punjabi farmer. We walk around his land and, as we go, he tells us how he did it. He says he started in 1951 with 20 acres.

"I am the son of a small farmer. We were refugees from Pakistan. Nothing was with us. We lost everything in Pakistan. It pinches me that now the government wants to interfere and split up our holdings."

Jaghit Singh says that: "The common man's fate changed in 1966/67. People were actually hungry in those days. Three years back they were paying one rupee for a single grain of triple dwarf wheat. UP 308 sold for 250 rupees a kilo. I obtained seed from a friend and multiplied it out. I used to sell it for 100 rupees a quintal. There was more money to be made of course in those days from selling for seed purposes, than selling food-grains. Everybody wanted the new seeds."

Jaghit Singh was a powerful advocate of the importance of fertilizer. He split his fertilizer applications into three, giving one-half at the time of sowing, one-quarter before the first irrigation and the last quarter at the fifth or sixth irrigation. He used 90 to 100 lb of nitrogen per acre, 50–60 lb of phosphate and about 60 lb of potash. He attempted to take account of the need for micro-nutrients and trace elements as well, though he recognized that at the moment there were practical limitations to this level of sophistication.

He had a new combine harvester and he showed it to us, standing in a new concrete yard. "Old people," he said, "didn't believe that the same machine could do cutting and threshing and bagging." Use of the combine gave him an important price advantage over other farmers. He could market his crop while others were still threshing. This meant he could command a scarcity premium before the price fell to its support level, as the great glut of wheat from the rest of the Punjab came on the market.

He had a new combine harvester... standing in a new concrete yard.

Singh was building a new house; he had hired an architect from Chandigarh; he had dug a swimming pool and, when the tubewell was finally electrified, he would *probably use the machine to fill up the pool besides irrigating the crops. He had been in Montana, in the United States, on an International Farm Exchange Programme; had a daughter five years old and a son one year old. Modern farmer, modern man. Huge radiogram in the sitting-room; cassette tape-recorder, new record albums. Seeds of change indeed.[29]*

A widely accepted point of view in the development community is that poverty, especially in rural areas, is severe and worsening, and that the demand for food is increasing. Therefore, we must look to the modernization of agriculture, through applications of science and technology, for solutions.

We next turn to two experts who see the results of new technologies as encouraging. The first is the former president of the World Bank, Robert McNamara:

Clearly, the bulk of the poor today are in the rural areas. All of our analysis indicates that this is likely to continue to be the case during the next two or three decades....Within the rural areas the poverty problem revolves primarily around the low productivity of the millions of small subsistence farms....

Disparities in income will simply widen unless action is taken which will directly benefit the poorest. In my view, therefore, there is no viable alternative to increasing the productivity of small-scale agriculture if any significant advance is to be made in solving the problems of absolute poverty in the rural areas....

Without rapid progress in smallholder agriculture throughout the developing world, there is little hope either of achieving long-term stable economic growth or of significantly reducing the levels of absolute poverty....

There is ample evidence that...small-scale operations need be no barrier to raising agricultural yields.

There is ample evidence that modern agricultural technology is divisible, and that small-scale operations need be no barrier to raising agricultural yields.

The question, then, is what can the developing countries do to increase the productivity of the small farmer. How can they duplicate the conditions which have led to very rapid agricultural growth in a few experimental areas and in a few countries so as to stimulate agricultural growth and combat rural poverty on a broad scale?[30]

The second statement is from the Food and Agriculture Organization (FAO), the United Nations organization that is primarily concerned with food production. The following excerpt is from a 1979 report about raising the world's food production to adequate levels by the end of the century.

By the end of this century...world population will surpass 6 billion, against less than 3 billion twenty years ago and 4.3 billion today; the labour force will increase to over 2.5 billion or 40 percent more than today. The agricultural sector must be able to produce the food needed for the expanding population, 90 percent of which is in developing countries, and absorb in gainful employment a good part of the increase in the labour force.... At the same time, it must always be remembered that agriculture, as the chief user of land, carries most of the responsibility for safeguarding this heritage. Additional production of food and agricultural raw materials must not be obtained by misusing the land and the sea....

A sustained higher growth of production can come only by a modernization of the production process, i.e., purchased inputs must be increased and resources used more intensively in conjunction with an expansion of the land base....

The rapidly rising demands for agricultural products in the face of limited natural resources call for an increasing reliance on science and technology. The man/land ratio in developing countries is expected to fall from 0.9 ha in the mid-1970s to 0.5 ha…by the year 2000 and water resources which are easy to develop and use are becoming scarce. Research must play a fundamental role in increasing agricultural production, basically by raising yields. The agriculture of the future in developing countries must become more science-based…as has been the case with the agriculture of developed countries.[31]

Point of View Number 2

New Technologies Can Promote Needed Social and Political Change

Although many proponents of Green Revolution technologies do not devote much attention to social and political change, the following statements emphasize these concerns strongly. The first is from a Mexican development economist, Dr. Edmundo Flores, who drafted this scenario in 1972:

In the next fifteen years agricultural surplus stocks will increase and though their prices will decline steadily, no one will buy them. By then, international food grants will have come to a stop and world trade, in the midst of a grave depression, will be confined to the sale of tropical commodities to the temperate and cold regions….

The demonstration effects of progressive surplus stockpiling (i.e., the social awareness resulting from the tradition-shattering aspects of the green revolution), the paralysis of international trade, and rising unemployment will corrode the status quo…and sooner or later will lead to a redistribution of <u>productive land</u> so as to unload on the farmers the food surpluses and, at the same time, improve their social status.

This will be followed by full employment policies in industry and modern services and by the organization of societies based on true equality. The abundance of food will permit the construction of the necessary overhead facilities, cities, schools, universities and research centers without atavistic fears of rationing and inflation.

In providing the means to kill hunger, the Green Revolution will destroy many vested interests.

Thus, in providing the means to kill hunger, the Green Revolution will destroy many vested interests. It will force the reappraisal of the problem of landless peasants, of the unemployment of workers and of the alienation of the masses. And in the final analysis, it will precipitate a prodigious economic, social and political transformation in the developing countries.[32]

While most of the developments foreseen by Flores have not occurred, this does not necessarily reveal a fundamental flaw in his assessment. Rather, it may be that the amount of time in which such a major transformation would occur is greater than originally anticipated.

Next, an Indian scientist describes a grass-roots experience. Dr. M. S. Swaminathan, the director general of the International Rice Research Institute (IRRI) located in the Philippines, is a contributor to Green Revolution technologies. He introduced dwarf wheat into India and implemented successful village-level programs that used high-yielding varieties. In 1964, he developed the National Demonstration Project in India, which enabled scientists to test and demonstrate directly the validity of experimental findings on high-yielding varieties in farmers' fields. Dr. Swaminathan writes:

The term "Green Revolution" has been used in different senses by different people…. Some have used it to imply that the technologies associated with the "Green Revolution" have built-in seeds of discrimination against small farmers, because they are capital-intensive, labor-displacing, and ecologically damaging. These statements have been made, I believe, in ignorance of what has really happened. For instance, in the Punjab or the western part of India, more jobs have been generated.... In the Indo-Gangetic basin...the capital required may still be beyond the means of a small farmer, but it is not really so high as to make it difficult to organize a reasonable credit-supply system. Some farmers have standardized the construction of a tube well made of bamboo and, including a one or two horse-power pump, it costs about 40 to 50 dollars....

These are the kinds of changes which enabled the northern part of India to double its wheat production within a few seasons. Had the technology been confined to a few farmers, it would have been impossible for production to go up from about 12 million tons to 26 million tons within four crop seasons....

In our discussions of the Green Revolution, we should either clarify the issues or avoid referring to it; disparagement has already done a lot of damage in terms of development planning....

There is a desire for change, there is a desire to get higher yields and income. In my view, this represents the most important positive change that has taken place in the Indian rural scene.[33]

Point of View Number 3

Technology Conserves, Not Destroys, the Environment

To the charge that agricultural technologies are ecologically insensitive, Norman Borlaug answers:

I want it to be perfectly clear that I am opposed to the reckless and careless use of chemicals either industrial or agricultural. However, we must also recognize that we need agricultural chemicals to produce and protect our food, fiber, and timber....

In the next forty years world food and fiber production must be increased more than it was increased in the 12,000 year period from the discovery of agriculture up to 1975.[34]

Borlaug also sharply criticizes the solutions to ecological problems proposed by "environmentalists":

Environmentalists today seek a simple solution to very complex problems. The pollution of the environment is the result of every human activity as well as the whims of nature. It is a tragic error to believe that agricultural chemicals are a prime factor in the deterioration of our environment....

DDT, because it is a name popularly known to most segments of the public, has been the first target. Once that is accomplished, the so-called ecologists will work on hydrocarbons, then organo-phosphates, carbamates, weed killers and, perhaps, even fertilizers will come under the assault of their barrage of misinformation.

If this happens—and I predict it will if most DDT uses are canceled—I have wasted my life's work. I have dedicated myself to finding better methods of feeding the world's starving populations. Without DDT and other important agricultural chemicals, our goals are simply unattainable—and starvation and world chaos will result....

The agricultural chemical industry has been the whipping boy of environmentalists.

The agricultural chemical industry has been the whipping boy of environmentalists, whose views have been so short-sighted that they haven't bothered to examine some key facts:

1. *To produce food for ourselves and other nations, we required 290 million acres of farmland last year.*

2. *To get the same yield while relying on the technology we used 30 years ago—when most of today's pesticides and fertilizers were nonexistent—we would have required nearly 600 million acres, or twice the amount used last year.*

3. *This would have resulted in a huge loss of forest and grass lands which not only would have further crowded some animal species into extinction but would have caused other problems as well.*

4. *Pesticides, therefore, have actually helped prevent the development that environmentalists fear most—diminishing species of wildlife....*

Let's get our priorities in perspective. As much as I favor wildlife, man must come first. We must feed ourselves and protect ourselves against the health hazards of the world. To do that, we must have agricultural chemicals. Without them, the world population will starve.[35]

Sterling Wortman and Ralph Cummings, Jr., two agricultural specialists who have extensive field experience in both the United States and abroad, hold views similar to Borlaug's. Their book, *To Feed This World*, specifically addresses the small farmer's concerns and the "food-population-poverty problem."

While intensification of agriculture probably has degraded land in some areas, leveling, irrigation, drainage, and careful management of fields has probably resulted in a net improvement of most of the agricultural lands involved. Land values have generally increased, making reinvestment in maintenance or improvement of agricultural areas a more attractive proposition. The Morrow plots at the University of Illinois, continuously cropped and monitored for over a hundred years under various levels of fertilizer, provide evidence that chemical fertilizers under proper management will not "burn out" the soil. In fact, some of the worst environmental abuse is occurring under traditional, not intensive, agriculture. The spread of the Sahara Desert and soil erosion and flooding in Asia, partially due to overgrazing or deforestation, are evidence of the heavy price often paid when traditional agriculture is asked to attempt to sustain increasing numbers of people.[36]

School of Thought: More Food Needs to Be Produced, But Not by the Modern Agricultural Techniques Currently in Use

The second school of thought agrees that food production is a key ingredient in ending hunger. However, it promotes different agricultural methods: It advocates the use of more organic methods of production than do "Green Revolution" technologies, ones that do not depend upon the intensive use of energy, chemicals, or pesticides. Proponents of this alternative approach to agricultural production argue that it has the merit of being ecologically sound, sustainable over a long period of time, and potentially as productive as more mechanized forms of farming.

Point of View Number 1

Green Revolution Technologies Are Not Safely Transferable, Nor Can the Same High Levels of Production Be Sustained Indefinitely

Critics of the Green Revolution raise serious questions about its social, agricultural, and ecological effects.

TABLE F.3. TECHNOLOGICAL DEVELOPMENT, WESTERN STYLE—A CRITIQUE

Western Technology	Appropriate Technology
1 Big Fertilizer Factory in City	Small Bio-gas Fertilizer Plants for 26,000 Villages
Total Cost $140 Million	$125 Million
Cost of Imports $70 Million	Nil
Jobs Created 1,000	130,750
Energy Consumed 100,000 MWh/Year	Energy Generated 6,000,000 MWh/Year
Fertilizer Produced 230,000 Tons	230,000 Tons

Source: Anne Buchanan, *Food, Poverty and Power* (Nottingham, England: Russell Press, Ltd.), 107.

Of the excerpts that follow, one focuses on the American agricultural system (which provided a model for the Green Revolution), and raises questions about how well this system is working, even in the favorable environment of the United States. A second excerpt points to adverse long-term consequences from an initially successful project in Peru. Additional material highlights what are seen to be social inequities produced by the Green Revolution.

The Cornucopia Project was designed to study the American food system and identify problems and solutions based on organic methods. The following excerpt reflects the viewpoint both of Cornucopia Project work and of the authors, Robert Rodale and Thomas Dybdahl:

The abundance of food in America is being achieved at a very high cost.

We are kidding ourselves. And especially we are pulling the legs of future generations of Americans in a way our children won't appreciate when they get old enough to know who did them dirty. For the truth is that the abundance of food in America in 1981 is being achieved at a very high cost—not so much in dollars, but in soil, in irreplaceable underground water, in squandered oil, wasted gas and environmental degradation that nature will be able to repair only many decades after the current American food machine grinds to a halt....

Even here in the United States, where population growth is considered moderate, we still have almost 5,000 more mouths to feed every day. And because of erosion and the building-over of farmland, we are losing the productive equivalent of 25 square miles of agricultural land every day....

The increasing use of herbicides, pesticides and chemical fertilizers has led to the contamination of both soil and water, and to the destruction of wildlife. The environmental damage caused by these substances costs an estimated $839 million annually. That figure does not include the cost of any harm done to the health of people.

Increased pesticide use also tends to encourage the development of stronger pests, which in turn calls for more powerful pesticides. Already, to grow our crops we use approximately 6.25 pounds of pesticide for every person in the country....

Up to now, producers, processors, shoppers and sellers of food have largely been blind to the dimensions of the trap they are heading into. Like rubber bands pulled well beyond their normal lengths, parts of the system are being stretched. Rather than asking whether the whole system is arranged illogically and being used in

118

wrong ways, everyone makes adjustments. Already, some of the tiny bands have snapped. And some of the bigger ones are being pulled beyond the safety point.[37]

Dr. Asit Biswas and Margaret Biswas, both researchers and consultants, have specialized in problems involving interrelationships among agriculture, energy, and the environment. Asit Biswas's account of the Canete Valley experience in Peru points out the detrimental effects of pesticides:

The Canete Valley in Peru is an example of an ecological disaster that could occur due to heavy reliance on pesticides.

The cost of greater application of pesticides increased tremendously, and gradually all useful insects were destroyed.

During the period 1949–1956, the use of pesticides was constantly increased to control the cotton pests. New pests appeared in the crops because of the destruction of predators and parasites, and the pests themselves started to develop resistance to the chemicals used. The cost of greater application of pesticides increased tremendously, and gradually all useful insects were destroyed. By 1956, the situation had become critical and nearly 50 percent of the crop failed.

The use of pesticides as the exclusive form of control was banned in 1957. Synthetic organic insecticides were completely prohibited, and mineral insecticides were used. Enemies of cotton pests were re-introduced and cropping practices were changed, based on a study of the ecology of the cotton fields. The equilibrium of the valley's ecosystem was eventually restored several years later.[38]

Point of View Number 2

The Green Revolution Has Widened the Gap Between Rich and Poor

Some critics feel that the social costs of the Green Revolution greatly outweigh its benefits. Among them is Jagjivan Ram, then India's minister of agriculture who asserted in 1975 that the Green Revolution adversely affected the lowest stratum of rural Indian society. An excerpt from a 1975 article in the *International Journal of Health Services* presents Ram's position:

As the Indian Minister of Agriculture and Food, Jagjivan Ram, pointed out at the end of 1969, the beneficiaries of the "Green Revolution" are not the peasants who live miserably on a few rupees a month, but the privileged strata of large and medium-sized landholders. While 22 per cent of the families own no land and 47 per cent own less than 0.4 hectare (1 acre), 3 or 4 per cent of the large landholders with political power and influence are in a position to appropriate for themselves all the resources and technical assistance put at the disposal of farmers by the governmental agencies.

As a consequence of…the "Green Revolution," class conflicts have sharpened considerably.

As a consequence of the application of the "Green Revolution," class conflicts have sharpened considerably in the region in India "benefited" by it. Only the farmers from the upper strata of rural families are in a position to carry out the improvements indispensable for increasing crop yields. The medium-sized and small farmers do not have the resources at their disposal for investing in irrigation and other improvements the "Green Revolution" demands. The large landholders and businessmen, whenever possible, practice usury with interest rates reaching as high as 36 per cent. Attracted by the profit opportunities derived from the "Green Revolution," a new social group inserts itself in the rural areas—capitalists, businessmen, and retired bureaucrats who appropriate the lands of the medium-sized farmers and poor peasants and finally expel them. Large mechanized agricultural estates belonging to industrialists alternate with poor peasants living in semifeudal conditions.[39]

In the excerpt concluding this section, Pierre Spitz, as director for Asia of the Food Systems and Society research project at the United Nations Research Institute for Social Development in Geneva, points to ways in which the Green Revolution has magnified social inequality:

The "green revolution", by magnifying inequalities and aggravating the effects of the process of dispossession on the lives of the poorest, helps to exacerbate structural violence....

A geneticist does not operate in an economic and social vacuum. His selection criteria vary according to the category of peasants with whom he is concerned and their farming systems. Furthermore, he may work in a laboratory cut off from the rural masses but very close to industrial interests. When this is the case, he will tend to propose universal solutions which do not take much account of local ecological, economic and social conditions. [40]

Francine Frankel's *India's Green Revolution* reveals both favorable and unfavorable aspects of India's experience in Ludhiana, the Punjab state.

On virtually all indices of agricultural modernization Ludhiana has scored spectacular progress. Even to cite the statistical record, a dull but obligatory exercise in empirical studies, is, in the case of Ludhiana to make an eloquent statement of the agricultural transformation occurring in the district. Among the most striking changes are the following. Between...1960–61 and 1968–69, the area under irrigation increased from 45 percent to 70 percent, mainly as the result of the rapid installation of tubewells....Consumption of fertilizer increased more than 13 times, from 17.6 pounds to 242 pounds per cultivated acre. More dramatic still...between 1965–66 and 1968–69, the acreage under the new Mexican dwarf varieties expanded from a minuscule 170 acres to an overwhelming 420,000 acres, or an area accounting for 90 percent of the total acreage under wheat. Finally, and the surest measure of success, yields per acre in Ludhiana increased from an average of 1,385 pounds in 1960–61 to over 3,280 pounds in 1968–69 (i.e., by over 120 percent). Moreover, during the last few years, Ludhiana has seen a trend toward mechanization which promises even greater efficiency in the exploitation of the new technology for intensive cropping. Exact estimates of the number of tractors now in use in the district are difficult to come by, but in April 1969 they were not less than 2,500 and possibly as many as 5,000, most representing purchases over the past two years....

If one reviews the experience of Ludhiana as a whole, it appears that most classes of cultivators have made some gains as a result of the green revolution. Nevertheless, the benefits have been heavily weighted in favor of the large farmer (the cultivator with 25 to 30 acres or more) who has been able to exploit the full potential of the new technology for multiple cropping and diversification of the cropping pattern by large capital investments in land improvement and mechanization. Although 15 to 25 acre farmers have also experienced absolute increases in output and income, the gap between the large and medium farmers has undoubtedly widened. Small farmers, those with 10 to 15 acres have so far made only marginal gains, and ultimately they may find their farm operations overcapitalized and uneconomic. Some farmers with less than 10 acres have experienced an absolute deterioration in their economic position with the increasing difficulty of finding leased land on reasonable terms. The condition of landless laborers has improved, but at a proportionately smaller rate than that of large landowners, and these gains are threatened by the rapid drive toward more complete mechanization. [41]

A society's agricultural methods depend on its resources, preferences, and level of development. Most Third World countries use more human labor and fewer machines to produce food. Right: *Harvesting rice, India* (Marcello Bertinetti/Photo Researchers); next two-page spread: *Ancient Incan farming methods, Peru* (Loren McIntyre/Woodfin Camp & Assoc.).

The benefits have been heavily weighted in favor of the large farmer.

Modern technology, according to one school of thought, is the best way to grow more food in developing countries. In 1949, Truman's "Point Four" address declared: "Greater production is the key to prosperity and peace. And the key to greater production is a wider and more vigorous application of modern scientific and technical knowledge." Left: *Grinding corn, El Salvador* (Alon Reininger/Contact for Woodfin Camp & Assoc.); above: *Shelling corn, Peru* (Loren McIntyre/Woodfin Camp & Assoc.); next two-page spread: *Harvesting wheat, India* (Robert Frerck/Woodfin Camp & Assoc.).

Energy is a factor in food production. Different agricultural technologies need different amounts and types of energy. Traditional dry-land Asian rice culture uses about 1 calorie of energy (human labor) to produce about 20 calories of rice. Modern U.S. corn production uses about 1 calorie (fuel, fertilizer, heat) to produce 1 calorie of corn. Beef production and deep-sea fishing use 10–20 calories of energy to yield 1 calorie of food. Photos, both Japan. Left: *Planting vegetables in dry areas* (Mike Yamashita/Woodfin Camp & Assoc.); above: *Planting rice in wet areas* (Mike Yamashita/Woodfin Camp & Assoc.).

*How much land is available for growing food?
Of the more than 13 billion hectares of land in
the world, the total amount of potentially
cultivable land on earth is generally agreed to
be about 3.2 billion hectares, only about 1.4
billion of which are now being cultivated. Thus,
apparently, the area upon which food can be
grown could be more than doubled. However,
other factors can make the planet's stock of
agricultural land seem either scarce or abundant, depending on one's point of view.* Left and
next two-page spread: *Farms in U.S.* (Dick
Durrance/Woodfin Camp & Assoc. and
Robert Frerck/Woodfin Camp & Assoc.);
above: *Farm in Japan* (Mike Yamashita/
Woodfin Camp & Assoc.).

The term "Green Revolution" now refers to almost any package of modern agricultural technologies introduced into the Third World. Many of these technologies were first developed in the United States. Critics of the Green Revolution question its ecological effects, both in the U.S. and Third World nations. Robert Rodale and Thomas Dybdahl report on the Cornucopia Project, designed to study the American food system and to identify problems and organic solutions: "The abundance of food in America…is being achieved at…[the cost of] environmental degradation that nature will be able to repair only many decades after the current American food machine grinds to a halt…. [W]e are losing the productive equivalent of 25 square miles of agricultural land every day." Photos, all in U.S. Left: Combining wheat (Jim Balog/Black Star); above: Harvesting corn (Craig Aurness/

Woodfin Camp & Assoc.); next two-page spread: Harvesting wheat (Jeff Jacobson/Archive); following two-page spread: Harvested corn (Craig Aurness/Woodfin Camp & Assoc.).

What is the effect of the American-based "Green Revolution" technologies on the environment? Advocates of these methods, including Norman Borlaug, believe that technology can conserve, even enhance, environmental resources: "To produce food for ourselves and other nations, we required 290 million acres of farmland last year. To get the same yield while relying on the technology we used 30 years ago...we would have required nearly 600 million acres, or twice the amount used last year. This would have resulted in a huge loss of forest and grass lands which not only would have further crowded some animal species into extinction but would have caused other problems as well." *Left: Testing new plant breeds in hydroponic solutions* (Fred Ward/ Black Star); *above: More hydroponics* (Terrence Moore/Woodfin Camp & Assoc.); *next two-page spread: A complex irrigation*

system, California (Baron Wolman/Woodfin Camp & Assoc.); *following two-page spread: Irrigating a wheat terrace, China* (Lowell Georgia/Photo Researchers).

141

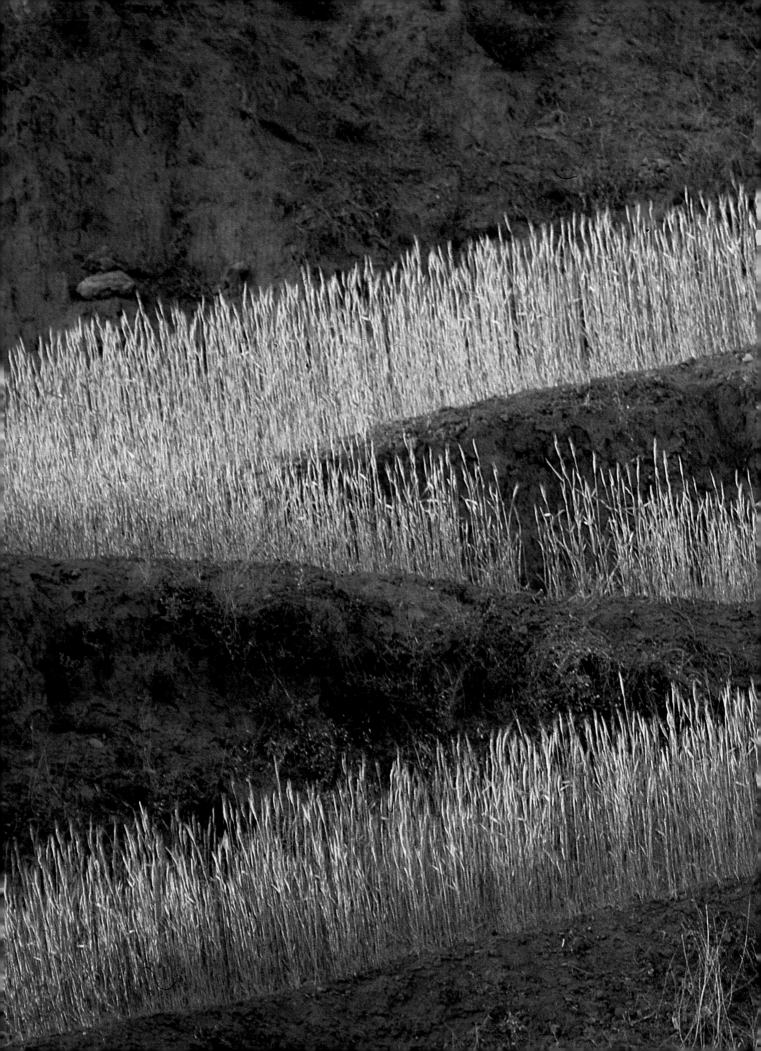

Water is essential to food production. The earth
has about 14,000 cubic kilometers [km 3] of
fresh rainwater, in the form of stable runoff,
that humans could use. Of this, 9,000 km 3
might be called the potentially usable world
water resource, from which all needs will have
to be met for some years to come. If present
trends continue, predicts Robert Ambroggi, all
of the available fresh water in the world will be
in use shortly after the year 2000. More efficient
irrigation methods are being developed, but
some parts of the world are already severely
short of water and are drawing from underground pools at a rate faster than the water can
be replenished. Left: *Primitive irrigation, Egypt*
(E. Erwitt/Magnum Photos); above, top: *A
pump-and-hose contraption makes use of a
narrow irrigation ditch* (Mark Godfrey/
Archive); above, bottom: *A water wheel irri-
gates a rice paddy, China* (Paolo Koch/Photo

Researchers); next two-page spread: *Water
is drawn by the bucketful, Guatemala* (Alon
Reininger/Contact for Woodfin Camp
& Assoc.).

In many water-short areas, desertification—productive land turning to desert—is becoming a severe problem. Experts differ on the long-term consequences of this problem. Robert Katz represents the optimistic view: "Ruined land can be reclaimed, water tables raised (or lowered). We can make rain. Soil erosion is preventable.... To the many admonitions that our planet's resourcefulness is waning fast, there is much one can oppose." The UN Conference on Desertification represents the pessimistic view: "More than one third of the earth's land is arid....[M]any vulnerable areas are even now being turned into desert. This process... threatens the future of...that 14 per cent of the world's population who live in the drylands." Photos, Somalia. Left: *Searching for water in the drylands* (Mike Yamashita/Woodfin Camp & Assoc.); above: *Bringing water back from a distant source* (Alain Nogues/Sygma);

next two-page spread: *Desert village* (Mike Yamashita/Woodfin Camp & Assoc.); following two-page spread: *A waterless landscape* (Mike Yamashita/Woodfin Camp & Assoc.).

FIGURE F.13. TRENDS IN GRAIN
PRODUCTION AND USE (U.S. AND REST OF
THE WORLD)

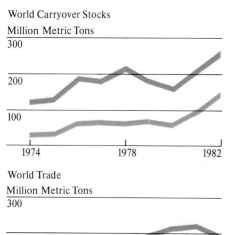

World Grain Production
Billion Metric Tons

World Utilization
Billion Metric Tons

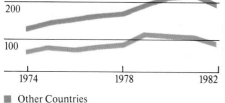

World Carryover Stocks
Million Metric Tons

World Trade
Million Metric Tons

■ Other Countries
■ United States

Source: U.S., Department of Agriculture, *1983 Handbook of Agricultural Charts*, Agriculture Handbook, no. 619 (Washington, DC: U.S. Government Printing Office, December 1983), 66.

The United States produced nearly 22 percent of the world's grain in 1982–1983 and held 58 percent of world grain stocks. This nation dominates the world grain trade.

Basic Information on Food Storage and Security

"Food security" means that adequate daily consumption of food at the national, village, and family level is assured, even in years of a bad harvest. Vast areas of the world—inhabited by hundreds of millions of people—are highly vulnerable to food shortages, as several major famines in the 1970s and yearly seasonal hunger in many regions indicate. World food security has been the as-yet-unrealized goal of many people working to end hunger.

All observers agree that a key—perhaps *the* key—component of any program of world food security is an effective system of food storage, which can serve as a buffer against lean times.

Grains have been the focus of food-security systems, both historically and currently. This is because grain can be stored; it contains a relatively high nutrient density per unit weight; and it is relatively inexpensive to ship. Thus, many consider grain reserves—stocks that can be drawn upon in lean times—as a cornerstone of a food-secure world. Small stocks can be used to fight famine; and if grain reserves are large enough, they can be put on the market to increase supply and stabilize prices in lean years.

The Global Impact of Fluctuations in Food Production

The production of food fluctuates more than the production of any other basic commodity. There are variations in the availability of labor, the flow of raw materials, market conditions, and all the variables of industrial production. Above all, food production is subject to weather conditions and other hazards in almost every part of the world. Rainfall, sunlight, frosts, insect invasions—all affect the production of food crops, even in highly sophisticated agricultural systems.

Weather changes can devastate an entire year's harvest. When bad weather hits a small or poor country, a localized famine may result. When several major food-producing countries are affected at the same time, this can drastically alter both internal food availability in those countries and world market prices.

Between 1978 and 1979, for instance, Soviet grain production fell from 237 million metric tons to 179 million metric tons.[42] This forced the Soviets to buy heavily on the international grain market. As a result, food prices rose worldwide, which hindered poor people's access to food, especially in poor countries. Only about 12 to 13 percent of world grain enters international trade, but that percentage is crucial.[43] Considering the number of countries that depend on food imports, a small percentage change in production by a major exporter such as the United States or a major importer such as the USSR, can produce a significant impact on the world market. When crop failures strike one of these grain giants, people in Africa, Latin America, and Asia feel the effects.

The Presidential Commission on World Hunger describes this problem:

In the recent past, world production shortfalls of less than 10 percent have been linked to price increases for wheat and rice of 200 percent or more. Modest shortages, which may raise the cost of a loaf of bread in the United States by a cent or two a loaf, can result in severe shortages in Bangladesh, or Mali, or Guyana....

Richer customers can easily—and unknowingly—draw supplies away from the poorest people simply by offering a higher price. At the height of the 1972–74 food crisis, U.S. grain was being sold on commercial terms to feed European cattle while food aid shipments to people in the poorest countries were being trimmed back because budgetary allowances had not anticipated the higher cost of grain.[44]

Since Biblical times, men and women have found ways to store food as protection against a poor crop. Every society has developed institutions and technologies to keep food for times of scarcity. Some types of food, such as fresh milk, can be stored for only a very short time. Others, such as processed milk (yogurt, cheese, dried milk) can be stored much longer. Grain, more than any other food, can be stored for a very long time without losing its nutritional content. There are many ways of storing grain, ranging from the flour and cereals stored in a household pantry, to the bins and shelves of retail stores, to the cribs and granaries of farmers, to the grain elevators of rural communities, all the way to the massive storage facilities of the multinational grain companies and of some governments

An adequate food reserve should correspond to population and food-consumption increases. The amount of grain storage necessary to guarantee world food security is 17 to 18 percent of total annual world consumption, according to the Food and Agriculture Organization.[45] At the 1981 level of consumption, this reserve was estimated to be about 250 million metric tons.[46]

An adequate food reserve should correspond to population and food-consumption increases.

Grain that was stored in statistically measured national and corporate storage systems dropped well below that level during the period from 1960 to 1980. By 1980 the world had just forty-six days' worth of grain supplies stored. In 1981 and 1982, bumper crops in the United States pushed stocks upward again. By the end of 1982, there were more than 150 million metric tons stored in the United States alone.[47] (See Table F.4.)

TABLE F.4. INDEX OF WORLD FOOD-SECURITY, 1960–1983

Year	World Carryover Stocks of Grain	Grain Equivalent of Idled U.S. Cropland	Total	World Consumption
	(Million Metric Tons)			(Days)
1960	200	36	236	104
1965	142	70	212	81
1970	164	71	235	75
1971	183	46	229	71
1972	143	78	221	67
1973	148	25	173	50
1974	133	4	137	41
1975	141	3	144	43
1976	196	3	199	56
1977	194	1	195	53
1978	221	22	243	62
1979	197	16	213	54
1980	183	0	183	46
1981	221	0	221	56
1982[a]	260	13	273	66
1983[b]	191	92	283	68

(a) preliminary
(b) projection

Source: Lester R. Brown et al., *State of the World 1984* (New York: W. W. Norton, 1984), 187.

One way to ensure greater world food security is to improve the world's ability to store grain once it is harvested. As much as 20 percent of the world's grain—about 250 million metric tons—is destroyed by pests, rot, and other problems following the harvest, according to the Food and Agriculture Organization. The percentage losses incurred by other more perishable food crops, such as potatoes, are probably even higher. Substantial food losses could be avoided via a relatively small investment in improved storage and handling, especially in the developing countries.[48]

It costs about $10 per ton for bulk storage of grain.

It takes money and resources to store grain—buildings, labor, and, in sophisticated systems, mechanisms for maintaining low humidity and temperature and for moving the grain in and out of storage. It costs about $10 per ton per year for bulk storage of grain. Using this estimate, the cost of world food security (approximately 250 million metric tons), based on 1981 consumption levels, would be about $2.5 billion per year.[49]

A number of worldwide storage schemes, to be managed internationally, have been proposed to supplement those already present at the national and local levels. The FAO, under Sir John Boyd Orr, the first director general, offered the first such proposal in 1946:

There has never been enough food in the world....

The limiting factor is not the physical capacity to produce enough food but the ability of nations to bring about the complex economic adjustments necessary to make adequate production and distribution possible....

Food is more than a trade commodity; it is an essential of life.[50]

Since 1946, many discussions, studies, and negotiations have addressed the question of international grain reserves. In 1974, the World Food Conference discussed a plan to create an internationally coordinated reserve of possibly up to 60 million tons, which would stabilize world market prices and prevent a resurgence of the kind of global food shortage experienced in 1972–1974.[51] This reserve was to be financed primarily by the rich nations, to be held nationally by both exporting and developing countries. Although more than 100 nations agreed to this proposal and there are continuing discussions of implementation, it has yet to be implemented.

Aside from the issue of whether international grain reserves are a good idea, there is an ongoing debate about how they could best be organized. The debate on this issue is summarized briefly in this excerpt from Philip H. Trezise's *Rebuilding Grain Reserves:*

What is the objective of a grain reserve policy to be: to ensure against famine, to stabilize cereal markets ...or both?

What is the objective of a grain reserve policy to be: to ensure against famine, to stabilize cereal markets (prices) generally, or both? If the objective is to prevent famine, the major effort must be directed toward a few regions where crop failures could lead directly to mass starvation. Stable prices, or more accurately the avoidance of large jumps in grain prices, are also important to these regions since they import part of the grain they require on commercial terms. But the goal of achieving more stable cereal prices depends most of all on the economic objectives, the crop prospects, and the agricultural policies of the higher-income industrial countries, which account for most of the world's trade in grains....

How large a reserve is necessary? This will depend, of course, on how much insurance is desired against which risks. There is no simple formula. Moreover,

158

reserves most probably will not be costless. The participants will need to decide what they are prepared to spend or invest collectively in an arrangement and under what cost-sharing procedure. And if the aim is to reduce the range of price fluctuations, what limits should be set? Or, put more directly, when should grain be bought for stocks and when should it be sold? Should the indicator be market price or should it depend on physical quantities of grain produced or put in stocks?

Who should hold reserves—international agencies, governments, private firms, farmers? Where should reserves be located? What countries must participate to make a reserve scheme viable? What of the USSR and the People's Republic of China, both of whom are important elements in the grain trade?

What rules would govern the release of reserves against famine? Should local grain stocks be exhausted and available foreign exchange assigned to commercial purchases before other reserves are committed? Would the existence of reserves discourage the advances in farm productivity that probably must underpin any long-term solution to the food problems of the poorer and more populous developing countries? If so, could this consequence be avoided by other policy measures?[52]

Schools of Thought on Food Storage and Food Security

This section presents two differing approaches for reaching the same end goal of a food-storage system that can ensure the world true food security. What distinguishes the two approaches is their view on how best to create such a system—through large-scale internationally coordinated reserves or through a network of local and national storage facilities.

While in some respects this issue is the most technical of all to be examined in this book (as the differing perspectives about it make clear), at the heart of the debate are very human questions regarding local responsibility, the effects of large-scale planning and distribution, and the role of the individual in making decisions that affect his or her life.

School of Thought: Establishing a Large-Scale Internationally Coordinated Grain-Reserve System Is a Necessary Step in Ending World Hunger

Point of View Number 1

We first present the views of those who want to establish a large-scale internationally coordinated grain-reserve system. Their primary concern is with providing famine relief and meeting production shortfalls. They also want reserves used to stabilize the market, which would benefit individual farmers.

International Reserves Are an Essential Part of a Program to End World Hunger

President Carter's Commission on World Hunger devoted Chapter 3 of its final report to the subject of food security. The commissioners vigorously debated the issue of international grain reserves,[53] ultimately deciding that international reserves were an essential part of a program to overcome world hunger:

The lives of the 800 million estimated to be living in absolute poverty are put at risk every time there is a drought in Kansas, or floods in India, or a late frost in the Ukraine. The world must prepare itself for these irregular, but inevitable, setbacks. It must store food against a time of scarcity....

World food security and grain reserves have multiple goals. In addition to feeding hungry people in a disaster situation, reserves invariably have consequences and implications for other areas, such as consumer price stability, farm price stability, and income stability for farm people. As part of a larger international food system, these goals in turn influence the location of food shortages and hunger. An effective grain reserve system therefore must include international, national, and regional reserves, coordinated in such a way as to reduce the risk of hunger anywhere in the world.[54]

IFAD (International Fund for Agricultural Development) Assistant President Sartaj Aziz was formerly deputy secretary general of the World Food Conference. In 1975 he obtained agreement for the support of an internationally coordinated system of national stock policies. This system, he believed, "could, if properly implemented, at least assure the adequate availability of physical supplies at all times." Summarizing the major conclusions of the World Food Conference, Aziz said:

First, it agreed on the nature and magnitude of the food problem, and emphasized that famine and hunger, which have haunted men and nations throughout history, have now taken on an unprecedented urgency and can only be dealt with by concerted worldwide action.

Second, it reaffirmed that the only long-term solution is increased production in developing countries, because no amount of food aid or other palliatives can solve the problem in a fundamental sense. It also agreed that the task of increasing production has to be undertaken in a broad developmental framework. This does not only mean providing fertilizers, pesticides, technology and investment, but involving the large masses of people, particularly the small farmer and the landless labourer, in the process of development and employment.

The Conference also accepted that in the meantime a system of world food security must be created. The proposed system consists of four main elements: the improved coordination of stock policies, a longer term food aid policy, better arrangements for dealing with emergencies and a food information and early warning system. Even while trying to increase production to meet demand, there will be price fluctuations and supply shortfalls. Unless this kind of integrated food security policy can be evolved, the world cannot be safeguarded against ups and downs or avoid periodical shortages or famines.[55]

Point of View Number 2

An Internationally Coordinated System of Food Security Should Regulate the Market

Proponents believe that such a system would stabilize prices, thus reducing the costs to Third World countries that must import food, thereby freeing funds for development. In 1978, Brennon Jones, while working for Bread for the World, argued this point:

Without emergency reserves, poor nations are at the mercy of world market prices. Grain prices tripled and quadrupled in the 1972–73 market year, with wheat rising from $60 a ton to $200, and rice from $130 to more than $500 a ton.

But the developing nations still had to buy much of their own food. When a nation such as India is forced to spend over $500 million of its scarce foreign exchange on U.S. food purchases—as it did in 1974—that is money that is not available for making desperately needed long-term agricultural production and development gains.[56]

160

Farmers Will Benefit from an International Reserve System

Barbara Ward addresses the impact of an international reserve system on the individual farmer. Ward, who died in 1981, was described as "one of the most widely read and influential writers on economic and international affairs in the English-speaking world."[57] For a number of years she focused her attention on the need to close the gap between the developed and developing worlds through economic aid.

Let us look at the way markets operate at a time of increasing food shortage. The very small farmer cannot enter the market at all because, over and above what he grows for subsistence, he has no money, no "effective demand". If his own plot does not feed his family, in a pure market system, he starves. Next, the expectation of shortage begins to push up prices and as they rise, more and more of the poor and semipoor find a minimum diet beyond their reach. Meanwhile, those with economic power—in this case, large farmers and merchants—are buying all the grain they can hoard in order to force up prices still further and enlarge their own returns. The cycle of deprivation extends to an ever wider group. Finally, at the peak of the shortage, between harvests, the majority are malnourished, a minority (or sometimes a majority) die and a small elite make large fortunes.

If, in the following years, there are a succession of excellent harvests and even gluts, these same farmers will be in the forefront of those demanding government intervention to keep prices up and to introduce public purchase and storage—on the lines of American policy in the 1950s and the 1960s. But if no such measures are introduced, the farm community will see the prices fall drastically and the smallest farmers will reach ruin by another route.[58]

The adverse impact of rapidly fluctuating prices is not limited to only Third World farmers. United States Congressional Representative John LaFalce of New York speaks for the concerns of farmers in the United States:

As we all know, the American farmer has been recently buffeted by abrupt and often times severely damaging changes in the markets, as prices have rapidly fallen or risen with little prior warning. A U.S. contribution to an international food reserve could help level out the demand for U.S. agricultural products, by absorbing substantial amounts of U.S. foodstuffs, when this country enjoys bumper harvests and by providing a surplus fund in times of acute scarcity, when various buyers are clamoring for scarce American grains. This stabilization of the marketplace could help provide the American farmer with the necessary assurance that his products would always find a buyer at a fair price to the farmer.[59]

School of Thought: Establishing a Large-Scale Internationally Coordinated Grain Reserve Is Not Desirable

Many experts believe that a large-scale internationally coordinated grain reserve would make matters worse. Some fear that such reserves might reduce incentives for local storage, some think they would interfere with free enterprise. Others point to the national level as the most effective one for food-storage systems.

Internationally Coordinated Grain Reserves Could Reduce Incentives for Local Storage

Medard Gabel is an example of those who fear that such a worldwide system would take away people's sense of purpose and initiative. In *Ho-Ping: Food for Everyone*, Gabel writes:

Location of short-term food storage facilities would be primarily in the food-poor countries and as decentralized as possible, i.e., either farmer, co-op, or village-held storages. The reasons for this are twofold, one logistical, the other psychological. If food is stored near to where it most likely will be needed, then the time, energy, and organization required to get it when it actually is needed will be reduced. The second reason is that the comfort of knowing that your family is not going to go hungry or starve will have an unknown but powerful psychological effect on the entire world.[60]

As Gabel's quotation suggests, those who hold this point of view do not so much *oppose* international storage as they strongly *favor* local storage. They believe that the only equitable and workable solutions to the food-storage problem are at the local level. They oppose an international approach on the grounds that it will shift attention, resources, control, and incentives away from the local level.

Michael Lipton, writing in the *Guardian*, shares this view:

Often…the economics are much more attractive for locally made improvements to traditional structures than for such innovations as metal bins, where cost of materials and transport tend to mean that only big structures pay—and only bigger farmers benefit.…

For all the variations over space and time, a few lessons seem to apply to all who seek to advise and improve Third World storage. First, concentrate less on the big Government stores, and much more on farm family stores, where about 70 percent of grain is normally found.[61]

Activist Susan George helped prepare a "counter-report" for the World Food Conference and has authored several books on hunger. In the following quote from *Feeding the Few: Corporate Control of Food*, she brings her knowledge and concern for the small rural farmer to bear on the issue of grain reserves:

Farmers would rather have their grain close to hand, they only sell to far-off storage centers if in dire need of cash; and even if they do have surpluses to sell, the local processor can frequently offer them a better deal than the distant central facility (if only because of transport costs). Central storage is a failure because it is under-used (only to 14% of capacity in one African country) but also because the moment it <u>does</u> begin to fill up, infestations and fungi spread rapidly so that actually <u>more</u> food is often lost in "modern" post-harvest systems than in "backward" ones. Centralized storage is also costly in terms of foreign exchange, provides almost no employment and <u>its use adds at least 20% to the final cost of food</u> to the consumer. On-farm storage, on the other hand, has a great many advantages—the farmer has experience and knowledge of local building and pest control materials, he provides his own labor, his family constantly oversees the condition of the stored grain, no money is spent on transport and next to none on capital requirements, [and] anything that does spoil is not wasted but is fed to animals.[62]

Point of View Number 2

An International Grain-Reserve System Would Interfere with the Market and Private Enterprise

Supporters of this point of view include United States Senator Robert Dole, whose minority statement to President Carter's Commission on World Hunger addressed the subject of international grain reserves:

The best reserve possible is the promotion of effective grain production around the

Concentrate less on the big government stores, and much more on farm family stores.

world and insurance of an effective grain marketing system—not by imposing restrictive reserve standards that have negative effects on those responsible for food production. I feel huge reserves would be counterproductive. The world could end up with less grain rather than more, because large reserves tend to depress producer prices, destroy production incentives and disrupt markets....

A free-enterprise system of agriculture is the best mechanism to attain maximum production at the lowest possible price. Government programs that try to manipulate and regulate the market no matter what their goals purport to be more times than not end up as "disasters."[63]

The American Farm Bureau Federation expressed similar views in the 1978 congressional hearings on a proposed international emergency wheat reserve:

We are opposed to deliberate public policies designed to set up food reserves. The normal carryover stocks held by farmers and the grain industry, the fact that major crops are produced over wide geographic areas and the flexibility of a livestock economy provide assurance to domestic consumers and foreign buyers of an adequate supply of food.

We will continue to oppose the creation of government reserves. If short-term reserves are accumulated because of excessive production, inadequate demand, or both, we believe such reserves should be held by farmers.

In order to provide opportunity for more orderly marketing and to avoid government-controlled reserves, we favor programs to encourage and assist farmers to increase on-the-farm storage.[64]

The federation then commented:

Government-managed reserve stocks of farm commodities are both unnecessary and undesirable. Government-held reserves are not needed for the protection of our customers here or abroad. Users of U.S. agricultural commodities have a great deal of protection in the productivity, diversity, and flexibility of American agriculture. While we oppose government-held reserve stocks, we believe needed reserves can and should be maintained by farmers, handlers, and processors. Farmers and the trade have demonstrated their willingness to maintain larger reserves if the U.S. government does not take over this function.[65]

Opponents of international reserves are also concerned that national self-reliance will be badly damaged by an international system. United States Department of Agriculture Secretary John R. Block expresses the views of the Reagan Administration, which strongly supports the free market and strongly opposes internationally coordinated reserves:

Our grain reserve policies are based on our belief that the responsibility for carrying reserves of food for the world should not be borne by the United States alone. It should be shared by all major countries.

We continue to oppose internationally-coordinated reserves. Our emphasis is toward encouraging other countries to establish national grain reserves to enhance domestic, regional, and global food security.

We have met our own responsibility. U.S. grain reserves have helped stabilize food supplies and prices worldwide. Our Food Security Reserve of 4 million tons of wheat and the farmer-owned reserve are intended to help us meet our future international

We are opposed to deliberate policies designed to set up food reserves.

The responsibility for carrying reserves of food for the world should not be borne by the United States alone.

trade and food aid commitments. It is time for others to begin to carry their share of the burden....

The burden in the end lies with the governments of the food deficit developing countries. It is up to them to make the tough decisions necessary to meet the goal of greater food self-reliance—to be able to grow or trade for the needs of their individual countries. [66]

Point of View Number 3

National-Level Food-Storage Systems Are Most Effective

However, it is not only conservative thinkers who want to limit international grain reserves. The FAO is responsible for the International Undertaking on Food Security, adhered to by over fifty-five countries and endorsed by the World Food Conference. [67] As early as 1976, economist Onno van Teutem was reminding Third World nations that an international system, even one that worked perfectly, could not be expected to take the place of effective national-level systems. The food crisis of 1972–1974 illustrated the danger of relying too heavily on international stocks. In his view:

It would be wrong to expect too much for any such [international] agreement in the way of benefits for developing countries. Basic improvement in national food security arrangements of developing countries will surely continue to depend largely on their own internal food production as well as on the effectiveness of complementary action to stabilize national food supplies....

It is sometimes asserted that food-deficit countries cannot afford to hold stocks, since current production cannot meet current needs; that the availability of adequate food supplies from the main exporting countries precludes the need for establishing organized national food-stock systems in developing countries; or, conversely, that the low level of world stocks calls for immediate steps by developing countries to build up their own reserves.

It would be wrong for developing countries to conclude that large food suppliers will solve the problems.

These reactions are only natural, for the latest food crisis found the world unprepared to deal with the resulting problems, in much the same way as the energy crisis suddenly confronted economies built up on the basis of an abundance of cheap fuel supplies. In other words, the developing countries, which are the ones that risk food shortages, must find new ways of living with new realities. It would be wrong for them to conclude that the large food suppliers will solve their problems. [68]

Robert Paarlberg, a political scientist writing for the Overseas Development Council, is also a strong supporter of national-level solutions. In his view, although international reserves may not do harm, at the level where real needs must be met they are irrelevant:

Even if the many barriers to creating an IGR [International Grain Reserve] were somehow overcome, such a reserve might prove to be of only limited value in the larger struggle to provide food security for the world's poor, and especially for those 800 million living in "remote villages"....Most of those who are chronically undernourished would profit little from a lessening of price fluctuations in the world grain market. Within the low-income countries, most of the food that is consumed does not come from an "integrated" commercial market, let alone the international market. More than 1 billion of the people living in these countries, including most of those who are undernourished, subsist largely from their own production, much of which takes the form of non-cereal crops which are not traded in the international market....The poorest countries, where hunger is

164

most widespread, are those which participate least in world food markets. For the citizens of these countries, an IGR scheme primarily designed to stabilize world market prices can provide only marginal benefits beyond the ports and major cities....

A more promising path to global food security may be found not at the global level, through international food initiatives such as the IGR, but at the national level, through policy initiatives that can be undertaken unilaterally by individual states. It is at the national level that the most potent instruments—price, tax, monetary, budget, and public investment policies—are available for increasing food security. These national policy instruments have far greater reach into the rural food economy than any that might be conferred upon a global food authority through international agreement.[69]

The most potent instruments for increasing food security are at the national level.

Food Distribution

Schools of Thought on Distribution

In the following pages, we briefly explore a range of viewpoints concerning food that look at questions other than production and storage. We have grouped them under the broad heading of *Distribution*.

The schools of thought presented here focus on varying aspects of the distribution question: the system for distributing food; the issue of land distribution; and the distribution of political power among and within nations.

Each of these schools of thought is worthy of its own book; and indeed, many such books have been written. Most of this section could have focused on an in-depth examination of the schools of thought on the economics of the food system, the pros and cons of land reform, or the implications of political oppression and power within Third World agricultural societies.

However, the rest of this chapter does not provide a complete overview of any of these important subjects. Rather, it identifies them as entities in their own right that are worthy of further exploration.

School of Thought: For Hunger to End, the Efficiency of the Food System Must Be Improved

This first school of thought on distribution looks at the food system. The system is complex, and those who are concerned with ending hunger need to understand it. Breakdowns in distribution can cause localized hunger when there is plenty of food available elsewhere. Misguided government policies can make it more difficult for farmers to produce, distribute, and sell their products.

Point of View Number 1

Ineffective Food Distribution Can Be a Factor in Creating Hunger

A vivid example of this argument is a dispatch filed in 1972 by a *Newsweek* reporter from the Sahel region of Africa, during the severe drought:

"Sure, the food is pouring in," observed British Red Cross liaison officer George Bolton, "but how the hell are we going to get it to the people who need it? There isn't a tarred road within a thousand miles of Juba." Bolton wasn't exaggerating. While I was in Juba, I witnessed the arrival of 5,000 gallons of cooking oil, which had been diverted from the nearby state of Rwanda. Since the rickety old ferry was

FIGURE F.14. A VIEW OF THE FOOD-PRODUCTION SYSTEM

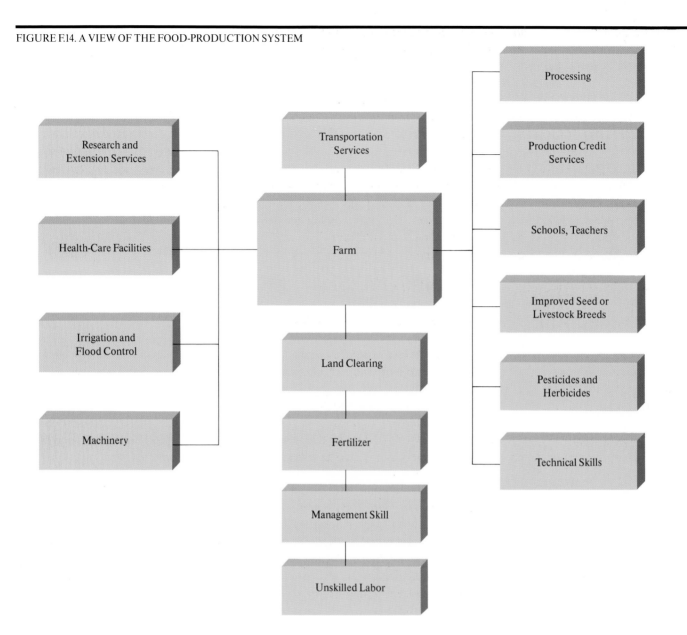

Source: Daniel N. Lapedes, ed., *McGraw-Hill Encyclopedia of Food, Agriculture and Nutrition* (New York: McGraw-Hill, 1977), 7.

Production of food depends upon a complex food-supply system. Pictured here are elements of this system in a modern industrial nation. According to some experts, hunger in the Third World is due partly to a failure to understand the food-supply system and manage it effectively.

not strong enough to carry the oil shipment across the White Nile so it could be distributed to the needy in the interior, the oil was promptly unloaded on the riverbank and stored in Juba.

And this was not an isolated incident. I saw warehouses in Juba overflowing with millet, dried fish, cooking utensils, agricultural tools and medical supplies—all useless because nothing could be delivered to the people who needed it.[70]

According to C. Peter Timmer, Walter Falcon, and Scott Pearson, a clear under-standing of the food system must be at the heart of any rational policy directed at ending hunger. The food system is the crucial link between government policies and the people they are intended to serve, and—more importantly—between those who produce food and those who eat it. Timmer, Falcon, and Pearson discuss the functions of the food system and its importance for food policy:

The failure of government policies to deal more effectively with hunger—despite trends showing greater availability of food—reflects a lack of understanding of the direct and indirect causes of hunger and its relationship to a country's food system.

All food systems must accomplish similar tasks. By organizing the production or provision of food, its marketing, and its consumption by the citizens of the society, food systems around the world end up having much in common. The choices a society faces in organizing these tasks are completely analogous to the larger economic choices faced by any society whether socialist or capitalist: what to produce, how to produce it, and for whom. Different societies make fundamentally different choices in each area and yet have food systems that are understandable within a common methodology of food policy analysis.

The macro perspective places the food system squarely in the context of economic growth and efforts to alleviate poverty. These efforts involve strategies for raising productivity in the agricultural sector, for it is there that much poverty is found. A healthy and dynamic rural sector is essential to reducing hunger, but the policies that create such rural dynamism do not all emanate from agricultural planning offices. Most of the economic environment required to stimulate efficient resource allocation, labor productivity, and more jobs is created by macroeconomic policy.

Using macro policies to alleviate poverty in the long run is only part of an effective food policy. Reaching the poor in the short run is always difficult because of their weak link to the food system and the rest of the economy. Poor consumers have different diets from those who are better-off, and their income sources are usually much less secure. Similarly, very small farmers often do not control adequate resources in the form of land, water, or credit to participate fully in the potential of new agricultural technology. The task is to find interventions in the micro environment that can protect their welfare while the macro forces strengthen their links to the economy in the long run.[71]

Many developing nations have attempted to solve the hunger problem by substituting central planning for the functioning of the market—an approach that often is supported by development organizations and specialists. However, many analysts believe that the foundation of an effectively functioning food system is an effectively functioning free market. Sterling Wortman and Ralph Cummings, Jr., suggest that if the free market in Third World nations were unimpeded by govern-ment regulations, it might support efficient food production and distribution.

Studies of marketing systems in Asia, Africa, and Latin America indicate that, at existing levels of production, private marketing systems are surprisingly effective.

The food system is the crucial link between government policies and the people they are intended to serve.

The foundation of an effectively func-tioning food system is an effectively functioning free market.

167

Prices in the markets appear to be influenced by aggregate supply and demand for the region and country. Price differences from one market to another infrequently exceed transportation costs by a large margin (when large differences occur they are usually due to the availability of small volumes during the off-seasons, during times of shortage, or when the government has artificially restricted commodity movements). While prices in the off-season are usually higher than at harvest time, the differences seldom exceed storage costs substantially (costs which include charges for the high interest rates and high rates of loss prevailing in low-income countries). On the average, the profits from holding commodities do not appear to be excessive for the management performed and the risk assumed. In markets that have large numbers of small traders, evidence of price rigging is remarkably rare, although there are some notable monopolies of some perishable products (for example, potatoes). Studies of marketing margins reveal that the share of the retail price going to the wholesaler (above transportation and storage costs and market fees) is usually small.

Thus, the private marketing systems appear to operate effectively <u>in the absence of monopolies</u>. Imperfections in the private marketing system seem to be largely due to inherent uncertainties of supply and demand and to seasonal scarcities of stocks. These uncertainties arise from forces over which private traders have limited control. However, even in normal times and especially in times of extreme shortage or of rapid growth in production, problems do appear which may require government intervention.[72]

Point of View Number 2

Government Intervention in Food Distribution Does Harm

Governments can make it difficult for farmers to produce, distribute, and sell their products, as this litany of examples from the World Bank's *World Development Report 1981*, illustrates:

Many countries pursue policies that discriminate against farmers. In every country, farmers—and particularly smallholders—require a credible framework of incentives if they are to increase their output. Incentives depend primarily on prices, but other factors are also important. In many countries, official prices exceed world prices at official exchange rates; yet delays in payment for crops, and costly inefficiencies in transport, storage and marketing significantly reduce the prices farmers actually receive. Food prices in the free market commonly exceed official prices, but are unstable and unpredictable and depend on private trade and distribution which is often officially discouraged. Government domestic procurement and distribution, on the other hand, is frequently inadequate to support prices at harvest time, and a major drain on the budget and scarce administrative resources. Erratic import procurement can also destabilize prices. And even when farmers do increase their incomes, there are often few consumer goods and services available in rural areas....

Inequitable land tenure excludes the landless poor from productive employment.

Inequitable land tenure arrangements can both reduce incentives (when, for example, tenants do not receive the benefits of innovation and increased production) and exclude the landless poor from productive employment and higher incomes.

The discrimination against farming goes beyond the incentive system. Agricultural extension services are frequently underfinanced and inadequately staffed, often as the result of neglect rather than any deliberate intention to downgrade agriculture.[73]

In the area of land distribution, we examine the view that land reform is the key to ending hunger.

This school of thought addresses the distribution of land. According to proponents, the system of land ownership plays a major role in determining whether the food system works well or poorly. They hold that redistribution of land and equitable land tenure must be key factors in any successful program to end hunger. Where land reform has been implemented, it has produced good results.

Point of View Number 1

Land Reform Is Essential to Successful Development

Law professor Roy Prosterman has devoted his life to the study of land reform issues. In his view land reform must be at the core of any effective development policy.

Land reform is possible, has worked, and has achieved both massive increases in production and dramatically improved distribution of that production to the people who are cultivating the land.

A high proportion of the hungry are non-land-owning rural poor. Their access to food depends heavily on gaining access to ownership of the land on which food is produced. Approximately 87–100 million families in the less developed world are non-land-owning families that are landless laborers or tenant farmers. The tenant families are being charged forty or fifty percent of what they produce by the landlord for the right to farm the land. The landless laborers make a dollar a day in the field, and they can only find employment during the peak season.

Also, the motivation of cultivators to adopt high-productivity technologies depends on their being assured the benefits of increased production through land ownership.

And another point—if new technologies come before land reform, the situation often becomes worse for the landless. Pressure builds until a land redistribution becomes inevitable. But now that you've put the inputs in, you're going to have greater resistance on the part of the landowner, and the price of land is going to be higher. You've put in a billion dollars worth of technology, and thereby increased by two billion dollars the price you're going to have to pay the landlords for their land.

You need both [land] ownership and technology. The two go together and complement one another.

Before any technologies can really be effective in increasing food production, there needs to be a welcoming environment. That means egalitarian land tenure. Much of Africa already has egalitarian tenure. What they need is to supply the inputs and technical support that go with ownership to permit full realization of the productive potential of the small owners. You need both ownership and technology. The two go together and complement one another.[74]

Sterling Wortman and Ralph Cummings, Jr., also emphasize the central role of land in the food system. To them, land is more than just a factor of production and a source of wealth in developing nations; it is also a principal source of social status:

Land tenure is central in determining <u>who</u> benefits from increases in productivity. Land is an essential ingredient in agriculture and thus in rural life. It influences the amount of a farmer's production. It influences employment. It also influences status in the community. Together, wealth and status go a long way toward establishing a rural person's contribution to, as well as claims on, society. As Solon Barraclough states: "Farm size is a crucial development issue not because of economies or diseconomies of scale but because land ownership in traditional societies is practically synonymous with control of labor, wealth, social prestige,

169

and political power…the ability to make others do one's will." Phillip Raup also puts the issue succinctly: "Land tenure institutions define a farmer's status. They create the framework of expectations within which hopes and fears motivate him to economic activity." Evidence from many nations suggests that rising agricultural productivity may be possible under a variety of land tenure conditions. However, a relatively equitable land tenure system is a requisite to ensuring broad partici-pation of the rural population in the economic and political process of a country.[75]

Point of View Number 2

Land Reform Programs Have Produced Good Results

The 1980 *World Development Report* addresses this issue:

Although most farms in developing countries are small, the small minority of large farms account for most of the area. Yet there is wide-ranging evidence that (com-paring similar types of agriculture) smaller farms outperform larger farms in value added per acre. For example:

India. The Farm Management Studies of the 1950s, covering about 3,000 farms in six states, found that the larger the farm, the smaller its output per acre. Nor has the green revolution—high-yielding varieties of seed—changed this conclusion. The National Council of Applied Economic Research surveyed 4,000 households throughout the country in 1968–69, 1969–70 and 1970–71; more than 2,500 of them were farming throughout the period. Although the productivity gap between large and small farms tended to narrow as the green revolution spread, it remained significant—even after controlling for differences in land quality and irrigation. The proportion of land under high-yielding varieties did not vary by farm size. Tests relating capital and labor use to farm size showed that as farms became larger, they used proportionately less capital and labor—and particularly the latter, which costs less on small farms making use of family labor than on large farms relying mainly on hired labor.

The intensity with which land and labor were used declined sharply and con-sistently as farm size increased.

Brazil. The World Bank and SUDENE, the official regional development authority, carried out a detailed study of 8,000 farms in the poor northeastern region in late 1973 and early 1974. It revealed that the intensity with which land and labor were used declined sharply and consistently as farm size increased. Depending on the subregion, small farms applied 5 to 22 times as much labor per hectare as large farms, although the proportion of high- or medium-yielding soils did not vary significantly with the size of the farm. Small farms tended to employ more labor than profit maximization would warrant, probably in part because family members have difficulty in obtaining employment elsewhere, while large farms employed less.

Such studies suggest that redistribution of land in larger farms into smaller ones in many cases would increase output and employment (and of course equity) significantly. But there are important qualifications. [Emphasis added] For example, where literacy rates are low among small farmers, middle-size farms tend to be quicker to adopt innovations. After a certain point fragmentation inhibits productivity growth, and significant land is lost through field boundaries (for example, in parts of Asia a holding of one hectare may comprise 15 or 20 tiny parcels). For some combinations of crops and soils, mechanization—and thus large fields—may increase output: research in South Asia provides little support for the yield-increasing effect of tractor cultivation, which may simply cause agricultural laborers to get fewer days of work. But where labor is in relatively short supply, and timely cultivation and harvesting are critical to increasing yields, large mechanized farms may be economically rational.[76]

170

School of Thought: For Hunger to End, Inequitable Power Structures Must Become More Equitable

This school of thought addresses the distribution of economic and political power. Proponents argue that hunger will not be ended without fundamental changes in the power structure. In their view, technologically oriented programs that ignore this are just superficial tinkering or smokescreens created by the powerful to hide the true causes of hunger.

Point of View Number 1

Hunger Will Not End Without Changes in the Power Structure

In the 1890s, peasants in imperial Russia faced a similar situation to that which peasants now face in many nations. They worked the land to produce food, and they starved. Leo Tolstoy wrote of this situation in 1893. His words still have meaning for modern political leaders and development specialists who share his view that the power structure must change before people can have food:

Feed the people! Who then has taken it upon himself to feed the people? It is we, the civil servants, who have taken it upon ourselves to feed the very men who have always fed us and who go on feeding us every day.... It can be said that bread, not to mention all other forms of wealth, is produced directly by the people.... How is it then that this bread is to be found, not in the possession of the people, but in our hands, and that, by a peculiar and artificial process, we have to return it to the people, calculating so much for each person?... Must we delude ourselves by saying that the people were poor merely because they have not yet had time to adjust to our civilization, but that, come tomorrow, we shall set about imparting all our knowledge to them, concealing nothing, and that then they will doubtless cease to be poor.... Do not all enlightened folk continue to live in the towns—for what they claim to be a very exalted purpose—and to eat in the towns the sustenance which is brought there and for want of which the people are dying? And these are the circumstances in which we have suddenly started to assure ourselves and everyone else that we are very sorry for the people and that we want to save them from their wretched plight, a plight for which we ourselves are responsible and which is indeed necessary to us. Here is the cause of the futility of the efforts made by those who, without changing their relationship with the people, wish to come to their help by distributing the riches which have been taken from them.[77]

For those who believe that redistribution of power is a prerequisite for development, any talk about food-production technologies, food storage and security, or an efficient food-distribution system is just a smokescreen generated by the powerful. History offers few examples of powerful people willingly giving up their power. In an article aptly entitled "Politics First," Solon Barraclough writes:

How [development] proceeds depends to a large extent on how power is distributed among different social groups.

Development is not just economics or sociology or technology but history. How it proceeds depends to a large extent on how power is distributed among different social groups. The immediate outlook for most of the rural poor in the developing countries is for continued poverty and increased repression. This problem is not going to be solved merely by greater investments in technological improvements of the green revolution or by more abundant credit and technical assistance. Rural development for the low-income majorities requires fundamental and often revolutionary reforms in social institutions....

We would be naive or hypocritical to believe that helping governments implement conservative development strategies of technological modernization and economic growth, which do not consider the welfare and participation of the rural poor as real high-priority goals, will in some miraculous fashion directly benefit more than a very few of the poverty-stricken small farmers and landless labourers.[78]

171

Frances Moore Lappé and Joseph Collins echo Barraclough's views. Lappé, perhaps best known as the author of *Diet for a Small Planet,* works with Collins at the San Francisco-based Institute for Food and Development Policy. In *Food First* they write:

Focusing narrowly on production totals transforms rural development into a technical problem—one of getting the "right," usually foreign-made, inputs to the "progressive," invariably well-placed farmers. We refer to this production focus as <u>narrow</u> precisely because it ignores the social reality of hunger—that the hungry are those with control over little or no food-producing resources. Until control over productive resources is democratized such "agricultural modernization" will remain but a mirage of rural development—a mirage that undermines the interests of the majority of the rural population in order to serve those of a few—large landholders, moneylenders, industrialists, bureaucrats, and foreign investors.[79]

Point of View Number 2

The Powerless Must Become Independent and Self-Reliant

What is the solution to this dependence of the powerless? Those who are concerned about the distribution of power see the answer as self-reliance at the individual, local, and national levels. People will not have food until they have power. Susan George puts it this way:

My personal feeling is that very little can be done to help the rural poor without overwhelming social changes in their own countries. Most projects can therefore be little more than palliative measures serving the elites, in the final analysis, as alibis for maintaining the status quo. Thus I would urge other people to give support to national liberation and minority political groups whose goal is to change the whole society....

Underdeveloped countries would do well to imitate China and rely on their own strength rather than on the aid of the West.

The UDCs [underdeveloped countries] would do well to imitate China and rely on their own strength rather than on the aid of the West. Any real progress in eliminating hunger will mean social change; any massive commitment of Western aid will require a political and economic return.... The only available choices are self-reliance or dependency. If governments of poor nations continue to walk the road of food aid, the MNCs [multinational corporations] or the World Bank, they do so in the full knowledge that solutions offered for their problems will continue to be technocratic and exploitative and that all the strings will be pulled by outsiders. Doubtless for such governing elites even total loss of dignity and national self-hood is preferable to loss of power and of a comfortable life.

Others have learned that there is honor in austerity, that charity is no substitute for justice and that nothing can equal the people's strength when their leaders have the courage to speak a single word to their would-be masters: No.[80]

China is the shining success story for many who believe that redistribution of power and greater self-reliance must precede meeting food needs. This section concludes with a quotation from the man responsible for much of the development of modern China, Mao Tse-tung:

We stand for self-reliance. We hope for foreign aid but cannot be dependent on it; we depend on our own efforts, on the creative power of the whole army and the entire people....

On what basis should our policy rest? It should rest on our own strength, and that means regeneration through one's own efforts. We are not alone; all the countries

172

and people in the world opposed to imperialism are our friends. Nevertheless, we stress regeneration through our own efforts....

In the fight for complete liberation the oppressed people rely first of all on their own struggle and then, and only then, on international assistance. The people who have triumphed in their own revolution should help those still struggling for liberation. This is our internationalist duty. [81]

Conclusion

In this chapter, we have explored the question of how to improve the availability of food on the planet. We have examined the basic information on food production, food storage and security, and food distribution. And we have heard from the major spokespeople of the international schools of thought on high-technology agriculture, organic farming, international grain reserves, food security at the local level, land reform, the impact of political power within and among nations, and more.

When we began this chapter many pages ago, we started with the words, "Hunger exists when there is not enough food for the people who need it." While there are many differing interpretations about how best to remedy that situation, it is heartening to note that virtually all the voices we have heard agree that it *can* be remedied.

Indeed, as we noted in *Basic Facts on Food Production,* ours is an incredibly fertile and productive planet. At a time when 13 to 18 million of us are dying yearly as a consequence of the persistence of hunger, this earth is already producing enough food to feed more than 6 billion people—hundreds of millions more than are now alive. While there are many problems yet to overcome and many policies and programs yet to enact, it is not because of absolute scarcity of food that hunger persists.

While there are many problems to be overcome, it is not because of absolute scarcity of food that hunger persists.

We have enough. And we can grow more.

The question is, "Which pathways will nations and the world community pursue to ensure that enough food in the right places is available to all?" As the experts in the previous pages have indicated, there is no scarcity of answers to that question.

NOTES

1   United Nations, Food and Agriculture Organization, *Monthly Bulletin of Statistics* 5, no. 11 (November 1982): 19.

2   Calculations based on Population Reference Bureau, *1982 World Population Data Sheet* (Washington, DC: Population Reference Bureau, 1982); United Nations, Food and Agriculture Organization, *Monthly Bulletin of Statistics* 5, no. 11 (November 1982): 19; U.S., Department of Agriculture, *Composition of Foods,* Agriculture Handbook, no. 8, by Bernice K. Watt and Annabel L. Merrill (Washington, DC: U.S. Government Printing Office, 1963), 66; and FAO and WHO recommendations for daily caloric intake, in George Thomas Kurian, *The Book of World Rankings* (New York: Facts On File, 1979), 306.

3   Terry N. Barr, "The World Food Situation and Global Grain Prospects," *Science* 214 (4 December 1981): 1087, 1088.

4   Ibid., 1088.

5   Michael F. Lofchie and Stephen K. Commins, "Food Deficits and Agricultural Policies in Tropical Africa," *Journal of Modern African Studies* 20, no. 1 (1982): 1.

6   Barr, "World Food," 1088; and Keith O. Campbell, *Food for the Future* (Lincoln, NB: University of Nebraska Press, 1979), 23, 24.

7   Lester R. Brown, *By Bread Alone* (New York: Praeger, 1974), 205, 206.

8   Yujiro Hayami and Vernon W. Ruttan, *Agricultural Development: An International Perspective* (Baltimore, MD: Johns Hopkins University Press, 1971), 70–71.

9   Sterling Wortman and Ralph W. Cummings, Jr., *To Feed This World: The Challenge and the Strategy* (Baltimore, MD: Johns Hopkins University Press, 1978), 59.

10 Julian L. Simon, "World Food Supplies," *Atlantic Monthly,* July 1981, 76. (Revised from *The Ultimate Resource,* Princeton, NJ: Princeton University Press, 1981.)

11 Robert Katz, *A Giant in the Earth* (New York: Stein and Day, 1973), 109, 111, 112.

12 M. Rupert Cutler, "The Peril of Vanishing Farmlands," *New York Times,* 1 July 1980, A19.

13 United Nations, General Assembly, *Report of the United Nations Conference on Desertification* (A/CONF. 74/36), 1977, 2.

14 Robert P. Ambroggi, "Water," *Scientific American* 243, no. 3 (September 1980): 101–103.

15 Ibid., 103.

16 Tom Fulton and Peter Braestrup, "The New Issues: Land, Water, Energy," *Wilson Quarterly* 5, no. 3 (Summer 1981): 125–26.

17 United Nations, Food and Agriculture Organization, *Energy for World Agriculture,* FAO Agriculture Series, no. 7 (1979): 42.

18 Ibid., 47.

19 B. A. Stout, *Energy Use and Management in Agriculture* (Belmont, CA: Wadsworth, Breton Publishers, 1984), 21.

20 David Pimentel et al., "Food Production and the Energy Crisis," *Science* 182 (2 November 1973): 448.

21 Vernon W. Ruttan, "Agricultural Research and the Future of American Agriculture," *The Future of American Agriculture as a Strategic Resource,* eds. Sandra S. Batie and Robert G. Healy (Washington, DC: The Conservation Foundation, 1980), 145.

22 United Nations, Food and Agriculture Organization, *The State of Food and Agriculture 1982,* FAO Agriculture Series, no. 15 (1983): 30; and United Nations, Food and Agriculture Organization, *Energy for World Agriculture,* 125.

23 United Nations, Food and Agriculture Organization, *The State of Food and Agriculture 1982,* 68.

24 Independent Commission on International Development Issues, *North-South: A Program for Survival* (Cambridge, MA: MIT Press, 1980), 100.

25 S. H. Wittwer, "Food Production: Technology and the Resource Base," *Science* 188 (9 May 1975): 583.

26 Robert Katz, *A Giant in the Earth* (New York: Stein and Day, 1973), 40–41.

27 Harry S. Truman, "The Faith By Which We Live," Inaugural Address, Washington, DC, 20 January 1949, *Vital Speeches of the Day* 15, no. 8 (1 February 1949): 227, 228.

28 Daniel Benor and James Q. Harrison, *Agricultural Extension: The Training and Visit System* (Washington, DC: World Bank, May 1977), 51–52.

29 Stanley Johnson, *The Green Revolution* (New York: Harper & Row, 1972), 178–79.

30 Robert S. McNamara, *The McNamara Years at the World Bank: Major Policy Addresses of Robert S. McNamara, 1968–1981* (Baltimore, MD: Johns Hopkins University Press, 1981), 244–45, 246, 248.

31 United Nations, Food and Agriculture Organization, "Agriculture: Toward 2000," prepared for the Twentieth Session, Rome, 10–29 November 1979 (C 79/24), July 1979, vii, xv, xvi.

32 Katz, *Giant in the Earth,* 197–98.

33 M. S. Swaminathan, "The Green Revolution Can Reach the Small Farmer," *Hunger, Politics and Markets,* ed. Sartaj Aziz (New York: New York University Press, 1975), 83–84.

34 Norman E. Borlaug, "Using Plants to Meet World Food Needs," *Future Dimensions of World Food and Population,* ed. Richard G. Woods (Boulder, CO: Westview Press, 1981), 175, 181.

35 ——, "Without Pesticides, 'The World Population Will Starve,'" *U.S. News & World Report,* 1 November 1971, 93.

36 Wortman and Cummings, *To Feed This World,* 64.

37 Robert Rodale and Thomas Dybdahl, "The Coming Food Crunch," *Cry California,* Summer 1981, 7, 9, 10.

38 Asit K. Biswas, "Agricultural Development and Environment," *Mazingira,* no. 11 (1979): 11–12.

39 Silvio Almeida et al., "Analysis of Traditional Strategies to Combat World Hunger and Their Results," *International Journal of Health Services* 5, no. 1 (1975): 128.

40 Pierre Spitz, "Silent Violence: Famine and Inequality," *International Social Science Journal* 30, no. 4 (1978): 884–85.

41 Francine R. Frankel, *India's Green Revolution: Economic Gains and Political Costs* (Princeton, NJ: Princeton University Press, 1971), 12–13, 39.

42 U.S., Department of Agriculture, *USSR: Review of Agriculture in 1981 and Outlook for 1982* (Washington, DC: U.S. Government Printing Office, May 1982), 20.

43 ——, *Foreign Agriculture Circular* (FG-29-82), 15 September 1982, 4.

44 U.S. Presidential Commission on World Hunger, *Overcoming World Hunger: The Challenge Ahead* (Washington, DC: U.S. Government Printing Office, March 1980), 89, 90.

45 United Nations, Food and Agriculture Organization, *Agriculture: Toward 2000* (Rome: FAO, 1981), 10.

46 Derived from U.S., Department of Agriculture, *Foreign Agriculture Circular,* 4.

47 "The Somber Waves of Grain," *Newsweek,* 17 January 1983, 52.

48 United Nations, Food and Agriculture Organization, *The State of Food and Agriculture 1980,* FAO Agriculture Series, no. 12 (1981): 23.

49 Uwe Kracht, World Food Council, Rome, correspondence with The Hunger Project, 15 September 1981.

50 United Nations, Food and Agriculture Organization, *Proposals for a World Food Board,* 1 October 1946, 1, 3, 5.

51 A. Doak Barnett, *China and the World Food System,* Monograph no. 12 (Washington, DC: Overseas Development Council, April 1979), 21, 22; and "We Need Development for Sheer Survival," *Ceres* 8, no. 1 (January–February 1975): 27.

52 Philip H. Trezise, *Rebuilding Grain Reserves: Toward an International System* (Washington, DC: Brookings Institution, 1976), 3.

53 Commissioner Robert Dole wrote a minority opinion opposing the commission recommendation in favor of an international reserve. See U.S. Presidential Commission on World Hunger, *Overcoming World Hunger,* 207–209.

54 U.S. Presidential Commission on World Hunger, *Overcoming World Hunger,* 90.

55 "We Need Development for Sheer Survival," *Ceres,* 24.

56 U.S., Congress, House, Committee on International Relations and the Committee on Agriculture, *International Emergency Wheat Reserve,* statement of Brennon Jones, 95th Cong., 2nd sess., 13 June 1978, 11.

57 *Current Biography 1977,* s.v. "Ward, Barbara (Mary)," 424.

58 Sartaj Aziz, ed., *Hunger, Politics and Markets* (New York: New York University Press, 1975), xi–xii.

59 U.S., Congress, House, Committee on International Relations and the Committee on Agriculture, *International Emergency Wheat Reserve,* statement of Hon. John J. LaFalce, 9.

60 Medard Gabel, *Ho-Ping: Food for Everyone* (Garden City, NY: Doubleday, Anchor Press, 1979), 221.

61 Michael Lipton, "Salting Grain Away," *Guardian,* 30 July 1979, 13.

62 Susan George, *Feeding the Few: Corporate Control of Food* (Washington, DC: Institute for Policy Studies, n.d.), 61–62.

63 U.S. Presidential Commission on World Hunger, *Overcoming World Hunger,* 208.

64 U.S., Congress, House, Committee on International Relations and the Committee on Agriculture, *International Emergency Wheat Reserve,* 143.

65 Ibid.

66 U.S., Congress, House, Committee on Agriculture, *World Hunger Situation,* statement by John R. Block, 97th Cong., 1st sess., 22 July 1981, 278, 281–82.

67 Onno van Teutem, "Grain Stock Policies in Developing Countries," *Science and Public Policy: Journal of the Science Policy Foundation* 3, no. 3 (June 1976): 208; and Aziz in "We Need Development," 24.

68 van Teutem, "Grain Stock Policies," 208, 209.

69 Robert Paarlberg, "A Food Security Approach for the 1980s: Righting the Balance," *U.S. Foreign Policy and the Third World: Agenda 1982,* eds. Roger D. Hansen et al., Overseas Development Council (New York: Praeger, 1982), 80, 81.

70 Julian L. Simon, "World Food Supplies," *Atlantic Monthly,* July 1981, 74. (Revised from *The Ultimate Resource,* Princeton, NJ: Princeton University Press, 1981.)

71 C. Peter Timmer, Walter P. Falcon, and Scott R. Pearson, *Food Policy Analysis* (Baltimore, MD: Johns Hopkins University Press, 1983), 13.

72 Wortman and Cummings, *To Feed This World,* 366–67.

73 World Bank, *World Development Report 1981* (New York: Oxford University Press, 1981), 105.

74 Roy L. Prosterman, unpublished interview with Ted Howard of The Hunger Project, San Francisco, May 1982.

75 Wortman and Cummings, *To Feed This World,* 271.

76 World Bank, *World Development Report 1980* (New York: Oxford University Press, 1980), 42.

77 Leo Tolstoy, *La Famine,* in Pierre Spitz, "Silent Violence: Famine and Inequality," 890.

78 Solon L. Barraclough, "Politics First," *Ceres* 7, no. 5 (September–October 1974): 28.

79 Frances Moore Lappé and Joseph Collins, *Food First* (New York: Ballantine, 1982), 128.

80 Susan George, *How the Other Half Dies* (Montclair, NJ: Allanheld, Osmun, & Co., 1977), 261, 251 (respectively).

81 Mao Tse-tung, *Quotations from Chairman Mao Tse-tung,* ed. Stuart R. Schram (New York: Bantam, 1972), 110, 99 (respectively).

Because food shortages occur in vast areas of the inhabited world, food security is a major priority in the effort to end hunger. And food storage—especially grain reserves—is a key component of any program of food security. "Food security" means the assurance of an adequate daily consumption of food at the national, village, and family level, even in years of a bad harvest. Weather changes, such as droughts, can devastate an entire year's harvest. The result may be a localized famine or—if several major food-producing countries are affected simultaneously—a dramatic altera-tion in world food availability and world prices. This is what happened in 1983, when a disloca-tion of the world's largest weather system, El Niño, resulted in high winds and floods, which contributed to increased drought around the globe. Right: *The effects of El Niño in Botswana* (Thomas Nebbia/Woodfin Camp & Assoc.).

Some believe that only a large-scale internationally coordinated grain reserve can ensure
true food security. But critics, fearing that such
a reserve would only reduce incentives for local
and national storage, see storage at the local
level as the solution. Medard Gabel writes: "If
food is stored near to where it most likely will
be needed, then the time, energy, and organization required to get it when it actually is needed
will be reduced.... Left: *A thatched-hut granary
in Benin* (Wendy Watriss/Woodfin Camp &
Assoc.); above, top: *Grain is stored in a clay-
walled hut, Nigeria* (Marc & Evelyne Bernheim/
Woodfin Camp & Assoc.); above, bottom:
*Corn is stored in grassy pouches hung from a
tree, Ivory Coast* (Marc & Evelyne Bernheim/
Woodfin Camp & Assoc.); next two-page
spread: *Sacks of peanuts form a different kind
of pyramid, Nigeria* (John Moss/Photo
Researchers).

*International reserves, say their advocates, are
central to ending hunger. The U.S. Presidential
Commission on World Hunger concludes:
"Reserves invariably have consequences and
implications for other [than just local] areas,
such as consumer price stability, farm price stability, and income stability for farm people."*
Above: *Primitive granary, Ivory Coast* (Marc &
Evelyne Bernheim/Woodfin Camp & Assoc.);
right: *Modern granary, New Jersey* (Sylvia
Johnson/Woodfin Camp & Assoc.).

Under the broad heading of distribution, various viewpoints concerning food are explored. They focus on the system for distributing food, the issue of land distribution, and the distribution of political power among nations. Hunger will not be ended simply by producing enough food. A Newsweek reporter's dispatch from the Sahel region of Africa illustrates the problem: "I saw warehouses in Juba overflowing with millet, dried fish, cooking utensils, agricultural tools and medical supplies—all useless because nothing could be delivered to the people who needed it." Left: On foot: bringing the crop to market, China (Larry Mulvehill/ Photo Researchers); above, top: By oxen: bringing the crop to market, China (Lowell Georgia/Photo Researchers); above, bottom: By boat: bringing the crop to market, Mexico (Mark Godfrey/Archive); next two-page spread: Containerized freight, U.S. (Jeff Jacobson/Archive).

Many developing nations have attempted to solve the hunger problem by substituting central planning for the functioning of the market—an approach that often is supported by development organizations and specialists. However, a number of analysts believe that the foundation of an effectively functioning food system is an effectively functioning free market. They suggest that, if the free market in Third World nations were unimpeded by government regulations, it might well support more efficient food production and distribution. Above, top: *Produce trucks, California* (Chuck O'Rear/ Woodfin Camp & Assoc.); above, bottom: *Railway freight cars, U.S.* (Chuck O'Rear/ Woodfin Camp & Assoc.); right: *Loading grain aboard ship, Australia* (Robert Frerck/ Woodfin Camp & Assoc.); next two-page spread: *A floating market in Kashmir* (Robert Frerck/Woodfin Camp & Assoc.).

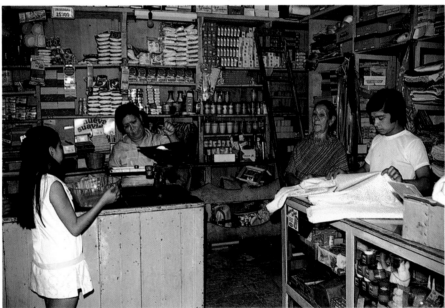

"All food systems must accomplish similar tasks," say economists C. Peter Timmer and colleagues. "By organizing the production or provision of food, its marketing, and its consumption by the citizens of the society, food systems around the world end up having much in common. The choices a society faces in organizing these tasks are... what to produce, how to produce it, and for whom." Left: *A Third World market features local produce* (Andy Levin/ Black Star); above, top: *Haitian market* (© Chuck Fishman/Contact); above, bottom: *Corner store, rural Mexico* (Marc & Evelyne Bernheim/ Woodfin Camp & Assoc.); next two-page spread: *Modern supermarket, U.S.* (Sepp Seitz/Woodfin Camp & Assoc.). *Chickens compete with people for food, but cows can live on forage.* Following two-page spread: *Chickens, U.S.* (Julie Habel/Woodfin Camp & Assoc.); third two-page spread: *Cattle, U.S.* (Mark Godfrey/Archive).

193

*Distributing food means distributing power,
according to one school of thought. Hunger can
be ended only through fundamental changes in
the social structure and the redistribution of
political power. In 1893, Leo Tolstoy wrote: "It
can be said that bread, not to mention all other
forms of wealth, is produced directly by the
people.... How is it then that this bread is to be
found, not in the possession of the people, but
in our hands, and that, by a peculiar and artificial process, we have to return it to the people,
calculating so much for each person?"* Left:
Cooking in an African village (B. & C. Alex-
ander/Black Star); above: *Cooking in a Guatemalan village* (Albert Moldvay/Woodfin
Camp & Assoc.).

People must have power in order to have food, assert Frances Moore Lappé and Joseph Collins: "Focusing narrowly on production totals transforms rural development into a technical problem—one of getting the 'right,' usually foreign-made, inputs to the 'progressive,' invariably well-placed farmers. We refer to this production focus as <u>narrow</u> precisely because it ignores the social reality of hunger— that the hungry are those with control over little or no food-producing resources." Left: A Jamaican family eats dinner on a crowded stairway (Alon Reininger/Contact for Woodfin Camp & Assoc.); above: *Mealtime for California farm workers* (Chuck O'Rear/ Woodfin Camp & Assoc.).

In answer to the question, "Can we improve the availability of food on the planet?" nearly all the major spokespeople addressing this issue say "yes." The question then, is not "can we?" but rather "which pathways will nations and the world community pursue to ensure that enough food in the right places is available to all?" Ours is an incredibly fertile and productive planet. At a time when 13–18 million are dying yearly because of hunger, this earth is already producing enough food to feed more than 6 billion people—hundreds of millions more than are now alive. It is not because of absolute scarcity of food that hunger persists. We have enough. And we can grow more. Overleaf: *An African farmer displays her harvest* (Wernher Krutein/Photovault); left: *Iowa corn* (Craig Aurness/Woodfin Camp & Assoc.); above, top left: *Alfalfa crop* (John Blaustein/Woodfin Camp & Assoc.); above, top right: *Safflower crop* (John Blaustein/ Woodfin Camp & Assoc.); above, bottom left: *Bananas* (Andy Levin/Black Star); above, bottom right: *Wheat harvest* (Lowell Georgia/Photo Researchers); Overleaf two-page spread: *A once-barren Bali hillside has been transformed into fertile terraced farmland* (Mike Yamashita/Woodfin Camp & Assoc.).

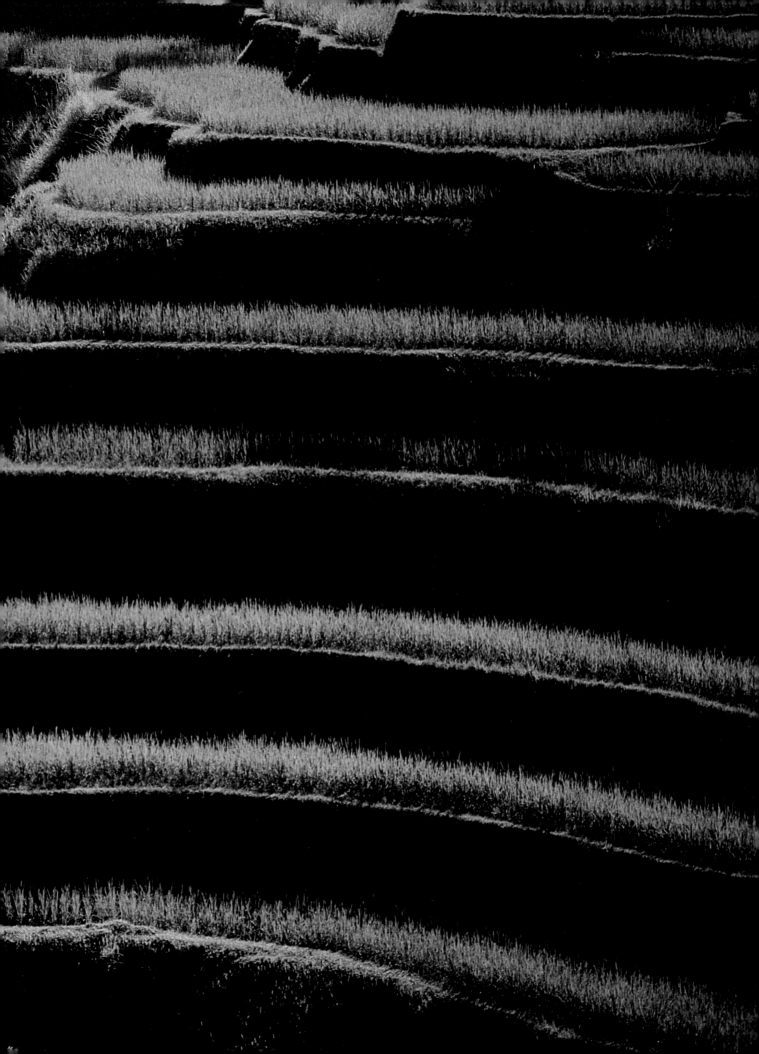

Foreign Aid

We now turn to the third major issue surrounding hunger—foreign aid.

Today, after more than three decades of various foreign-aid approaches and programs have provided us with much learning and experience, we can view the question of foreign aid through a wide array of perspectives. As we shall see in the following chapter, individuals from all schools of thought agree that economic development in Third World countries is an issue of major importance.

The question these experts ask is: How can we best achieve that development? Specifically, do foreign-aid programs, as presently carried out, really contribute to promoting development and alleviating hunger? Or are there other approaches and directions that would be more effective?

The chapter begins with a *Basic Facts* section, which offers a brief history of foreign aid, starting with the United States Marshall Plan and Point Four programs. It discusses the spectacular success of the Marshall Plan, as well as the new directions that foreign aid has taken in recent years in moving away from the Marshall Plan concept of industrialization and large-scale construction projects.

The remainder of the *Basic Facts* section presents current data on foreign-aid programs, including which nations and groupings of nations contribute the most money to foreign aid. The fair-share contribution of developed nations to aid programs is a frequently discussed issue.

Is foreign aid a contribution to ending hunger, irrelevant, or actually an impediment?

The chapter next reviews two schools of thought on foreign aid. The first holds that foreign aid has been effective in the past and is needed to promote development, which will lead to the end of hunger. The views of foreign-aid specialists in the First and Third Worlds, and of political leaders and United States students who have worked abroad, are presented. Case studies are offered to concretely illustrate the successes of aid programs. The basic argument is that foreign-aid programs not only contribute to national development, stability, and self-sufficiency in recipient nations, but also benefit donor nations. The beneficial results of food-aid programs in the Third World receive special attention.

A second school of thought holds that foreign-aid programs have either made no difference or have actually been an impediment to development. In examining this school of thought, we will hear from individuals who represent very different ends of the economic and political spectrums. Proponents of a "free market," such as economist Peter Bauer and Edward J. Feulner of the Heritage Foundation, argue that foreign aid diverts resources away from the private sector and gives the responsibility for promoting development and ending hunger to government, rather than to private enterprise. At the other end of the spectrum, Frances Moore Lappé, Joseph Collins, and Denis Goulet discuss the shortcomings of foreign aid from a "grass-roots development" perspective. In their view, foreign aid discriminates against the poor and undermines the potential for self-reliant development. They do not necessarily oppose government participation in development; in fact, they often cite China as a promising model. Proponents of both the "free market" and the "grass-roots development" perspectives agree that incentives and self-reliance must be important parts of any development program, and that foreign aid promotes neither. Like the advocates of foreign aid, the opponents also offer concrete examples from the Third World that support their points of view.

Basic Facts

Large-scale foreign aid is a relatively new phenomenon in international affairs. The first major government-to-government aid program was the United States Marshall Plan, which was initiated in 1948, following the end of World War II.

The rationale for the program was outlined by General George Marshall at Harvard University on June 5, 1947:

It is logical that the United States should do whatever it is able to do to assist in the return of normal economic health in the world.... Our policy is directed not against any country or doctrine but against hunger, poverty, desperation and chaos. Its purpose should be the revival of a working economy in the world so as to permit the emergence of political and social conditions in which free institutions can exist....

An essential part of any successful action on the part of the United States is an understanding...of the character of the problem and the remedies to be applied. Political passion and prejudice should have no part. With foresight, and a willingness on the part of our people to face up to the vast responsibility which history has clearly placed upon our country, the difficulties I have outlined can and will be overcome.[1]

This address contained the ideas of the Marshall Plan, which became a prototype for later aid programs. The plan was originally proposed for a four-year period at a maximum cost of approximately $17 billion. It came to a successful conclusion nine months ahead of schedule, at a cost of approximately $13 billion.[2]

Like many subsequent aid programs, the Marshall Plan combined both humanitarian and political objectives. Its purpose was to rebuild war-torn Europe and, in the process, to block the spread of communism. The Marshall Plan gave major emphasis to loans and grants for repair and construction of industrial plants and infrastructure.[3]

Here is a brief summary of some of the areas in which the plan succeeded:

By 1951, Europe's overall production was up 37 percent. Industrial output in OEEC [Organization for European Economic Cooperation] countries had risen from 87 percent of its pre-war level in 1947 to 134 percent in 1951.

Steel production, which was approximately 30 million tons in 1947, had nearly doubled by 1951.

Textile products (cotton, wool) greatly increased while in some cases others (rayon) nearly doubled. Cement production doubled. Petroleum refining increased sixfold from 250,000 barrels a day to 1.5 million a day.

Agricultural output climbed 10 percent above its pre-war level. The Gross National Product gained more than $30 billion.

Inflation was brought under control. The economic level was ahead of pre-war days. Trade increased among the European countries and with the United States.[4]

The Point Four program—the first major aid program for the Third World—was initiated by the United States in 1949. It supported relatively small technical-assistance projects for a number of developing nations.

The first government foreign-aid program was the U.S. Marshall Plan, initiated in 1948.

The Marshall Plan combined both humanitarian and political objectives.

211

FIGURE FA.1. DISTRIBUTION OF U.S. FOREIGN ASSISTANCE, BY REGION (PERCENTAGES)

■ Middle East[a]   ■ Latin America
■ Asia   ■ Africa
■ Europe[b]   ■ Other[c]

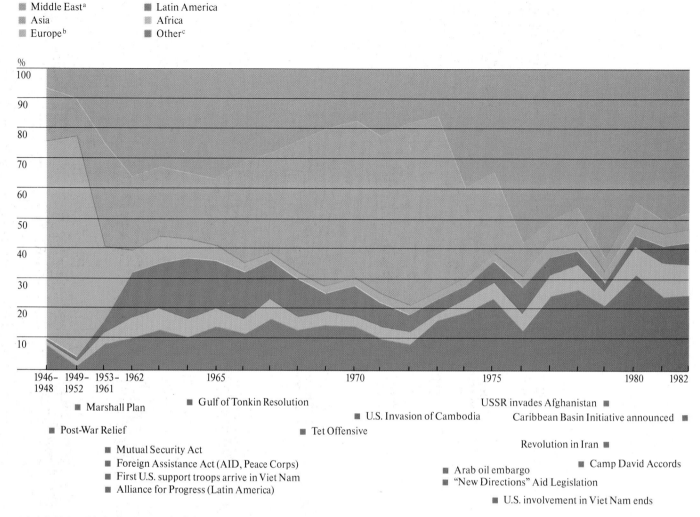

■ Marshall Plan   ■ Gulf of Tonkin Resolution   USSR invades Afghanistan ■

■ U.S. Invasion of Cambodia   Caribbean Basin Initiative announced ■

■ Post-War Relief   ■ Tet Offensive

■ Mutual Security Act   Revolution in Iran ■

■ Foreign Assistance Act (AID, Peace Corps)   ■ Camp David Accords

■ First U.S. support troops arrive in Viet Nam   ■ Arab oil embargo

■ Alliance for Progress (Latin America)   ■ "New Directions" Aid Legislation

■ U.S. involvement in Viet Nam ends

a. Includes Egypt and the South Asian countries of Afghanistan, Bhutan, Bangladesh, India, Nepal, Pakistan, and Sri Lanka.
b. Includes Canada and Oceania.
c. Interregional and centrally funded programs and contributions to multilateral banks.
Note: Data are based on fiscal-year commitments.

Source: Overseas Development Council, *U.S. Foreign Policy and the Third World: Agenda 1983,* eds. John P. Lewis and Valeriana Kallab (New York: Praeger, 1983), 286–87.

FIGURE FA.2. TRENDS IN U.S. FOREIGN ECONOMIC AND MILITARY ASSISTANCE

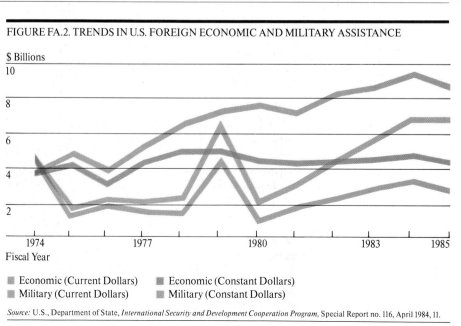

$ Billions

Fiscal Year

■ Economic (Current Dollars)   ■ Economic (Constant Dollars)
■ Military (Current Dollars)   ■ Military (Constant Dollars)

Source: U.S., Department of State, *International Security and Development Cooperation Program,* Special Report no. 116, April 1984, 11.

Since these early beginnings, dollar volume of aid, numbers of donor nations and organizations, and types of programs have grown significantly. This growth has been accompanied by an intense and continuing debate about the purpose of aid, the appropriate structure and focus of aid programs, the relative advantages of bilateral and multilateral aid, and especially the role that politics should play in allocating funds.

There has been debate about the purpose, structure, and management of aid programs, as well as the role of politics in allocating aid.

Since the Marshall Plan and the Point Four program, the focus of aid-giving programs has changed. Before 1970, aid agencies reacted to the Marshall Plan's successful reconstruction of Europe by directing their Third World development programs toward large-scale capital development. The theory was that building dams, highways, factories, and other modern facilities would create economic growth in the developing countries, thus raising the income of all. But in practice, while economic growth did result, income often failed to "trickle down" to benefit the poor. By 1973, Robert McNamara, then president of the World Bank, noted in a major policy speech: "The data suggest that the decade of rapid growth has been accompanied by greater maldistribution of income in many developing countries, and that the problem is most severe in the countryside."[5]

The shortcomings of capital-intensive aid programs caused a gradual shift toward programs that emphasized direct assistance designed to meet "basic human needs" at the local level. According to John Sewell, president of the Overseas Development Council, the goal of this approach is:

[To make] the quality of life of men, women, and children the focal point of decisions about the development process.... [It] urges commitment to the elimination of the worst aspects of absolute poverty on an accelerated basis.... It is intended to improve the income-earning opportunities of the poor, the public services that reach the poor, the flow of goods and services to meet the needs of all members of the household, and the participation of the poor in making the decisions which affect them.... Basic needs are... generally understood to encompass minimum levels of personal consumption and access to essential health, education, and other social services.[6]

The basic-human-needs approach is a recognition that no single comprehensive program is applicable throughout the world. Different regions of the world require different types of programs, and local aid-recipients must be personally involved if self-reliance is to be achieved.

Today, most of the world's foreign-aid money comes from the seventeen member nations constituting the Development Assistance Committee (DAC) of the OECD. The OECD is a group of developed—mostly Western—nations that have joined to support one another in promoting economic growth. DAC members coordinate their foreign-aid policies. Members of DAC are Australia, Austria, Belgium, Canada, Denmark, Finland, France, West Germany, Italy, Japan, the Netherlands, New Zealand, Norway, Sweden, Switzerland, the United Kingdom, and the United States. In 1981, the seventeen DAC nations contributed $25.6 billion in foreign aid, or 72 percent of the world total.[7] This amounted to an average of $37.75 from each person in these seventeen nations.[8]

Most foreign-aid money comes from OECD (Western industrialized) nations.

The Organization of the Petroleum Exporting Countries (OPEC) is a second and relatively new group among the major aid-donors.[9] The largest donations within OPEC by far have come from the Arab members. In 1981, OPEC members contributed $7.8 billion, or about 22 percent, of all development aid.[10] This is $22.80 of aid per capita for OPEC-member countries, and $158.57 per capita for Arab OPEC nations.[11]

FIGURE FA.3. OFFICIAL DEVELOPMENT
ASSISTANCE (ODA) FROM MAJOR
DONOR GROUPS ($ BILLIONS AND
PERCENTAGES, 1981)

Net ODA
($ Billions)

Net ODA
(as Percentage of GNP)

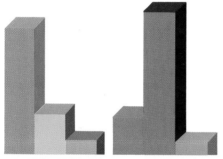

■ DAC Countries[a]   25.6
▢ OPEC Countries[b]   7.8
■ Centrally Planned Economies[c]   2.1

■ DAC Countries[a]   0.35
■ OPEC Countries[b]   1.46
▢ Centrally Planned Economies[c]   0.14

a. Including the United States.

b. Saudi Arabia net ODA in 1981 was $5.8 billion, or 4.77 percent of GNP; the United Arab Emirates net ODA was $0.8 billion, or 2.88 percent of GNP; and Kuwait net ODA was $0.7 billion, or 1.98 percent of GNP.

c. Figures for the USSR and Eastern Europe.

Source: Overseas Development Council, *U.S. Foreign Policy and the Third World: Agenda 1983*, eds. John P. Lewis and Valeriana Kallab (New York: Praeger, 1983), 273.

The third group of major donors consists of Bulgaria, Czechoslovakia, the German Democratic Republic, Hungary, Poland, Romania, and the USSR (i.e., the centrally planned economies). In 1981, these countries contributed $2.1 billion in development assistance, or 6 percent of the world total. This came to $5.50 on a per capita basis.[12]

In recent years, considerable debate has occurred as to the "fair share" of resources that developed nations should transfer to the developing world through aid. In 1970, the United Nations set 0.7 percent of GNP as the standard amount that each developed nation should contribute to development assistance.[13]

In 1981, five DAC members—the Netherlands, Sweden, Norway, Denmark, and France—surpassed the United Nations standard. This represented a significant increase from 1970, when no DAC nation donated 0.7 percent of its GNP to foreign aid. Over the decade, the total contribution (as a percentage of GNP) of all DAC countries grew slightly: from 0.34 percent to 0.35 percent.[14]

In 1980, six OPEC nations—Iraq, Saudi Arabia, Kuwait, Qatar, the United Arab Emirates, and Libya—surpassed the United Nations standard. Qatar led these nations, contributing 4.8 percent of its GNP to foreign assistance.[15] Almost all OPEC aid funds have been allocated to Arab countries.[16]

A distinction is often made between *bilateral* and *multilateral* aid. *Bilateral* aid refers to the direct transfer of goods and services from one government to another. For instance, Canada might send surplus wheat to Egypt; the United States could give Costa Rica a loan to purchase farm equipment; France could send Somalia a team of doctors. *Multilateral* aid refers to contributions from several countries to an institution, which then allocates the assistance to the recipient. The World Bank is the largest multilateral aid-giving institution. In fiscal year 1982 it dispensed $10.3 billion in loans to Third World nations.[17] Other multilateral agencies include the International Monetary Fund, the Inter-American Development Bank, and the United Nations Development Program. Both bilateral and multilateral aid are used to fund similar types of programs, including agricultural training, food aid, construction, and educational programs. In 1981, bilateral

TABLE FA.1. ASSISTANCE FROM MULTILATERAL INSTITUTIONS TO DEVELOPING COUNTRIES ($ MILLIONS)

	Concessional 1970	1980	Total 1970	1980
WORLD BANK GROUP	163	1,650	739	5,111
International Development Association	163	1,543	163	1,543
International Finance Corporation	—	—	68	295
World Bank	—	107	508	3,273
IMF Trust Fund	—	1,636	—	1,636
United Nations	498	2,487	498	2,487
International Fund for Agricultural Development	—	45	—	45
REGIONAL BANKS	225	614	326	1,619
Inter-American Development Bank	224	326	308	893
Asian Development Bank	1	149	16	477
African Development Bank and Fund	—	96	2	193
Caribbean Development Bank	—	43	—	56
European Communities	210	1,013	221	1,270
Arab/OPEC Funds	—	294	—	422
Total	1,096	7,739	1,784	12,590

Source: Overseas Development Council, *U.S. Foreign Policy and the Third World: Agenda 1983*, eds. John P. Lewis and Valeriana Kallab (New York: Praeger, 1983), 281.

TABLE FA.2. OFFICIAL DEVELOPMENT ASSISTANCE (ODA) FROM SELECTED
COUNTRIES IN 1981

	ODA (Million Dollars)	Share in World ODA (Percentage)	ODA as Percentage of GNP
United States	5,783	16.1	0.20
France	4,177	11.7	0.73
West Germany	3,181	8.9	0.47
United Kingdom	2,195	6.1	0.44
Japan	3,171	8.9	0.28
Canada	1,189	3.3	0.43
Saudi Arabia	5,798	16.2	4.77
Kuwait	685	1.9	1.98
USSR	1,661	4.6	0.15
East Germany	194	0.5	0.16

Source: Rutherford M. Poats, *1982 Review: Development Co-operation* (Paris: Organisation for Economic Co-operation and Development, November 1982), 183.

and multilateral aid from all DAC sources totaled $25.6 billion. Of this amount, 71 percent was bilateral aid and 29 percent was multilateral aid.[18]

In terms of total dollars expended per year, the United States has been—and continues to be—the largest donor of foreign aid in the world. In 1981, United States aid programs amounted to $5.8 billion.[19] However, the percentage of GNP that the United States has allocated to aid has declined steadily since World War II: Whereas the United States contributed an average of 1.6 percent of its GNP to foreign aid during the Marshall Plan era, by 1981 its contribution was down to 0.2 percent.[20] In terms of percentage of GNP, this decline placed the United States as sixteenth among the seventeen DAC nations.[21]

In terms of total dollars, the United States has been the world's largest donor of foreign aid.

In order to meet the United Nations standard of 0.7 percent in 1983, the United States would have required a foreign-aid budget of $20.5 billion. And in order to provide an aid program comparable to the Marshall Plan, in terms of percentage of GNP, the United States would have required a budget of about $47 billion.[22]

Aid comes not only from countries, but also from private voluntary organizations (PVOs—also referred to as nongovernmental organizations, or NGOs). These organizations often make sizeable contributions: In 1981, funds expended by Western-based PVOs exceeded $2 billion.[23] In its recent directory, the Technical Assistance Information Clearing House listed 497 organizations in the United States that administer or fund projects overseas.[24] Well-known agencies range in size from CARE (income of $283 million) and Catholic Relief Services (income of $364 million) to groups such as Oxfam America (income of $5 million).[25]

Typically, grants from most private voluntary organizations go to small-scale projects that are designed to directly benefit the poorest groups in the Third World. A large percentage of these funds is devoted to agricultural and rural development.

In 1981, United States citizens contributed more than $1 billion to PVOs. Although the United States ranks low in development aid as a percentage of GNP, among Western countries it ranks eighth in contributions to PVOs as a percentage of GNP.[26]

In 1981, U.S. citizens contributed more than $1 billion to private voluntary organizations.

FIGURE FA.4. TRENDS IN BILATERAL AND MULTILATERAL AID ($ BILLIONS AND PERCENTAGES)

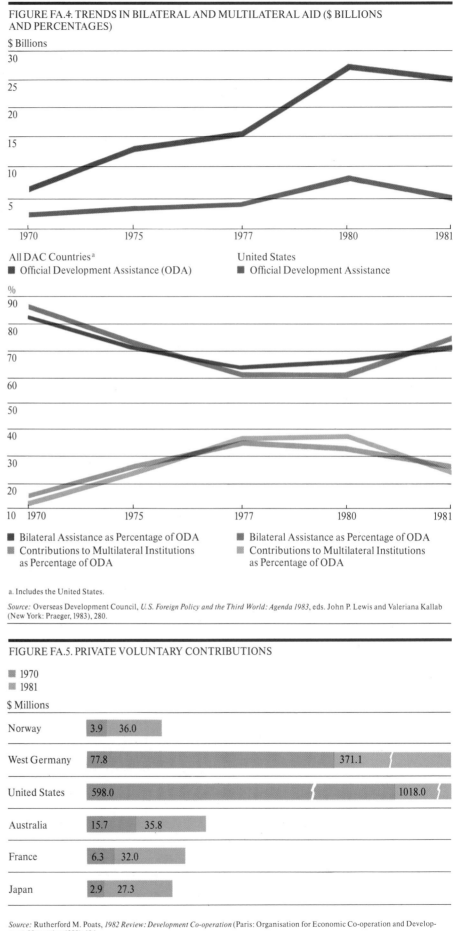

$ Billions

All DAC Countries[a]
■ Official Development Assistance (ODA)

United States
■ Official Development Assistance

■ Bilateral Assistance as Percentage of ODA
■ Contributions to Multilateral Institutions as Percentage of ODA

■ Bilateral Assistance as Percentage of ODA
■ Contributions to Multilateral Institutions as Percentage of ODA

a. Includes the United States.

Source: Overseas Development Council, *U.S. Foreign Policy and the Third World: Agenda 1983*, eds. John P. Lewis and Valeriana Kallab (New York: Praeger, 1983), 280.

FIGURE FA.5. PRIVATE VOLUNTARY CONTRIBUTIONS

■ 1970
■ 1981

$ Millions

Norway	3.9	36.0
West Germany	77.8	371.1
United States	598.0	1018.0
Australia	15.7	35.8
France	6.3	32.0
Japan	2.9	27.3

Source: Rutherford M. Poats, *1982 Review: Development Co-operation* (Paris: Organisation for Economic Co-operation and Development, November 1982), 194.

Schools of Thought on Foreign Aid

After nearly four decades of global foreign-aid activity, there is a wealth of both successes and failures to point to regarding the impact of aid on development and ending hunger. Given that both the positive and negative effects of aid programs are so tangibly visible, it is not surprising that case studies are often cited to bolster the viewpoints of those involved in promoting or criticizing foreign aid.

In the remainder of this chapter, we will present a number of these case studies. Taken as a whole, they point out both the problems and opportunities that seem inherent in foreign-aid projects.

The first school of thought we examine is one that argues that foreign aid has an important, effective role to play in the development programs of Third World nations. The evidence and case studies cited support the view that aid has been effective in combating hunger.

The alternative perspective is provided by the school of thought that argues that foreign aid has either made no difference or has actually impeded development. This school of thought holds that the poorest of the poor—the intended beneficiaries of the programs—are often left worse off than before the aid was given. Again, evidence and case studies are cited, this time to support the argument that in some instances, aid programs have actually created *more* hunger and starvation, not less.

School of Thought: Foreign Aid Has Been Effective in the Past. It Is Needed to Promote Development and End Hunger

In this first school of thought, we hear from a variety of voices—many of them officials with foreign-aid agencies—who argue the following points of view: Foreign-aid programs contribute to national development, stability, and self-sufficiency in recipient nations and encourage the people of these nations to stand on their own feet economically, agriculturally, and politically. Such programs also benefit donor nations by providing motivation for leaders and people of developed nations to support development programs and contribute to the end of hunger. Finally, food-aid programs, in particular, produce both immediate benefits (by saving lives) and long-term benefits (by improving agricultural systems).

Point of View Number 1

Foreign-Aid Programs Contribute to National Development, Stability, and Self-Sufficiency in Recipient Nations and Encourage Economic, Agricultural, and Political Independence

Hollis B. Chenery implemented foreign-aid policies while he was assistant administrator of the United States Agency for International Development (USAID) and while he was at the World Bank. These policies particularly emphasized providing economic assistance for capital growth in both industry and food production.

Foreign aid is the central component of world development. The poorest countries, even before the oil crisis, were dependent on a long-term inflow of capital and the U.S., until 10 years ago, was the leader in supplying them....Contributing to capital formation, technical assistance, transfer of technology to the least-developed countries, is essential, whether your goals are purely economic, or political or security objectives.[27]

Although direct connections between foreign-aid programs and the successes of various countries are difficult to prove, some reports suggest such a relationship. Here is an excerpt from a 1980 USAID *World Development Letter:*

Development is occurring. Many of the countries of Southeast Asia have achieved a level of development few would have predicted a decade ago. India is now surviving a drought on the strength of its own home-grown food. Population growth rates have dropped dramatically in Thailand, Indonesia, Colombia, the Dominican Republic, South Korea, the Philippines and Panama, among others. More than 30 countries are establishing health care systems that were virtually non-existent in the past. Third World nations are increasingly able to borrow in private capital markets for development projects.[28]

Former AID official John Sommer's article, "Does Foreign Aid Really Help the Poor?", provides specific examples of how foreign-aid programs have contributed to economic development:

Foreign aid has proved successful in many areas of the world.

To the extent that a country's economic growth is a precondition for helping its poor people, foreign aid has proved successful in many areas of the world. For example, India, described until recently as the world's archetypical "basket case," last year achieved the ability to produce all the food grains it will need for the next 20 years, according to the World Bank. While this achievement is due primarily to India's own efforts, it also is due in part to the United States and other donors for new high-yield varieties of wheat and rice, for the creation of Indian agricultural training and research institutions, for expansion of fertilizer production, and for the needed storage facilities. India is not alone. Korea, in the 1950s, also was known as a "basket case." In 1963, its per capita income was $82; by 1980 it was $1,500. The country is now a world competitor in several industries, with exports totaling over $15 billion. Nine Korean companies are listed among the Fortune 500. Visitors returning to Korea quickly see how much better off rural areas, too, have become. To Korea's achievements the United States contributed policy guidance on land reform and capital mobilization, and financial assistance for fertilizer production, irrigation, and management training, among many other forms of assistance. In 1980 Korea "graduated" from the AID rolls.[29]

Many leaders of OPEC nations also believe that foreign aid contributes to national development. Ibrahim Shihata, director general of the OPEC Fund for International Development, discusses some of the reasons why the OPEC nations have a strong commitment to giving aid:

I would like to turn now to the role of OPEC member countries in the cooperation with other Third World nations through the difficult years to come. Since some OPEC members initiated their aid programs in the 1960's, their role has generally been seen as providers of funds on concessional terms. This is certainly a role which some of them will continue to play as long as they are in a position to do so. However, it cannot, and should not be envisaged as the only role to be expected from these countries in a lasting and balanced framework of cooperation....

It must only be stressed that the high level of OPEC aid has been provided out of deep concern for the welfare of the South and the need for fostering self-reliance among its countries. OPEC countries are continuing their efforts to foster solidarity and enhance aid efforts through new initiatives. In early 1980, these countries substantially modified the Agreement Establishing the OPEC Fund, converting it from an international account of temporary character to an on-going international agency for development finance with open-ended resources which so far exceed US$4 billion.[30]

218

The results of USAID's programs for food production and nutrition are described in a USAID report, excerpted here:

U.S. assistance for food production and nutrition programs has resulted in substantial progress. Some examples:

AID-supported agricultural research in Sri Lanka resulted in the introduction of 12 new high-yield varieties of rice. These new rice strains increased rice production in Sri Lanka 23% per hectare. Currently, 72% of Sri Lankan farmers are using these or other high-yield varieties.

Working with the government of Bangladesh, the World Bank, and other donors, AID helped create a food security program to prevent famine. The key elements included establishing floor prices to encourage agricultural productivity and expanding grain storage capabilities. Since 1975, Bangladesh's storage capacity has tripled. The country can now store 1.8 million tons of food. These public stocks help tide Bangladesh over during lean harvest seasons. Maintaining incentive prices has allowed farmers to invest in new high-yield seeds, fertilizer, and irrigation pumps, all of which have helped increase food production.

AID's long-term support for agricultural research and extension services, credit and marketing systems, and basic infrastructure helped Indonesia achieve self-sufficiency in rice production in 1982.[31]

Stories of how aid programs have totally revolutionized lives come from all over. Mike Haverstock, writing in *Americas*, reports on a successful project, supported by the Rockefeller Foundation, in Cali, Colombia:

For four centuries Cali, Colombia, was one of thousands of sleepy pueblos of Hispanic America, with little to distinguish it from all the rest. Then, about the time World War II was over, there occurred in Cali and the surrounding green fields and blue skies of the Cauca Valley something like the spark from a flint that starts a fire. A veritable conflagration of progress has followed....

Go-getters among the region's landowners were successful in persuading the Rockefeller Foundation to locate the International Center for Tropical Agriculture near Palmira, less than an hour by good road from Cali, where many of the scientists who work at the Center live. Their research at the Center is an important reason why farmers of the Cali area are reporting increasing yields, and little in the way of insect pests or plant diseases with which they are unable to cope.

Cali's bankers note that earnings from agriculture have been reinvested locally in industry. There have been sizeable international investments as well, such as Inter-American Development Bank and World Bank financing for the huge hydroelectric installations not far from the city. Cali's installed power capacity has jumped from 28,000 kilowatts in 1953 to 650,000 kilowatts today. And the artificial lake created as part of the hydroelectric installation has become a recreational facility, a place to swim and fish on weekends.

International investment is also helping to regulate the flow of the Cauca River. Through construction of a system of dams, dikes, and canals, the local Corporation of the Cauca Valley plans to bring an additional one million acres of farmland into production by 1984. To assure the region's continued importance as a producer of paper, Cartón de Colombia, the city's foremost manufacturer of paper products, has set the goal of reforesting seventy-five thousand acres of land by the end of the century.

U.S. assistance for food production and nutrition programs has resulted in substantial progress.

Research...is an important reason why farmers of the Cali area are reporting increasing yields.

The well-planned infrastructure improvements have helped create a base for industrialization and an investment climate that is the pride of the city's businessmen. Before World War II, Cali manufactured almost nothing. Since then scores of Colombian companies have come to the area, and scores more have sprung up locally. Some forty international companies have opened factories in the Cali area, making the city an important producer of chemicals, paper, and rubber products, as well as processed food and drink.[32]

Richard Critchfield writes about Java, a success story, in *The Christian Science Monitor*:

Thirty percent of all homes in the 35 Javanese villages have been rebuilt from bamboo huts to masonry houses.

In just the past 3 to 5 years, 30 percent of all homes in the 35 Javanese villages have been rebuilt from bamboo huts to masonry houses. The average village now has 11 TV sets and 46 motorcycles. In the 35 villages, there was a total of 40 minibuses, 21 trucks, and 12 privately owned cars (something unheard of 10 years ago)....

The rich are getting richer faster; but the poor are getting richer, too. I put the question to several hundred villagers, including some of the poorest landless laborers I could find: "Well, are you better or worse off than you were 10 years ago?" Without a single exception, they said they were better off. Some laughed that anyone would be so foolish as to ask....

Infant mortality, always a good indicator of how the poorest are faring, is dropping. So is fertility.

Rural industries have doubled or tripled in the past 10 years, in terms of craftsmen employed, volume of goods sold, and incomes.

Village primary school attendance has shot up from about 10 percent to 50 percent as 31,000 new schools were built, 196,000 new teachers hired at quadrupled salaries, and 200,000,000 new textbooks handed out in the past five years.[33]

In a similar vein, Alexanderina Shuler writes about education programs in AID's publication, *Agenda*:

An important part of AID's promotion of technology transfer is training abroad and in the United States. Since 1941, more than 200,000 individuals from foreign countries have received formal and nonformal training in food production, nutrition, population planning, health and education under the U.S. assistance program. The students return to their home countries to become government leaders, university professors, bank presidents and scientists.

A fundamental problem in most developing countries is the lack of trained middle-level manpower. More welders, mechanics and other skilled workers are needed. AID is helping fill the gap. In Morocco, for instance, two AID-funded centers are teaching women electronics, drafting, accounting and stenography. The centers also help graduates find jobs.

Education can make a difference:

A Moroccan mother taught modern methods of hygiene and food preparation discovers her children are healthier.

Because he received training in carpentry, a formerly unemployed worker in Nigeria now has a marketable skill that enables him to provide his family with adequate food, clothing and shelter.

220

Education and training is a means and objective of national development. It provides people with the knowledge they need to cope with real problems, boosting chances for a successful shift to a more productive and just society.[34]

Point of View Number 2

By Economically Benefiting Donor Countries, Foreign-Aid Programs Provide Greater Motivation for Rich Nations to Contribute to the End of Hunger

The domestic benefits of foreign aid can be direct and tangible, as the next three statements point out. The first is from Edmund Muskie, a former United States senator from Maine who served as secretary of state in 1980.

American foreign assistance dollars are investments we make in others and in ourselves. These U.S. investments mean security aid to nations whose independence is threatened by outside intervention. These investments mean economic development for poorer nations. They help developing countries buy American equipment to build highways and dams, help hire American experts to strengthen their institutions, help them produce the food and the jobs that increase living standards for their people. And these investments directly benefit our own people.

Seventy cents of every dollar we commit for country-to-country development programs are spent here in the United States. They purchase American goods and American services, from farm equipment to technical training. These purchases amounted to nearly $2 billion last year alone. Our Agency for International Development has spent over $650 million for goods and services just in California over the past 10 years. Well over another billion dollars last year went to American farmers for grain and other agricultural commodities.[35]

The second statement comes from James Bednar of USAID:

Look into some obscure corners and you're likely to find evidence of the U.S. foreign assistance program. Take home improvement, for instance.

Orientation and education techniques perfected in Latin America have helped prepare families in U.S. public housing for new responsibilities.

Self-help home improvement programs, now common in America's inner cities, on Indian reservations, and in Puerto Rico and the U.S. Virgin Islands, were born out of this country's work in developing nations. Starting with the Marshall Plan in Germany right after World War II and continuing today under the AID program, the United States has provided technical and financial aid to help people improve homes and rehabilitate entire communities. Under the so-called "aided self-help" approach, tenants or owners do their own work with materials supplied by the government. It is relatively inexpensive and encourages community involvement and home ownership. In U.S. cities, similar programs have concentrated on rebuilding deteriorated houses and apartments. The family orientation and education techniques perfected in Latin America have helped prepare families in U.S. public housing for new responsibilities when their projects are converted to cooperative ownership....

In still another health-related area, some American children are drinking vitamin A fortified low-fat milk today as a result of AID-sponsored research in the 1960s. Working in Brazil, Washington University researchers proved that vitamin A could be added to low-fat milk, thus helping prevent blindness. Previously, scientists believed that fat was necessary to absorb vitamin A effectively.

The results of an AID nutrition project in Chile have been used in U.S. research and feeding programs, for, among others, migrant workers, American Indians and

221

other low-income groups. Even the food in U.S. hospitals, prisons and other institutions is better because of research AID helped support. In 1969, General Foods developed a macaroni-like food from corn, soy and wheat. It is seven times as nutritional as conventional pasta—and costs less. [36]

The third statement on domestic benefits comes from a USAID *World Development Letter,* which challenged critics of international aid. It responded to typical questions asked by citizens about foreign aid and pointed out that critics of aid-giving nations were getting much more than they realized from assistance programs:

About a year ago, World Development Letter answered a series of questions actually asked by a woman from Missouri in a letter to one of her senators. These were commonly asked questions about the U.S. foreign assistance program, and we added a few that other correspondents had posed.

"We have to work five months out of every year just to pay our taxes. Are we going to bankrupt the United States so we can support the world?"

The per-person annual cost of all foreign economic assistance is about $34. Most of that $34 is spent in the United States for goods and services that mean jobs and income for Americans.

The U.S. foreign aid program bought almost $50 million in goods, services and agricultural products in Missouri.

Take Missouri for example. The U.S. foreign aid program bought almost $50 million in goods, services and agricultural products in Missouri during 1980 for use in the less developed countries. Of the total, $41.6 million went to Missouri farmers and food processors for grain and other agricultural commodities under the Food for Peace program. The balance, $8 million, went to Missouri manufacturers and other firms for supplies used in overseas economic development programs administered by the Agency for International Development. The foreign aid program bought more from other states than it did from Missouri in 1980: $96 million from California, $173 million from New York, $145 million from Kansas, $114 million from Texas— to name a few.

"I just don't understand why we have a foreign aid program. We have a lot of poor people in the United States, too. America can take care of itself; let developing countries take care of themselves."

Progress in the Third World serves the U.S. national interest. Apart from our traditional humanitarian concerns, as these nations develop they become bigger customers for our farms and industries; they become bigger markets for American investments and more accessible sources of raw materials essential to our economy and our national defense.

For example: 40% of U.S. exports go to developing countries, and 42% of our raw materials and commodities come from the Third World.

U.S. exports to developing countries exceed our exports to all of industrialized Europe and are four times greater than our exports to Japan. Some 2 million American jobs now depend on exports to the Third World. One out of every 10 acres of American farmland produces for export to those countries. At the end of 1982, a cumulative $53.15 billion was invested by U.S. companies in the Third World.

The U.S. depends on Third World countries for 100% of our natural rubber; 96% of our tin, essential to the electronics industry; 88% of our bauxite, vital to our aircraft industry; 75% of our cobalt, needed by the steel and nuclear industries. [37]

Benefits to donor nations from foreign aid also can be measured in ways other than products sold and jobs created. In the following passages, two Americans who volunteered in aid programs in the Third World tell their stories. Each benefited personally from the interaction with different peoples and cultures. The lessons they learned abroad and brought back to their homes and communities in the United States can give us a greater understanding and awareness of Third World issues.

Participants in aid programs have benefited personally from interacting with different peoples and cultures.

We begin with Laurel Schneider, who recounts her work in Thailand.

I was … afraid at first in the camp. So much need! These were the refugees I'd always heard about in church and had glimpsed on the news—the world's poorest, most desperate people—stripped even of their homeland. And who was I, what was I, to do anything about it? Where should I give? What should I give?

I'd go into the camp in the morning, teach English at my appointed hours, and for the rest of the time I'd nervously walk around the camp wondering how to be more "useful."

The refugees were … friendly, but I didn't know how to talk to them, and I was afraid to open up. At last it was the refugees who rescued me. After one of my English classes, one young man came up and shyly invited me to his "home" for lunch. I had been warned against eating in the camp ("the water is contaminated and they can't really wash their dishes and you've seen what their 'fresh' rations look like…"), but I gratefully accepted. And at that moment everything got turned around. This young man and his family had nothing, and yet around their little pot of rice and stew (broth made from the bits of rationed chicken) they offered me everything. They heaped into my bowl whatever nutrition there was in their meal and when I looked from my fleshy arms to their thin limbs, I started to raise my voice in protest, but it got stuck in my throat by the shining of their eyes and the indelible smiles on their faces. Suddenly, I somehow realized that the privilege of giving was another one I had taken for granted. So we sat and ate, and I've never had a better meal.

After that I began to relax. I realized that my defenses were making me the loser. I discovered that the more I opened myself up to the camp, the more I myself became enriched. Instead of giving a little and losing it all as I had feared, the little I gave seemed to come back to me three-hundred fold.

The "global family" is no longer an intellectual ideal in my mind. It is flesh and blood, and I am given the honor of being a member of it. Wherever I go I will carry the love and memory and responsibility that comes of being a brother or sister. I pray to God that I am equal to it and that someday I can do for them and their children what they have done for me.[38]

Former Senator Paul Tsongas of Massachusetts had a similar experience:

My 2 years as a Peace Corps volunteer in a small Ethiopian town were a learning experience that surpassed any formal study before or after it. There I lived and learned with students whose lives had been vastly different from my own. I was a Peace Corps teacher, but I hope my Ethiopian friends know how much they taught me.

My years as a Peace Corps volunteer were a learning experience that surpassed any formal study.

We had a very personal sense of depending on each other, so it was natural for us to know that nations also must depend on each other. Nothing before or after that time has shaped my view of the world so deeply.[39]

Food-Aid Programs Produce Both Short- and Long-Term Benefits

One of the most well-known types of foreign aid is "food aid"—the physical transfer of food from one country to another. The United States has one of the world's major food-aid programs: PL (Public Law) 480. The objective of the program is "the provision of humanitarian food aid, the furtherance of international economic development, the expansion of U.S. agricultural and commercial export markets and the promotion of U.S. political interests."[40]

In the following three excerpts, we examine the point of view that food aid can and does literally save lives by providing famine relief and supplements to meet nutritional deficiencies. We also hear from proponents of food aid who argue that over the long term, "food-for-work" programs can contribute to the establishment of systems that will increase food production.

M. Peter McPherson, the administrator of USAID and a former Peace Corps volunteer, discusses the purposes and accomplishments of food-aid programs:

It goes without saying that food aid is not a substitute for social and economic progress and cannot be expected to provide long term solutions to the hunger problem. However, the generous quantities of food aid that the U.S. has sent overseas can be credited with saving millions of lives over the past 25 years.

Furthermore, as food aid has become better-integrated with our overall development assistance programs, it has proven increasingly important for its developmental as well as its humanitarian impacts.... [Food aid] not only introduces extra quantities of food into national food systems, but provides local currencies that are being used for food production and other development activities; it saves foreign exchange, which would otherwise be allocated for food imports, and also affords an opportunity to discuss host country agricultural policies.... [Other] programs which support expanded and improved agricultural progress and policies allow us to increase further the development impact of food aid....

Agricultural commodities ... go directly to nutritionally vulnerable groups through school feeding programs, maternal and child health programs, and related efforts to reach pregnant and nursing women. They also support food-for-work programs to supply food to the needy in rural areas while supporting productive projects....

Food aid still has an important contribution to make in alleviating hunger in poor countries.

In view of anticipated rates of population growth, and recognizing how difficult it may be to maintain steadily rising increases in the rate of food production— particularly in Africa—food aid still has an important contribution to alleviating hunger in poor countries, particularly among those groups that are most susceptible to malnutrition.[41]

Here is a similar point of view from Philip Johnston, executive director of CARE, a private voluntary organization that has played a major role in distributing food aid under PL 480. In 1984, CARE distributed 854,824,000 pounds of food to 22 million people worldwide. The value of food, health supplies, and services delivered by CARE to people in 38 countries was placed at $257 million. In this quotation Johnston provides background on CARE programs and discusses some of the accomplishments of food aid.

CARE exists to help the poor of the developing world to achieve sustained improvement in their lives and to offer relief in times of crisis when there is acute suffering and life is threatened. Food aid can be instrumental to both purposes.

FIGURE FA.6. U.S. PUBLIC LAW 480 (FOOD AID) PROGRAM (1960–1981)

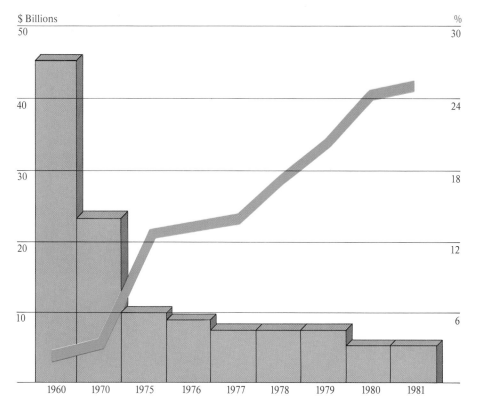

■ Total Agricultural Exports in Billions of Dollars
■ Public Law 480 as Percentage of Total

Source: Overseas Development Council, *U.S. Foreign Policy and the Third World: Agenda 1983*, eds. John P. Lewis and Valeriana Kallab (New York: Praeger, 1983), 236.

One of the most well-known types of foreign aid is "food aid"—the physical transfer of food from one country to another. The United States has one of the world's major programs, PL (Public Law) 480. This chart pictures food aid as a percentage of total U.S. agricultural exports.

For 38 years, CARE has distributed food in more than 50 countries, assisting several hundred million people. As a resource food offers certain advantages: it is one of the most effective means of targeting resource transfer to the most disadvantaged and improving income distribution; it can be a net additional resource with positive consequences; it can promote labor-intensive technologies and thereby broaden the participation of the rural poor in the economic life and development of their communities and regions; it can be a direct and effective means of combating acute malnutrition and severe food shortages; as a versatile resource, it can be used in a variety of ways in promoting and supporting development activities.

To produce positive outcomes, food-aid programs must be carefully planned.

Current knowledge and experience indicate that to produce positive outcomes, the use of food aid requires that it be programmed under certain conditions and with certain precautions; to do otherwise runs the risk that it becomes a costly and ineffective intervention that can create dependency and act as a disincentive to local food production. The objectives of CARE's policy on food assistance are to promote and contribute to its most effective use and to ensure that CARE's food aid projects are undertaken in a manner and under conditions that are most likely to produce positive results.

CARE's policy on food assistance includes the following program principles:

priority to low-income food-deficit countries and the most disadvantaged segments of the population therein

adherence to development criteria

community participation

treatment of the total costs of food aid programming

inclusion of process and impact evaluation

internal commitment to advocating important food aid issues

application of minimum standards regarding food aid programming, including a clear statement of the project's framework and minimum expectations, assessment of potential impact on domestic agricultural production and consumption, and compliance with rigorous standards of accountability.

CARE's staff is proud of our hard-earned reputation for cost-effective delivery, and of the many commendations we have received for scrupulously monitoring every facet of our programs, from shipping to food preparation at project sites.

A purpose of Public Law 480 is to use the abundant agricultural productivity of the U.S. to combat hunger.

Much of the food for CARE programs comes from the U.S. Government. The Food for Peace Act, established by Congress in 1954 as Public Law 480, states in its preamble several related purposes: to expand national trade (Title I), to use the abundant agricultural productivity of the U.S. to combat hunger and encourage economic growth in developing countries (Title II), and to develop and expand export markets for U.S. agricultural commodities (Title III).

The food for CARE programs comes exclusively from Title II. The largest share of this food has been for mothers and children through health centers and elementary schools, although a substantial amount is used in food-for-work development programs.

Even school and mother-child feeding programs have an undeniable long-range development impact. School lunches, for example, are an enormous incentive to school enrollment and attendance in developing countries, and economic and social development are greatly enhanced by a literate population.

Although we are aware of the complexities food-for-work programs present, we continue to support the concept of food-for-work as one approach to providing a mechanism for poor people to participate in greatly needed community development projects. For example, through CARE food-for-work projects in India and Guatemala, we help farmers irrigate and terrace their land, doubling or even tripling land use.

What's more, each additional crop planted provides another season's work for the landless, who are totally dependent on agricultural activities for their livelihood. In these instances, food-for-work not only increases food production, it also improves the quality of life for landless laborers.

CARE will pursue food-for-work programs where conditions are favorable, and we hope to find more ways to couple food aid with community development needs in poor countries.

Food aid is not the only assistance required by the poorest people on our planet, but it has helped millions survive, regain their health, and provide a better life for their children. It represents an agricultural abundance that is ours to share and, while we need to monitor its effectiveness, I know many would join me in saying that we should not abandon it or the millions who benefit from it.[42]

One major use of food aid is for famine relief and emergency assistance. The following paper published in 1981 describes a program in Kampuchea (Cambodia), which many say saved virtually an entire population from starvation.

Many say famine relief in Kampuchea saved virtually an entire population from starvation.

The Cambodian people have been saved from the famine, disease and economic prostration which one year ago threatened their very survival. With the assistance of a worldwide relief effort—unparalleled in history for its size and scope— Cambodia has begun the laborious work of reconstruction. Significant steps in this direction were taken during 1980, leading to guarded optimism for 1981. However, serious problems remain which only continued international assistance can overcome.

The international relief effort contributed more than $800 million in aid to Cambodia through multilateral, bilateral and private channels. The efforts mounted by the United Nations agencies—led by UNICEF and the International Committee of the Red Cross—supplied approximately $500 million by the end of 1980. The countries which support the Heng Samrin government, particularly the Soviet Union and Vietnam, provided an estimated $200 million in assistance.

Significant funds were also donated by the private voluntary agencies. Organizations like Oxfam, World Relief and others throughout the world raised funds totaling approximately $100 million. Most of these funds were channeled to Cambodia or Thailand in programs which were coordinated with the larger international operations....

The key to Cambodia's recovery lies in its agriculture, and it was in this area that the international aid programs made an extremely important contribution. In late 1979, after a decade of war, killing, social upheaval and famine, the Cambodian countryside was terribly devastated. Whereas before 1970 nearly 2.5 million hectares (one hectare equals 2.5 acres) were farmed and large amounts of rice exported, in 1979 no more than 700,000 hectares were planted. The meager harvest at the beginning of 1980 was exhausted by early spring, leaving Cambodia dependent upon international assistance.

By contrast, this year's harvest has been successful. A Food and Agriculture Organization (FAO) team which surveyed Cambodia just before the 1980 harvest reported that 1,190.8 million hectares of rice were under cultivation. The team estimated that Cambodia's food deficit during 1981 would be less than one-half of the previous year's shortfall.

The Cambodian people showed great determination in using the aid…to bring about this remarkable agricul-tural recovery.

The Cambodian people showed great determination in using the aid from the international community to bring about this remarkable agricultural recovery. Despite logistical and administrative difficulties, the U.N. organizations and voluntary agencies, along with Vietnam, supplied Cambodia's farmers with more than 70,000 metric tons of rice seed, as well as a vast array of agricultural implements and fertilizer.…

In retrospect, the relief operation appears to have been a great success. But as the year progressed this was not always clear. In fact, the effort was surrounded by problems and controversy commensurate with the scale of operations, particularly over the question of food distribution.…

At an international conference on Cambodian relief held in Geneva in May, western governments which were providing a significant proportion of the funding for the relief effort complained vociferously about the administrative, logistical and political problems which they believed were hampering the relief effort. Some of these complaints were quietly echoed to the Cambodian authorities by the relief organizations. The response was positive. As the spring and summer progressed, the Heng Samrin government took steps which ironed out many of the administrative problems, and the aid began to flow more smoothly. This became clear when the agricultural supplies needed by the farmers were distributed efficiently and quickly. The improved distribution also reflected the impact of the port and transportation equipment donated by the international community.

By the end of 1980 aid officials and journalists were reporting marked improve-ments in the health and nutritional status of the Cambodian people, although a very small percentage of children recently surveyed by UNICEF were classified as "severely undernourished."[43]

School of Thought: Foreign-Aid Programs Either Have Made No Difference or Have Been an Impediment to Development

The second school of thought holds that foreign aid is far from a necessary ingredient in ending hunger—in fact, it can often cause more harm than good. The following points of view articulate the beliefs that: Aid alone is insufficient to spark economic development; aid disrupts the recipient nation's economic system and its people's ability to become self-reliant; and it often gives greater power to the corrupt elites and governments who are partly responsible for the hunger in the first place.

Point of View Number 1

Countries Will Either Develop or Not Develop, Regardless of Foreign Aid

One perspective on foreign aid is that its most fundamental premise—that injections of external capital and assistance can make the difference in spurring on development—is flawed. As Edward J. Feulner, president of the Heritage Foundation, says, "Aid is neither a necessary or [sic] a sufficient condition for economic development. I can cite a number of countries that did not have it. A number of countries that have had it have not advanced into the developed arena."[44]

British economist Peter Bauer, one of the most creative thinkers on the limitations and shortcomings of foreign aid as a useful tool of development, agrees. His basic argument is that countries will develop or not, irrespective of whether aid is present. Further, aid can actually impede development by discouraging free enterprise. With Basil Yamey, Bauer writes:

Although the case for official transfers is largely taken for granted, various arguments or rationalizations are often advanced. These are addressed primarily to audiences not yet firmly committed.

The central argument for foreign aid has remained that without it Third World countries cannot progress at a reasonable rate, or cannot progress at all. But not only is foreign aid patently not required for development, it is, in actual fact, much more likely to obstruct it than to promote it.

Large parts of the Third World made rapid progress long before foreign aid.

It diminishes the people of the Third World to suggest that, although they crave material progress, unlike the West they cannot achieve it without external doles. Of course, large parts of the Third World made rapid progress long before foreign aid—witness Southeast Asia, West Africa, and Latin America. The emergence of hundreds of millions of people, both in the South and in the West, from poverty to prosperity has not depended on external gifts. Economic achievement has depended, as it still does depend, on people's own faculties, motivations, and ways of life, on their institutions and on the policies of their rulers. In short, economic achievement depends on the conduct of people, including governments. External donations have never been necessary for the development of any country, anywhere. There are, of course, a number of Third World countries or societies which have not progressed much in the postwar period. This lack of progress reflects factors which cannot be overcome by aid, and are indeed likely to be reinforced by it.[45]

Garrett Hardin sees no correlation between receiving aid and becoming developed:

We've had a salutary lesson in the development of India and China during the past three decades. Since 1950 India has received massive foreign aid from many countries, but China from only one country (the Soviet Union) and that only until 1957. At the outset the two countries were equally miserable and had equally poor prospects. Today? Without question the people of China are far better off. Foreign aid did not rescue India from poverty; lack of aid did not handicap China. In fact, it may be that China did so well precisely because she was not "helped" by "aid."[46]

Point of View Number 2

Foreign-Aid Programs Ignore the Crucial Development Factors: Entrepreneurial Skills and Motivation

Peter Bauer elaborates on this point:

If all conditions for development other than capital are present, capital will soon be generated locally, or will be available to the government or to private businesses on commercial terms from abroad.... If, however, the conditions for development are not present, then aid—which in these circumstances will be the only source of external capital—will be necessarily unproductive and therefore ineffective....

229

If a country, or rather a people, cannot readily develop without external gifts, it is unlikely to develop with them. A low level of material achievement is a symptom, an effect of the absence or the weakness of the forces behind material progress; foreign aid focuses on symptoms and effects and diverts attention from the determinants of development....

People react to poverty and material backwardness in different ways. Some may not even notice it. Such a response may be part of a wider attitude of unquestioning acceptance of the nature of things, a reaction which is especially likely if comparisons with other people are not readily available. Some may accept poverty consciously, either in the form of resignation or by unwillingness to change modes of conduct. Some may attempt to improve their position through beggary or blackmail. Finally, some may attempt to improve their economic performance. Only the last of these responses can lead to sustained material progress. And it is the one least likely to be encouraged by an insistence on foreign aid as allegedly necessary for material advance.[47]

Point of View Number 3

Foreign Aid Diverts Human and Financial Resources Away from the Private Sector to Governments of Developing Nations

Bauer and Yamey explain:

The unfavorable effects [of aid] have been serious in many countries. Aid must bear a heavy share of responsibility for the adoption and pursuit of detrimental economic policies in many Third World countries. The transfer of aid resources to a recipient government increases its economic power vis-à-vis its subjects, enables it more readily and extensively to carry out its chosen policies, however unfavorable their effects may be, and makes it easier for it to mask or conceal their ill effects, at least for a time. Moreover, some of the policies detrimental to economic advance, such as economic planning, have been advocated by those responsible for the distribution of aid. Aid has also discouraged the prudent conduct of economic affairs in that, for instance, the emergence of balance-of-payments difficulties could itself be used as an argument for further aid.[48]

In the same vein, Bauer—with John O'Sullivan—argues that at both the individual and the institutional levels, foreign-aid programs prevent or destroy self-reliance:

Aid encourages the delusion that a society can progress from indigence to prosperity without...economic effort and achievement.

Aid encourages the delusion that a society can progress from indigence to prosperity without the intermediate stage of economic effort and achievement. Insistence on the need for external donations obscures the necessity for the people of poor countries themselves to develop the faculties and attitudes and to adopt the conduct and the mores required for sustained material progress—if this is what they wish to do. (Of course, they may reasonably prefer to remain poor and to hold on to their traditional ways.) Aid also subtly confirms and perpetuates ideas and modes of conduct which obstruct economic development—notably the idea that an improvement in one's fortunes depends on other people, the state, the rich, one's superiors, local rulers, or foreigners.[49]

Bauer's final argument, with Yamey, is that foreign aid is a principal source of the conflict between countries of the North and South:

Official Western aid has now gone to the Third World for about thirty years, more than a human generation. Over this period major deficiencies, even startling anomalies, have become apparent. These untoward results might not matter much if the policy had served to promote the well-being of the peoples of the Third World, but it has not done so. Only exceptionally and in the most propitious circumstances can aid promote or accelerate economic advance, and then merely to a minor extent.

The effects of foreign aid have been quite different. It is foreign aid that has brought into existence the Third World (also called the South). It thus underlies the so-called North-South dialogue or confrontation. Foreign aid is the source of the North-South conflict, not its solution. The paramount significance of aid lies in this very important, perhaps momentous, political result.

A further pervasive consequence of aid has been to promote or exacerbate the politicization of life in aid-receiving countries. This major result has gravely damaged the interests of the West and the well-being and prospects of the peoples of Third World countries.[50]

Point of View Number 4

Foreign-Aid Programs Promote the Interests of Donor Countries, Thereby Undermining Developing Countries' Potential for Self-Reliance

The previous viewpoint challenged the assumptions underlying foreign aid, from the perspective of "free market" economics. The following excerpts also challenge these assumptions; but these challengers mostly do not share this "free market" approach. Indeed, much of their criticism is that aid is a tool used by capitalist governments, particularly the United States, to maintain their global authority.

This is the view of Pierre Spitz, who, as director for Asia of the Food Systems and Society research project at the United Nations Research Institute for Social Development in Geneva, writes:

Aid from the rich countries has made it possible to promote, not the development of the poor countries, but a certain type of industrial and agricultural growth, the unequally distributed benefits of which have enabled the dominant social classes in the poor countries to strengthen their domination....The rich countries are thus afforded fresh opportunities to make further profits, as is shown by the substantial growth of arms sales throughout the world.[51]

Michael Hudson, an economist, thinks that aid programs do the poor more harm than good:

One is...tempted to question just what the term aid has come to mean. Etymologically speaking, to aid means to add to, that is, to help. Retrospectively and prospectively, however, what has been helped by U.S. aid programs is the U.S. balance of payments, U.S. industry and commerce, and U.S. long-term strategic goals. The flow of scarce foreign-exchange resources has been from the aid-borrowing countries to the United States. This "aid" has been imposed upon them in the form of a contractual debt service which represents an immense mortgage upon their future balance-of-payments receipts, as well as an immense opportunity-cost of not having acted earlier to guide their economies towards self-sustaining growth....

As events have turned out, technological aid has helped to displace rural peasants and throw them into mushrooming urban slums. The food deficit economies have become increasingly unbalanced and unstable, and in many cases increasingly militarist in nature, particularly for the "forward defense" countries bordering the Soviet Union and China. The strategy of U.S. foreign aid has thus been designed by its diplomats in keeping with its own world policies rather than with a view towards the needs or capabilities of the aid-borrowing countries.[52]

231

Foreign Aid Goes Mainly to Political Allies and the Elite of Developing Countries Rather Than to the Needy

Frances Moore Lappé, Joseph Collins, and David Kinley, authors with the San Francisco-based Institute for Food and Development Policy, point to what they consider to be a gap between the humanitarian rhetoric of U.S. foreign-aid programs and the way foreign-aid funds are actually allocated:

The biggest single chunk of our bilateral aid dollars—namely, one third—goes to the Economic Support Fund, a program which most Americans have never even heard of. According to congressional legislation, the Economic Support Fund "provides balance of payments, infrastructure and other capital and technical assistance to regions of the world in which the United States has special foreign policy and security interests."

The Economic Support Fund is disbursed as grants rather than loans and without the slightest reference to poverty criteria or its impact on the poor. Eighty-six percent of the Economic Support Fund proposed for FY 1980 is allocated to the Middle East. Egypt and Israel alone receive 77 percent. Through the Economic Support Fund these two countries would receive more than all development projects funded by AID anywhere in the world....

While not focused on the poorest countries, our aid dollars certainly are focused. About that there is no dispute....

Three of the top recipients of U.S. aid dollars...aren't even third world countries.

Of the almost 100 countries that receive aid from AID, only 10 receive over half of all bilateral economic assistance in FY 1980 appropriations requests.... Three of the top recipients of our aid dollars—Israel, Turkey and Portugal—aren't even third world countries....

Yes, our aid dollars are focused. They are concentrated in those countries which the U.S. administration identifies as being of strategic importance.[53]

A similar point of view is that those who principally benefit from foreign aid are the elite responsible for the persistence of hunger and poverty. Advocates of this view ask: Who really gets the aid? Not the poor, say the authors whose works appear in this section; rather, the beneficiaries are the elite who run Third World governments. Indeed, foreign aid frequently helps them maintain their power, which they often use for self-aggrandizement and exploitation, and which contributes to the persistence—not the alleviation—of poverty and hunger. Bauer and Yamey represent this view:

Foreign aid does not go to the pitiable figures we see on aid posters or in aid advertisements—it goes to their rulers. The policies of these rulers who receive aid are sometimes directly responsible for conditions such as those depicted. This is notably so in parts of Africa and Southeast Asia. But even where this is not so the policies of the rulers, including their patterns of public spending, are determined by their own personal and political interests, among which the position of the poorest has very low priority. Indeed, to support rulers on the basis of the poverty of their subjects does nothing to discourage policies that lead to impoverishment. Many Third World governments have persecuted and even expelled the most productive groups, such as the Chinese in Vietnam and Indonesia, or the Asians in East Africa. On the criterion of poverty, such governments then qualify for more aid, because incomes in their countries have been reduced.

These anomalies or paradoxes are obscured when it is suggested that giving money to the rulers of poor countries is the same as giving it to poor, even destitute people. Giving money to governments is certainly not the same thing as helping the poor. On the contrary: Western aid to Third World governments, especially in Asia and Africa, has extensively supported disastrous economic policies, which have greatly aggravated the lot of the poorest. Dr. Nyerere of Tanzania has for many years been a much favored aid recipient. Apart from large-scale collectivization of farming, his government has forcibly moved millions of people into so-called socialist villages, often far from their homes. These policies have had devastating effects on food production. President Mobutu of Zaire, another recipient of extensive aid, has expelled large numbers of traders. This had led to enforced reversion to subsistence production over large areas, causing much hardship and deprivation.[54]

Susan George, who works with the Transnational Institute in Paris, looks beneath the publicity that sometimes surrounds aid projects and finds that local people are often the victims, rather than the beneficiaries, of these projects:

The latest annual report of the French Caisse Centrale de Coopération Economique lists under food crop projects a 20 million franc operation in Upper Volta [now Burkina Faso] for the irrigated cultivation of green beans. Never mind that these vegetables are not eaten by Voltaics but by Europeans as an off-season, luxury dish; never mind that the peasant cultivators get only about 5–7% of the final purchase price—this is supposed to be a "development" project—even a food project. This agency has apparently no inkling that "food" and "cash" crops are not determined by edibility or non-edibility, but rather by who does the eating! What about national sovereignty? One might argue that the government of Upper Volta should be the judge of how aid money is used. At the risk of encouraging interference in the internal affairs of this or any other country, I'd argue it should certainly not be the sole judge. Given facts established (by the World Bank), i.e. that Voltaics eat on average only 78% of the necessary daily caloric ration; that life expectancy is 42 years, etc. a foreign government or a multilateral agency has the duty to finance only projects improving nutritional levels or to abstain. If the government wants green beans, it should plant them on its own time and use its own money.

At the multilateral agency level, examples also abound—displacement of thousands of peasants by massive dam projects, disproportionate aid to particularly repressive governments that have no intention of allowing their own people to satisfy their "basic needs" or to "participate" in any meaningful way....

How, for instance, can the World Bank write with a straight face (in the 1980 Annual Report, p. 97) that because of a $37 million IDA credit, "about 430,000 rural (Bangladesh) households will have access to irrigation facilities through a project that provides for 8500 new low-lift pumps ...(and various other project components)"? Such a description is at best ingenuous, at worst dishonest considering everything that has been written (by Hartman and Boyce and others) about monopolisation of pump irrigation by the largest farmers at the head of wholly fictitious "cooperatives"; and the way in which these irrigation projects have contributed to the dispossession of small farmers and to land concentration in Bangladesh.

Are IBRD, IDA, FAO and the others prepared to submit to impartial and public evaluation of their food production projects? Or is the public (whose taxes ultimately finance most agency work) to accept on faith IBRD's numerical fantasies ("430,000 households") as a substitute for proof?[55]

Frances Moore Lappé and her colleagues see further evidence of the dangerous and corrupting effects of foreign aid:

Local people are often the victims, rather than the beneficiaries, of aid projects.

Just over 50 percent of all official aid from the West goes to 66 low-income countries. This amounts to $7.60 per person. The people of 69 middle-income countries receive $18.20 per person in aid.

FIGURE FA.7. HOW MUCH AID GOES TO THE POOREST COUNTRIES?

GNP (per Capita)

$301.00 $1,150.00 $2,540.00

Aid (per Capita)

$7.60 $18.20 $3.00

▪ Low-Income Countries
▪ Middle-Income Countries
▪ Newly Industrialized Countries

Source: New Internationalist, no. 126 (August 1983): 10–11.

Instead of helping, we hurt the dispossessed majority.

Field investigations and other research have led us to realize that U.S. foreign assistance fails to help the poor because it is <u>of necessity</u> based on one fundamental fallacy: that aid can reach the powerless even though channeled through the powerful. Official foreign assistance necessarily flows through the recipient governments, and too often (particularly in those countries to which the United States confines most of its aid) these governments represent narrow, elite economic interests. We have learned that additional material resources are usually not needed to eliminate hunger. In fact, the influx of such outside resources into those countries where economic control is concentrated in the hands of a few bolsters the local, national and international elites whose stranglehold over land and other productive resources generates poverty and hunger in the first place. Instead of helping, we <u>hurt</u> the dispossessed majority.

Tubewells designed to benefit the poorest farmers in a Bangladesh village become the property of the village's richest landlord; food-for-work projects in Haiti intended to help the landless poor end up as a boon to the village elite; rural electrification justified as a prerequisite to jobs in rural industries results in the elimination of jobs for thousands of poor rural women in Indonesia.[56]

Writing in the New York Times with Nick Allen, Lappé recalls similar abuses in Central America:

We studied a Guatemalan agribusiness project that is the type of United States Government-subsidized "free-enterprise" venture that the Administration is promoting in its Caribbean Basin plan. (The plan would offer tariff and tax incentives for corporate investment in "nontraditional" agriculture, such as cucumbers, pineapples, tomatoes, and cut flowers.)

In 1975, Alcosa, a Guatemalan subsidiary of Hanover Brands, based in the United States, began contracting with peasants to grow cauliflower and broccoli, which were processed and shipped frozen to North American supermarkets. Alcosa is partly financed by the Latin American Agribusiness Development Corporation, a consortium of big banks and agribusiness firms supported by the Agency for International Development....

Alcosa, the [AID] study says, recruited poor highland farmers who gave up their corn, bean and cabbage patches to specialize in cauliflower. While at first their income increased, by 1980 many farmers were suffering substantial losses. They were able to survive only by going heavily into debt to Alcosa for hybrid seeds and insecticides and to itinerant merchants for other goods. While Alcosa loans were interest-free, "Alcosa paid itself first, even if that meant... 3 months of no-income farming."

When Alcosa stopped buying vegetables in one village, the farmers protested that "there was nothing to eat."... "Their children had been forced to quit school and leave home to seek work as farm labor or domestic servants,"...

Rather than a different kind of aid, what is needed is a different kind of recipient.

In one village out of 17, the Alcosa project did succeed both for the company and the farmers. What made the difference was a strong peasant cooperative that had enough clout to negotiate a better contract with the company. Since the co-op had its own agronomists, farmers did not have to rely on Alcosa's advice. The agronomists said: Use smaller doses of cheaper insecticides and intersperse corn with cauliflower. Thus, the farmers did not have to give up their staple food crop....

When will we learn that, rather than a different kind of aid, what is needed is a different kind of recipient? As long as recipients of our aid, in Central America and elsewhere, are governments protecting economic and political structures that deny power to most citizens, that aid—military or economic—will not only fail to end the problems of hunger and poverty but rather will aggravate inequalities at their core.[57]

Point of View Number 6

Food Aid Takes Away Recipients' Dignity and Motivation

The final point of view we will examine in this chapter concerns the perceived problems and negative effects of food aid.

We begin with a quotation from Mahatma Gandhi, who looks at the effect of food give-away programs on the individual:

My ahimsa would not tolerate the idea of giving a free meal to a healthy person who has not worked for it in some honest way and, if I had the power, I would stop every sadavrata (free distribution of meals)....It has degraded the nation and it has encouraged laziness, idleness, hypocrisy and even crime...Do not say you will maintain the poor on charity.[58]

Dr. Siegfried Bethke, a former administrator of the West Africa Branch of the World Food Program, feels that foreign food-aid takes away the incentive for local food production. As "Food Aid: For Peace or Patronage?" explains:

In an internal FAO report, written in August 1977 [and later made public], Dr. Bethke said "in the Region at large...out of 55 operational projects only four, possibly five or six—in two or three countries—may be considered as satisfactory.... The whole of the rest vary from unsatisfactory to very bad." The reasons he suggests for this low success rate are, first, that the region is potentially self-sufficient in food but that food aid acts as a disincentive to production through "market displacement"; second that the administrative and logistic requirements for the distribution of project food aid are so heavy that at best it often fails to reach its target groups, and that at worst corrupt use and sales of food aid are widespread.[59]

Frances Moore Lappé agrees:

For every pound of P.L. 480 cereals imported, there was a net decline of almost one-half pound in Indian domestic production.

Dumping large quantities of low-priced American grain in underdeveloped countries makes it economically impossible for the small domestic producers to compete. Unable to get a fair return for their grain, such producers are frequently forced to sell their land and become landless (and often jobless) laborers. A study in 1969 concluded that for every pound of P.L. 480 cereals imported, there was a net decline of almost one-half pound in Indian domestic production over the following two years, because of the reduced return to the farmer....

Although the disincentive effect of food aid on local production continues to be debated, a 1975 U.S. government (General Accounting Office) research survey concluded, "Leading world authorities now indicate that such food assistance by the United States and other countries has hindered the developing countries in expanding their food production and thus has contributed to the critical world food situation."[60]

Staff members of World Neighbors report another instance of how foreign aid causes severe problems. In February 1976, an earthquake struck Guatemala. Following the quake, a number of agencies undertook an extensive food-distribution program. Within two weeks, the rural people asked that the give-aways be stopped. So did the Guatemalan government, which passed a decree

235

prohibiting importation of food for relief programs three months later. In a letter to headquarters, World Neighbors staff members Roland Bunch, Mary McKay, and Paul McKay addressed the problems that led to this decision, and drew some general conclusions about food aid:

Food being brought into an area inevitably reduces the demand for locally produced food. This is especially true when large quantities are involved.... This distribution of imported food lowers prices of locally produced food.... This may take away from the people their previous ability to provide for themselves and create a new, unnecessary dependency.

With lowered prices for basic grains there is also less incentive on a national level to produce these grains. With time, the producers of basic grains will turn to producing other crops, causing a lowered national food production. Thus the country as a whole becomes more dependent on food imports.

Nutrition programs based on free foreign food convince many mothers that their children can only be healthy if they consume the foods given away in the program. Often these foods are not available or would be prohibitively expensive if the family were to try to buy the same thing locally. Thus instead of teaching a woman how she can feed her child well using things the family has produced or purchased locally, this approach takes away the family's dignity and, in effect, says that they are not capable of feeding their children adequately without outside help.

Food distribution programs are more expensive than are effective long-term development programs. It is much less expensive to teach a man to double his wheat harvest than it is to continue to give him the extra wheat he needs. But cheaper still is teaching a local extensionist who can then teach his neighbors. Compare this to the cost of feeding him and all of his neighbors!

Once people become accustomed [to] (or even dependent) upon food distribution, the institution involved is often very bitterly resented when the day comes when the food must be terminated. People often come to feel the food is their right rather than a privilege or temporary good luck. To some extent the tendency to see gifts as their right can result from the psychological need to maintain personal dignity or self-respect. If I feel people owe me something (because of some social injustice, etc.) then I don't have to feel bad about accepting it....

Food distribution programs make future development work which does not involve free goods much more difficult. Afterwards when there is need to build a road or a school for a village or you try to get a group of women together for a nutrition class, the first question is, "If we do this, what will we be given." People with long-term development programs in Honduras have complained that, since Hurricane Fifi and the emergency effort which followed it, long-term nutrition and agricultural programs have been practically impossible because the people are only interested in what those from the outside are willing to give them. In terms of a proverb already heavily over-used, they have been given so many fish that they have no interest in learning how to fish.

Food distribution programs tend to reward poverty. Since they are designated to help the poorest, we know of examples where the poorest farmer who never did anything to help himself got the help and his neighbor who had been attending agricultural classes and using soil conservation techniques and improved farming methods received nothing. Psychologists will tell us that we are using positive reinforcement, the most effective modifier of human behavior we know, to encourage people to remain poor.

Food distribution programs are more expensive than long-term development.

236

Food distribution creates a feeling of inadequacy. Just imagine how you would feel if you could not provide for your family without receiving a hand-out.

The relief programs... strongly affected how local people have chosen their leaders. Instead of looking to honest, hard-working leaders with good judgement, the people have often followed the men who were able to secure for their followers the largest amount of goods. These men, all too often, are those who are deceitful, who have painted the conditions in their villages as black as possible, who fibbed about what help they had already received, and who didn't mind cheating when filling out forms.[61]

This section concludes with two case studies that, according to their authors, demonstrate how food-aid programs discriminate against the poor. Both describe programs in Bangladesh. The first discusses a tubewell irrigation project. Betsy Hartmann and James Boyce write:

Two case studies demonstrate how food-aid programs discriminate against the poor.

Project aid reached Katni in the form of a deep tubewell for irrigation, one of 3000 installed in northwestern Bangladesh by a World Bank project. On paper, the tubewell will be used by a farmers' cooperative formed especially for the purpose. According to the press release which announced the project, each tubewell "will serve from 25 to 50 farmers in an irrigation group." In reality, the tubewell in our village was the personal property of one man: Nafis, the biggest landlord of the area. The irrigation group, of which Nafis was supposedly the manager, was no more than a few signatures he had collected on a scrap of paper....

The tubewell was by far Nafis's greatest patronage plum. Although each tubewell cost the donors and the government about U.S. $12,000, Nafis paid less than $300 for his, mostly in bribes to local officials. The tubewell sits in the middle of a 30-acre tract of Nafis's best land. Since it will yield enough water to irrigate twice that area, Nafis says the smaller farmers who till adjacent plots will be able to use his water—at a price. But the hourly rate he intends to charge is so high that few of his neighbors are interested. As a result his tubewell will not be used to its full capacity.

At first we were surprised that the beneficiary of the World Bank's aid should be the richest man in our village, but on closer inspection we learned that this was not so strange. A foreign expert working on the project told us, "I no longer ask who is getting the well. I know what the answer will be, and I don't want to hear it. One hundred percent of these wells are going to the big boys. Each thana (county) is allotted a certain number of tubewells. First priority goes to those with political clout: the judges, the magistrates, the members of parliament, the union chairmen. If any are left over, the local authorities auction them off. The rich landlords compete, and whoever offers the biggest bribe gets the tubewell. Around here the going price is 3000 taka (less than U.S. $200)."...

First priority goes to those with political clout: the judges, the magistrates, the members of parliament, the union chairmen.

For the poor of our village, the only conceivable benefit of the project will be the employment generated by Nafis's extra rice crop. Nafis plans to work part of his tubewell land with hired labor and to lease part to sharecroppers. (Since the yield on this irrigated land will be higher, Nafis intends to take two-thirds rather than his customary one-half of the crop: "After all," he says, "I bought the well.")[62]

The second case study concerns the inappropriateness of a food-for-work program and the graft it encouraged. Barry Newman writes in *The Wall Street Journal:*

Two truths have been revealed in recent years to the savants of economic development: Foreign aid works best when it goes straight to the poor; and expensive machinery has no place in countries where millions of the unemployed are willing to work with their hands.

Paying hungry people with donated food to build roads and dig canals by hand would seem a perfect dovetailing of these maxims. The idea is called Food for Work. It is being put into practice near this village [Mukundupur, Bangladesh] a few miles from the River Ganges.

In the mud and stubble of a paddy field, 60 women in cotton saris are digging a pit. Some are barely more than children, others are bent and gray. With heavy-bladed hoes they lift clods into baskets, hoist them to their jute-padded hips and dump them onto a heap of earth. A young man in white bell-bottom trousers stands nearby with a clipboard, supervising.

The women are rebuilding a three-mile road, long washed out, that once linked Mukundupur with the highway to Pabna, a market city to the west. Each worker is expected to move 50 cubic feet of earth in a day. For that she will get six pounds of wheat from the United States....

Food for Work in Bangladesh, the largest program of its kind, gives a month's work and 240,000 metric tons of wheat to 2.4 million landless peasants, tiding them over the leanest time of year. Half the wheat comes as a gift through the United Nations, and the rest is a gift from the United States. It is meant to go directly to the poor in a country where most food aid is rationed to the middle class. And the food is used for building things that the poor themselves presumably need.

Food for Work, in short, is the ideal food-aid program. Or it would be, that is, if it weren't also something of a fiasco.

"It's a stupid idea based on office theory," concludes a British aid worker.

There are three problems. First, roads and canals don't do much for those who don't own land, and half the population of over 90 million is in that category; roads and canals do help landowners, who, with Food for Work, thus get a bonus of free labor. Second, a good number of the roads and canals built through Food for Work aren't built properly and quickly fall apart.

And third, an appalling amount of the food intended for the hungry is some-how spirited away, apparently by those same landowners and their allies in local government.

A confidential report to the U.S. Agency for International Development says Food for Work strengthens an "exploitative semi-feudal system" in the villages of Bangladesh and "speeds up the polarization process in rural areas."

"The economic-development benefits resulting from FFW are related to land utilization," reports AID consultant Hjalmar Brundin, "and therefore they scarcely—and only in the best of cases—indirectly benefit the landless."

"Misappropriation," Mr. Brundin adds, casts doubt on Food for Work's effectiveness even as a simple relief operation. The consultant says his figures show "a very strong indication that less than 70% of the wheat withdrawn for FFW finds its way to the laborers." Of 240,000 tons, in other words, about 80,000 tons are stolen.[63]

238

Conclusion

In this chapter, we have examined basic information on foreign aid and reviewed alternative interpretations of the track record of foreign-aid programs. We now have nearly four decades of experience with major foreign-aid programs. During this period, the number and diversity of participating nations—both donor and recipient—have grown. So have philosophies of giving aid, types of programs, and numbers of participating organizations. The history of foreign aid provides numerous success stories and stories of failure. There is a rich store of lessons to be learned and a diverse body of knowledge and experience. But what are the lessons, and what is the knowledge that can provide a foundation for more effective development assistance in the future?

More than any other issue explored in this book, foreign aid provides an illuminating study of how the same body of historical experience can offer persuasive evidence to support many different perspectives on an issue. Both proponents of foreign aid and its critics support their points of view with field experience, and both may be reporting accurately. A project in India produced brilliant results. A similar project in Africa had no impact. One in Latin America left participants worse off than they had been. Are there meaningful generalizations to be made about foreign aid as a whole or can the subject be examined only on a case-by-case basis?

The entire field of foreign aid has changed dynamically, both in theory and practice, since the early days of the Marshall Plan. At that time, many felt that it was sufficient to simply transfer to the Third World what had worked in Western Europe. But decades of hard-earned lessons have made it clear to all that the "development" process involves more than simply making inputs of capital, resources, or technology available. Aid programs that ignore local cultures, questions of who controls the economic and political power in a village or a nation, and the desires of the proposed beneficiaries of the program are likely to fail.

What all perspectives do seem to agree on is that Third World economic development is a matter of real urgency today. How should this development best be achieved—through transfers of resources in foreign-aid programs? Through free market economics? Through indigenous grass-roots development? Or, when necessary, through revolutionary movements such as those of China, Cuba, and, more recently, Nicaragua? We will continue to encounter these questions in the chapters on *National Security* and *The New International Economic Order*.

What all perspectives seem to agree on is that Third World economic development is a matter of real urgency today.

NOTES

1 George C. Marshall, "European Unity," *Vital Speeches of the Day* 13, no. 18 (1 July 1947): 553, 554.

2 Agency for International Development, "The Marshall Plan: The Plan," *War on Hunger* 11, no. 6 (June 1977), 22.

3 For further information, see Agency for International Development, "The Marshall Plan: The Speech" and "The Marshall Plan: The Plan," *War on Hunger* 11, no. 6 (June 1977).

4 Agency for International Development, "The Marshall Plan: The Plan," 22.

5 Robert S. McNamara, *The McNamara Years at the World Bank: Major Policy Addresses of Robert S. McNamara, 1968–1981* (Baltimore, MD: Johns Hopkins University Press, 1981), 242.

6   Overseas Development Council, *The United States and World Development: Agenda 1980,* eds. John W. Sewell et al. (New York: Praeger, 1980), 91.

7   Unless otherwise noted, the currency unit is United States dollars.

8   Overseas Development Council, *U.S. Foreign Policy and the Third World: Agenda 1983,* eds. John P. Lewis and Valeriana Kallab (New York: Praeger, 1983), 274, 276.

9   OPEC was created in 1960 to coordinate the petroleum policies of Third World oil-producing nations. OPEC members are Algeria, Ecuador, Gabon, Indonesia, Iran, Iraq, Kuwait, Libya, Nigeria, Qatar, Saudi Arabia, United Arab Emirates, and Venezuela. In the early 1970s the OPEC nations, acting as a cartel, raised oil prices sharply, causing shortages, inflation, and other problems in the oil-consuming nations.

10   Overseas Development Council, *U.S. Foreign Policy…1983,* 274.

11   Derived from Ibid.; World Bank, *World Development Report 1983* (New York: Oxford University Press, 1983), 183; and Population Reference Bureau, *1981 World Population Data Sheet* (Washington, DC: Population Reference Bureau, 1981). Arab OPEC nations are Algeria, Iraq, Kuwait, Libya, Qatar, Saudi Arabia, and the United Arab Emirates.

12   Overseas Development Council, *U.S. Foreign Policy…1983,* 274; and Population Reference Bureau, *1981 World Population Data Sheet.*

13   United Nations, General Assembly, *Resolutions,* Supplement no. 28 (A/8028), 15 September–17 December 1970, 43. For more information, see United Nations, Department of Public Information, *Everyone's United Nations* (E.79.I.5), December 1979, 117–22.

14   Overseas Development Council, *U.S. Foreign Policy…1983,* 276.

15   John P. Lewis, *1981 Review: Development Co-operation* (Paris: Organisation for Economic Co-operation and Development, November 1981), 78.

16   Ibid., 115.

17   A. W. Clausen interviewed in "What It Will Take to End Worldwide Recession," *U.S. News & World Report,* 15 November 1982, 65.

18   Overseas Development Council, *U.S. Foreign Policy…1983,* 280.

19   Ibid.

20   Derived from chart, "U.S. Economic Assistance as a Percent of GNP: Gross Obligations and Loan Authorization Basis," Bureau for Program and Policy Coordination, Office of Planning and Budgeting, Agency for International Development; and Overseas Development Council, *U.S. Foreign Policy…1983,* 273.

21   Overseas Development Council, *U.S. Foreign Policy…1983,* 276.

22   Derived from Population Reference Bureau, *1983 World Population Data Sheet* (Washington, DC: Population Reference Bureau, 1983).

23   Overseas Development Council, *U.S. Foreign Policy…1983,* 282.

24   Technical Assistance Information Clearing House, *U.S. Nonprofit Organizations in Development Assistance Abroad: TAICH Directory 1983,* eds. Wynta Boynes et al. (New York: American Council of Voluntary Agencies for Foreign Service, 1983), vii.

25   Ibid., 82, 89, 334.

26   Overseas Development Council, *U.S. Foreign Policy…1983,* 277.

27   Hollis B. Chenery in "Foreign Aid: Debating the Uses and Abuses," *New York Times,* 1 March 1981, E5.

28   Agency for International Development, *World Development Letter* 3, no. 10 (12 May 1980): 39.

29   John G. Sommer, "Does Foreign Aid Really Help the Poor?" *Agenda* 4, no. 3 (April 1981): 3.

30   Ibrahim Shihata, "OPEC and the Third World," *IFDA Dossier* 24 (July–August 1981): 68, 69.

31   Raisa Scriabine, Agency for International Development, Washington, DC, correspondence to The Hunger Project, San Francisco, 3 December 1984.

32   Mike Haverstock, "Cali: City on the Move," *Americas* 34, no. 2 (March–April 1982): 3, 5, 7.

33   Richard Critchfield, "It's Time to Give Foreign Aid a Good Name," *The Christian Science Monitor,* 13 July 1979, 13.

34   Alexanderina Shuler, "Making a Difference," *Agenda* 3, no. 8 (October 1980): 4.

35   Edmund S. Muskie, "The Secretary of State on Foreign Aid," *World Development Letter* 3, no. 19 (29 September 1980): 76.

36   James Bednar, "Foreign Aid: Generosity Returned," *Agenda* 3, no. 10 (December 1980): 3, 4, 5.

37   Agency for International Development, *World Development Letter* 4, no. 13 (24 June 1981): 49–50. Years and figures updated by Raisa Scriabine, Agency for International Development, Washington, DC, correspondence to The Hunger Project, San Francisco, 3 December 1984.

38   Laurel Schneider, "Thai Refugee Report," *Tucker* 5, no. 1 (Fall 1981): 2–3.

39   U.S., Congress, Senate, *Congressional Record,* 96th Cong., 1st sess., 1979–1980, 125, pt. 28, statement of Senator Paul Tsongas, 37331.

40   Overseas Development Council, *U.S. Foreign Policy and the Third World: Agenda 1982,* eds. Roger D. Hansen et al. (New York: Praeger, 1982), 139.

41   U.S., Congress, House, Committee on Agriculture, *World Hunger Situation,* 97th Cong., 1st sess., 22 July 1981, testimony of M. Peter McPherson, 300–301, 302.

42   Philip Johnston, CARE, New York, correspondence to The Hunger Project, San Francisco, 29 November 1984.

43   Jeremy Mark, "Cambodia: Hope for a Future," *1981 World Refugee Survey* (New York: United States Committee for Refugees, 1981), 21–23.

44   Edward J. Feulner in "Foreign Aid: Debating the Uses and Abuses," *New York Times,* 1 March 1981, E5.

45   Peter T. Bauer and Basil S. Yamey, "Foreign Aid: What Is at Stake?" *Public Interest,* no. 68 (Summer 1982): 57.

46   Garrett Hardin, "The Toughlove Solution," *Newsweek,* 26 October 1981, 45.

47   Peter T. Bauer, *Dissent on Development: Studies and Debates in Development Economics* (Cambridge, MA: Harvard University Press, 1972), 97–98, 100, 101.

48   Peter T. Bauer and Basil S. Yamey, "The Third World and the West: An Economic Perspective," *The Third World: Premises of U.S. Policy*, ed. W. Scott Thompson (San Francisco: Institute for Contemporary Studies, 1978), 116–17.

49   Peter T. Bauer and John O'Sullivan, "Foreign Aid for What?" *Commentary* (December 1978), 47.

50   Bauer and Yamey, "Foreign Aid," 53–54.

51   Pierre Spitz, "Silent Violence: Famine and Inequality," *International Social Science Journal* 30, no. 4 (1978): 889.

52   Michael Hudson, "The Political Economy of Foreign Aid," *The Myth of Aid,* eds. Denis Goulet and Michael Hudson (New York: IDOC North America, 1971), 78, 79.

53   Frances Moore Lappé, Joseph Collins, and David Kinley, *Aid as Obstacle: Twenty Questions about Our Foreign Aid and the Hungry* (San Francisco: Institute for Food and Development Policy, 1980), 15, 17.

54   Bauer and Yamey, "Foreign Aid," 61.

55   Susan George, "Dear Friends and Colleagues of the North-South Food Roundtable," *Development: Seeds of Change* 1 (1982): 79, 80.

56   Lappé et al., *Aid as Obstacle,* 10–11.

57   Frances Moore Lappé and Nick Allen, "Central American Victims," *New York Times,* 28 May 1982, A27.

58   S. P. Varma, "Gandhi and Contemporary Thinking on Development," *IFDA Dossier,* no. 37 (September–October 1983): 30. The word *ahimsa* expresses an ethical precept central to Buddhism and Hinduism. It is usually translated as "nonviolence." Gandhi applied this precept to mean peaceful struggle against casteism and colonial domination, as well as positive inner virtue that cares for the welfare of all.

59   "Food Aid: For Peace or Patronage?" *Reading Rural Development Communications,* Bulletin 10, July 1980, 10.

60   Lappé et al., *Aid as Obstacle,* 94–95, 97–98.

61   Roland Bunch, Mary McKay, and Paul McKay, "Problems with Food Distribution Programs: A Case in Point," occasional paper (Oklahoma City, OK: World Neighbors, 1978), 1–2.

62   Betsy Hartmann and James Boyce, *Needless Hunger: Voices from a Bangladesh Village* (San Francisco: Institute for Food and Development Policy, 1979), 48–49, 50.

63   Barry Newman, "World Hunger: Graft and Inefficiency in Bangladesh Subvert Food-for-Work Plans," *The Wall Street Journal,* 20 April 1981, 1.

Most experts agree that Third World countries need economic development. But do foreign-aid programs promote or hinder the goals of development and ending hunger? On this question, there is little agreement. Right: *Distributing U.S. corn-soya-milk, Somalia* (William Campbell/Sygma); next two-page spread: *UN grain stockpile, Somalia* (David Kryszak/ Black Star).

The Point Four program was the first major aid program for the Third World. It supported technical assistance projects in agriculture, education, and rural development. Later programs placed a greater emphasis on large-scale capital development and security assistance projects in agriculture, education, and rural development. Since 1970, there has been a shift toward programs designed to meet basic human needs. European and OPEC nations, UN agencies, and private voluntary organizations have become increasingly active participants in these programs. Here is how John Sewell, president of the Overseas Development Council, describes the goals of the basic-needs approach: "[To make] the quality of life of men, women, and children the focal point of decisions about the development process.... [It] urges commitment to the elimination of the worst aspects of absolute poverty on an accelerated basis.... It is intended to improve the income-earning oppor-tunities of the poor, the public services that reach the poor, the flow of goods and services to meet the needs of all members of the household, and the participation of the poor in making the decisions which affect them." Left: Refugees lining up for food, Chad (Jane-Evelyn Atwood/Cosmos for Woodfin Camp & Assoc.); above, top: Save the Children distribution truck and children, Zimbabwe (Wernher Krutein/Photovault); above, bottom: UNICEF school, Burkina Faso (Wernher Krutein/Photovault).

Critics question whether self-sufficiency in developing countries can ever be achieved through foreign aid. They find aid ineffective in sparking economic development and say that it actually disrupts recipient nations' economic systems and their peoples' ability to become self-reliant. According to a former administrator of the World Food Program in West Africa, no more than six out of fifty-five projects in his region were successful. What caused the low success rate? The fact that "food aid acts as a disincentive to production" and "the administrative and logistic requirements for the distribution of project food aid are so heavy that at best it often fails to reach its target groups, and that at worst corrupt use and sales of food aid are widespread." According to a U.S. General Accounting Office report, "Leading world authorities now indicate that…food assistance by the United States and other countries has hindered the developing countries in expanding their food production and thus has contributed to the critical world food situation." Photos: All Ethiopia. Overleaf two-page spread: Wollo Wollo refugee camp (C. Steele-Perkins/ Magnum Photos); above: Cartons of food from the U.S. arrive for distribution (C. Steele-Perkins/Magnum Photos); right: Distributing food at a refugee camp (C. Steele-Perkins/ Magnum Photos).

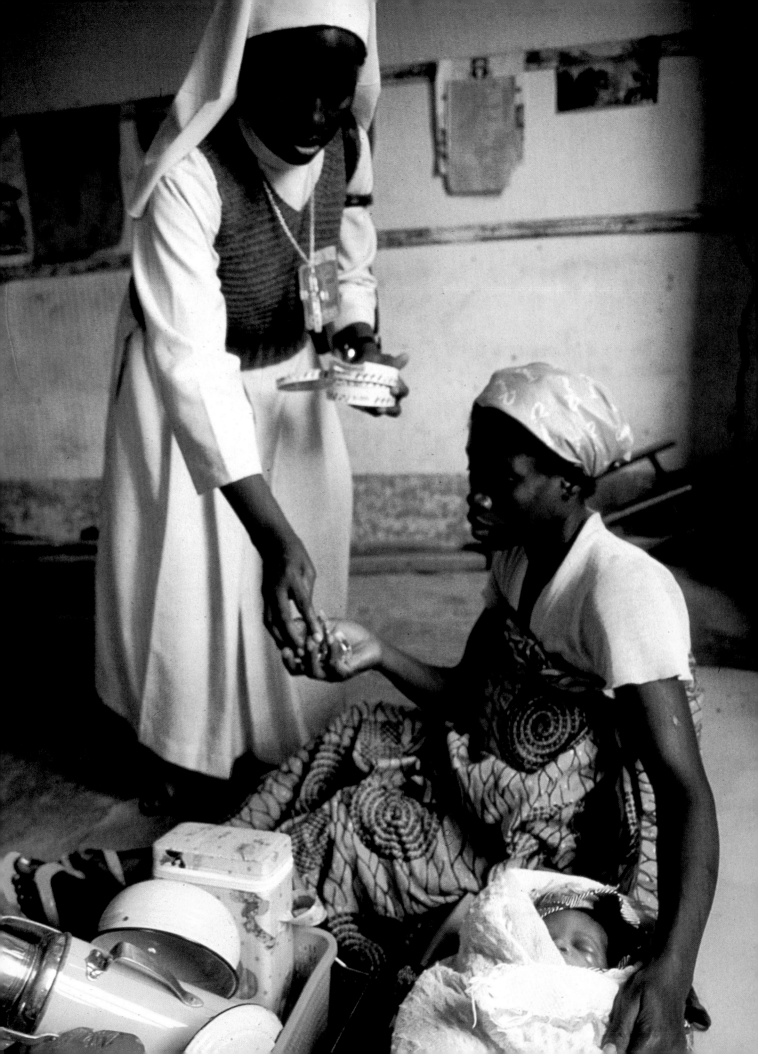

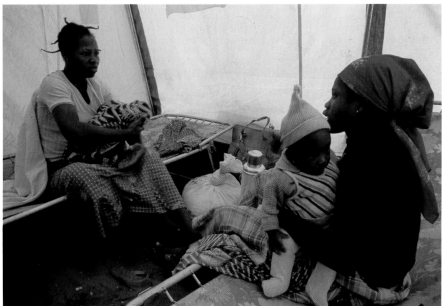

Foreign-aid programs, say proponents, do contribute to the meeting of basic needs, self-sufficiency, and national development. They also say that timely food aid for famine relief has saved thousands of lives. They support these views with statistics and specific success stories.

Richard Critchfield writes about Java in The Christian Science Monitor: "In just the past 3 to 5 years, 30 percent of all homes in the 35 Javanese villages have been rebuilt from bamboo huts to masonry houses." USAID's publication, Agenda, reports that "more than 200,000 individuals from foreign countries have received formal and nonformal training in food production, nutrition, population planning, health and education under the U.S. assistance program. The students return to their home-countries to become government leaders, university professors, bank presidents and scientists." Overleaf two-page spread: *Women carrying grain, Burkina Faso* (Wernher Krutein/

Photovault); left: *A mother receives treatment for her four-day-old infant, Ghana* (C. Steele-Perkins/Magnum Photos); above, top: *Doctor treating child, Somalia* (Kevin Fleming/ Woodfin Camp & Assoc.); above, bottom: *Hospital for refugee mothers, Ghana* (C. Steele-Perkins/Magnum Photos); next two-page spread: *USAID construction project, El Salvador* (S. Meiselas/Magnum Photos); following two-page spread: *Building a highway through the jungle, French Guyana* (S. Salgado Jr./Magnum Photos).

Self-reliance—China's experience seems to illustrate the value of government policies based on this goal. As Mao Tse-tung declared: "We stand for self-reliance. We hope for foreign aid but cannot be dependent on it; we depend upon our own efforts, on the creative power of the whole army and the entire people.... On what basis should our policy rest? It should rest on our own strength, and that means regeneration through one's own efforts." In order to further its development, China accepted assistance from the USSR and is now seeking closer ties with the West. China's ambivalence reflects the debate about foreign aid. All points of view seem to agree that Third World economic development is a matter of real urgency. But how should this development be achieved? Through foreign-aid programs? Through free market economics? Through indigenous grass-roots development? Or, when necessary, through revolutionary movements such as those in China,

Cuba, and Nicaragua? Experts differ on the answers to these fundamental questions. Photos: All China. Left: *Building project, Qianing Province* (Owen Franken/Sygma); above, top: *Men and women repairing a road* (E. Arnold/Magnum Photos); above, bottom: *Threshing by traditional methods* (Paolo Koch/Photo Researchers); next two-page spread: *"Barefoot doctor" and patient* (E. Arnold/Magnum Photos).

National Security

Central to the following discussion is the question, "What is national security and how can we best ensure a secure and stable world?" This question is viewed in terms of very distinct perspectives, each of which leads to differing policy recommendations about where to place our global priorities.

Many people believe that an effective way to end hunger is to shift spending priorities from national security to development. Since the money spent on national security is allocated primarily to military forces, the high cost of military establishments is a major point of contention.

Those who favor reallocating military funding do not normally question the need for national security. Rather, they question the cost effectiveness of military forces, and they point to other things that money now allocated to the military could buy if priorities were reordered. They compare the prices of aircraft carriers with agricultural implements, submarines versus school houses, and tanks versus tube-wells. Reducing or eliminating military spending, they suggest, would free ample funds for promoting development and ending hunger.

Should military budgets be reallocated to development or are strong military forces a prerequisite to development?

Another major school of thought supports the current levels of military spending, and even seeks to increase them. Adherents of this approach focus on the necessity of a strong military establishment. A nation is thought to be secure when its government is able to defend itself against military attacks and revolutions. A strong military establishment is viewed as the most effective—perhaps the only—way to achieve the goal of national security. If military forces are strong enough, they will rarely have to fight; their presence alone will be sufficient to deter potential aggressors and revolutionaries.

Economists sometimes describe the debate over military expenditures versus food and development as the "guns vs. butter" debate. This view implies that only a finite pool of resources is available, which can be used for ending hunger *or* for military spending. Much of the data in this chapter on military expenditures represents this "either/or" orientation. But some people who favor strong military forces believe that the world has sufficient resources to have both guns *and* butter—that is, to support a strong military establishment *and* to end hunger. These people also question whether reductions in military expenditures would necessarily lead to commensurate increases in funds for ending hunger. In fact, they claim there is no evidence to suggest that such would be the case.

There is little agreement about the facts of national security and military spending—in particular, about the degree to which military forces in the United States, the USSR, or other nations contribute to national security. In fact, no one even agrees on the *definition* of national security. So what *can* be more or less documented as fact? The size of national military establishments; the extent to which they have grown; and how much all this costs.

The *Basic Facts* section concentrates on important trends related to aspects of national security. One involves the size of military establishments, which grew rapidly during 1960–1980, but less rapidly than global population and GNP. However, weapons are now far more destructive than ever before, and they can be delivered more accurately. Another significant trend is increases in military spending by developing nations.

This chapter reviews two basic schools of thought. The first holds that too much money is being spent on the military, and that priorities must be reordered if hunger is to end. This position is represented by: the Brandt Commission report; economist Murray Weidenbaum, national security analyst Thomas Wilson, former World Bank President Robert McNamara, and hunger expert Frances Moore Lappé; and, from the Third World, UNESCO Director General Amadou-Mahtar M'Bow and director of the Institute for the Study of Rural Resources in Bangladesh, Muzammel Huq. The major points of view are, first, that funds now allocated to military spending should be reallocated to programs that would directly contribute to ending hunger and enhancing the quality of life; second, that the relationship between true "national security" and large military expenditures is questionable; and third, that large military forces in Third World nations perpetuate and even create conditions that contribute to hunger and poverty.

A second school of thought holds that reducing military spending in the United States and in Third World nations would ultimately set back efforts to end hunger. Proponents of this position believe that a strong United States defense establishment and military assistance to allies who need it must be the highest priority. Viewpoints include those of present and former high-level officials of the United States government—Ronald Reagan, Richard Nixon, Henry Kissinger, Alexander Haig, and Maxwell D. Taylor. They believe that Soviet-dominated communism poses the most serious threat to attaining a secure, stable world order in which hunger can be ended and that the United States has a special responsibility to deal with that threat. They also believe that Third World nations must have strong military forces and support from the United States to protect themselves against external threats and to maintain the internal political stability necessary for development. Soedjatmoko, an Indonesian scholar and rector of the United Nations University, and Julius Nyerere, president of Tanzania, present a Third World perspective: Developing nations need a degree of internal unity and stability in order to be viable. This requires military forces and less tolerance of dissent than is acceptable in democratic Western nations.

Basic Facts

The Global Military Establishment: How Big? Growing How Fast?

In 1981, it was estimated, there were about 25 million people in the world's regular armed forces.[1] This was over 6 million more than in 1960. The average annual growth rate of military personnel for this period was about 1.5 percent. (During the same period, the world's population grew at an average rate of 2.0 percent per year.)[2] Including reserves, paramilitary forces, and civilians needed to produce weapons and services for the military, about 100 million people were involved in military-related activities in 1981–1982.[3]

From 1960 to 1980, the world's annual military expenditures (measured in constant 1979 dollars) grew from $298 billion to $495 billion annually.[4] During the first sixty years of the twentieth century, military expenditures increased by a factor of 10 (see Figure NS.1). By 1982, the nations of the world were spending about $1 million a minute on their military establishments.[5] The average yearly rate of growth for military spending was about 2.5 percent. (The gross world product, measured in constant 1979 dollars, grew at an average rate of about 4.6 percent per year during this period.)[6]

Because of developments in nuclear technology, the largest increase, by far, has occurred in the destructive potential of weapons.

In 1981, there were about 25 million people in the world's regular armed forces.

Between the bomb that levelled Hiroshima and the Poseidon warhead, the yield-to-weight ratio has increased 150-fold. A heavy bomber was necessary to carry the 5-ton city-destroying bomb of 1945. Now one Poseidon submarine carries 16 missiles, each with 10 warheads, and each warhead with over three times the explosive force of the Hiroshima bomb. That adds up to a larger explosive force than was used by all the munitions in World War II.[7]

The United States and the USSR possess about 16,500 nuclear weapons between them.

Between them, the United States and the USSR now possess approximately 16,500 nuclear weapons, along with the appropriate delivery systems (long-range bombers, ground- and submarine-launched ballistic missiles, and air-launched cruise missiles). If current trends continue, the number could reach 26,000 or more by 1985. Not only has there been a major growth in destructive power, but there also have been significant improvements in delivery systems. For example, inter-continental missiles can now travel 6,000 to 8,000 miles in half an hour and deliver their nuclear payloads with a high degree of accuracy.[8]

In 1980, 54 percent of the world's military budget was spent by the United States and the USSR, combined. The expenditures of their allies in NATO and of the Warsaw Pact raised the total to 76 percent of the world's outlay.[9]

Developing nations, as well, spend substantial sums on their military forces. According to the Overseas Development Council, in 1971 developing countries spent $47.3 billion (in constant 1979 dollars) on their military, a figure that accounted for more than 17.3 percent of the world's military expenditures. By 1980, spending had reached $142.4 billion and the proportion had risen to more than 21 percent. Some of the poorest nations regularly allocate between 2 and 10 percent of their GNP for military purposes. In 1980, Oman was the leading spender among developing countries, with a military budget equal to 24.6 percent of its GNP. By comparison, U.S. military spending amounted to 5.5 percent of its GNP.[10]

Exports and Imports of Armaments

The world trade in conventional arms (measured in constant prices) more than tripled between 1960 and 1980.[11] On the export side, in 1980 the NATO countries originated somewhat more than half (53.2 percent) of the export volume, and the Warsaw Pact countries originated 38.8 percent, according to U.S. government figures.[12] Arms exports by non-NATO and non-Warsaw Pact countries have risen, as well. However, exports from these sources were still under 10 percent of the total in 1980.[13] Figure NS.4 summarizes information on arms transfers.

By 1978, Third World nations accounted for three-fourths of world arms imports.

On the import side, Third World nations accounted for less than half of arms imports in 1960, but by 1978 accounted for three-fourths of the volume.[14] In some of the more advanced nations, a growing domestic arms-production capability is augmenting the imports.[15] According to the United States Arms Control and Disarmament Agency, the value of arms and military equipment produced in the Third World more than quintupled during the 1970s: from less than $1 billion in 1970 to over $5 billion in 1979.[16]

Military Training Programs

Both the United States and the USSR offer extensive military-training programs to their allies in Third World nations. According to an article in *Defense 82*, in 1981 about 10,100 foreign military personnel were trained in the United States, and about 11,400 were trained in the USSR.[17]

FIGURE NS.1. WORLD MILITARY EXPENDITURES (1908–1976)

$ Billions (Constant 1973)

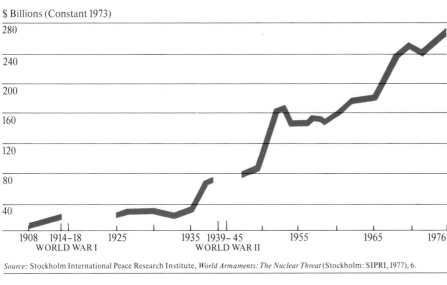

Source: Stockholm International Peace Research Institute, *World Armaments: The Nuclear Threat* (Stockholm: SIPRI, 1977), 6.

FIGURE NS.2. WORLD MILITARY EXPENDITURES (1972–1984)

■ World   ■ Developed   ■ Developing

$ Billions (Current)   Ratio Scale*

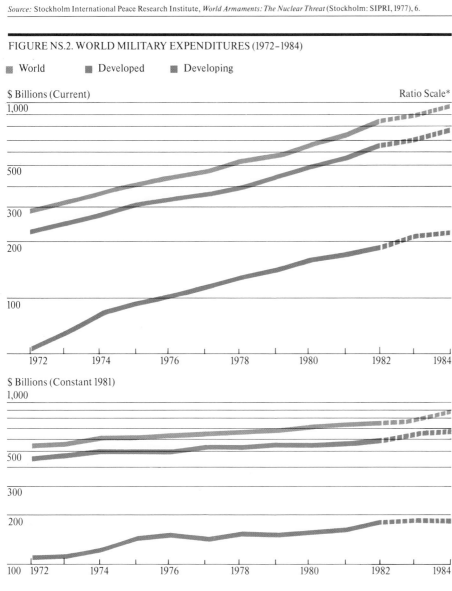

$ Billions (Constant 1981)

*On a ratio (or semilog) scale, an equal slope anywhere on the chart means an equal growth rate.

Source: U.S. Arms Control and Disarmament Agency, *World Military Expenditures and Arms Transfers, 1972–1982,* ACDA Publication 117, April 1984, 2.

This chart shows the changes in regional spending that underlie overall world trends. Growth in military budgets has been pronounced in the Middle East and, to a lesser degree, in Africa.

FIGURE NS.3. MILITARY EXPENDITURES BY REGION (1972–1982)

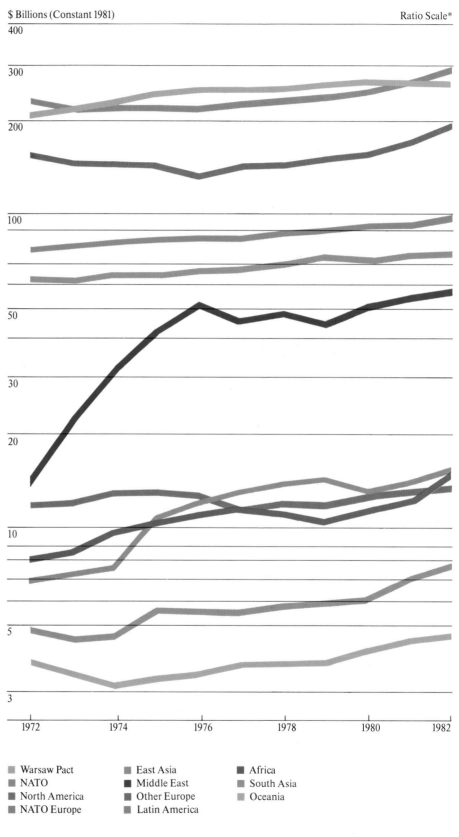

$ Billions (Constant 1981) Ratio Scale*

Warsaw Pact · East Asia · Africa
NATO · Middle East · South Asia
North America · Other Europe · Oceania
NATO Europe · Latin America

* On a ratio (or semilog) scale, an equal slope anywhere on the chart means an equal growth rate.

Source: U.S. Arms Control and Disarmament Agency, *World Military Expenditures and Arms Transfers, 1972–1982,* ACDA Publication 117, April 1984, 2.

FIGURE NS.4. WORLD ARMS TRANSFERS (1971 and 1980)

$ Billions (1979)

| 1971 Recipient Region | 1971 Supplying Country | 1980 Recipient Region | 1980 Supplying Country |

a. Other[a] **e.** Far East **i.** China **m.** Czech.
b. Africa[b] **f.** Middle East/N. Africa **j.** USSR **n.** W. Germany
c. L. America **g.** Developed Countries **k.** U.S. **o.** U.K.
d. S. Asia **h.** Other[c] **l.** Italy **p.** France

a. Albania, Bulgaria, Cyprus, Fiji, Papua-New Guinea, Portugal, Romania, Turkey, and Yugoslavia.
b. Excluding countries of North Africa (Algeria, Egypt, Libya, Mauritania, Morocco, Sudan, and Tunisia).
c. Other suppliers, supplying 2% or more of the market in 1971 included Canada, the United Kingdom, Poland, France, and West Germany.
Note: "Arms transfers" indicates actual deliveries (through either sales or aid), as distinguished from sales orders, contracts, or agreements, or the value of aid programs that may result in a future transfer of goods. The data include deliveries of military equipment only; they do not include the value of training, technical and other services, and consumables.

Source: Overseas Development Council, *U.S. Foreign Policy and the Third World: Agenda 1983* (New York: Praeger, 1983), 266.

FIGURE NS.5. SHARES OF WORLD ARMS IMPORTS (1982)

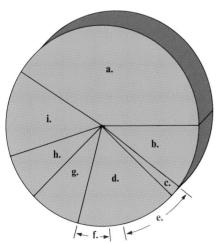

a. Middle East 41.9%
b. East Asia 9.8%
c. North America 1.9%
d. All Europe 18.3%
e. NATO 11.4%
f. Warsaw Pact 6.1%
g. Latin America 7.6%
h. South Asia and Oceania 5.5%
i. Africa 14.9%

Source: U.S. Arms Control and Disarmament Agency, *World Military Expenditures and Arms Transfers, 1972–1982,* ACDA Publication 117, April 1984, 6.

Schools of Thought on National Security

What should be the size of military budgets and how effectively are military funds being used?

In this chapter's presentation of schools of thought and points of view, we devote special attention to people who address issues of national-security policy from the vantage point of the United States. For example, we present the opinion of those who criticize the military expenditures of the United States but not of the Soviet Union. Similarly, it is largely the proponents of the United States' national-security policy, rather than spokespersons for the Soviet Union, who are called upon to present their cases. We have taken this approach because most of the policy debate in this country reflects this emphasis.

The fundamental questions involve the size of military budgets, alternative uses for the money, and the effectiveness of military establishments. Costs are a particularly significant issue because of the great disparity between funding for development (food, education, and so forth) versus funding for the military.

Proponents of reduced military spending include not only those who favor reallocating military funds in order to end hunger, but also those who favor reallocations to other purposes. Still other advocates are simply opposed to military spending as a matter of general principle. All these critics question both the effectiveness and the size of military establishments. They offer evidence that large military forces add little to real peace or security.

Advocates of high levels of military spending often argue that the size of military budgets should be determined by "what is needed" to protect the nation. They believe that before hunger can end, we must have a peaceful and secure world. They tend to be deeply concerned about geopolitical and strategic questions, in particular about threats to world security posed by the Soviet Union and its allies. In their view, the United States plays a special role in maintaining peace and stability, because no other nation has the power to counter the perceived Soviet threat and to maintain the balance of power. Third World nations need strong military forces, otherwise their governments will not be able to maintain internal stability and territorial integrity. Hunger often increases amidst the chaos and social upheaval that accompany revolutions. Therefore, unless nations are internally stable and free from external threats, policies to end hunger will not succeed.

School of Thought: Too Much Money Is Being Spent on the Military; Priorities Must Be Reordered If Hunger Is to End

As already noted, proponents of this school of thought question military spending from several points of view. They hold that military budgets could be reallocated to other, more beneficial projects. They question the relationship between large military forces and real security. Finally, they express doubts about the benefits of military assistance to the people of Third World nations.

Point of View Number 1

Money Now Spent on Military Forces Could Liberally Fund Projects to End Hunger and Otherwise Improve the Quality of Life

The Brandt Commission report is often cited in support of this point of view. Here is a brief excerpt:

Our survival depends not only on military balance, but on global cooperation to ensure a sustainable biological environment, and sustainable prosperity based on equitably shared resources. Much of the insecurity in the world is connected with the divisions between rich and poor countries—grave injustice and mass starvation causing additional instability. Yet the research and the funds which could help to put an end to poverty and hunger are now pre-empted by military uses. The threatening arsenals grow, and spending on other purposes which could make them less necessary is neglected. If military expenditures can be controlled and some of the savings related to development, the world's security can be increased, and the mass of mankind currently excluded from a decent life can have a brighter future.[18]

The Brandt Commission also makes specific comparisons between military and nonmilitary spending alternatives:

1. *The military expenditure of only half a day would suffice to finance the whole malaria eradication programme of the World Health Organization, and less would be needed to conquer river-blindness, which is still the scourge of millions.*

2. *A modern tank costs about one million dollars; that amount could improve storage facilities for 100,000 tons of rice and thus save 4000 tons or more annually: one person can live on just over a pound of rice a day. The same sum of money could provide 1000 classrooms for 30,000 children.*

3. *For the price of one jet fighter (20 million dollars) one could set up about 40,000 village pharmacies.*

4. *One-half of one per cent of one year's world military expenditure would pay for all the farm equipment needed to increase food production and approach self-sufficiency in food-deficit low-income countries by 1990.*[19]

Economist Murray Weidenbaum discusses the effect of large military budgets on the domestic economy. Weidenbaum, a former chief economist of the Boeing Corporation, a frequent contributor to publications of the American Enterprise Institute for Public Policy Research, and chairman of President Reagan's Council of Economic Advisors from January 1981 through August 1982, is an expert on the economics of military spending. He writes:

The costs of defense are usually described in so many billions of dollars. They can more meaningfully be expressed in thousands of men and women pulled away (voluntarily or otherwise) from civilian pursuits, millions of man-years of industrial effort, millions of barrels of oil pumped from the earth, and thousands of square yards of planet space filled with equipment and debris. In short, the real cost of military activities should be measured in human and natural resources and in the stocks of productive capital absorbed in producing, transporting, and maintaining weapons and other military equipment.

It is in the sense of alternative opportunities lost that military spending should be considered—the numbers of people employed by the military, the goods and services it purchases from the private sector, the real estate it ties up, and the technology devoted to it. Not only do we lose the opportunity for civilian use of goods and services, but we also lose the potential economic growth that these resources might have brought about.

For example, the production of a missile, which will eventually be exploded or buried, may entail the same amount of economic activity as the production of machinery for a factory producing new railroad cars, which will continue to enhance the nation's productive capacity.[20]

The views of Inga Thorsson, whose experience is based on service in the Swedish parliament and the foreign ministry, coincide with those of the Brandt Commission and Weidenbaum. Thorsson believes that military budgets should be reallocated

The costs of defense…can more meaningfully be expressed in thousands of men and women pulled away…from civilian pursuits.

to the task of ending poverty, and that the claim that military spending fosters economic growth is specious. Her article, excerpted below, is aptly titled, "The Arms Race and Development: A Competitive Relationship."

Common sense alone tells us that military preparations are an economic burden. The arms race and development are to be viewed in a competitive relationship, particularly in terms of resources. Or to put it another way: the arms race and underdevelopment are not two problems; they are one. They must be solved together, or neither will ever be solved.

It is a historical fact that governments have, over the past 30 years, spent vast resources on armaments, resources which—on grounds of morality, on grounds of equal human justice, on grounds of enlightened self-interest—ought to have been directed to ending world poverty and building for human and material development. In this way world armaments are among the causes of poverty and underdevelopment....

Military spending inhibits the capital investment required for development.

Military expenditures do not foster growth. Through their inflationary effects... and the general economic and political malaise to which they contribute, military spending inhibits the capital investment required for development. Through the drain on the most valuable research talents and funds, it restrains productivity gains and distorts growth in science and technology. The military sector is not a great provider of jobs. On the contrary it is shown that military spending is one of the least efficient kinds of public spending. It drains away funds that could relieve poverty and distress. The very nature of military spending heightens tensions, reduces security and underpins the system which makes even more arms necessary.[21]

Amadou-Mahtar M'Bow, director-general of UNESCO, is a historian and educator who grew up in a rural village in the Sahel region of Senegal. Like many Third World leaders, M'Bow is deeply concerned about the arms race, which he sees as damaging the development prospects of Third World nations. Reallocating military budgets, he says, could change the face of the earth:

If only a proportion of the material and human resources devoted to preparation for war were assigned to the cause of development, it would suffice to change the face of the earth, lessen the widening gulf between rich and poor countries, and reduce the areas of poverty which continue to exist in many industrialized countries. A great number of essential activities, in the fields of nutrition, health, literacy, the development of education, the training of scientific and technological personnel, the establishment of research centres, cultural development, and the safeguarding of the environment, are curbed or even blocked, solely for lack of material resources. This in turn aggravates inequalities, and brings about new situations of tension....

The arms race is not only fraught with the most terrible danger to human life; it also determines investment choices and sets a premium on economic structures which, having become essential to the life of nations, subsequently make it all the more difficult to carry out the conversion of the arms industry to non-military activities.[22]

Point of View Number 2

The Relationship between "National Security" and Large Military Forces Must Be Questioned

The people who support reallocating military spending to development needs question the relationship between "national security" and large military forces. From this perspective, there is a need to challenge commonly held assumptions

FIGURE NS.6. HOW MUCH EXPLOSIVE POWER DO WE HAVE?

"The arms race is . . . fraught with the most terrible danger to human life. . . ." Graphics like this are used by opponents of military spending and nuclear weapons to emphasize the dangers to humanity posed by the arms race. The chart shows the world's current firepower compared with the firepower of World War II.

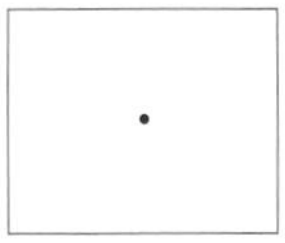

The single dot in this square represents all the firepower of World War II: 3 megatons.

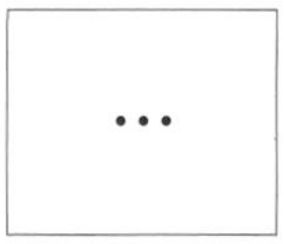

The three dots in this square represent the destructive power of the weapons on just one Poseidon submarine: nine megatons. This is equal to the firepower of three World War IIs and enough to destroy over 200 of the Soviet Union's largest cities. The United States has thirty-one such subs and ten similar Polaris subs.

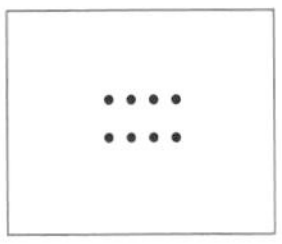

This square, enclosing 24 megatons, represents one new Trident submarine with the firepower of eight World War IIs. This is enough firepower to destroy every major city in the northern hemisphere.

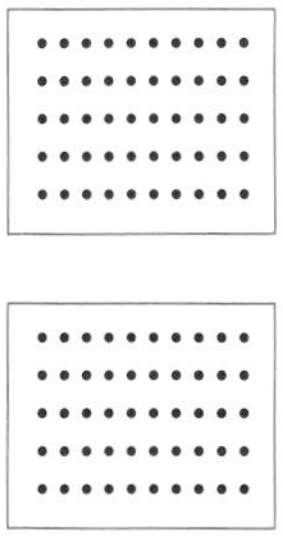

These two squares (300 megatons) represent enough firepower to destroy all the large and medium-size cities in the entire world. The present nuclear arsenal is about 18,000 megatons, which equals 6,000 World War IIs; the United States and the Soviet Union share this firepower with approximately equal destructive capability.

Source: Jim Geier, Burlington, VT, 1981.

about what national security really means. One person who holds this view is Thomas Wilson, a former member of the U.S. State Department. The following excerpt comes from an essay that was prepared for United States President Jimmy Carter's Commission on World Hunger.

By habit we think of national security in terms of military forces and capabilities....

But national security has another face. It means a capacity to live in peace....

The most promising initiative for reversing the current drift into deeper crisis is seen to be a sustained attack on the quintessential symbol of human poverty: chronic malnutrition....

The relevance of world hunger to increased security ... is the opportunity it offers for visible and positive political action.

The relevance of world hunger to increased security, then, is the opportunity it offers for visible and positive political action to enhance the world's capacity to live in peace by resolving contemporary world problems. Underlying this relationship is an historic convergence of two sets of interests with dramatic potential for human affairs: Political action to relieve global problems simultaneously serves both the interests of national security and the interests of people—collectively and individually....

Public perception of the direct connection between world hunger and national security could be the wellspring for that extra measure of political will needed to overcome hunger and get on with the rest of the global agenda as well.[23]

Next, Robert McNamara focuses on the statistical relationship between underdevelopment and violence. McNamara wrote *The Essence of Security,* excerpted here, shortly after his resignation in 1968 as United States secretary of defense. It was part of a set of "reflections in office," and it shows the new directions he would initiate during his thirteen years as president of the World Bank. Although he believed that statistical analysis must be used with caution, he concluded that "security is development," and used the following figures as evidence:

The rich nations...possess 75 percent of the world's wealth, though roughly only 25 percent of the world's population. Since 1958 only one of these 27 nations has suffered a major internal upheaval on its own territory....

Since 1958, 87 percent of the very poor nations, 69 percent of the poor nations and 48 percent of the middle-income nations suffered serious violence. There can be no question but that there is a relationship between violence and economic backwardness....

Our security is related directly to the security of the newly developing world....

Security is development, and without development there can be no security.[24]

Issue analyst Lane Vanderslice makes a similar point in a background paper written for Bread for the World. The purpose of this Washington-based lobby is to influence United States public policy related to hunger; thus it initiated a campaign in the fall of 1983 to pass a "Human Needs and World Security Bill," which is intended to redirect security (military) assistance to development assistance.[25] Vanderslice wrote his paper, "Real Security in an Insecure World," to support this proposed legislation.

"Security"...is "the state or feeling of being free from fear, care, danger, etc."

"Security," Webster's dictionary says, is "the state or feeling of being free from fear, care, danger, etc." "Development," it says, is "a stage of growth."

"Security aid," on the other hand, is aid the U.S. government gives to foreign regimes, usually to help them purchase U.S.-made weapons. Some "development aid" is designed to bring health, clean drinking water, agricultural skills and other self-help tools to people of the Third World.

Development aid, ironically, often contributes to the security of the world, while security aid often undermines it.

Three years ago, U.S. security aid to foreign governments was almost equal to U.S. development aid. Since then, security aid has been increased by 73 percent and has become the fastest-growing part of the U.S. budget; development aid has grown by only 10 percent, barely enough to keep up with inflation.

But, contributing to efforts that help a country's poor people overcome poverty is an essential part of that country's security. An overarmed country is not truly secure if its people are poor and malnourished. By helping poor people obtain basic needs, a contribution is made to the <u>real</u> security of a nation. The U.S. will strengthen its own security by contributing to development assistance since hunger and poverty are major sources of social unrest in the world today.[26]

Point of View Number 3

Military Assistance to Developing Nations Does Not Necessarily Benefit the People of Those Nations

The following quotation from the Committee on Poverty and the Arms Trade describes a mythical Third World nation, Magweta, where the effects of military aid are both costly and pernicious:

After World War II Magweta finds itself with a small foreign exchange surplus and rudimentary armed forces and police force. The country's economy is based on agriculture, predominantly small farms run by one family, but also including a few large estates primarily producing cash crops for export. A civilian political grouping has recently come to power with a policy of rapid industrial development, basing its appeal on nationalistic sentiment among the people.

To transform the country the ruling group starts to import large quantities of machinery including small amounts of arms, although the cost of the latter is reduced by a grant of military aid from a Western power. Many of the ruling group have been educated in the West and have acquired a Western lifestyle; they set the pace by purchasing cars, radios, and similar luxuries which others in the higher echelons then seek to acquire. The politicians make patriotic speeches which justify the expansion and re-equipping of the military.

After a few years the foreign exchange position has seriously deteriorated and a loan is obtained from the IMF. Exports are encouraged and a major effort is made to expand the production of cash crops through the use of improved agricultural techniques. Selective restrictions are placed on imports in order to stimulate local production but arms imports continue to increase.

Although there is a short-term improvement helped by some direct foreign investment, a steady decline in the price of cash crop exports, relative to manufactured imports, results in a second application for a loan. This is granted on condition that the currency is devalued and import restrictions removed. At the same time government expenditure must be reduced and a suitable climate created for foreign investment. This the government reluctantly accedes to.

FIGURE NS.7. THE POVERTY-REPRESSION-MILITARIZATION CYCLE IN THIRD WORLD NATIONS

Purchase of Arms and Luxuries

Lack of Foreign Exchange

Repression and Concentration of Power and Wealth in the Hands of the Elite

International Loans; Policies for Increasing Exports

Loss of Food Production for Local Consumption and Impoverishment of the Society

Revolt; Political Opposition

Source: Committee on Poverty and the Arms Trade, "Magweta or How Does the Arms Trade Affect Development?" *Development: Seeds of Change* 1 (1982): 35.

The result of this policy is the destruction of embryonic local industry as large foreign concerns, relying heavily on advertising and the lure of the Western image, flood the markets. Several large tracts of land, some of which were previously farmed under the traditional system, are bought up by a few individuals and firms and converted to produce more crops for export. Employment in traditional agriculture stagnates, and the most vigorous young people leave the land to move into the urban areas where most of the wealth is concentrated. Rural society declines and shanty towns grow in the shadow of the westernised cities.

Living conditions deteriorate for the bulk of the population and political unrest breaks out in the poorer areas of the cities. The president declares an emergency and has the opposition suppressed. Union leaders and political opponents are arrested and detained without trial, students are attacked and several newspapers closed down as censorship is introduced. The gap between the rich and the poor widens. Those who have "made it"—the richer farmers, senior civil servants, army officers and the handful able to obtain managerial positions in the new foreign-owned factories—enjoy a high and rising standard of living, along with the substantial expatriate community brought in by the multinational corporations and aid programmes.

As the division between rich and poor becomes more apparent,... violence—both criminal and political—increases.

As the division between rich and poor becomes more apparent, with the number of urban unemployed rising rapidly and conditions in the rural areas worsening, violence—both criminal and political—increases. The richer groups take to barring their windows and hiring private security guards, and there is a growing clamour for "law and order." The military and para-military forces are expanded and armed with newly imported weaponry, while foreign advisors come to train them in "counter insurgency." Occasional attempts at reform are opposed by the military and by pressure from outside interests.

Eventually the existing government is ousted and a more forceful, military-backed grouping takes over political power. With the industrial section of the economy expanding but earlier loans falling due, yet another overseas loan is applied for and obtained. In return there is a relaxation of the laws governing the repatriation of profits and a guarantee that "law and order" will be maintained and foreign business interests protected. With a military aid package forming part of the loan agreement, massive orders are placed for new armaments, including tanks and other major arms, so that the armed forces can be expanded and "brought up to date." One result of this is an increase in arms purchases by two neighbouring countries as they observe the continuing militarisation of Magweta. The ground-work for a local arms race has been laid.

At this point the burden of the grotesquely expanded military on the economy is enormous and over 30% of all imports are armaments. The government spends more on the armed forces than on education or health. In addition a great deal more is spent on "civilian" projects directly related to the increasing militarisation of society, such as roads capable of carrying tanks and new airstrips. Meanwhile strikes in the towns and military reprisals in the countryside against suspected opposition plays havoc with production of food and other necessities of life.

In development terms, poverty and all its attendant miseries have been increased, despite the annual increase in GNP. Unemployment is up to around 30%, millions live in urban squalor without proper housing, food, clean water, or sanitation. Many more—the majority—live in varying degrees of rural poverty. Civil and political rights have become non-existent and the whole society is caught in a disastrous cycle maintained only by naked force and the systematic use of torture. The poverty-repression-militarisation cycle is well under way.

Clearly this is a simplified description of the "under-development" process taking place, but its essential elements hold true for a number of Third World countries, particularly those in Latin America and Southeast Asia. [27]

For Muzammel Huq, director of the Institute for the Study of Rural Resources in Bangladesh, the fiction of Magweta is a reality. Here is how he expresses his general concerns about the effects of military assistance:

Perhaps the time has come for every nation to re-examine the whole concept of national security. Whose security is being defended, that of an economic or political class, or that of the entire population of the country? Wages are kept down and cheap labour enclaves maintained, strikes are prevented and supplies of raw material are obtained from the Third World at low prices, all in the name of national security. This is a dangerous concept which must be abandoned.

Militarization of the police and of paramilitary organizations is going ahead at a tremendous pace in the Third World today. And this militarization is required to support the internal power structure and to maintain the status quo within various developing countries. [28]

Frances Moore Lappé and her colleagues also point to a Magweta-like reality. They write:

Few realize that the U.S. government, through more than a dozen channels, gives economic and military assistance to regimes that it identifies as serving its interest. None of these channels are considered part of our foreign assistance. Yet their impact on the lives of the vast majority of people in the Third World is both more sweeping and profound.

Probably more than through aid or direct coup d'etat interventions—such as Iran (1953), Guatemala (1954), the Dominican Republic (1965) and Cambodia (1970)—the U.S. government influences what goes on in numerous countries by propping up regimes through non-aid economic channels and through military assistance and sales. The U.S. government invariably uses such power to support economic and political "stability." In many countries "stability" means maintaining a situation in which the majority are deprived of basic human needs and rights. For this reason, U.S. influence in many cases is opposed to the well-being of the poor majority....

But genuine development requires that the poor and their allies organize to achieve a more equitable sharing in control over resources. It is precisely such popular efforts that our military aid helps to suppress. [29]

School of Thought: Reducing Military Spending in the United States and in Third World Nations Would Ultimately Set Back Efforts to End Hunger; a Strong United States Defense Establishment and Military Assistance to Allies Who Need It Must Be the Highest Priority

In this school of thought, we look at the opinions of those who favor high levels of military spending. Although the experts and lay people who hold this view think that a strong United States defense establishment and military assistance to allies are important ingredients in ending hunger, they generally do not include this point as a major theme in their argument. Rather, they present national security as a matter of the highest priority and suggest that once this goal is achieved, other social benefits will follow.

The Soviet Threat Requires a Strong U.S. Military Establishment

In the view of those who advocate a strong military establishment, the perceived threat posed by the Soviet Union is the major issue. U.S. President Ronald Reagan emphasized this in a 1981 speech to Congress:

I believe that my duty as President requires that I recommend increases in defense spending over the coming years. I know that you're all aware— but I think it bears saying again— that since 1970 the Soviet Union has invested $300 billion more in its military forces than we have. As a result of its massive military buildup, the Soviets have made a significant numerical advantage in strategic nuclear delivery systems, tactical aircraft, submarines, artillery, and anti-aircraft defense. To allow this imbalance to continue is a threat to our national security.[30]

Journalist Norman Podhoretz expresses his concern for human rights. He sees communism as a threat to individuals as well as nations, and he alleges that communist regimes perpetrate conditions in which human suffering, including hunger, flourishes:

A word also needs to be said about the obstacle posed by Communism—again, whether or not allied to the Soviet Union—to the development of institutions under which human rights can flourish. Human rights have invariably fared worse under Communism than under the regimes it has replaced. Are the Cubans today better off than they were under Batista? Ask the many thousands who have already left and the countless others who are clamoring to get out. Are the South Vietnamese better off under the rule of the North than they were under Thieu? Ask the boat people. Are the Cambodians better off as Kampucheans? Ask the grave. These are the most hideous illustrations of the rule, but it is important to understand that the horrors perpetrated by the Communists in power are not accidental or arbitrary. They follow from the totalitarian nature of Communist regimes.[31]

The United States Must Shield Weaker Nations from Soviet Aggression

Some advocates of the high-defense-level school of thought feel that the United States should also shield weaker nations from what they regard as Soviet aggression. Former President Nixon is one who represents this point of view:

Now some might ask, what is wrong with being second? Isn't it jingoistic and nationalistic for the United States always to have to be number one?

The answer to that question is that the day the United States becomes the second strongest nation in the world, peace and freedom will be in deadly jeopardy everywhere in the world.

We do not seek power for its own sake. What we seek is the assurance that our survival and that of other free nations will never be threatened by some other nation whose intentions are less peaceful than ours, and whose military forces are more powerful than those of the United States.

History has taught us again and again that war is caused not by the strength of one nation alone, but by the weakness of one nation in relation to another....

Strength and resolution command respect. They are an incentive for negotiation leading to peace. But weakness and naive sentimentality breed contempt. They are an open invitation to pressure tactics and aggression leading to war.[32]

278

Americans should not feel guilty about expanding their power in the world, according to Samuel P. Huntington, who, at the time of this quotation, had been a member of the faculty at Harvard's Center for International Affairs since 1964. Historically, the expansion of American power has benefited the human race.

The United States is, in practice, the freest, most liberal, most democratic country in the world with far better institutionalized protections for the rights of its citizens than any other society. As a consequence, any increase in the power or influence of the United States in world affairs generally results—not inevitably, but far more often than not—in the promotion of liberty and human rights in the world. The expansion of American power is not synonymous with the expansion of liberty, but a significant correlation exists between the rise and fall of American power in the world and the rise and fall of liberty and democracy in the world....

In the early 1960s Latin America became the focus of large-scale economic aid programs, military training and assistance programs, propaganda efforts, and repeated attention by the President and other high-level American officials. Under the Alliance for Progress, American power was to be used to promote and sustain democratic government and greater social equity in the rest of the Western Hemisphere. This high point in the exercise of United States power in Latin America coincided with the high point of democracy in Latin America. This period witnessed "the Twilight of the Tyrants": it was the age in which at one point all but one of the ten South American countries (Paraguay) had some semblance of democratic government.[33]

To understand fully the rationale for United States foreign and military policy during the Nixon and Ford administrations (1968–1976), we must look at the views of Henry Kissinger. The former United States secretary of state emphasizes the importance of maintaining the balance of power as a foundation for peace and progress. In his view, a strong military establishment and its judicious use in international affairs are essential:

The peace we seek...must rest on something more tangible than a hope or a fear of holocaust. It must also reflect a military and geopolitical equilibrium. The notion of balance of power has always been unfashionable in America. But it is the precondition of security, and even of progress. If the mere avoidance of conflict becomes our overriding objective, and if our own military power is disparaged, the international system will be at the mercy of the most ruthless....

The United States must proceed simultaneously on three fronts:

First, we must maintain a military balance that does not tempt aggression against our friends or allies, against our vital interests, or in the extreme case against ourselves.

Secondly, beyond resisting naked aggression, we have a stake in the principle that political or economic pressure, or military or terrorist blackmail, should not become the arbiter of the world's political disputes. The geopolitical equilibrium must be maintained lest radical forces hostile to the West gain such momentum that they appear as the irresistible wave of the future.

And thirdly, on the basis of a balance thus achieved and preserved, we must be ready to explore routes to genuine peaceful coexistence. The great powers, having learned that they cannot dominate one another, must practice moderation and ultimately cooperation. The creativity of a world of diversity and peaceful competition can be the basis of unparalleled human progress. A stable balance is the

Historically, the expansion of American power has benefited the human race.

The peace we seek...must rest on something more tangible than a hope or a fear of holocaust.

most hopeful—perhaps the only—basis for the control and ultimately the reduction of weapons of mass destruction.

The quests for security and for peace are inseparable.

Too often these requirements are posed in the alternative. But the quests for security and for peace are inseparable; we cannot achieve one without the other. No democracy can court conflict. Our government will have support in resisting challenges to our vital interests only if confrontation is seen to have been unavoidable. Our people have a right to expect of their government that it will explore all avenues to a genuine peace. And our allies will insist on it.[34]

Paul Dietrich addresses America's moral responsibilities in leadership. Dietrich was president of Citizens for Reagan, the largest independent campaign committee supporting President Reagan in the 1980 elections, as well as president of the Washington-based John Davis Lodge Center for International Studies. He is currently publisher and editor in chief of *Saturday Review* magazine. The following statement reveals his specific concern with defending United States policy in Central America:

America's concern for El Salvador, Central America and the Caribbean is a morally acceptable, legitimate undertaking. History demonstrates with a clarity that is irresistible, that no matter how ill-fed, ill-clothed, no matter how illiterate or how miserable people have been under their traditional governments, they will be more miserable under Communist governments.

The fact is that Communism and Marxist-Leninist governments make things worse, not better. Communism, when it arrives at political power, does not produce an economic order that can support a population. It does not produce a social system that provides equal opportunity, or a good life for everyone. It simply does not work as a humane system. Everybody understands that the number of refugees which pour out of Communist countries decade after decade proves the inhumanity of the system and its incompatibility with human survival and human realizations.

The last reason why it is morally acceptable for the U.S. to participate in the problems of this area and their solutions is that the strength of the United States is inextricably and inevitably involved with the defense of freedom in present times. When the U.S. protects its own national security, it is, in fact, engaging in a morally acceptable enterprise.[35]

Point of View Number 3

Third World Nations Need Strong Military Forces to Protect Themselves from Outside Threats

To advocates of a strong military posture, the view that Third World nations can work out their own destinies, without protection from external threats, is naive.

Alexander Haig, former secretary of state in President Ronald Reagan's Administration, makes this viewpoint clear in testimony given at his confirmation hearings:

[Our long term objectives are] the eradication of hunger, poverty, and disease; the expansion of the free flow of people, goods, and ideas; the spread of social justice; and through these and similar efforts, the improvement of the human condition....These desirable and critical objectives are impossible to achieve in an international environment dominated by violence, terrorism, and threat.[36]

In a 1981 United States Department of State policy paper on Central America and the Caribbean, Thomas O. Enders expresses a similar view:

280

First, we will help threatened countries to defend themselves. Once insurgents take arms with outside support, there is no alternative to an armed response....

Second, we will help threatened countries to preserve their people's right to self-determination: political and social progress—the involvement of broader sections of the public in decisionmaking through legitimate elections, or the carrying out of appropriate land reforms, or containment of violence from whatever quarter—must go hand in hand with military assistance.

Third, we will help countries...to achieve economic success. However well they do against the armed threat, genuine stability can only be based on economic prosperity.[37]

Latin America, especially El Salvador, provides the latest testing ground for a policy whose premise is that both external and internal forces are influential in creating revolutionary situations. According to this policy, the United States should provide counterbalancing forces wherever communist countries are contributing to a revolutionary situation. The report of the National Bipartisan Commission on Central America, chaired by Henry Kissinger, explains the rationale for this policy:

Major Themes

The crisis in Central America is acute. Its roots are indigenous—in poverty, injustice and closed political systems. But world economic recession and Cuban-Soviet-Nicaraguan intervention brought it to a head.

The crisis will not wait. It must be addressed at once and simultaneously in all its aspects. Ultimate resolutions depend on economic progress, social and political reform. But insurgencies must be checked if lasting progress is to be made on these fronts.

Indigenous reform, even indigenous revolution, is no threat to the U.S. But the intrusion of outside powers exploiting local grievances for political and strategic advantage is a serious threat. Objective of U.S. policy should be to reduce Central American conflicts to Central American dimensions.

United States has fundamental interests at stake: Soviet-Cuban success and resulting collapse of Central America would compel substantial increase in our security burden or redeployment of forces to detriment of vital interests elsewhere....

Central Americans desperately need our help and we have a moral obligation to provide it. The U.S. and other nations can make a difference. But in the end solutions will depend on the efforts of Central Americans themselves....

Security Issues

In El Salvador there are two separate conflicts: (1) between those seeking democratic reform and those seeking to retain their privileges; (2) between Marxist-Leninist guerrillas and those who oppose Marxism-Leninism.

In discussing the latter we identify three general propositions about such guerrilla movements:

Political and social progress must go hand in hand with military assistance.

281

1. They depend on external support. Without it they are unlikely to succeed.

2. They develop their own momentum which reform alone cannot stop.

3. Victorious, they create totalitarian regimes, even though they have enlisted support of democratic elements in order to project democratic, reformist image.

External support comes from Soviet Union, Cuba and now Nicaragua. Cuba has developed into a leading military power through Soviet assistance. Since Sandinista victory, Soviets have come around to support Cuban strategy of armed road to power in Central America.[38]

Point of View Number 4

Well-Funded Military-Assistance Programs Help Developing Nations Build Internal Security and Stability

Proponents of this view often reject the opinions of those who are concerned about repression by the military. They feel that the United States, with its long history of stability, has a totally different situation from that of developing nations. Therefore, the standards that Americans apply to their government may not be applicable to other parts of the world.

Soedjatmoko, a scholar and Indonesian political leader, recognizes that the Third World has different factors to consider. He is sensitive to the problems faced by developing nations in striking a reasonable balance between freedom and order:

Especially in those countries in which there is in the political culture no tradition of legitimate dissent, the absolute priority to development given by developmental governments strengthens their inclination to look at criticism or dissent as obstruction of a legitimate and unobjectionable enterprise. Dissent, therefore, is treated as subversion rather than as a way in which society ensures the best possible consideration of the largest range of policy options....In addition, it was often found necessary for the state itself to handle some of the larger and urgent economic development tasks, either in the absence of a strong, experienced private entrepreneurial class or, in some cases, because of ideological preferences....

Development can take place under conditions of order and stability.

Also, it is under conditions of order and stability that the political institutionalization necessary for the perpetuation of the state and the safeguarding of the continuity of the development effort can take place....

These perceptions of order and stability merged with concepts of national security which were shaped by earlier experiences of sometimes long wars of independence, post-independence external threats, secession movements, and other forms of civil strife, including subversion and insurgency. These have made nation building, national integration and unity a constant preoccupation. It might be useful at this point also to remind ourselves that the U.S.A. was barely nine years old when Congress passed the "infamous" Alien and Sedition Acts, which introduced a system of terror into the country.[39]

Julius Nyerere, another leader with practical experience in nation building, echoes this theme. The tasks of building nations and meeting basic human needs, he believes, require unity and stability:

Once the first free government is formed, its supreme task lies ahead—the building up of the country's economy so as to raise the living standards of the people, the eradication of disease and the banishment of ignorance and superstition. This, no less than the struggle against colonialism, calls for the maximum united effort *by the whole country if it is to succeed. <u>There can be no room for difference or division.</u>*

In Western democracies it is an accepted practice that in times of emergency opposition parties sink their differences and join together in forming a national government. <u>This is our time of emergency</u>, and until our war against poverty, ignorance and disease has been won—we should not let our unity be destroyed by a desire to follow somebody else's "book of rules."[40]

Paul Dietrich feels that revolutions often slow down the development process, exacerbating poverty and human suffering rather than remedying them. Therefore, the United States should support governments that are threatened by revolution. In support of this view, Dietrich points to some hard, practical realities:

As [Crane Brinton] demonstrated in his careful study of modern revolution; revolutions, in fact, take place not when things become worse and worse until they reach a point where people can no longer stand them. Revolutions take place at a time when things are getting better. They take place when regimes are less repressive, when people are less miserable and when there are rising expectations and changing views about government, society and economic distribution.

Revolutions are not caused by social injustice although social injustice is not a good thing. Revolutions are caused by revolutionaries. Revolutionaries are people. They are not social forces. They are people with guns. Revolutions are caused by violence and terrorism. They are brought about by popular fronts. In Central America and El Salvador revolutionaries utilize the instruments of terror to destroy the already weak societies and institutions of government and undermine the already weak bases of order in that society.

Revolutions are not caused by social injustice.... Revolutions are caused by revolutionaries.

Governments like that of El Salvador are especially vulnerable to terrorist subversion for three reasons. First, because up until the recent elections, they were not chosen by the people, none of them had any persuasive claim to have a popular mandate for their program.

Second, in a society where order is the central value, the inability for the government to maintain order becomes, in itself, a reason for abandoning the government. If a government cannot govern and there is no alternative claim to legitimacy then any claim to legitimacy is lost.

Therefore, the weaker the government institution becomes and the more central the value of order becomes, the more vulnerable the entire government becomes if it is not able to maintain order.

That is exactly what terrorism does—it destroys the ordinary cause of life in the society.[41]

Andrew K. Semmel, a foreign affairs specialist with the United States Defense Security Assistance Agency, responds to critics of the military-assistance program:

In the conduct of United States foreign and defense policy, few programs have evoked as much controversy or been characterized by as much misperception as our security assistance program. Conversely, few programs have generated as many positive contributions to our national security or as many improvements to global stability as the security assistance we have provided to other countries....

Foreign Military Sales are not inherently destabilizing or evil, and United States arms sold abroad are rarely used in conflict; they have had a far more important role in deterring conflict, as in Korea. Therefore, we need to inform and better explain our security assistance to the American public and to the Congress which represents it, if we hope to further our foreign and defense objectives. The quality of United States foreign policy and the improvement of our defense posture, in no small way, may be dependent on the success of this effort.[42]

Point of View Number 5

Military-Assistance Programs Can Contribute Directly to Development, Since Indigenous Military Forces Play a Positive Role in the Development Process

Those who hold this view point out that members of the military forces are among the most educated, professional, and nationally conscious members of society in developing nations. The excerpts that follow emphasize this point.

Analyst Emile Benoit studied the relationship between defense and economic growth in Third World nations. He writes:

Defense programs directly contribute various useful inputs into LDC [Less Developed Countries] civilian economies, particularly manpower training which may considerably improve the productivity of military manpower for civilian occupations after demobilization. Especially where the military takes its recruits in substantial numbers from self-subsistence agricultural pursuits, it may find it necessary to provide them with some element of general education and will as a matter of course inculcate such rudimentary but important industrial and urban skills and attitudes as: following and transmitting precise instructions; living and working by the clock; noticing and reading signs; spending and saving money; using transportation (bicycles, motorcycles, autos, buses, boats, planes, etc.); working with, repairing, and maintaining machinery; listening to radio; becoming interested in national and even international news; etc.

In addition, the military may supply dual use infrastructure, such as airfields, ports, and communication networks, which may sooner or later be used in part by civilians, especially in outlying areas. The military contribution to civilian relief and rehabilitation after natural disasters may be quite important in LDCs. Its mapping, hydrological, meteorological, and other R&D is usually more important than the work done by civilian agencies in these fields.

"Civic action" programs in many LDCs utilize defense resources directly to meet civilian goals.

Food, clothing, shelter, and medical services provided by military personnel does to some extent substitute for provision by the civilian economy of comparable goods and services to civilians. Beyond this, "civic action" programs in many LDCs utilize defense resources directly to meet civilian goals—as in pre-release training of military personnel for civilian functions, military construction of schools, clinics, roads, etc. solely for civilian use, use of the military for public health work, reforestation, public education, and other essential civilian functions. All this is in addition to the primary economic contribution of the defense program in assuring a minimum of physical security in the absence of which the political structure and hence also the civilian economy would falter and ultimately disintegrate.[43]

John Spanier, a professor of international relations, presents a similar point of view:

In a far less developed society, the military has an advantage over its civilian competitors. Armies are, by and large, microcosms of modern industrial societies.

284

They are technically and rationally oriented to their occupational activities. They cannot function without engineers, mechanics, communications specialists, and so forth; even the operation of jeeps, tanks, guns, and other military equipment by the ordinary soldier demands elementary "industrial" skills. Military units have, in fact, on occasion been used for such tasks as the construction of roads, bridges, and harbors (recall the role of the U.S. Army Corps of Engineers in the development of the American West)....

The army in a new nation is often said to be in a good position to organize the nation for its economic "takeoff" and to surmount the turbulent transition from the traditional agrarian to modern society. An army is founded on centralized command, hierarchy, and discipline, the very characteristics that communist parties claim will allow them, and only them, to modernize an underdeveloped nation successfully and rapidly. The army may, in fact, be the only organization that can compete with the communists in the capacity to break the power of the landowning classes, carry out land reforms, organize the nation's human and natural resources for development, and control the unhappy masses from whom capital savings must be collected.[44]

The army may be the only organization which can break the power of land-owning classes.

United States General Maxwell D. Taylor has extensive credentials: He served as a combat officer in World War II and Korea; as President John Kennedy's chairman of the joint chiefs of staff; as ambassador to Viet Nam in 1964–1965; and as a special consultant to President Lyndon Johnson. In this excerpt, he reiterates some of the points made by Benoit and Spanier:

The armed forces have an occasional opportunity to demonstrate civic responsibility through participation in nonmilitary activities such as disaster relief and programs for environmental and urban improvement. They have many assets applicable to such purposes—organization, trained manpower, and experience in construction, telecommunications, public health, transportation, and flood control. Abroad they have had a long record of performance in repairing the devastation caused by wars in which they have taken part, often learning by direct participation that it is more difficult to rebuild than to destroy a country. They engaged in the rehabilitation of the Axis nations after World War II and later in both South Korea and South Vietnam they conducted civic action programs in cooperation with the inhabitants which resulted in the construction of thousands of homes, schools, hospitals, churches, bridges, and market places.[45]

Another opinion as to why military power is important has to do with military coups, which occur frequently in Third World nations. Coups are often cited as an adverse consequence of building up military forces. But Robert Lincoln, a former official of the United States Information Agency, suggests that before we condemn military coups, we should look carefully at their causes and consequences. In some cases a military coup may be exactly what is needed to keep the development process moving forward.

Because takeover of civilian governments can tempt the military anywhere, it is important for American professional military—coming from a culture where the coup is so alien—to examine all foreign coups in depth. This need for careful examination clearly applies to the coup in Turkey on 12 September, 1980....

Americans take an automatically negative attitude even when the coup happens to be performed by honorable men, by any definition, and for recognized democratic reasons, such as alleviation of national chaos. That democracy cannot thrive in chaos seems sensible enough, and in the case of the Turkish coups, chaos beforehand was almost beyond belief.[46]

In contrast to the mythical Third World nation Magweta, introduced earlier in this chapter to illustrate the viewpoint that *opposes* military assistance, here are two real-life examples that illustrate the *positive*, constructive roles played by national military establishments.

The first report is from India:

The [Indian] army is the largest single organization in the country dealing with Adult Education. And what goes on in the army educational field has naturally far-reaching effect.…The training as a whole (that) Jawans (Indian G.I.s) get changes the whole concept of their life. When they go back to the village on leave or on retirement they bring about a change in the atmosphere of the village community; through them the education they receive in the army filters down to the village population. And of course they set an example, standing for a national approach to problems and bringing to bear on problems an objective outlook free of parochial loyalties…(Within the army itself, the soldiers) speak the same language. Hindustani or simple Hindi is the common language of the army and it has proved to be the greatest single factor in the spread of a common language in India.[47]

The second is from Burma:

The military often expands into economic development activities.

In a number of countries—Burma is a pertinent example—the armed forces maintain their own economic enterprises, which range from manufacturing plants to department stores. In Burma, the Defense Service Institute, which was mainly concerned with supplies to the military establishment, was expanded in 1961 to include the Burma Economic Development Corporation. Through this device, the army controls commercial concerns involved in steel production, pharmaceuticals, cement, and shipping. Generally, such economic enterprises are designed to assist the army in performing its military functions and they do not necessarily contribute to economic growth. The military often expands into economic development activities, however, particularly in land reclamation work.

As a result, the military develops a pool of trained managers who are available for public and private industries. These are either retired officers or officers who have been assigned to governmentalized industries. In Indonesia, Israel, and Egypt, for example, former army officers are to be found in key managerial posts of governmental industries. Alternative ways of training such managers are available, and in some new nations, e.g., Egypt, national schools of economic administration are being developed.[48]

Interestingly, both the proponents as well as most opponents of reordered military priorities share a common assumption, which defines the parameters of the debate: the belief that there is not enough—that one can have guns or butter, but never both. Hardly anyone has ever questioned this assumption.

However, R. Buckminster Fuller did so, and in the process put a whole other light on the subject. Fuller begins by challenging widely accepted views about wealth—views that lead to what he sees as the erroneous conclusion that scarcity is a major problem in the world. Concerns about scarcity, which affect most individuals and nations, lead to world views and choices that emphasize protecting one's security and choosing between seemingly competing claims for scarce resources (such as between guns and butter). But, Fuller argues, wealth is *not* money—it is the combination of physical energy (as matter or radiation) and the knowledge of human beings. Thus, since matter and energy can never be destroyed but only changed to the other form (matter into energy or energy into matter), and since human knowledge and experience can only increase the potential for wealth,

286

therefore creation in the world is virtually unlimited. He concludes:

In general we have the capability, which can be fully realized within ten years, of producing and sustaining a higher standard of living for all humanity than that ever heretofore experienced or dreamt of by any.

This is not an opinion or a hope—it is an engineeringly demonstrable fact. This can be done using only the already proven technology and with the already mined, refined, and in-recirculating physical resources.

This will be an inherently sustainable physical success for all humanity and all its generations to come.[49]

The major problem, Fuller argues, is that we simply are not aware of the wealth that exists around us, or of how to use existing design technologies to make this wealth available for human well-being. Although Fuller does not specifically discuss military and development spending in this context, some have suggested that his perspective on the world's available resources serves to make the guns versus butter dichotomy obsolete as a forum for discussion.

The planet Earth's four billion billionaires have not yet been notified of their good fortune. Their heritage probating is being postponed by the lawyers for the now inherently obsolete power structures of all kinds—religious, political, financial, professional, and academic—all of which exploitative systems are organized only to take biased advantage of all scarcities, physical and metaphysical.

Evolution has now accelerated into revolution, which, if it goes bloody, will render all humanity extinct, but if it goes via the design revolution, all humanity will win. This is a new kind of revolution; it is one that, instead of revengefully pulling down the top fortunate few, will elevate all the heretofore unfortunates and the fortunates alike to new and sustainable heights of realized life far superior to those previously tenuously attained by the most privileged few.[50]

Conclusion

In this chapter we have examined the basic facts and figures of national security and have reviewed the two major schools of thought regarding the priority that military spending should have on the planet. What emerges are two distinct perspectives about what national and planetary security is, and how best to achieve it.

Proponents of strong military forces often describe themselves as "realists." We must deal with the world as it is, they say, not with the world as we would wish it to be. In these dangerous times there is no higher priority than ensuring national security. While development and ending hunger can obviously bring about a more secure and harmonious world, they are no substitute for military strength.

Those who favor reallocation of military spending to development also have as their goal the creation of a secure and stable world. From their perspective, it is not weapons that ensure peace, but the removal of some of the root causes of the world's underlying tensions—inequities in wealth, hunger, lack of essential human needs being fulfilled. Ending hunger and resolving other important social ills, they say, is a prerequisite to true national security and stability.

We began this chapter by noting that, for all the current debate and discussion

We have the capability…of…sustaining a higher standard of living…than that ever heretofore experienced.

Both proponents and opponents of military spending have as their goal creation of a secure and stable world.

287

about "national security," there is still no agreed-upon definition of the term. It has been our intention to map out the differing perspectives on the subject, the better to promote a fuller understanding of the essence of national security.

We are not saying that through understanding will come a resolution of the divergent views about the subject. What we are saying is that by making available the range of interpretations, approaches, and dimensions of thinking on this vital issue, the possibility for a breakthrough in thinking about national security will emerge.

NOTES

1   Ruth Leger Sivard, *World Military and Social Expenditures 1983* (Washington, DC: World Priorities, 1983), 32.

2   Ibid.

3   Ruth Leger Sivard, *World Military and Social Expenditures 1982* (Leesburg, VA: World Priorities, 1982), 6.

4   Sivard, *Expenditures 1982,* 26. National military expenditures are current and capital expenditures to meet the needs of the armed forces. They include military assistance to foreign countries and the military components of nuclear, space, and research and development programs.

    In *World Military and Social Expenditures 1982* (Leesburg, VA: World Priorities, 1982), Sivard notes that a standard definition of military expenditures, as paraphrased above, is used by the members of NATO, but that major differences in national accounting systems make it impossible to achieve general uniformity.

    In Warsaw Pact and other communist countries, the scope of the accounting for military programs is not clear, and data are necessarily highly speculative.

5   Ibid., 6.

6   Ibid., 26.

7   Ruth Leger Sivard, *World Military and Social Expenditures 1981* (Leesburg, VA: World Priorities, 1981), 15.

8   Ibid.

9   U.S. Arms Control and Disarmament Agency, *World Military Expenditures and Arms Transfers, 1971–1980,* ACDA Publication 115, March 1983, 27.

10 Overseas Development Council, *U.S. Foreign Policy and the Third World: Agenda 1983,* eds. John P. Lewis and Valeriana Kallab (New York: Praeger, 1983), 260, 261.

11 Sivard, *Expenditures 1981,* 6, 9.

12 U.S. Arms Control and Disarmament Agency, *World Military Expenditures…1971–1980,* 30.

13 Sivard, *Expenditures 1981,* 6, 9.

14 "A Choice of Securities," *Ceres* 14, no. 3 (May–June 1981): 50.

15 U.S. Arms Control and Disarmament Agency, *World Military Expenditures and Arms Transfers, 1969–1978,* ACDA Publication 108, December 1980, 19.

16 Ibid.

17 Andrew K. Semmel, "Helping Others Help Us," *Defense 82* (November 1982): 13.

18 Independent Commission on International Development Issues, *North-South: A Program for Survival* (Cambridge, MA: MIT Press, 1980), 124–25.

19 Ibid., 14.

20 Murray L. Weidenbaum, *The Economics of Peacetime Defense* (New York: Praeger, 1974), 28–29.

21 Inga Thorsson, "The Arms Race and Development: A Competitive Relationship," *Development: Seeds of Change* 1 (1982): 12, 15.

22 Amadou-Mahtar M'Bow, "The Will for Peace," *Unesco Courier,* April 1979, 4, 5.

23 Thomas W. Wilson, Jr., "Hunger, Politics, and Security," *Food and People,* eds. Dudley Kirk and Ellen K. Eliason (San Francisco: Boyd & Fraser, 1982), 390, 395.

24 Robert S. McNamara, *The Essence of Security* (New York: Harper & Row, 1968), 146, 149.

25 Lane Vanderslice, "Real Security in an Insecure World," Background Paper, no. 69 (Washington, DC: Bread for the World, October 1983): 1.

26 Ibid.

27 Committee on Poverty and the Arms Trade, "Magweta or How Does the Arms Trade Affect Development?" *Development: Seeds of Change* 1 (1982): 34–35.

28 Muzammel Huq, "The Structure of Hunger," *Unesco Courier,* September 1980, 16.

29 Frances Moore Lappé, Joseph Collins, and David Kinley, *Aid as Obstacle: Twenty Questions about Our Foreign Aid and the Hungry* (San Francisco: Institute for Food and Development Policy, 1980), 123–24, 24 (respectively).

30 U.S., Ronald Reagan, "Address Before a Joint Session of the Congress on the Program for Economic Recovery," 18 February 1981, *Public Papers of the Presidents of the United States, 1981,* 112.

31 Norman Podhoretz, "An Overview of American Foreign Policy: The Present and Future Danger," *Congressional Policy: A Guide to American Foreign Policy and National Defense,* ed. Paul Dietrich (Washington, DC: National Center for Legislative Research, 1982), 17.

32 U.S., Richard Nixon, "Radio Address on Defense Policy," 29 October 1972, *Public Papers of the Presidents of the United States, 1972,* 1066, 1067.

33 Samuel P. Huntington, *American Politics: The Promise of Disharmony* (Cambridge, MA: Harvard University Press, 1981), 248–49, 251.

34 Henry Kissinger, *For the Record: Selected Statements, 1977–1980* (Boston: Little, Brown & Company, 1981), 191–93.

35 Paul Dietrich, ed., "Central America: El Salvador," *Congressional Policy: A Guide to American Foreign Policy and National Defense* (Washington, DC: National Center for Legislative Research, 1982), 202–203.

36 U.S., Department of State, *Opening Statement at Confirmation Hearings,* delivered by Secretary of State Alexander Haig, Current Policy, no. 257 (9 January 1981): 2.

37 U.S., Department of State, *Tasks for U.S. Policy in the Hemisphere,* address by Thomas O. Enders, Current Policy, no. 282 (3 June 1981): 2.

38 "Summary of Kissinger Commission Report," *Congressional Quarterly,* 14 January 1984, 64, 65.

39 Soedjatmoko, *Development and Freedom,* Ishizaka Lectures 2 (Tokyo: Simul Press, 1980), 17, 18.

40 Julius K. Nyerere, "One Party Government," *Spearhead: The Pan-African Review* 1, no. 1 (November 1961): 8.

41 Dietrich, ed., "Central America: El Salvador," *Congressional Policy: A Guide to American Foreign Policy and National Defense,* 199–200.

42 Semmel, "Helping Others Help Us," 12, 20.

43 Emile Benoit, *Defense and Economic Growth in Developing Countries* (Lexington, MA: D. C. Heath & Company, Lexington Books, 1973), 17.

44 John Spanier, *Games Nations Play* (New York: Holt, Rinehart & Winston, 1981), 381.

45 Maxwell D. Taylor, *Precarious Security* (New York: W. W. Norton, 1976), 64.

46 Robert A. Lincoln, "In Turkey: Preserving Democracy by Coup," *Army* 31, no. 8 (August 1981): 22, 23–24.

47   Edward Bernard Glick, *Peaceful Conflict: The Non-Military Use of the Military* (Harrisburg, PA: Stackpole Books, 1967), 154.

48   Morris Janowitz, *Military Institutions and Coercion in the Developing Nations* (Chicago: University of Chicago Press, 1977), 152–53.

49   R. Buckminster Fuller, *Critical Path* (New York: St. Martin's Press, 1981), 199.

50   Ibid., 200.

What makes a nation secure? Does a secure and stable world depend on military spending? Many people believe that shifting spending priorities away from national security and toward development is an effective way to end hunger. Others support—and seek to increase— current levels of military spending. In 1981– 1982, there were about 25 million people in the global military establishment proper and about 100 million people (including reserves, paramilitary forces, and civilians producing weapons and services for the military) in military-related activities. In 1960, the world's annual military expenditure was $298 billion; in 1980, it was $495 billion—an average annual growth rate of about 2.5 percent. Right: *NATO tank sign, West Germany* (Leif Skooglors/Woodfin Camp & Assoc.); next two-page spread: *Column of tanks crossing agricultural land* (© David Burnett/Contact).

Fundamental questions in the national security area involve the size of military budgets, alternative uses for the money, and the effectiveness of military establishments. Costs are a particularly significant issue because of the great disparity between funding for development (food, education, and so forth) and funding for the military. Left: *U.S. Marines in Lebanon* (J. Guichard/Sygma); above: *U.S. Air Force plane* (Wernher Krutein/Photovault); next two-page spread: *Soldier, Guatemala* (S. Meiselas/Magnum Photos); following two-page spread, clockwise from left, all El Salvador: *U.S. military advisors instruct local troops* (E. Richards/Magnum Photos); *Young recruits being trained* (S. Meiselas/ Magnum Photos); *National Guard training* (S. Meiselas/Magnum Photos); *Graduating cadets* (S. Meiselas/Magnum Photos).

One school of thought holds that too much money is being spent on the military; ending hunger depends on reordering priorities. The Brandt Commission reports: "Much of the insecurity in the world is connected with the divisions between rich and poor countries—grave injustice and mass starvation causing additional instability. Yet the research and the funds which could help to put an end to poverty and hunger are now pre-empted by military uses…. A modern tank costs about one million dollars; that amount could improve storage facilities for 100,000 tons of rice and thus save 4000 tons or more annually…. The same sum of money could provide 1000 classrooms for 30,000 children." Economist Murray Weidenbaum discusses the effect of large military budgets on the domestic economy. "The real cost of military activities should be measured in human and natural resources and in the stocks of productive capital absorbed in producing, transporting, and maintaining weapons and other military equipment…. For example, the production of a missile, which will eventually be exploded or buried, may entail the same amount of economic activity as the production of machinery for a factory producing new railroad cars, which will continue to enhance the nation's productive capacity."

Many people who favor "butter" in the "guns vs. butter" debate question the relationship between national security and large military forces. Issue analyst Lane Vanderslice writes: "'Security,' Webster's dictionary says, is 'the state or feeling of being free from fear, care, danger, etc.' 'Development,' it says, is 'a stage of growth.' 'Security aid,' on the other hand, is aid the U.S. government gives to foreign regimes, usually to help them purchase U.S.-made weapons. Some 'development aid' is designed to bring health, clean drinking water, agricultural skills and other self-help tools to people of the Third World. Development aid, ironically, often contributes to the security of the world, while security aid often undermines it…. The U.S. will strengthen its own security by contributing to development assistance since hunger and poverty are major sources of social unrest in the world today." Shortly after resigning as U.S. Secretary of Defense, Robert McNamara wrote: "There can be no question but that there is a relationship between violence and economic backwardness…. Our security is related directly to the security of the newly developing world…. Security is development, and without development there can be no security." All photos, El Salvador. This page, top to bottom: *Salvadoran army distributing food* (S. Meiselas/Magnum Photos); *Salvadorans working on AID project* (S. Meiselas/Magnum Photos); *Salvadoran school* (S. Meiselas/ Magnum Photos); opposite: *Election* (Bob Nickelsberg/Woodfin Camp & Assoc.).

The threat of communism is seen as the major issue by many proponents of strong military establishments. Journalist Norman Podhoretz writes: "Human rights have invariably fared worse under Communism than under the regimes it has replaced.... Are the South Vietnamese better off under the rule of the North than they were under Thieu? Ask the boat people. Are the Cambodians better off as Kampucheans? Ask the grave." Above: Ethiopian military on parade (William Campbell/Sygma); right: Ethiopian children wear Soviet emblem shirts (William Campbell/Sygma).

In addition to providing security, military forces may contribute directly to the economy in Third World nations. Analyst Emile Benoit writes: "Food, clothing, shelter and medical services provided by military personnel...to some extent substitute for provision by the civilian economy of comparable goods and services to civilians.... This is in addition to the primary economic contribution...assuring a minimum of physical security in the absence of which the political structure and hence also the civilian economy would falter and ultimately disintegrate." Left: *Rifle practice, Somalian military* (Alain Nogues/Sygma); above: *A Somalian mother nurses one child, while another looks on, rifle in hand* (Alain Nogues/Sygma).

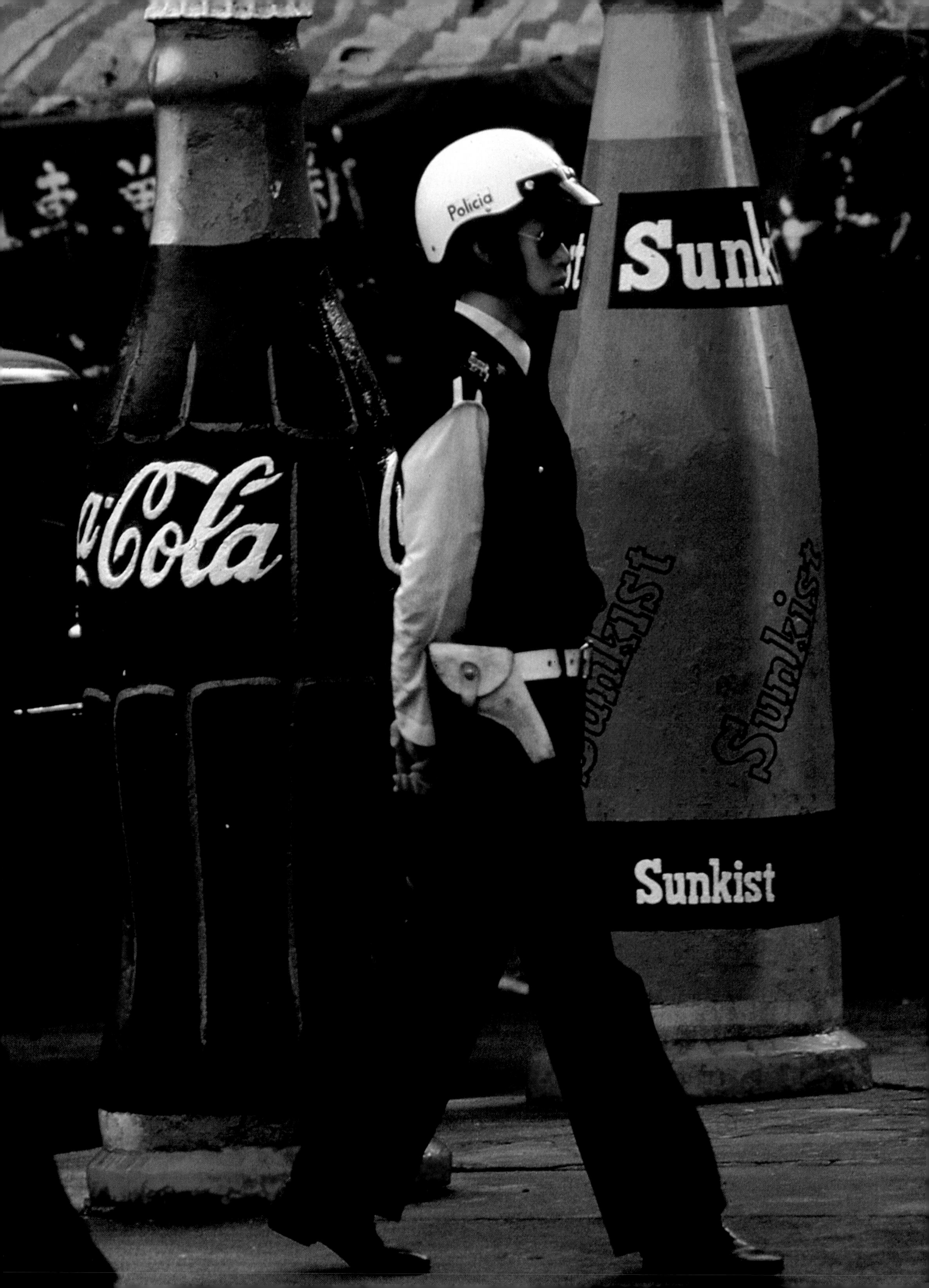
Policia
Sunk
Coca-Cola
Sunkist
Sunkist
Sunkist

Creating a climate safe for foreign investment
is an often stated goal of military security programs. But, according to the Committee on
Poverty and the Arms Trade, the results can
be "destruction of embryonic local industry as
large foreign concerns, relying heavily on advertising and the lure of the Western image, flood
the markets.... Rural society declines and
shanty towns grow in the shadow of westernised
cities." The committee believes that these conditions lead to political unrest, creating the need
for still larger military forces. Left: A Macao
policeman and Coca-Cola (P. J. Griffiths/
Magnum Photos); above, top: Magazine
stand, Thailand (John Blaustein/Woodfin
Camp & Assoc.); above, bottom: Cases
of soft drinks, Mexican village (Adriano
Heitmann/Archive).

Some leaders of Third World nations hold that strong military forces are necessary for the unity and stability essential to nation building. Tanzanian President Julius Nyerere states this view: "Once the first free government is formed, its supreme task lies ahead — the building up of the country's economy so as to raise the living standards of the people, the eradication of disease, the banishment of ignorance and superstition. This…calls for the maximum united effort by the whole country if it is to succeed. *There can be no room for difference or division.*" Left: *School, Haiti* (Charles Harbutt/Archive); above, top: *School, Pakistan* (© David Burnett/Contact); above, bottom: *School, Zaire* (James A. Sugar/ Black Star).

For all the current debate and discussion about "national security," there is still no agreed-upon definition of the term. It has been our intention to map out differing perspectives on the subject, the better to promote a fuller understanding of the essence of national security. We are not saying that through understanding will come a resolution of the divergent views about the subject. What we are saying is that, by making available the range of interpretations, approaches, and dimensions of thinking on this vital issue, we can allow the possibility for a breakthrough in thinking about national security to emerge. Left: *Antiballistic missile base, North Dakota* (R. Burri/Magnum Photos); above, top: *U.S. Air Force "mothball" fleet, Arizona* (R. Burri/Magnum Photos); above, bottom: *Military data bank, Washington, DC* (A. Webb/Magnum Photos); next two-page spread: *U.S. Army Rocket Museum, White Sands, New Mexico* (R. Burri/Magnum Photos).

New International Economic Order

We now turn to the final issue to be examined in this book—the New International Economic Order. Many of the economic news stories—such as "the Third World debt crisis"—that seem increasingly to make the front pages of our daily papers are at the heart of this issue.

In their concern about hunger, many experts and world leaders have focused on improving economic conditions in the Third World, since this is where most of the world's hungry people live. But while these experts and leaders agree on the need for improvement, they differ as to whether this improvement requires a fundamental change in the world economic system. Many who favor fundamental change support proposals for a "New International Economic Order" (NIEO).[1] Other observers, who regard the world's current economic arrangement as basically effective, feel that NIEO-type changes are unnecessary, and possibly are harmful for everyone, rich and poor alike.

In examining the New International Economic Order, we begin with a *Basic Facts* section, which includes a brief history of the NIEO concept, a primer on the workings of the international economic system, and some fundamental facts and figures. It devotes particular attention to ways in which Third World nations can accumulate productive capital, as well as to issues of trade and tariff reform.

Is the present economic order effective? Should there be fundamental change? What should be the role of multinational corporations?

The major schools of thought concerning the NIEO address four basic questions: Is the present economic order effective? Is there a need for fundamental change? What is the role of multinational corporations? And what are the possible obligations of former colonial powers to the Third World?

The school of thought favoring the reforms of the New International Economic Order holds that in order to promote development and to end hunger and poverty, a New International Economic Order must be established in place of the current international economic order. Speaking for this school of thought are analysts and political leaders from both developed nations and the Third World. They offer the points of view that the current economic order is not working, that fundamental change is needed, that multinationals must be stringently regulated, and that colonial powers have an obligation to redress past wrongs.

An alternative perspective is provided by the school of thought that holds that the present economic order is working well—and, if anything, it needs to be strengthened. Proponents argue that the proposals for a new international economic order are based on false premises, are impractical, and are potentially dangerous. Here too, analysts and political leaders from the developed countries and the Third World are represented. The viewpoints expressed fall into three categories. The first is that the present system works well—or at least as well as any system can. Proponents of this view generally favor a strong role for multinationals, pointing to Singapore, Taiwan, and South Korea as illustrations of the success of free enterprise. The second point of view holds that the causes of poverty lie within Third World nations and cannot be attributed to the international economic system. The third point of view regards the NIEO as irrelevant. It rejects conventional economic development as a goal for nations and argues for small-scale, self-reliant development activities at the village level.

Basic Facts

The NIEO concept emerged in 1974 at the Sixth Special Session of the United Nations. There, Third World nations (known as the "Group of 77")[2] joined to express their opposition to the workings of the current international economic system, which they claimed was unfair to their interests. Leaders of the Group of 77 were instrumental in the Sixth Special Session's adopting a declaration for the establishment of a New International Economic Order.[3]

Just who are the Third World, poor, or developing nations? We define them as "the 141 African, Asian, and Latin American member countries of the United Nations."[4] However, although we must refer to these nations as if they were a single entity in order to discuss the NIEO debate meaningfully, in actuality they are incredibly diverse—in terms of cultures, economic systems, political institutions, and levels of wealth. The map of the world in Figure N.1 illustrates this diversity. It classifies countries by income levels, and also distinguishes between oil importers and exporters and between the market and nonmarket economies of Europe.

The NIEO proposals made in 1974 and later advocate major reforms in the areas of resources, economic and technical assistance, trade, and monetary policy. In the area of resources, the proposals recommend stabilizing prices at high levels by linking export prices to import prices. In the area of economic and technical assistance, the proposals recommend increased economic aid and preferential tariff treatment, which would speed industrialization. In the area of trade, the proposals recommend governing multinational corporations by a strict international code of conduct. And in the area of monetary policy, they recommend giving Third World nations expanded voting rights in the International Monetary Fund, as well as an enlarged share of special drawing rights.[5]

Julius Nyerere, one of the most vocal Third World leaders, has described the Group of 77 as a "trade union of the poor":

Seventy percent of the world's population—the Third World—commands together no more than 12 percent of the gross world product. Eighty percent of the world's trade and investment, 93 percent of its industry, and almost 100 percent of its research is controlled—in the words of Barbara Ward—by the industrial rich.[6]

Since 1974, experts have debated and discussed the NIEO proposals in a number of conferences sponsored by the United Nations. These discussions have become known as the *North-South dialogue*.[7] There is little consensus, even among the leaders of developing countries, about what the world would look like if the NIEO reforms were made. Nonetheless, the NIEO is tremendously important to Third World nations as a negotiating *framework* for resolving such problems as world hunger and poverty. It is the very *system*, proponents of NIEO argue, that must be restructured. Historical wrongs must be righted, wealth must be transferred from rich to poor, and developing countries must be given far more voice and power in the world.

Some political and business leaders of wealthy nations, particularly of the United States, approach the NIEO proposals from an entirely different perspective. First, they claim that the "Third World" is a meaningless concept when it comes to formulating practical policies—Brazil, for example, has less in common with Burkina Faso (formerly Upper Volta) than with the United States. Second, the principal causes of poverty lie within the developing nations themselves. No international program can cure corruption and inefficiency or create the kinds of internal incentives necessary for promoting growth. Finally, these critics express

Greenland (Den.)

Iceland

Canada

United States

Swed[en]
Denmark
West Germany
Belgium
Netherlands
Ireland
United Kingdom
Luxembourg
Switzerland
France   Ita[ly]
Portugal   Spain

Gibraltar (UK)

Tunisia
Morocco
Algeria

Mexico

TROPIC OF CANCER

Cuba
Belize
Dominican Republic
Jamaica   Haiti
Guatemala
El Salvador   Honduras
Nicaragua
Costa Rica
Panama

Venezuela
Trinidad and Tobago
French Guiana (Fr.)
Colombia
Guyana
Suriname
Ecuador
Peru
Brazil

Western Sahara
Senegal
Cape Verde
Gambia
Guinea-Bissau
Guinea
Sierra Leone
Liberia
Ivory Coast   Ghana   Togo
Cameroon
São Tomé and Principe
Equatorial Guinea

Mauritania   Mali
Burkina Faso
Nig[er]
Benin

EQUATOR

Bolivia
Paraguay

TROPIC OF CAPRICORN

Uruguay
Chile   Argentina

FIGURE N.1. THE GROUP OF 77

The Group of 77 is the Third World's economic advocate. The term originated with the 77 nations supporting a common program at the first meetings of the UN Conference on Trade and Development (UNCTAD) in 1964. Now the group is much larger, but the original name is still used.

- Group of 77 Countries
- Group of 77 and Third World Countries

Source: U.S., Department of State, *Atlas of U.S. Foreign Relations,* by Harry F. Young (Washington, DC: Bureau of Public Affairs, U.S. Department of State, June 1983), 31.

FIGURE N.2. THE THIRD WORLD

*Defining the Third World is a controversial
task. A variety of criteria may be used, and
though these may clearly identify the core of
the Third World, its boundaries will vary from
one criterion to another. In this book, we use
"Third World" to mean the 141 African, Asian,
and Latin American member countries of the
United Nations.*

■ Third World Countries

Source: J. P. Dickenson et al., *A Geography of the Third World*
(New York: Methuen, 1983), xx.

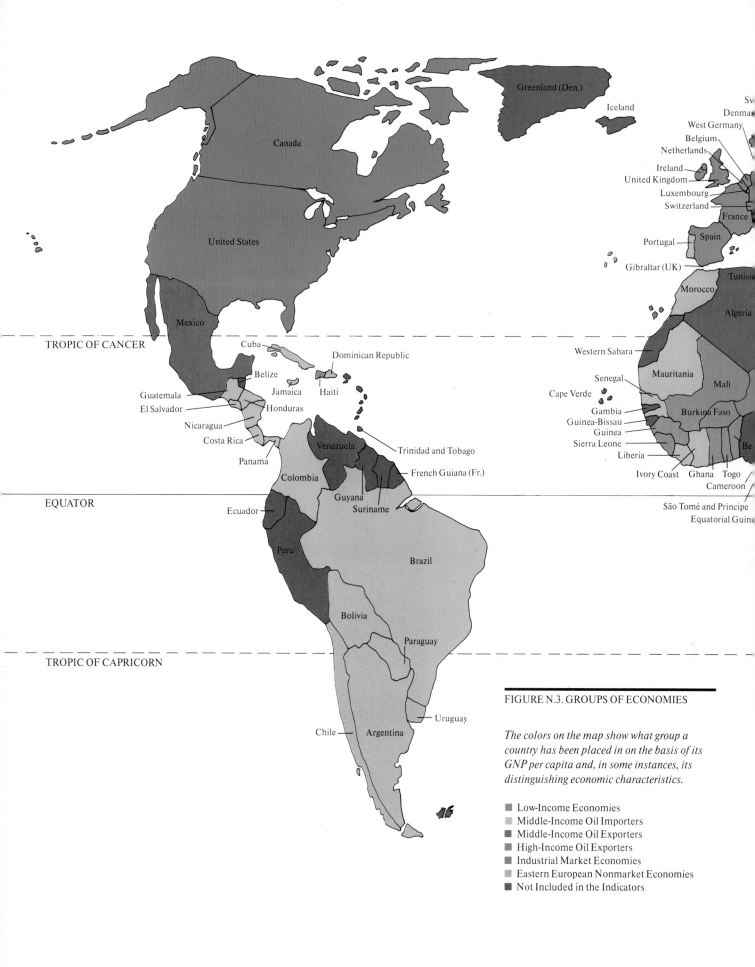

Greenland (Den.)

Iceland

Canada

United States

S...
Denma...
West Germany
Belgium
Netherlands
Ireland
United Kingdom
Luxembourg
Switzerland
France

Portugal
Gibraltar (UK)

Spain

Tunisia
Morocco
Algeria

TROPIC OF CANCER

Mexico

Cuba
Dominican Republic
Belize
Jamaica   Haiti
Guatemala
El Salvador
Honduras
Nicaragua
Costa Rica
Panama

Venezuela
Trinidad and Tobago
French Guiana (Fr.)

Colombia

Guyana
Suriname

Western Sahara

Senegal
Cape Verde
Gambia
Guinea-Bissau
Guinea
Sierra Leone
Liberia
Ivory Coast   Ghana   Togo
Cameroon

Mauritania
Mali
Burkina Faso

Be...

EQUATOR

Ecuador

Peru

Brazil

São Tomé and Principe
Equatorial Guine...

Bolivia

Paraguay

TROPIC OF CAPRICORN

Uruguay

Chile   Argentina

FIGURE N.3. GROUPS OF ECONOMIES

The colors on the map show what group a country has been placed in on the basis of its GNP per capita and, in some instances, its distinguishing economic characteristics.

- Low-Income Economies
- Middle-Income Oil Importers
- Middle-Income Oil Exporters
- High-Income Oil Exporters
- Industrial Market Economies
- Eastern European Nonmarket Economies
- Not Included in the Indicators

Source: World Bank, *World Development Report 1983* (New York: Oxford University Press, 1983), 142–43.

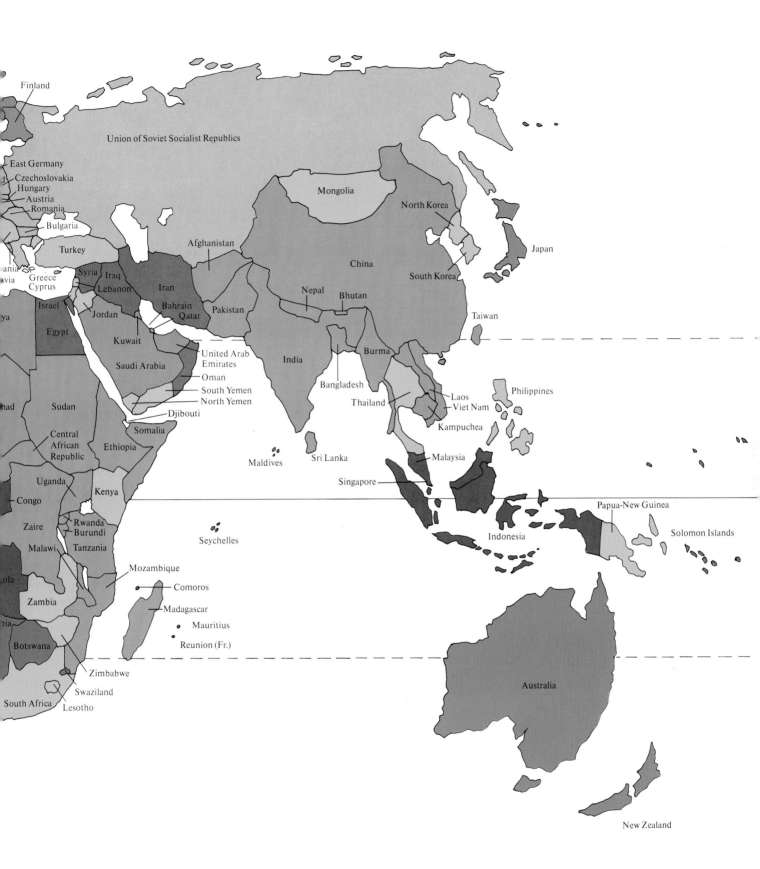

Finland

Union of Soviet Socialist Republics

East Germany
Czechoslovakia
Hungary
Austria
Romania

Bulgaria

Turkey

Greece
Cyprus

Israel

Egypt

Syria
Lebanon

Iraq

Iran

Jordan

Bahrain
Qatar

Kuwait

Saudi Arabia

United Arab
Emirates

Oman

South Yemen

North Yemen

Djibouti

Somalia

Sudan

Central
African
Republic

Ethiopia

Uganda

Kenya

Congo

Zaire

Rwanda
Burundi

Malawi

Tanzania

Zambia

Mozambique

Botswana

South Africa

Lesotho

Swaziland

Zimbabwe

Comoros

Madagascar

Mauritius

Reunion (Fr.)

Seychelles

Maldives

Sri Lanka

Afghanistan

Mongolia

China

Nepal

Bhutan

Pakistan

India

Bangladesh

Burma

Thailand

Laos

Viet Nam

Kampuchea

Malaysia

Singapore

Indonesia

North Korea

South Korea

Japan

Taiwan

Philippines

Papua-New Guinea

Solomon Islands

Australia

New Zealand

TROPIC OF CANCER

EQUATOR

TROPIC OF CAPRICORN

Greenland (Den.)

Iceland

Denm
West Germany
Belgium
Netherlands
Ireland
United Kingdom
Luxembourg
Switzerland
France

Portugal — Spain

Gibraltar (UK)

Tunis

Morocco

Alger

Canada

United States

Mexico

Cuba

Belize

Guatemala
El Salvador
Nicaragua
Costa Rica
Panama

Jamaica

Dominican Republic

Haiti

Honduras

Venezuela

Trinidad and Tobago

French Guiana (Fr.)

Colombia

Guyana
Suriname

Ecuador

Peru

Brazil

Bolivia

Paraguay

Uruguay

Chile — Argentina

Western Sahara

Senegal

Cape Verde

Gambia
Guinea-Bissau
Guinea
Sierra Leone
Liberia

Ivory Coast   Ghana   Togo
Cameroon

Mauritania

Mali

Burkina Faso

São Tomé and Principe
Equatorial Gui

FIGURE N.4. THE WORLD, ACCORDING TO
THE PHYSICAL QUALITY OF LIFE INDEX
(PQLI)

*The Physical Quality of Life Index (PQLI),
compiled by the Overseas Development
Council, is an indicator of human well-being.
Each country's PQLI is based on an average of
life expectancy at age one, infant mortality,
and literacy.*

■ PQLI of 90 or Above
■ PQLI of 78 to 89
■ PQLI of 56 to 77
■ PQLI of 31 to 55
■ PQLI of 30 or Below
■ Data not available

Source: Overseas Development Council, *U.S. Foreign Policy and
the Third World: Agenda 1983,* eds. John P. Lewis and Valeriana
Kallab (New York: Praeger, 1983), 208–209.

Finland

Union of Soviet Socialist Republics

East Germany
Czechoslovakia
Hungary
Austria
Romania
Bulgaria

Turkey

bania
avia

Greece
Cyprus

Syria
Lebanon

Iraq

Israel

Jordan

Egypt

ya

Kuwait

Saudi Arabia

United Arab
Emirates
Oman
South Yemen
North Yemen

Djibouti

Somalia

had

Sudan

Central
African
Republic

Ethiopia

Uganda

Kenya

Congo

Zaire

Rwanda
Burundi

Malawi

Tanzania

gola

Zambia

bia

Botswana

South Africa

Lesotho

Swaziland

Zimbabwe

Mozambique

Comoros

Madagascar

Mauritius

Reunion (Fr.)

Seychelles

Maldives

Afghanistan

Iran

Bahrain
Qatar

Pakistan

India

Nepal

Bhutan

Mongolia

China

North Korea

South Korea

Japan

Taiwan

Burma

Bangladesh

Thailand

Laos
Viet Nam

Kampuchea

Sri Lanka

Malaysia

Singapore

Philippines

Indonesia

Papua-New Guinea

Solomon Islands

Australia

New Zealand

321

FIGURE N.5. TWO MEASURES OF THE GAP
BETWEEN DEVELOPING AND DEVELOPED
COUNTRIES (1960-1981)

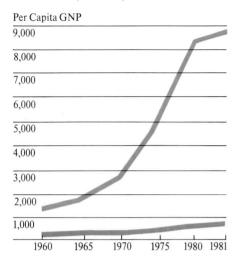

Per Capita GNP

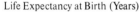

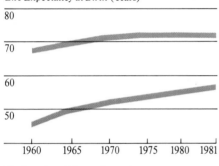

Life Expectancy at Birth (Years)

■ Developed Countries
■ Developing Countries

Source: Overseas Development Council, *U.S. Foreign Policy and
the Third World: Agenda 1982,* eds. Roger D. Hansen et al.
(New York: Praeger, 1982), 175; Overseas Development Council,
U.S. Foreign Policy and the Third World: Agenda 1983, eds. John P.
Lewis and Valeriana Kallab (New York: Praeger, 1983), 207.

FIGURE N.6. DEATH RATES PER
1,000 PEOPLE

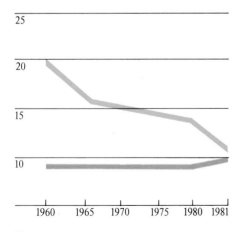

■ Developing Countries
■ Developed Countries

Source: Overseas Development Council, *The United States and
World Development: Agenda 1979,* eds. Martin M. McLaughlin et al.
(New York: Praeger, 1979), 176; Overseas Development Council,
U.S. Foreign Policy and the Third World: Agenda 1983, eds. John P.
Lewis and Valeriana Kallab (New York: Praeger, 1983), 207.

concern about *any* proposals for regulation of economic activity at the international level: There is no evidence, they say, that regulation or even redistribution would reduce poverty or narrow the gap between rich and poor in the long run.[8]

But both critics and advocates of NIEO agree on one point—that the gap in wealth between rich nations and poor nations is large, and is not noticeably declining. As Figure N.5 illustrates, the income gap clearly is widening; on the other hand, there has been some improvement in life expectancy and other indicators of well-being. Death rates in particular have dropped significantly, as Figure N.6 reveals.

The real, underlying issue is not so much the width of the "North-South gap" as it is the poverty in the South. The World Bank reported that in 1980 almost one billion people lived in absolute poverty, most of them in developing nations.[9] The illiteracy rate for developing nations exceeded 40 percent.[10] The 1983 Population Reference Bureau statistics show that nearly 600 million people live in countries where the average life expectancy is less than fifty years.[11] Most countries in which hunger persists as a basic issue are found in the Third World.[12]

The Brandt Commission describes life in the South:

Few people in the North have any detailed conception of the extent of poverty in the Third World or of the forms that it takes. Many hundreds of millions of people in the poorer countries are preoccupied solely with survival and elementary needs. For them work is frequently not available or, when it is, pay is very low and conditions are often barely tolerable. Homes are constructed of impermanent materials and have neither piped water nor sanitation. Electricity is a luxury. Health services are thinly spread and in rural areas only rarely within walking distance. Primary schools, where they exist, may be free and not too far away, but children are needed for work and cannot easily be spared for schooling. Permanent insecurity is the condition of the poor. There are no public systems of social security in the event of unemployment, sickness or death of a wage-earner in the family. Flood, drought or disease affecting people or livestock can destroy livelihoods without hope of compensation....

The poorest people in the world will remain for some time to come outside the reach of normal trade and communications. The combination of malnutrition, illiteracy, disease, high birth rates, underemployment and low income closes off the avenues of escape; and while other groups are increasingly vocal, the poor and illiterate are usually and conveniently silent. It is a condition of life so limited as to be, in the words of the President of the World Bank, "below any rational definition of human decency."[13]

The International Economic System

How does the international economic system work? Are international trade and politics linked to poverty and hunger? If so, how? Economists have produced a voluminous body of literature on these questions. Here are some facts and principles about which there is general agreement.

First let us look at how an economic system produces goods and services. For such a system to produce all the goods and services people want and need, many "factors of production"—labor, capital, technological know-how, resources, energy, and education—must come together in productive combinations. According to

322

some economists, economic growth depends mostly on capital. Capital is the physical ability to produce (in the sense of capital goods—electricity-generating plants, steel mills, trucks, lathes, tractors, and so on). Combined with labor and the other factors of production, capital generates output—products and services. Sometimes *financial* capital is referred to as "capital." However, financial capital is *money*, which often is used to buy capital goods.

If one assumes (as most economists do) that resources are limited, the production of goods always involves choice. To make a hoe, one must divert labor and resources away from growing grain. To build a steel mill, one must divert resources away from building a school or an apartment building.

How is capital created? By using productive capacity to produce *more* productive capacity, rather than to manufacture consumer products. By consuming less in the short term and investing the savings in capital goods, the long-term result will be more production and consumption. The more capital available, the more output can be produced; the more output produced, the more can be saved and invested. These increased investments can make more capital available for production in the future. That is what fuels economic growth.

Poor countries have very little capital. They can create more in five basic ways:

Poor countries have very little capital. They can create more in five basic ways.

1. Reduce consumption in the short term in order to invest from their own savings;

2. Receive aid in the form of physical capital or in the form of money that can be used to buy capital;

3. Borrow money to buy capital. This allows productive capacity to grow without reducing current consumption; however, the money must be paid for out of future consumption—when, presumably, there will be more output and saving will be easier;

4. Trade surplus products that can be produced with little capital (primarily agricultural products raised labor intensively) for capital;

5. Encourage investment from outside, thereby allowing savings from richer countries to be used for purchasing capital goods.

TABLE N.1. MEASURES OF THE GAP BETWEEN RICH AND POOR (1980)

	Richest Fifth of World Population	Poorest Fifth of World Population
GNP per Capita (Dollars)	9,469	206
Government Education Expenditures per Capita (Dollars)	497	6
Teachers per 1,000 School-Age Population	40	12
Women in Total University Enrollment (Percentage)	43	27
Adult Literacy (Percentage)	97	42
Government Health Expenditures per Capita (Dollars)	432	2
Physicians per 10,000 People	21	3
Life Expectancy (Years)	74	53
Infant Deaths per 100 Births	2	12
Calories per Capita as Percentage of Requirements	134	90
Protein Supply per Capita (Grams)	99	48
Population with Safe Water (Percentage)	96	39

Source: Ruth Leger Sivard, *World Military and Social Expenditures 1983* (Washington, DC: World Priorities, 1983), 25. Copyright © 1983 World Priorities, Leesburg, VA 22075.

TABLE N.2. MAJOR DEVELOPING-COUNTRY DEBTORS

	External Public Debt Outstanding[a]		External Public Debt as Percent of GNP		Public Debt Service[b] as Percent of Exports of Goods and Services		Average Annual Growth of Public Debt 1970–1981
	1970	1981	1970	1981	1971	1980	(Percentage)
	($ Billions)						
Brazil	3.2	44.0	7.2	16.4	14.8	34.4	26.8
Mexico	3.2	42.6	9.7	26.4	22.7	31.8	26.5
Korea, Rep.	1.8	20.0	20.9	29.9	19.2	12.2	24.5
India	7.9	17.9	14.9	10.3	22.3	8.6[c]	7.7
Indonesia	2.4	15.5	27.1	20.0	7.8	8.0	18.3
Algeria	0.9	14.4	18.5	34.6	5.8	24.9	28.2
Egypt	1.6	13.9	23.8	52.2	28.8	15.6	21.4
Israel	2.3	13.9	41.3	64.2	11.8	11.6	17.9
Turkey	1.9	13.8	14.4	19.9	11.9	16.8	20.0
Venezuela	0.7	11.4	6.6	17.7	3.8	13.3	28.4
Argentina	1.9	10.5	7.6	14.6	20.3	17.7	16.9
Yugoslavia	1.2	5.3	8.5	8.4	5.5	3.5	14.4
Chile	2.1	4.4	26.2	15.3	21.2	21.9	7.2
Total, 13 Developing Countries	31.2	227.5	13.2	20.0[d]	14.3	17.7	19.8

(a) Disbursed (long-term and medium-term); includes publicly guaranteed private debt.
(b) Repayments of principal (amortization) plus interest payments.
(c) 1979 figure.
(d) Estimate.

Note: The countries in this table are the thirteen largest holders of debt, both public and private, although data on privately held debt are not available for all countries. Of the countries that did report private debt, Argentina had $12.2 billion, Brazil $19.8 billion, and Yugoslavia $10.9 billion in 1981. Total public debt for the developing countries in 1981 was $368 billion; total reported debt disbursed (public and private) in 1981 was $462 billion; and total reported debt outstanding (disbursed and undisbursed, public and private) was $592.7 billion.

Source: Overseas Development Council, *U.S. Foreign Policy and the Third World: Agenda 1983,* eds. John P. Lewis and Valeriana Kallab (New York: Praeger, 1983), 200.

Solutions 2 through 5 require interactions with the international trade and aid systems. Because the poor countries are frustrated by these interactions, they call for a new international economic order. In the text that follows, each of the five ways of creating capital is discussed.

Growth from Own Savings. About 85 percent of the capital investment in the poor countries comes from their own internal savings.[14] Since income is so low in these countries, savings rates are relatively low, and capital growth is slow. Moreover, simply keeping the consumption rates constant for poorer countries' rapidly growing populations requires fully two-thirds of their economic growth. Contrast that with the one-fourth required in rich countries, where savings are higher and population growth rates are lower.[15]

Foreign Aid. Of the monies invested in developing countries, 15 percent comes from someone else's savings—i.e., external resources.[16] In 1981, about 30 percent of these external resources came in the form of official development assistance (foreign aid) from DAC countries (see Figure N.8). Most of this assistance was devoted to increasing or improving publicly owned capital, such as roads, railroads, ports, dams, and communications systems.

Borrowing. An increasing proportion of capital investment in developing countries is financed by borrowing, either from public sources (such as other governments or the World Bank) or from private sources (primarily from commercial banks). After the oil price increases of the early 1970s, the Third

TABLE N.3. RELATION BETWEEN INTEREST PAYMENTS ON EXTERNAL DEBTS AND
EXPORT EARNINGS FOR SOME MAJOR DEBTOR COUNTRIES

Country	Total External Debt (Billion Dollars)	Estimated Export Earnings (Billion Dollars)	Share of Export Earnings to Pay Interest[a] (Percentage)
Brazil	93.5	17.5	64
Mexico	86.6	22.2	47
South Korea	40.3	19.4	25
Argentina	38.5	9.2	50
Venezuela	31.5	12.9	29
Indonesia	28.8	16.8	21
Poland	27.0	10.2	31
Turkey	23.6	5.2	54
Philippines	22.7	5.7	47
Yugoslavia	20.0	10.3	23
Chile	18.7	4.1	54
Thailand	13.5	8.4	19
Peru	12.5	3.7	41
Malaysia	11.3	12.4	11
Taiwan	8.5	27.5	4
Ecuador	7.1	2.1	38

Source: Lester R. Brown et al., *State of the World 1984* (New York: W. W. Norton, 1984), 17.

(a)   Assumes interest rate of 12 percent; total debt service, including principal repayment, is of course much larger.

World's level of borrowing increased rapidly, not only to pay for new capital, but
also to pay for oil imports to keep already-installed capital operating. Many loans
to developing countries come on "concessional" terms, which means that the
interest rates are lower than commercial rates and the payback periods are
longer. However, loans do have to be repaid; and loan repayments have become
a substantial burden on the economies of borrower nations. The trends in foreign
indebtedness appear in Figure N.9 and Table N.2.

Trade.   Of the money flowing into Third World countries from abroad, 80 percent
is earned by the exports of these countries.[17] But such exports comprise a relatively small fraction—only about one-fourth—of total world trade, the great bulk
of which goes to the developed countries. Only 7 percent of world trade takes
place *between* the Third World nations.[18] (See Table N.4.)

*Eighty percent of the money flowing
into Third World countries is earned
by exports.*

Most Third World exports are "primary products"—minerals and agricultural
products that have been directly extracted from the resource base with minimal
human or mechanical processing. In 1980, developing countries depended on
primary products for 79 percent of their export earnings.[19] Half these countries
earn at least 50 percent of their export money from a single product—usually
coffee, sugar, or minerals.[20]

TABLE N.4. TRADE FLOWS AS A PERCENTAGE OF WORLD TRADE (1980)

(Percentage) From	To	North	South	Total
North		50	24	74
South		19	7	26
		69	31	100

Source: World Bank, *World Development Report 1981* (New York: Oxford University Press, 1981), 12.

This map shows the distribution of geographically allocated direct net investment flows to the Third World from major source countries, 1979–1981 (in percentages).

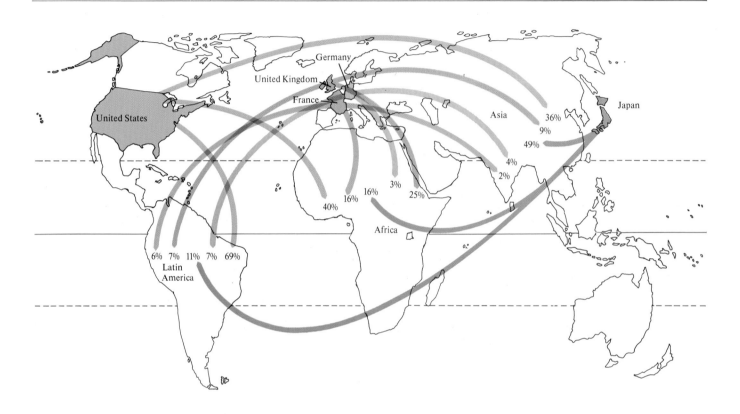

Source: South, no. 32 (June 1983): 55.

FIGURE N.8. COMPOSITION OF DEVELOPMENT ASSISTANCE COMMITTEE RESOURCES TO DEVELOPING COUNTRIES

Percent

- Private Investment and Lending
- Private Export Credits
- Private Voluntary Agency Grants[a]
- Nonconcessional Official Flows
- Official Development Assistance (ODA)

1964–1966 Average   1970   1975   1981

a. Data on private voluntary grants are not available for 1964–1966 average.

Source: Overseas Development Council, *U.S. Foreign Policy and the Third World: Agenda 1983,* eds. John P. Lewis and Valeriana Kallab (New York: Praeger, 1983), 275.

It makes sense that a large amount of primary products flows from the South. By trading resource-intensive goods for capital-intensive goods or for capital itself, Third World countries can build up the productive capacity of their economies. However, the terms of trade for their products are getting worse. Petroleum and manufactured goods—that is, what poor countries import—have risen in price much faster than have agricultural products or basic minerals. For example, from 1970 to 1980 the price of coffee rose nearly four times, sugar rose by a factor of 6.5, copper by 1.6, iron ore by 2.3, and tea by 2.1. Petroleum, however, rose by a factor of 22.3.[21] Because the terms of trade are getting worse, the amount of money flowing into the developing countries is consistently less than the amount of money flowing out. Debt has financed the difference.

Manufacturing capacity in the Third World has grown, and exports of products such as textiles, radios, fertilizers, and shoes have risen in value from $13 billion in 1970 to $91.6 billion in 1979.[22] But 50 percent of the South's manufactured exports are exported by South Korea, Taiwan, Singapore, and Hong Kong.[23]

Private Investment. In 1981, about half of the DAC external resources going into the South came from private investors—primarily, commercial banks and multinational corporations—that finance and/or build productive capital in Third World countries (see Figure N.8). Ownership of this capital is partially or wholly external, and, of course, profits from its operation flow back to the owners. However, the contributions to the countries that are invested in may be large— through creation of jobs, wages, resource development, and royalties on extracted resources. Foreign investments can also generate the need for supporting industries and services that may be domestically owned.

In summary, the developing countries feel that the conditions imposed upon them by the current international economic order discriminate against them so much that fundamental changes must be made if hunger and poverty are ever to be eradicated.

Trade and Tariff Reform

Proposals for reforming the international economic order invariably include removing impediments to trade. What are the nature and impact of these impediments? For centuries, nations have attempted to regulate international trade in ways that would especially benefit their own citizens. Traditionally, this has occurred in three ways. The first is tariffs—import taxes on goods from other countries, designed to make foreign goods more expensive and thus to promote the sales of domestic industries. The second is quotas—limits on the amounts of foreign goods that can be imported. The third is subsidies—allowances to domestic producers that let them offer their goods on the international market at prices lower than those of other nations.[24]

More than 200 years ago, Adam Smith argued that all interferences with free trade harm the system as a whole. Without such interferences, every producer in the world would be able to offer wares in a free, competitive marketplace, and every consumer would be able to choose freely among all goods. At one time or another, most nations have erected one or more barriers to free trade; but since 1945, the world has moved increasingly toward lowering national trade barriers.[25]

In 1948, a number of developed countries agreed on a new framework, called General Agreement on Tariffs and Trade (GATT), for addressing questions involving trade barriers.[26] GATT has produced a long series of international

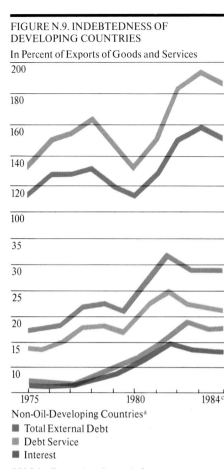

FIGURE N.9. INDEBTEDNESS OF DEVELOPING COUNTRIES

In Percent of Exports of Goods and Services

1975   1980   1984[c]

Non-Oil-Developing Countries[a]
- Total External Debt
- Debt Service
- Interest

25 Major Borrowing Countries[b]
- Total External Debt
- Debt Service
- Interest

a. Excluding China.

b. These countries are Algeria, Argentina, Brazil, Chile, Colombia, Egypt, Hungary, India, Indonesia, Israel, Malaysia, Mexico, Morocco, Nigeria, Pakistan, Peru, Philippines, Portugal, Romania, South Africa, South Korea, Thailand, Turkey, Venezuela, and Yugoslavia.

c. Projections.

Source: International Monetary Fund, *World Economic Outlook,* Occasional Paper no. 27 (April 1984): 62.

Percentage of World Production

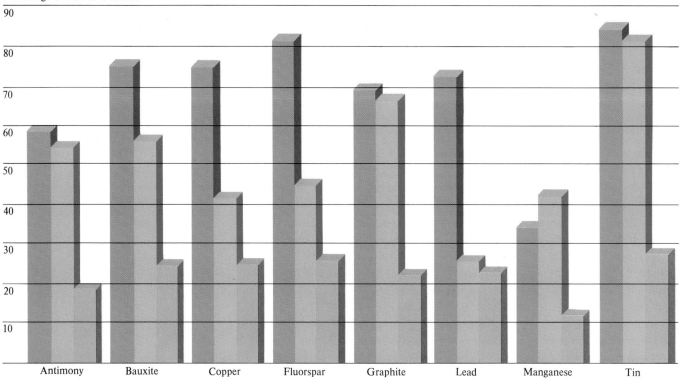

The North's Consumption of Strategic Materials
The South's Output of Strategic Materials
United States's Consumption of Strategic Materials

Source: Third World Foundation, *Third World Diary 1981* (London: Radnor House, 1980).

negotiations, which gradually have resulted in reciprocal tariff cuts. More than eighty nations, both rich and poor, have joined GATT; its member nations now account for 80 percent of international trade.[27] As a result of GATT negotiations (in forums with names such as the Kennedy Round and the Tokyo Round), the United States—historically, a high-tariff nation—reduced tariff rates on dutiable imports to less than 10 percent. (Compare this to the roughly 60 percent rate in 1934, at the time of the Trade Agreements Act.)[28] In the past, GATT dealt only with manufactured goods, and tariffs on them have been decreasing. After the Tokyo Round in 1979, GATT nations agreed to apply the same tariff and non-tariff concessions to agricultural products—the main exports of the Third World.[29] Before this agreement, Third World countries found GATT's principles of reciprocity and nondiscrimination largely meaningless, as they had little to offer at the bargaining table. As the Pakistani representative said at the 1961 GATT ministerial meeting, "It is like asking a person who has no income to produce evidence of his earnings if he wants to earn more."[30]

Frustrated with GATT, Third World nations pressed for an alternative approach. The response was the establishment of the United Nations Conference on Trade and Development (UNCTAD), which held its first meeting in 1964.[31] UNCTAD can only make recommendations, but it has greatly influenced how individual United Nations member states have structured their individual national-development policies: It led to one of the first organized expressions of Third World views on international trade, and provided a first "test-bed" for the NIEO.

Within UNCTAD, a theory gradually gained ground: The world economy should be adjusted—beyond protective trade barriers for the rich countries, even beyond free trade—to protect the poor countries actively. Even if trade were free, the argument goes, stronger competitors will systematically squeeze the poor countries out of the market. In order to establish an environment that supports development, the international system must be structured to give developing countries some form of "protection" from such competition.

Schools of Thought on the New International Economic Order

At the heart of the NIEO debate is the question: For poor nations to develop their economies and end their poverty, what needs to be done—and by whom? Another frequently asked question is: Who is responsible for the present situation?

For poor countries to develop their economies and end their poverty, what needs to be done—and by whom?

Proponents of the NIEO, in its various forms, believe that poor nations are that way because the system is stacked against them and because they are exploited by richer, more powerful nations. They also lack the capital resources and, in some cases, the natural and human resources needed for development. Accordingly, the system needs to be changed, and wealth needs to be redistributed. Some Third World leaders blame colonialism for the present state of affairs. Others point to multinational corporations as exploiters and impediments to development.

Critics of the NIEO emphasize two points: the responsibility of Third World nations for their current problems, and the importance of individual initiative in the context of a free-market economy. Poor countries, these experts believe, are that way principally because of their leaders' decisions and quality of leadership. Can the United States, they ask, really be blamed for the excesses of an Idi Amin or the economic incompetence of a Julius Nyerere? The solution is less rhetoric, fewer government regulations, more equitable systems of taxation, and, in general, more opportunity for individuals and enterprises to play roles in the economy that will generate wealth and improve well-being.

In addressing the NIEO debate, we will examine certain schools of thought and points of view that touch on four basic questions:

1. Does the present economic order meet the development needs of Third World nations and offer them an opportunity for a better future?

2. Where change is needed, must it be fundamental or should it be incremental? What changes will really produce results?

3. What is the role of multinational corporations in the present economic order? What should their role be in the future?

4. Do former colonial powers have an obligation to their former colonies? If so, what is the nature of that obligation?

School of Thought: To Promote Development and to End Hunger and Poverty, a New International Economic Order Must Be Established in Place of the Current International Economic Order

This school of thought holds that a New International Economic Order must be established. Supporting this stance are the following points of view: that "free markets" are biased against the Third World; that great changes— a "veritable revolution"— are needed to correct the problems of the current economic order; that an NIEO must have strong regulations that define and limit the role of multinationals in the Third World; and that former colonial powers have an obligation to redress the past wrongs done to their colonies.

Point of View Number 1

"Free Markets" Are Biased Against the Third World

How well does the present economic order meet the needs of Third World nations? Responding to the concerns expressed by the Group of 77, a group of twenty-one specialists from both industrialized and Third World nations was formed in 1974. Jan Tinbergen, a Nobel Laureate in economics, directed the group. Its report offered the following diagnosis of the economic maladies of the Third World:

[In the period following World War II, the poor nations] discovered that political liberation does not necessarily bring economic liberation and that the two are inseparable: that without political independence it is impossible to achieve economic independence; and without economic power, a nation's political independence is incomplete and insecure....

The poor nations have been forced to question the basic premises of an international system which leads to ever widening disparities between the richest and poorest nations and to a persistent denial of equality of opportunity. They contend that the "free" market is in fact not "free" but works to the advantage of the industrialized nations, who have used it to construct a protective wall around their affluence and life-styles. And even if it were "free," it would still work to the advantage of the industrialized nations because of their enormous political and economic strength.[32]

Citing some telling statistics, United Nations Development Program Director Bradford Morse observes:

The developing countries—with two-thirds of the world's population—produce less than one-third of the world's food, less than one-tenth of its industrial goods, and less than one-twelfth of its power output. That is an appallingly inefficient division of global labor—and a house divided with a vengeance.[33]

FIGURE N.11. THE GAP BETWEEN RICH AND POOR: A PRO-NIEO PERSPECTIVE

*This graph, emphasizing the gap between rich
and poor nations, is typical of the data that
proponents of the NIEO present to support
their position.*

■ Developing World
■ Developed World

The Developing World Has:

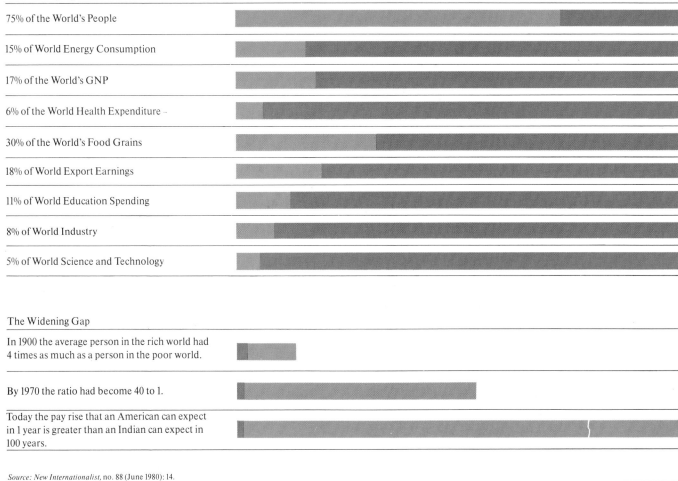

75% of the World's People

15% of World Energy Consumption

17% of the World's GNP

6% of the World Health Expenditure

30% of the World's Food Grains

18% of World Export Earnings

11% of World Education Spending

8% of World Industry

5% of World Science and Technology

The Widening Gap

In 1900 the average person in the rich world had 4 times as much as a person in the poor world.

By 1970 the ratio had become 40 to 1.

Today the pay rise that an American can expect in 1 year is greater than an Indian can expect in 100 years.

Source: New Internationalist, no. 88 (June 1980): 14.

FIGURE N.12. DETERIORATING TERMS OF TRADE OF THE NON-OIL-DEVELOPING COUNTRIES

*Data such as those pictured in this graph are
used by proponents of the NIEO to justify programs and policies that would stabilize the
terms of trade between the developed and*
*the developing countries. The data show that
the terms of trade of the non-oil-developing
countries have deteriorated to the lowest level
in 25 years. This situation reflects a precipitous*
*decline in the prices of their commodity exports
relative to the prices of their imports. These
countries are thus less able to pay for needed imports of food, raw materials, and capital goods.*

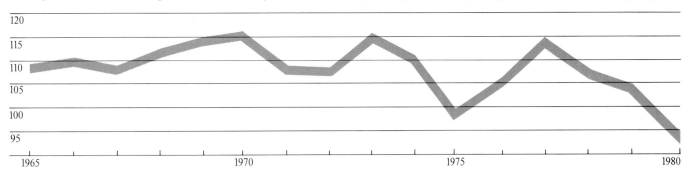

Note: Terms of trade are determined by the ratio of export prices to import prices and indicate what quantity of imports a country can receive in exchange for a given quantity of its exports. An index of 100 suggests that a given quantity of exports will exchange for a like amount of imports; an index below 100 indicates that a quantity of exports will exchange for a lesser amount of imports.

Source: Overseas Development Council, *U.S. Foreign Policy and the Third World: Agenda 1983,* eds. John P. Lewis and Valeriana Kallab (New York: Praeger, 1983), 197.

One problem with the current system, say NIEO proponents, is that so-called free markets are not really free, but are biased against the Third World. Former World Bank official Mahbub ul Haq puts it this way:

Developing countries contend that many market structures are biased against their interests. If this is not so, they argue, then why do they receive back only 10–15 per cent of the final price paid by consumers for their internationally traded commodities? Why only a 4 per cent share in new international reserve creation over the last twenty-five years? Why so little participation in international economic decision making?

The developed countries argue that they are not manipulating the market system, but they conveniently fail to explain why anyone should expect international market structures to work any better than national market structures, which also bypass the interests of the poor.[34]

Economic dependence is viewed as another endemic problem with the current international economic order. UN Ambassador Donald O. Mills of Jamaica, formerly chairman of the Group of 77, views dependence as a legacy of the colonial era:

The developed nations, particularly during the period of colonialism, carved out relationships and a global economic system that operate to our disadvantage.

Whatever the motivation behind the colonial system might have been in the beginning, we ended up with a system in which the colonies were used as plantations, by and large, to produce certain materials and supplies for the benefit of the metropolitan countries.

Many of our countries became heavily dependent on single commodities. Trade between developing countries was discouraged, as was our development of shipping, communications, banking services and all the rest.

After winning our independence, we still find ourselves on the losing end of an economic system that is very much a product of that historical situation.[35]

Great Changes— a "Veritable Revolution"—Are Needed to Correct the Problems of the Current Order

According to Kenneth Dadzie, former UN director-general for Development and International Economic Co-operation:

The old economic order is no longer viable and its system of management is no longer capable of achieving the necessary harmonisation of the interests of the major actors, let alone stimulating international development. We thus confront a major crisis in the world economy....in order to surmount this crisis, there is an inescapable need for decision-making to be shared by all groups of countries and for even international development to be made an explicit and central objective of international co-operation....the problems of the international economy are too pervasive to be tackled other than by global decision-making....there must be a veritable revolution in perspectives and perceptions.[36]

French President François Mitterand also believes that fundamental, not incremental, changes in the current economic order are called for. He addresses the need to reform the international monetary system:

Until the international monetary system is reformed, it will be impossible to have a policy for the Third World designed to solve the problem of hunger....

In my opinion, the problem of the Third World will not be solved until the industrial countries—the "haves"—find the courage, and therefore the wisdom, to impose new rules on themselves in their international monetary exchanges.[37]

The specific fundamental changes in the current economic order that have been proposed are broadly outlined in the statement of principles adopted at the Sixth Special Session of the UN General Assembly. This statement is generally regarded as the basic philosophical description of the NIEO. The following excerpt emphasizes some of the more specific proposals for reform of the international economy:

The new international economic order should be founded on full respect for the following principles.

The new international economic order should be founded on full respect for the following principles: ...

Equal participation of all countries in the solving of world economic problems in the common interest of all countries, bearing in mind the necessity to ensure the accelerated development of all the developing countries, while devoting particular attention to the adoption of special measures in favour of the least developed, land-locked and island developing countries as well as those developing countries most seriously affected by economic crises and natural calamities, without losing sight of the interests of other developing countries;

Every country has the right to adopt the economic and social system that it deems to be the most appropriate for its own development and not to be subjected to discrimination of any kind as a result;

Every country has the right to exercise permanent sovereignty over its natural resources and all economic activities....

Control of the activities of transnational corporations by taking measures in the interest of the national economies of the countries where such transnational corporations operate on the basis of the full sovereignty of those countries;

Right of the developing countries and the peoples of territories under colonial and racial domination and foreign occupation to struggle for their liberation and for the purpose of regaining effective control over their natural resources and economic activities; ...

Establishment of a just and equitable relationship between the prices of raw materials, primary products, manufactured and semi-manufactured goods exported by developing countries and the prices of raw materials, primary commodities, manufactures, capital goods and equipment imported by them with the aim of improving their terms of trade which have continued to deteriorate.[38]

Point of View Number 3

A New International Economic Order Must Have Strong Regulations That Define and Limit the Role of Multinationals in the Third World

NIEO proponents believe that such regulations are needed because multi-nationals, in their drive for profits, actually *create* conditions that exacerbate hunger and poverty. Here is how Richard J. Barnet of the Washington, DC-based Institute for Policy Studies sees it:

The Brandt Report distinguishes between the countries of the rich North and the poor South, and this map has become the symbol of real concern for the problems of the Third World and its interrelations with the more developed world. The map itself is based on the recently developed Peters Projection, rather than the more commonly used Mercator Projection. It provides a less Eurocentric representation of the world. Its surface distortions are distributed at the poles and the equator; the more densely peopled parts of the earth are, it is claimed, in proportion to one another.

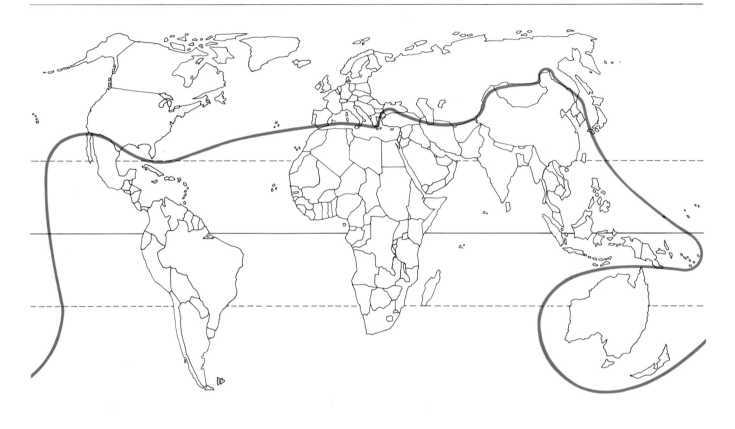

Source: J. P. Dickenson et al., A Geography of the Third World (New York: Methuen, 1983), 2.

FIGURE N.14. MULTINATIONAL CORPORATIONS

This map shows where just four multinationals,
Nestlé, Phillips, British American Tobacco, and
IBM, have subsidiaries—227 in 91 different
countries. Within the Third World each
provides a local base for marketing MNC
products in neighboring countries. Opponents
of MNCs use maps like this to support their view.

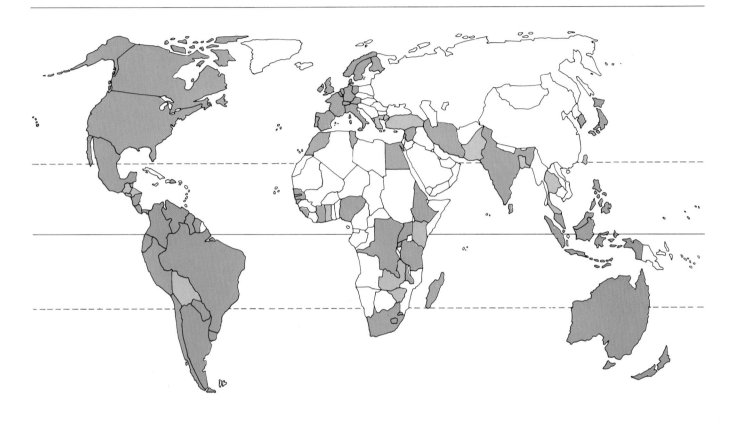

Number of the named four companies present:
- 4
- 3
- 2
- 1

Source: *New Internationalist*, no. 98 (April 1981): 13.

FIGURE N.15. EUROPEAN COLONIES IN AFRICA, ASIA, AND OCEANIA (1914)

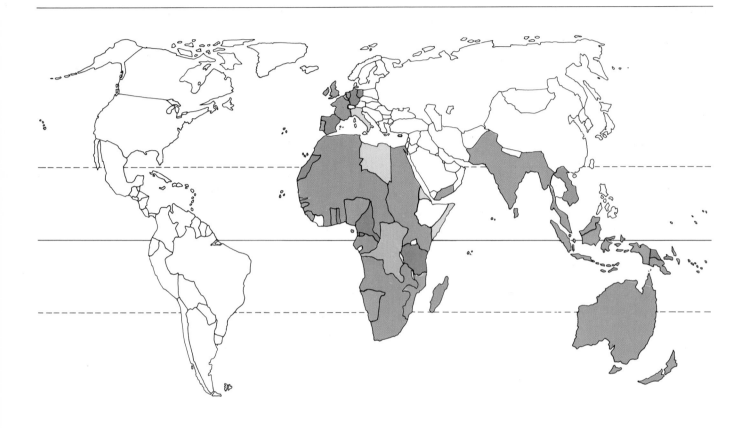

The Colonies as They Appeared in 1914:

- British
- French
- German
- Portuguese
- Dutch
- Italian
- Spanish
- Belgian

Source: New Internationalist, no. 98 (April 1981): 12–13.

The ultimate "food power" lies in the growing ability of these multinational corporations to control the production and marketing of food....

There is growing evidence from all over the world that food strategies that are highly profitable for the multinationals actually increase maldistribution of food and increase hunger. Many observers conclude that the bottom 20 to 60 percent of the population in various Third World "food deficient countries"... have less adequate and less nutritious diets than their parents and grandparents did.[39]

This antimultinational point of view is developed more fully in William W. Murdoch's *The Poverty of Nations:*

There seems little doubt that the TNCs [transnational corporations] in general are an obstacle to real development. The basic problem is that the goals of the TNC do not conform to the requirements of real development, particularly the needs of the poor majority in the LDCs [less developed countries]....

First, because the TNC is interested in producing the same sorts of goods [in LDCs] as it does in the West, using the same sorts of technology, it produces generally inessential and inappropriate goods in relation to LDC needs. It is the essence of TNC production and marketing techniques that these goods are oversophisticated, overelaborate, and highly packaged and promoted products. Rarely is the technology adapted to local needs and resources....

Rarely is the technology adapted to local needs and resources.

Secondly, while the activities of TNCs increase the power of some small local groups, they inhibit local businesses and the development of domestic entrepreneurship. They do this through the mechanisms already discussed— soaking up local capital, dominating the technology, taking over local firms, and so on.

Thirdly, TNC activities lead to a loss of national control over local productive assets and over important economic decisions, and there is evidence that this "denationalization" is increasing....

Finally, because they have economic power, TNCs are powerful social and political forces in many LDCs. At its most straightforward, this force is applied by making or withholding investments.... Investments have been withheld from leftist regimes and have expanded when rightist regimes took over. Political power accrues to the local groups that work closely with the TNCs, and at times this relationship has been bolstered by corporate bribery. In at least one case (ITT in Chile), there has been corporate collusion with the U.S. Central Intelligence Agency (CIA) in overthrowing a socialist government.[40]

In a minority report to the Presidential Commission on World Hunger, Eugene Stockwell of the World Council of Churches specifically addresses the negative impact of multinational corporations on the world's hungry people:

Too much corporate activity in today's world hurts rather than helps the world's hungry: the use of resources for the advantage of the wealthy rather than the poor, export cropping that uses land for corporate profits but not for feeding the hungry, the use of power and influence with developing country governments to secure privilege, and the creation by advertising of appetites for non-nutritional products and for products that militate against basic health and wellbeing.[41]

Former Colonial Powers Have an Obligation to Redress the Past Wrongs Done to Their Colonies

Isidoro Malmierca, the minister of foreign affairs of Cuba, feels this way:

The nonaligned countries have requested neither gifts nor alms.... [The] massive and sustained flow of resources of every kind ... [demanded by the nonaligned on behalf of the developing countries is] none other than the return of the resources drawn from our countries for centuries of colonial and neocolonial exploitation.[42]

The point of view that colonialism is the cause of poverty in the Third World both explains the problem and morally justifies redistributive programs. This viewpoint was articulated by the late Walter Rodney, a Guyanese scholar and political leader.

Colonialism created conditions which led not just to periodic famine, but to chronic undernourishment, malnutrition and deterioration in the physique of the African people. If such a statement sounds wildly extravagant, it is only because bourgeois propaganda has conditioned even Africans to believe that malnutrition and starvation were the <u>natural</u> lot of Africans from time immemorial. A black child with a transparent rib-case, huge head, bloated stomach, protruding eyes, and twigs as arms and legs was the favourite poster of [a large charitable operation which].... never bothered [European] consciences by telling them that capitalism and colonialism created the starvation, suffering and misery of the child in the first place.[43]

School of Thought: The Present Economic Order Is Working Well — If Anything, It Needs to Be Strengthened. The Proposals for a New International Economic Order Are Based on False Premises, Are Impractical, and Are Potentially Dangerous

This school of thought holds that the current economic order is effective, and that proposals for a new order are in fact dangerous. The following points of view are offered in support of this stance: that the current economic order is not the source of the serious economic problems faced by Third World nations; that the poverty of Third World nations is not due to developed nations plundering their resources; that developing countries do not all have the same needs; that multinational corporations are contributing to Third World development; that the NIEO debate is concerned only with economic justice between nations, and thus is irrelevant to the most important human issues of economic and social development; and that basic needs and human development, not economic growth, are the real issues.

The Current Economic Order Is Not the Source of the Serious Economic Problems Faced by Third World Nations

Although Overseas Development Council President John W. Sewell is inclined to support some NIEO proposals, he takes care to point out that Third World countries made real progress during the 1970s under the present system:

The progress achieved by the Third World as a whole in the 1970s was in some respects very striking. The annual GNP growth rate of the developing countries was 5.7 per cent (compared with 3.4 per cent in the industrial countries), and, despite the increase in protectionist measures in the mid-1970s, their aggregate manufactured exports increased at an annual rate of more than 10 per cent. It was also a remarkable achievement that the developing countries together managed to save and reinvest nearly a quarter of their national income—even while their oil-import bill skyrocketed to the detriment of their development progress and while official development assistance fell far short of the U.N. target set a decade ago. The progress of the developing countries was also impressive in terms of human well-being. Life expectancy in the Third World increased in two decades by as much as it increased in the industrialized nations in a century, and a number of major diseases, including smallpox, were virtually eradicated. The Physical Quality of Life Index (PQLI)—a composite measure incorporating indicators of infant mortality, life expectancy, and literacy—increased in the developing world from 39 in 1960 to 57 in the late 1970s.[44]

The World Bank sounded a similarly positive note in its 1980 *World Development Report:*

Considerable progress has been made in reducing the incidence of poverty over the past 30 years.... Progress would have been greater still but for the dramatic growth of population....

Since 1950 income per person in the developing world has doubled....

The proportion of people in absolute poverty in developing countries as a group is estimated to have fallen during the past two decades.... But because population has grown, the number of people in absolute poverty has increased.

There has also been progress in education. The proportion of adults in developing countries who are literate is estimated to have increased over the past three decades from about 30 percent to more than 50 percent; the proportion of children of primary-school age enrolled in school rose from 47 percent in 1960 to 64 percent in 1977....

The most striking advances against poverty have been in health. Average life expectancy in middle-income developing countries has risen nine years over the past three decades. In low-income countries, the increase has been even greater—15 years.[45]

William Simon, United States treasury secretary during the Nixon and Ford administrations, believes that the present economic order, while imperfect, is fundamentally sound and is far superior to any of the proposed alternatives. Simon is an active spokesperson for free-market solutions to development problems, as the following excerpt makes clear:

As the basis for cooperation between developed and developing countries evolves, we must preserve the fundamental principles—such as reliance upon market forces and the private sector—on which our common prosperity depends. Solutions must be dynamic and expansionary, so that all parties will benefit. Thus, we must seek increased production and improved efficiency, not just transfer of wealth....

The role of the private sector is critical. There is no substitute for a vigorous private sector mobilizing the resources and energies of the peoples of the developing countries. The technology and management expertise that the private sector commands in the industrial countries is badly needed by the LDC's and private markets can provide essential capital resources they need for investments.

A free market is not perfect but it is better than any alternative system....

To the degree elements of the New International Economic Order conflict with the basic principles of free markets and free enterprise, we must decisively reject them.[46]

Considerable progress has been made in reducing the incidence of poverty over the past 30 years.

There is no substitute for a vigorous private sector.

Economist Richard Cooper served as United States undersecretary of state for economic affairs in the Carter Administration. He is another critic of the NIEO:

Major changes in the system can have important implications for our own welfare.

We understand and sympathize with the aspirations of the developing countries. However, we also have an enormous stake in the continuing smooth functioning of the international economic system. We are the world's largest exporter and importer of both raw materials and manufactured goods, the largest overseas investor, and the largest international debtor as well as the largest creditor. Major changes in the system can thus have important implications for our own welfare.

As we look back over the past three decades, we believe that the system has responded flexibly, if not always smoothly, to major changes in the world, including the growing economic and political importance of the developing countries. We favor continued evolution of the system to meet new situations. But suggested changes must have a high probability of improving the system for everyone—if this is not the case, it makes no sense to disrupt a system which works reasonably well.[47]

Point of View Number 2

Third World Nations Are Poor, But Not Because Developed Nations Are Plundering Their Resources

Those who criticize the premises of the NIEO proposals offer this somewhat different point of view. Charles Krauthammer, writing in the *New Republic*, elaborates:

A more fashionable version of the argument that the West is responsible for third world poverty is based on a kind of ecological colonialism—the world is poor because the West is devouring its resources. The charge is usually directed at the US.... The Brandt report complains that one American uses as much energy as 105 Sri Lankans. It does not say that for every $1,000 of GNP produced, the US consumes two and a half barrels of oil, while for developing countries and Japan the average is about two. Given America's continental size and mechanized agriculture, the discrepancy is not unreasonable. Furthermore, the argument is that we are plundering (at $35 a barrel) the resources of others. But if we look at the relevant measure of plunder—oil imports—US consumption on a GNP basis is about half Japan's.

We are also accused of wasting the world's food. While US per capita caloric intake is high (though less than that of Bulgaria or Poland), the relevant fact regarding third world poverty is that the US is an enormous net food exporter. Some might feel guilty about eating a Big Mac while there is still hunger in the world. That may be an argument for greater generosity on the part of the US. It is not an argument that the US causes third world poverty.[48]

Point of View Number 3

Developing Countries Do Not All Have the Same Needs

Roger A. Brooks, a Heritage Foundation Roe fellow, expresses this point of view:

There is a wide diversity of interest among the various developing countries. The poorest countries seek increased official development assistance; middle-income countries seek balance-of-payments support and improved conditions for commodity trade; and the wealthier developing countries are most concerned about access to markets for industrial products, technology, and capital. Policies that might help one group of developing countries would be of limited value, or even detrimental to others.[49]

340

If the present economic order permits successful development, what are some of the notable successes? John Sewell identifies and comments upon some of them in the Overseas Development Council's *Agenda 1980*:

[The] average annual per capita GNP growth rates from 1960 to 1977 [of newly industrializing countries like Taiwan, South Korea, Brazil, Hong Kong and Singapore] were higher than that of the United States, even though their populations grew twice as fast. In all of the advanced developing countries (except Hong Kong) the share of industrial production within total gross domestic product is now higher than in the United States, and most of these countries performed at least twice as well as the United States in raising industrial productivity. Their export performance was even more striking: between 1967 and 1977, the average annual growth of their exports was 24 per cent (compared with 14 per cent in the United States and about 18 per cent in the industrialized countries as a whole).

Most of the advanced developing countries have changed from import-substitution to export-promotion policies. They have pursued outward-looking growth strategies that concentrate on exporting such low-cost consumer goods as apparel, footwear, and consumer electronics to the industrial countries. These countries are among the most rapidly growing markets for U.S. exports of agricultural products, machinery, transportation equipment, and high-technology goods and services, and they thereby contribute to the expansion of industry and the creation of jobs in the United States.[50]

The advanced developing countries contribute to the expansion of industry and the creation of jobs in the United States.

In an article on multinational corporations, Orville L. Freeman, secretary of agriculture during the Kennedy and Johnson administrations, and William Persen, Business International Corporation senior vice president, discuss Singapore's success, quoting Singapore's Prime Minister Lee Kuan Yew:

Lee Kuan Yew summarized Singapore's experiences as follows. "My experience leads me to conclude that developing countries can get their industries going with good indigenous managers, provided they have experienced foreign co-managers to show them what not to do in the early stages. Singapore's development would not have been possible if it had not been able to plug into the world grid of industrial powerhouses in America, Europe, and Japan." He noted that when Singaporeans went into joint ventures with U.S., European, and Japanese companies who provided the know-how, experience, and marketing, his country's enterprise failure fell from 38% to 7%, just 1% higher than the 6% failure rate of the wholly foreign-owned enterprises.[51]

Art Pine, a staff reporter for *The Wall Street Journal*, also discusses the successes and gains in Third World economies:

Over the past few years, South Korea and other advanced developing countries such as Mexico, Brazil and Taiwan have become formidable new rivals of the richer countries ... in steel ... shipbuilding, machine tools, construction and, more recently, electronics—basic industries that were once the richer countries' domain.[52]

Pine quotes Sir Roy Denman, the European Economic Community's ambassador to the United States, as saying that "The developing world is getting in the act...." Pine adds, "The suddenness of the developing countries' entry into these basic industries has caught the richer countries off guard."[53]

Multinational Corporations Are Contributing to Third World Development

Many experts feel that the multinational corporation is a powerful force for peace in the world today. For instance, Orville Freeman and William Persen present a new way of looking at multinationals: They say that multinationals may be the only genuinely apolitical and global organizations existing in the world today. As such, these corporations can provide leadership by moving beyond nationalism and addressing the global-level human concerns that affect us all.

An MNC [multinational corporation] is a company that produces and markets goods and services in more than one country, looks at the entire world as its area of operation, and acts accordingly....

These companies turn out about one-third of the world's gross product, about $1 trillion 250 billion worth of goods and services. For the last 20 years, the average growth of these companies has exceeded 10%, double the rate of economic advance in the industrial countries during the same period....

Since the end of World War II, the world has moved a long way from protectionism toward universalism and an open world for trade and investment. Multinational companies have been on the cutting edge of that development. Taking advantage of rapidly improving communications and transportation, MNCs have been a powerful force in hurdling national boundaries and restrictions, so that trade, commerce, goods, services, and ideas can flow more freely around the world to the benefit of all mankind....

The multinational corporation is a powerful force for peace in the world today.

The multinational corporation is a powerful force for peace in the world today. In its own interests, it seeks to minimize disruption and conflict between nation-states and to further a uniformity of tax, patent, and copyright laws, trade practices, and all the rules of the economic game worldwide, so it can reach out under common rules to serve the mass market.

In the global shopping center, which the world is increasingly becoming, antagonism between nations, jingoism, and restrictions on the flow of money, goods, people, or ideas are all anathema to the MNC. At the same time, its very process of reaching around the world, searching always for the most effective production constellation, brings the nations and the peoples of the world closer together, identifies the international problems that must be solved, develops a global social conscience, and experiments and tests the practicality of different organizational techniques to meet international problems.[54]

Economist Isaiah Frank speaks of the "quiet revolution" taking place between multinational corporations and the developing world. He raises the interesting possibility that negative views of multinationals may be based on past rather than present reality. Multinationals, says Frank, are capable of learning. So is their leadership. And so are the host countries with whom they work.

A quiet revolution is taking place in the relationship between multinational corporations and the developing world—they are learning to live together and like it.

This finding is one of the major conclusions of a study I recently conducted for the Committee for Economic Development and six of its overseas counterpart organizations. Despite much publicized conflicts, multinational corporations are becoming more sensitive to the political and social needs of the third world, while, at the same time, developing countries are demonstrating greater pragmatism and confidence in their negotiations with foreign firms....

The multinationals' attitude toward joint ventures has also changed. Although company opinion was divided, a substantial majority of firms are willing to accept some local equity participation. "We have fewer hang-ups on this subject today," said an executive of one firm whose historical position had been to insist on 100 percent ownership....

Just as transnationals have been increasingly accommodating to the changing realities in the third world, a significant evolution has been taking place in the attitudes of governments of developing countries. Longer contact and experience with multinationals have given host-country governments a better understanding of how the corporations operate and an appreciation that the relationship need not be of the zero-sum variety but can be one of mutual gain.[55]

Two case studies illustrate the constructive roles being played by the private sector in development. The excerpts, both from a conference report on the role of multinationals in development, describe the activities of two multinational corporations—Nestlé S.A. and Shell Petroleum.

Nestlé successfully participated in a Mexican rural development project:[56]

Summary of Case History: The Government of Mexico asked the Nestlé Company to participate in its Chontalpa Plan, a rural development program designed to help some 5000 families farming ejidos (Indian communal farms). Located in the humid tropics of the Gulf of Mexico, over 200,000 acres of land were reclaimed by the Government, which dammed the Grijalva River and brought settlers.

To aid dairy production, Nestlé first set up a pilot farm, and then worked with six of the twenty-two ejidos overseeing all technical aspects through its established Farm Technical Service, assisting ejido managers in administration, and guaranteeing private credit for operating capital (ejido land cannot be mortgaged).

The newly formed communities had little social cohesion, were fraught with dissent and nepotism, and few of the farmers were experienced in milk production. The Government was slow in draining the pastures, leading to excessive use of feed concentrates. All of these factors contributed to the unprofitability of the operation.

Nestlé responded by winnowing the number of farms to three, reducing its staff, simplifying production technology, and hiring a highly qualified project manager. The Government wrote off debts in arrears, prepared the pastures, and set up a single agency (instead of twelve as previously) to coordinate. The farmers elected new ejido leaders, took on more responsibilities instead of habitually relying on Nestlé technicians, eliminated overstaffing, and assigned more qualified workers to dairy production.

After five years, the operation became profitable for the ejidatarios (the dairy project was the first to achieve that in the Chontalpa Plan). Area milk supply was increased. Ejido leaders and managers gained experience. Nestlé did not obtain any significant new milk supply, hence no direct economic benefit. It did, however, render an effective service to the Mexican Government with which it must deal with regard to its other operations, and pioneered a method of producing milk in the tropics with pure-bred stock. The lessons learned were later applied with success by Nestlé in two other States of Mexico.

343

Discussion: The project produced more milk, thus reducing imports and improving nutrition. The company achieved its government relations objectives. The company stayed with the project without profit for a long time in part perhaps because of employee pride in their involvement in national development. It was a learning experience for both the company and the Government. There should have been a more patient pilot project before entering upon the large scheme. The operation was difficult, calling for frontier exploration, overcoming lack of skills. The Chontalpa Plan did not clearly define its objectives (subsequent projects did), and at first used technicians who lacked the experience necessary to handle the pressures of the newly settled ejidos.

A fundamental problem was that the idea for the project was imposed from the top (by the Government). Perhaps the company should have engaged an intermediary to involve the farmers in early decision making. That way the project might have cost the company less, the provision of infrastructure might have been more prompt, and unfamiliar people might not have been just thrown together. There would have been a sense of equity and of better understanding of the environment.[57]

Shell Petroleum successfully provided technical assistance in Nigeria:

As a public service, Shell Petroleum Development Co. developed a rural technical assistance program.

Summary of Case History: As a public service, Shell Petroleum Development Co. developed a rural technical assistance program. Its third project was carried out in the East Central State of Nigeria, centered on the town of Uboma, in association with the State Ministry of Agriculture. Drawing on experience in model projects in Italy and Portugal, planning was based on five principles: (1) long time-span to avoid the usual failure of crash programs to produce durable results; (2) area size that can be covered by one catalytic field agent (containing 10,000 to 15,000 people); (3) field personnel of high qualification; (4) thorough initial socio-economic survey; (5) beginning with confidence-building simple tasks.

A Nigerian agronomist was appointed Project Manager. His goal was to improve the yields of the major local food crops (yams, cassava, maize, beans, and vegetables) in an area of twenty-five square miles; improve diets through additional protein; increase incomes by improving cash crops (oil palm); and improve the quality of social services and infrastructure. Average farm size was eight acres of which some five were kept fallow under a rotation system.

After eight years, there were over 1600 acres in rice production (and two rice mills); 864 acres of improved oil palm; 2000 citrus and 70,000 pineapple stands, twenty-five hog or poultry farms, and seventeen farmer cooperatives which formed a Union. Cash incomes increased by 37 percent over the first ten years. The internal rate of return on Shell's investment was 30 percent.

Unlike prior cooperative efforts, the project recognized the viable social village structures, and worked with them—the kindred and ward groups and age grades, as well as Isusu Clubs (form of savings and loan associations). The oil palm improvement apparently worked for two reasons: it was subsidized by the Government; and the project staff convinced a few respected farmers and helped others calculate the benefits. Introduction of rice cultivation was made possible by government loans for land improvement, and by making the provision of desirable infrastructure such as bridges contingent on the farmers' agreement to switch from food staples such as yams. Sustained interaction between the Shell agent and the farmers appears to have been the most crucial attribute of the project, overcoming farmers' fears and suspicions of the Government.

Discussion: An eminently successful project. The company played the role of

344

intermediary as well as catalyst to coordinate the interplay of resources available in the area. It used excellent models of rural development which it had tested elsewhere. Its role was to finance an intermediary agent in the pursuit of rural development goals (its primary business being unrelated to agriculture).[58]

While the speakers we have presented thus far differ on the usefulness and effectiveness of the current international economic order, they do agree that economic development and growth should be a major goal for all nations.

The next two points of view argue that placing primary emphasis on conventional economic growth and development is irrelevant, and possibly harmful, to the eradication of hunger. For these people, the choice is not the current order versus the NIEO, but rather a new alternative altogether—one that is founded upon a new set of principles and values.

The NIEO Debate Is Concerned Only with Economic Justice between Nations. Thus It Is Irrelevant to the Most Important Human Issues of Economic and Social Development

The first point of view focuses on questions of effectiveness and economic justice *within* nations. Its proponents feel that since the causes of poverty and injustice are connected to effectiveness and economic justice within nations, it is at this level that they must be addressed. Susan George, a critic of traditional development approaches, writes in *Feeding the Few*:

The NIEO, as seen from the Southern hemisphere, is about economic justice on a world scale....

We owe to ourselves and to those who are struggling in the Third World for greater social and political justice a critical examination of what the NIEO may mean. Which social classes in the UDCs [underdeveloped countries] would most benefit from it? What are its prospects for fostering real development? To what degree might the acceptance of certain UDC proposals by the wealthy nations actually result in <u>greater manipulation and dependency</u> of the poor countries?...

Put more bluntly...who, exactly, is likely to see the money? In the most common instance, not the producers who do most of the work....In the Ivory Coast—a major coffee and cocoa exporter—the top 5% of the population receives 30% of the national income, while the bottom fifth of the population gets 4%. In Brazil...the figures are respectively 27% for the wealthiest 5% and 5% for the poorest 20%....

There are reservations to be made concerning the NIEO on grounds of gross inequalities of distribution inside many Third World societies, on grounds of the repressive nature of several governments that would most benefit and because the scheme as it stands would leave many nations out in the cold....These reservations do not imply that there should <u>not</u> be fairer prices for raw materials—simply that <u>of themselves</u> such adjustments would certainly not erase the problems of poverty and underdevelopment....

It is not enough that economic justice prevail between nations on a world scale. Before the NIEO can do much good for anyone but the elites, this justice must also obtain between the social classes in individual countries.[59]

Jean-François Revel, the former editor of *L'Express* (a French weekly news magazine) and the author of a book on totalitarianism, suggests that economic and technical assistance will make little difference if the recipient governments are badly governed. Leaders of Third World nations must place less emphasis on the rhetoric of "global negotiations" and more on political responsibility at home. "Third world demagogy," he says, "is the worst enemy of the Third World":

In a dictatorship, the most common type of regime in the Third World, the least one can ask of those in power is efficaciousness. But one finds, above all, incompetence and extravagance, not to mention corruption.

Many of the economic maladies of the Third World are related to politics. Argentina, whose economic level 40 years ago was comparable to that of Western Europe, has regressed into an underdeveloped state following the ravages of Peronism. This is the fruit of a clearly political decision. Nkrumah in Ghana, Nyerere in Tanzania, Toure in Guinea plunged their respective countries into decline by stupid administration or policies motivated purely by ideology. On the other hand, the Ivory Coast and Kenya, which were relatively well governed, were able to reverse and ameliorate the material condition of their citizens.[60]

Point of View Number 6

Basic Needs and Human Development, Not Economic Growth, Are the Real Issues

This point of view challenges the conventional idea of economic growth and development. Proponents argue that even if the international order worked equitably, it would still be an expression of the value system of the *developed* countries. The real issues are basic needs and human development, not economic growth. Moreover, the goals of human development and economic growth may be in conflict with one another.

E. F. Schumacher, best known to Americans for his book, *Small Is Beautiful*, which made him something of a folk hero with many, writes:

The heart of the matter, as I see it, is the stark fact that world poverty is primarily a problem of two million villages, and thus a problem of two thousand million villagers. The solution cannot be found in the cities of the poor countries. Unless life in the hinterland can be made tolerable, the problem of world poverty is insoluble and will inevitably get worse.

All important insights are missed if we continue to think of development mainly in quantitative terms and in those vast abstractions—like GNP, investment, savings, etc.—which have their usefulness in the study of developed countries but have virtually no relevance to development problems as such. (Nor did they play the slightest part in the actual development of the rich countries!) Aid can be considered successful only if it helps to mobilise the labour-power of the masses in the receiving country and raises productivity without "saving" labour. The common criterion of success, namely the growth of GNP, is utterly misleading and, in fact, must of necessity lead to phenomena which can only be described as neocolonialism.

I hesitate to use this term because it has a nasty sound and appears to imply a deliberate intention on the part of the aid-givers. Is there such an intention? On the whole, I think, there is not. But this makes the problem greater instead of smaller. Unintentional neocolonialism is far more insidious and infinitely more difficult to combat than neocolonialism intentionally pursued. It results from the mere drift of things, supported by the best intentions. Methods of production, standards of consumption, criteria of success or failure, systems of values, and behaviour

346

patterns establish themselves in poor countries which, being (doubtfully) appropriate only to conditions of affluence already achieved, fix the poor countries ever more inescapably in a condition of utter dependence on the rich.[61]

Discussion of this point of view concludes with the philosophy of A. T. Ariyaratne, follower of Gandhian principles and founder of the Sarvodaya Shramadana rural development movement in Sri Lanka. Table N.5 shows the difference between the present economic order and the economic order envisaged by Sarvodaya.

TABLE N.5. ECONOMIC ORDER IN SRI LANKA, PRESENT VS. SARVODAYA

Present Order	Sarvodaya Order
1. Strives to satisfy endless greed in man.	1. Principal attention is towards the satisfaction of human needs.
2. Encourages people to adopt an alien way of life patterned after industrial societies but which cannot be sustained by national resources.	2. Attempts to encourage people to adopt a sustainable and simple pattern of life on a foundation of spiritual, moral and cultural values and social realities.
3. Keeps faith in large scale projects, most modern technology, massive capital investments and market forces.	3. Puts faith in small scale projects, socially appropriate technologies, small scale capital investments and commercial institutions under people's control.
4. Gives first place to productions which bring in a cash income from which need satisfaction is expected to be done, and quality of life is measured quantitatively.	4. First place is given to productions which satisfy needs of people and the quality of life is measured qualitatively.
5. Land, labour, capital and entrepreneurship are considered to be the basic factors on which planning is done.	5. Nature, man, society and scientific knowledge are considered to be the principal factors on which economic progress is based.
6. Accepts the concept that after a certain age every person should personally receive a private salary or income and plans are made accordingly to generate employment.	6. Plans are made on the principle that every human being should participate in efforts to satisfy the basic human needs through righteous means of livelihood.
7. By depending on foreign aid, foreign debts, foreign management expertise, foreign technology and an import-export economic system Sri Lanka economy is tied to an international economic network which is controlled by industrialised countries.	7. Believes in establishing non-dependent relationships with foreign economies but by liberating from foreign economic strangleholds through self-reliance, National resource, National savings, National investments, National industries, National creativity, appropriate technologies and National self-sufficiency in basic needs.
8. Allows the benefits of natural and human resources to be sucked out of rural societies to urban and foreign exploitative organisations.	8. Strives to reactivate the rural economy by bringing in wealth into rural societies and retaining the wealth they justly produce.
9. Makes the human being a confused and restless person caught in a vicious economic cycle.	9. Helps the human being to be a contented and composed person who derives joy from work.
10. Helps a privileged minority to acquire a disproportionate amount of wealth and makes them wasteful, luxury-loving and playful individuals without a depth in life while the majority of people in the country are forced into situations lacking even the barest needs thus making them discontented, frustrated and angry.	10. Encourages all people in the country to fully satisfy their basic needs and build up for themselves a simple, contented, creative and cultured life.

Source: A.T. Ariyaratne, *In Search of Development* (Moratuwa, Sri Lanka: Sarvodaya Shramadana, 1982), 45–46.

In the Sarvodaya approach to social development, the words Sarva meaning "all" and Udaya meaning "awakening" are most significant. The ideas of self-development, self-fulfillment, self-reliance, self-realization and non-dependence, are all understood in the single word Udaya.[62]

Development is not measured purely from material standards but as a total awakening process contribution to total happiness. This definition goes beyond those that confine themselves to measuring development by gross national products, growth rates, per capita incomes and even the...Physical Quality of Life Index.[63]

Conclusion

The New International Economic Order, as we have seen, is not merely a set of detailed proposals for reforming the complex of monetary and financial interactions among nations. Any discussion of the world economy brings up a variety of views and perspectives about the goals of development, the responsibility of some nations for others, how best to promote justice and equity, and, ultimately, what is the end goal of human economic activity.

Here, as in the other chapters, proponents of different viewpoints approach the same body of information very differently. Do the results of development in the 1970s prove that the present economic order is working, or that it is a failure? Do development "successes" such as Singapore and South Korea prove that free enterprise works, or are they merely exceptions to the general conclusion that it doesn't?

While the debate about the New International Economic Order continues, particularly in forums such as the United Nations and its affiliated agencies, the fundamental structural changes envisioned by the early proponents of the NIEO do not seem imminent.

Nonetheless, the NIEO debate—as a framework for discussing some of the major economic issues that affect hunger and help to hold it in place—provides a valuable resource for ending hunger. By opening up a new way of speaking about and looking at issues on a global scale, the NIEO discussion has focused the attention of the world community on the role that the international economy can play in resolving the issue of the persistence of hunger.

NOTES

1   United Nations, General Assembly, *Declaration on the Establishment of a New International Economic Order* (A/AC. 166/L. 47), 30 April 1974, 2.

2   Wallace Irwin, Jr., *America in the World: A Guide to U.S. Foreign Policy* (New York: Praeger, 1983), 191.

3   United Nations, General Assembly, *Declaration*, 2.

4   Michael P. Todaro, *Economic Development in the Third World*, 2nd ed. (New York: Longman, 1981), xxxii.

5   United Nations, Development Program, *The United States' Stake in a New International Economic Order*, by Bradford Morse, n.d., 2–3.

6   Julius K. Nyerere, "A Trade Union for the Poor," *Bulletin of the Atomic Scientists* 35, no. 6 (June 1979): 38, 39.

7   For more information, see Martin M. McLaughlin, "The United States in the North-South Dialogue: A Survey," *The United States and World Development: Agenda 1979*, Overseas Development Council (New York: Praeger, 1979), 77–113.

8   For more information, see William L. Scully, "The Brandt Commission: Deluding the Third World," *Heritage Foundation Backgrounder*, no. 182 (30 April 1982): 1–23.

9   World Bank, *World Development Report 1982* (New York: Oxford University Press, 1982), 78.

10 Ibid., 24.

11 Derived from Population Reference Bureau, *1983 World Population Data Sheet* (Washington, DC: Population Reference Bureau, 1983).

12 A nation is defined as having ended hunger as a national issue when its infant mortality rate falls to 50 or below per thousand live births.

13 Independent Commission on International Development Issues, *North-South: A Program for Survival* (Cambridge, MA: MIT Press, 1980), 49–50.

14 Charlotte Waterlow, *Superpowers and Victims: The Outlook for World Community* (Englewood Cliffs, NJ: Prentice-Hall, 1974), 107.

15 Ibid.

16 Ibid.

17 Ibid., 101.

18 World Bank, *World Development Report 1981* (New York: Oxford University Press, 1981), 12.

19 Overseas Development Council, *U.S. Foreign Policy and the Third World: Agenda 1983,* eds. John P. Lewis and Valeriana Kallab (New York: Praeger, 1983), 242.

20 Waterlow, *Superpowers and Victims,* 101; and U.S. Presidential Commission on World Hunger, *Overcoming World Hunger: The Challenge Ahead* (Washington, DC: U.S. Government Printing Office, March 1980), 57.

21 Overseas Development Council, *U.S. Foreign Policy and the Third World: Agenda 1982,* eds. Roger D. Hansen et al. (New York: Praeger, 1982), 198.

22 Ibid., 202.

23 World Bank, *World Development Report 1982,* 132–33; and John Paxton, ed., *The Statesman's Year-Book* (London: Macmillan Press, 1981), 356.

24 Waterlow, *Superpowers and Victims,* 102.

25 Ibid., 102–103, 104.

26 Ibid., 102.

27 United Nations, Department of Public Information, *Towards a World Economy That Works* (DPI/666-80-40759), 1980, 69–70.

28 Paul A. Samuelson, *Economics,* 11th ed. (New York: McGraw-Hill, 1980), 660.

29 For more information, see John M. Letiche, ed., *International Economic Policies and Their Theoretical Foundations: A Source Book* (New York: Academic Press, 1982), 413–39.

30 David Millwood, *Help or Hindrance? Aid, Trade and the Rich Nations' Responsibility to the Third World* (Geneva, Switzerland: SODEPAX, 1971), 17.

31 Waterlow, *Superpowers and Victims,* 103.

32 Jan Tinbergen et al., *Reshaping the International Order: A Report to the Club of Rome* (New York: E. P. Dutton & Co., 1976), 15–16.

33 United Nations, Development Program, *The United States' Stake in a New International Economic Order,* 1.

34 Mahbub ul Haq, "A View from the South: The Second Phase of the North-South Dialogue," *The United States and World Development: Agenda 1979,* eds. Martin M. McLaughlin and the staff of the Overseas Development Council (New York: Praeger, 1979), 119.

35 Donald O. Mills, "Cry from Third World: 'Listen to Us!' " *U.S. News & World Report,* 31 July 1978, 61.

36 Global Negotiations Information Project, *Global Negotiations Action Notes,* no. 3 (19 January 1981): 3.

37 François Mitterand, "France in the World" (Address at New York University, 8 December 1980), 6, 7.

38 United Nations, General Assembly, *Declaration,* 3, 4.

39 Richard J. Barnet, "The Profits of Hunger," *Nation,* 9 February 1980, 129, 146.

40 William W. Murdoch, *The Poverty of Nations* (Baltimore, MD: Johns Hopkins University Press, 1980), 257–58.

41 U.S. Presidential Commission on World Hunger, *Overcoming World Hunger: The Challenge Ahead,* 76.

42 Carol Honsa, "Nonaligned Want a $300 Billion Slice of Pie," *The Christian Science Monitor,* 13 February 1981, 6.

43 Walter Rodney, *How Europe Underdeveloped Africa* (London: Bogle-L'Ouverture Publications, 1972), 258–59.

44 Overseas Development Council, *The United States and World Development: Agenda 1980,* eds. John W. Sewell et al. (New York: Praeger, 1980), 2.

45 World Bank, *World Development Report 1980* (New York: Oxford University Press, 1980), 35.

46 U.S., Congress, Senate, *Congressional Record,* 94th Cong., 1st sess., 1975, 121, pt. 27, statement of the Honorable William E. Simon, 35131.

47 U.S., Department of State, *North-South Dialogue,* Current Policy, no. 182 (15 May 1980): 3.

48 Charles Krauthammer, "Rich Nations, Poor Nations," *New Republic,* 11 April 1981, 21.

49 Roger A. Brooks, "Multinationals: First Victim of the U.N. War on Free Enterprise," *Heritage Foundation Backgrounder,* no. 227 (16 November 1982), 7.

50 Overseas Development Council, *The United States and World Development: Agenda 1980,* 3–4.

51 Orville L. Freeman and William Persen, "Multinational Corporations: Hope for the Poorest Nations," *Futurist* 14, no. 6 (December 1980): 10.

52 Art Pine, "Trade Threat: Third World's Gains in the Basic Industries Stir a Sharp Backlash," *The Wall Street Journal* (Western ed.), 13 April 1984, 1.

53 Ibid.

54 Freeman and Persen, "Multinational Corporations: Hope for the Poorest Nations," 3, 4.

55 Isaiah Frank, "Big Business in the Third World: Gains on All Sides," *The Christian Science Monitor,* 10 July 1981, 23.

56 These case histories were presented at a conference entitled "New Approaches to Agricultural and Rural Development: An International Conference on Multinationals." This conference was funded by both public and private services, among them Nestlé S.A.

57 George A. Truitt, ed., *Multinationals: New Approaches to Agricultural and Rural Development* (New York: Fund for Multinational Management Education, 1981), 21–22.

58 Ibid., 32–33.

59 Susan George, *Feeding the Few: Corporate Control of Food* (Washington, DC: Institute for Policy Studies, n.d.), 1, 2–3, 5, 7, 20.

60 Jean-François Revel, "How Well Is the Third World Governed?" *The Wall Street Journal,* 5 November 1981, 22.

61 E. F. Schumacher, *Small Is Beautiful* (New York: Harper & Row, Perennial Library, 1975), 193–94.

62 A. T. Ariyaratne, "A People's Movement for Self-Reliance in Sri Lanka," *Collected Works: Volume I,* ed. Nandasena Ratnapala (Dehiwala, Sri Lanka: Sarvodaya Research Institute, n.d.), 26.

63 A. T. Ariyaratne, *In Search of Development* (Moratuwa, Sri Lanka: Sarvodaya Shramadana, 1982), 32.

In their concern about hunger, many experts and world leaders have focused on improving economic conditions in the Third World, since this is where most of the world's hungry people live. But while these experts and leaders agree on the need for improvement, they differ as to whether this improvement requires a fundamental change in the world economic system. Right: Spinning, a traditional economic activity in India (Robert Frerck/Woodfin Camp & Assoc.).

The pro-NIEO school of thought holds that the current economic order is not working, that fundamental change is needed, that multinationals must be stringently regulated, and that colonial powers are obligated to redress past wrongs. An alternative school holds that the present system is working well, that multinationals play a strong, beneficial role in development, and that the causes of poverty are internal rather than consequences of the international economic system. Photos: Technology and economic activity in the Third World. Left: *Grinding grain, India* (Robert Frerck/Woodfin Camp & Assoc.); above, top: *Weaving cloth, Pakistan* (C. Harbutt/Magnum Photos); above, bottom: *Weaving a mat, Ecuador* (Victor Englebert/Photo Researchers); next two-page spread: *Metalworking, Burma* (Kal Muller/Woodfin Camp & Assoc.).

353

Most Third World exports are "primary products"—minerals and agricultural products that have been directly extracted from the resource base with minimal human or mechanical processing. In 1980, developing countries depended on primary products for 79 percent of their export earnings. Half of these countries earn at least 50 percent of their export income from a single product, usually coffee, sugar, or minerals. Left: *Cutting cane, Argentina* (J. Guichard/Sygma); above, top: *Bags of corn ready for shipping, Guatemala* (© Alon Reininger/Contact); above, bottom: *Packing corn, Nigeria* (William Campbell/Sygma); next two-page spread: *Crates of tea ready for shipping, Sri Lanka* (M. Serraillier/Photo Researchers).

Eugene Stockwell of the World Council of Churches criticized the role of multinationals in a minority report to the Presidential Commission on World Hunger. He said: "Too much corporate activity in today's world hurts rather than helps the world's hungry: the use of resources for the advantage of the wealthy rather than the poor, export cropping that uses land for corporate profits but not for feeding the hungry, the use of power and influence with developing country governments to secure privilege, and the creation by advertising of appetites for non-nutritional products and for products that militate against basic health and wellbeing." Above: *Picking tea, India* (George Holton/Photo Researchers); right: *Child picking tobacco, Honduras* (© Alon Reininger/Contact).

Some say colonialism is the cause of Third World poverty and that former colonial powers owe their former colonies reparations. According to Jamaican Ambassador Donald O. Mills, "[W]e ended up with a system in which the colonies were used as plantations, by and large, to produce certain materials and supplies for the benefit of the metropolitan countries.... After winning our independence, we still find ourselves on the losing end of an economic system that is very much a product of that historical situation." Left: *Sorting coffee, Haiti* (Thomas Nebbia/Woodfin Camp & Assoc.); above: *Coffee worker, El Salvador* (© Alon Reininger/Contact).

Proposed changes in the current economic order are presented in the statement of principles adopted at the Sixth Special Session of the UN General Assembly. One of the important principles is "Establishment of a just and equitable relationship" between the prices of goods exported by developing countries and the prices of goods and equipment imported by them. Above: *A traditional workshop, China* (B. Barbey/Magnum Photos); right: *Drying hemp, Haiti* (Thomas Nebbia/Woodfin Camp & Assoc.).

According to the World Bank, the current economic order is producing some beneficial results. In its 1980 World Development Report, the Bank states: "Considerable progress has been made in reducing the incidence of poverty over the past 30 years.... Progress would have been greater still but for the dramatic growth of population." Left: *Logging, China* (J. P. Laffont/ Sygma); above: *Timber factory, China* (J. P. Laffont/Sygma).

*What are some of the Third World successes of
the current economic order? John Sewell,
president of the Overseas Development Council,
reports that the "average annual per capita
GNP growth rates from 1960 to 1977 [of newly
industrializing countries] were higher than that
of the United States, even though their populations grew twice as fast.... Most of the
advanced developing countries have changed
from import-substitution to export-promotion
policies.... These countries are among the most
rapidly growing markets for U.S. exports of
agricultural products, machinery, transportation equipment, and high-technology goods and
services...."* Left: *Athletic shoes made in Korea*
(J. P. Laffont/Sygma); above, top: *Cotton
factory, China* (B. Barbey/Magnum Photos);
above, bottom: *Electronics factory, Korea*
(J. P. Laffont/Sygma); next two-page spread:
Steel/iron factory, China (H. Kubota/
Magnum Photos).

The NIEO debate, some say, ignores the important human issues of economic and social development. The real focus should be effectiveness and economic justice within nations. Susan George addresses this issue: "Which social classes in the UDCs [underdeveloped countries] would most benefit from it [the NIEO]?...Put more bluntly...who, exactly, is likely to see the money? In the most common instance, not the producers who do most of the work....In the Ivory Coast...the top 5% of the population receives 30% of the national income, while the bottom fifth of the population gets 4%....Before the NIEO can do much good for anyone but the elites,...justice must also obtain between the social classes in individual countries." Above: *Steelworker, Argentina* (J. Guichard/Sygma); right: *Iron/steelworker, Korea* (J. P. Laffont/Sygma).

Multinationals contribute to Third World development, according to experts such as Orville Freeman and William Persen. Their view is that multinational companies have been "a powerful force in hurdling national boundaries and restrictions, so that trade, commerce, goods, services, and ideas can flow more freely around the world to the benefit of all mankind." *And Isaiah Frank says, "A quiet revolution is taking place in the relationship between multinational corporations and the developing world—they are learning to live together and like it."* Left: *Texaco plant, Trinidad* (Adam Woolfitt/Woodfin Camp & Assoc.); above: *Shipping bauxite, Jamaica* (Dan Budnik/ Woodfin Camp & Assoc.); next two-page spread: *Loading goods for export, Korea* (J. P. Laffont/Sygma).

375

Economist Richard Cooper advises caution in changing an economic system that has worked "reasonably well." He says, "As we look back over the past three decades, we believe that the system has responded flexibly, if not always smoothly, to major changes in the world, including the growing economic and political importance of the developing countries. We favor continued evolution of the system to meet new situations. But suggested changes must have a high probability of improving the system for everyone—if this is not the case, it makes no sense to disrupt a system which works reasonably well. Left: *Soviet ship, Viet Nam* (P. J. Griffiths/Magnum Photos); above: *Automobile factory and ship, Detroit* (© Gianfranco Gorgoni/Contact).

While the debate about the NIEO continues, particularly in forums such as the United Nations and its affiliated agencies, the fundamental changes envisioned by early proponents do not seem imminent. Nonetheless, the NIEO debate—as a framework for discussing some of the major economic issues that affect hunger and help to hold it in place—provides a valuable resource for ending hunger. By opening up a new way of speaking about and looking at issues on a global scale, the NIEO discussion has focused the attention of the world community on the role that the international economy can play in resolving the persistence of hunger.
Left: *World Trade Center, New York* (Dan Budnik/Woodfin Camp & Assoc.); right: *UN headquarters, New York* (Jeffrey D. Smith/ Woodfin Camp & Assoc.); following two-page spread: *São Paulo slums, Brazil* (Claus Meyer/Black Star).

The End of World Hunger

As our examination of the five major issues surrounding hunger has demonstrated, there is no scarcity of thinking, approaches, and perspectives on the problem of the persistence of hunger.

Throughout the world, these varying points of view have generated a wealth of policies, projects, and experiments for eradicating hunger. Some have failed spectacularly; others have succeeded, producing results that have literally made the difference between life and death for tens of millions of people. All this has given the world community an expertise and a depth of knowledge and experience that have substantially advanced our progress toward the eradication of hunger from the planet.

"Progress" is a word that is not yet used comfortably in describing a problem as immense as the persistence of hunger and starvation. Only recently did the world's experts begin to agree on the extent of this problem. The notion of measuring the extent of hunger is also very recent; and measuring its elimination is so new as to be almost startling.

Since 1900, seventy-five countries have ended hunger within their borders as a basic, society-wide issue.

Yet in this century—quietly, and virtually without acknowledgment—many countries of the world have shown remarkable success in ending hunger. Since 1900, seventy-five countries have ended hunger within their borders as a basic, society-wide issue.[1] Forty-one of them have accomplished this feat since 1960.[2]

Today, more than half the world's population lives in countries that no longer suffer from the persistence of hunger.[3] What does it mean to say that hunger has ended as a basic issue in the lives of a people? How is this achievement indicated in concrete and measurable terms?

There are many ways to measure the existence of hunger in the world. One of the most widely accepted standards of measurement—used by numerous international agencies, including UNICEF and WHO—is the infant mortality rate (IMR). (As pointed out earlier, three out of every four who die of hunger are children.) The IMR measures the number of infants per thousand who are born live who die before their first birthday. Hunger exists as a chronic, persistent, society-wide condition when the IMR of a nation is greater than 50—that is, when more than 50 children per thousand die in the first year of their lives.[4]

All available data indicate that when the IMR goes down, the overall death rate among other age groups goes down as well. Thus, a society's changes or improvements that are reflected in a reduction of infant deaths are simultaneously reflected in a reduction of child and adult deaths.

The IMR can range widely from country to country. For example, in Japan and Sweden, where hunger has ended as a basic issue in the lives of the people, the IMR is 7; in Burkina Faso (Upper Volta), where hunger is widespread, the IMR is 210. That is, of every 1,000 babies born alive, 210 will die before their first birthday.[5]

India, whose population is equal to one-third of the population in all societies where hunger persists as a basic issue, has an IMR of 122.[6] While high, this is an

FIGURE E.1. INFANT MORTALITY DECLINE IN INDUSTRIALIZED COUNTRIES (1900–1980)

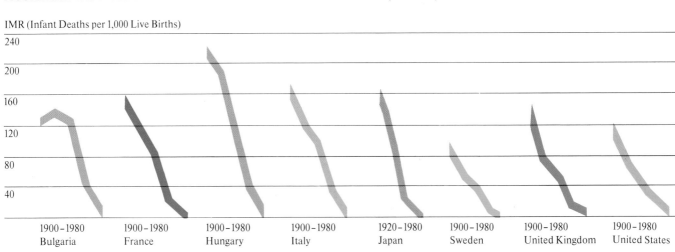

IMR (Infant Deaths per 1,000 Live Births)

240							
200							
160							
120							
80							
40							

| 1900–1980 | 1900–1980 | 1900–1980 | 1900–1980 | 1920–1980 | 1900–1980 | 1900–1980 | 1900–1980 |
| Bulgaria | France | Hungary | Italy | Japan | Sweden | United Kingdom | United States |

Source: United Nations, UNICEF, *The State of the World's Children 1984,* by James P. Grant, 6.

FIGURE E.2. AFRICA: INFANT MORTALITY RATES

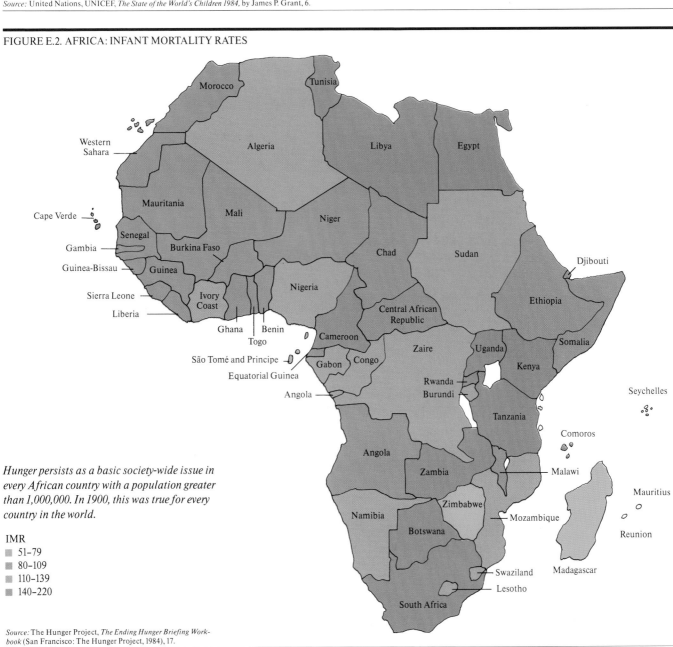

Hunger persists as a basic society-wide issue in every African country with a population greater than 1,000,000. In 1900, this was true for every country in the world.

IMR
- 51–79
- 80–109
- 110–139
- 140–220

Source: The Hunger Project, *The Ending Hunger Briefing Workbook* (San Francisco: The Hunger Project, 1984), 17.

improvement over 1960, when the IMR stood at around 157.[7] Many other nations have registered substantial drops in infant mortality in recent years. Figure E.1 shows estimates and projections of IMR by region for the years 1950–2025.

When a country has brought its IMR to a level of 50 or below, hunger as a basic, society-wide issue can be said to have ended.

When a country has brought its IMR to a level of 50 or below, hunger as a basic, society-wide issue can be said to have ended. This is not to say that no one goes hungry in countries with low IMRs. Pockets of hunger exist in the United States, for example, where the IMR is 11. Still, as an issue affecting the lives of the vast majority of the people—that is, as a persistent, chronic condition—hunger has ended in countries that have an IMR of 50 or below.

The seventy-five countries that have brought their IMR below 50 are, for the most part, countries that the world considers "developed." They are found in North America, Europe, and parts of Asia and Latin America. No country on the continent of Africa has yet achieved an IMR of 50 or below.[8]

In 1900, no country in the world had an IMR of 50 or below. For the first countries that ended hunger—nine of them reached this point by 1940—the process was a slow one. It required pioneering medical, educational, and developmental activities. Now, however, the process seems to be accelerating.

Hunger is ending in various climates, under a variety of political ideologies and economic systems, and using a wide range of agricultural techniques. While most of the seventy-five countries in which hunger has ended have a relatively high income level, there are important exceptions—such as Sri Lanka and China, both of which have per capita GNPs of around U.S. $300.[9]

All these countries brought their IMRs to 50 or below using various nutrition-improving measures along with basic preventive-health measures (such as immunization programs and clean-water supplies). Additional successful measures have included: increasing basic education and literacy; redistributing wealth, land, and power; promoting industrial development; increasing agricultural production; and improving food-distribution, -storage, and -delivery systems.

James P. Grant, executive director of UNICEF, explains how the synergistic process of development takes place:

A cat's cradle of...synergisms links almost every aspect of development: female literacy catalyses family planning programmes; less frequent pregnancies improves maternal and child health; improved health makes the most of pre-school or primary education; education can increase incomes and agricultural productivity; better incomes or better food reduces infant mortality; fewer child deaths tend to lead to fewer births; smaller families improve maternal health; healthy mothers have healthier babies; healthier babies demand more attention; stimulation helps mental growth; more alert children do better at school...and so it continues in an endless pattern of either mutually reinforcing or mutually retarding relationships which can minimize or multiply the benefits of any given input.[10]

There is no single prescribed way to achieve the end of the persistence of hunger in a society.

It is both important and heartening to note that there is no single prescribed way to achieve the end of the persistence of hunger in a society. Some countries focused on land reform, while others emphasized food subsidies, collectivized agriculture, or privately owned "family farms." For every country that saw a particular action as crucial to ending hunger, there is a country that ended hunger without it.

FIGURE E.3. ANNUAL GRAIN PRODUCTION IN CHINA (1949–1981)

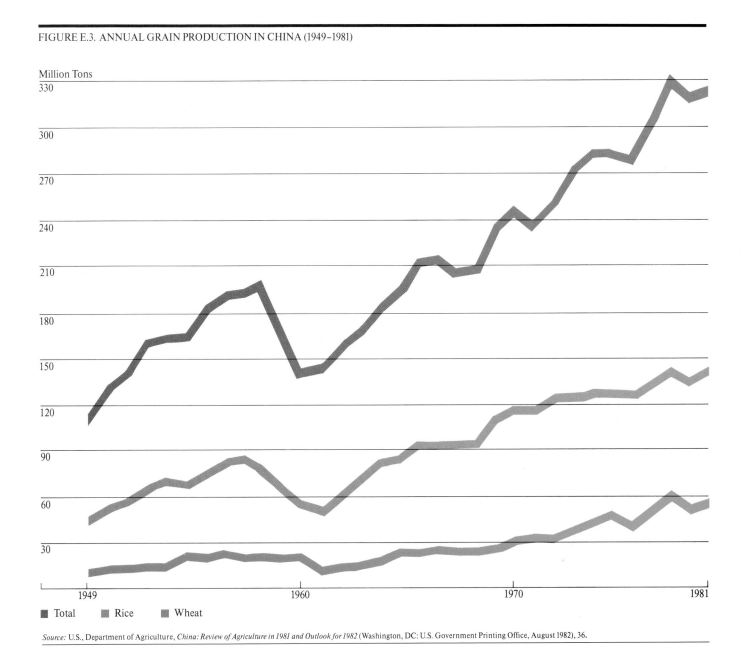

Million Tons

■ Total   ■ Rice   ■ Wheat

Source: U.S., Department of Agriculture, *China: Review of Agriculture in 1981 and Outlook for 1982* (Washington, DC: U.S. Government Printing Office, August 1982), 36.

Population planning, public health programs, and improved food production have all contributed to ending the persistence of hunger in China. These data show that grain production has nearly tripled in 30 years.

Three Asian countries—Taiwan, China, and Sri Lanka—provide fitting testimony to the plurality of contemporary models for ending hunger.

Where Hunger Has Already Been Ended

Taiwan

A successful land-reform plan was a key element in ending hunger in Taiwan.

A successful land-reform plan, supported with financial aid from the United States after World War II, was a key element in ending hunger in Taiwan. Before land reform, peasants paid more than 50 percent of their crops in rent to landlords—70 percent, in more fertile areas.[11] Once land ownership was transferred to the peasants, they no longer had to pay this sum.

To compensate the former landlords, the government set up a ten-year pay schedule, during which time the peasants gave certain percentages of their income to the government.[12] The government then used this money to pay the landlords for their land. Records show that even while they were paying these fees, a typical peasant family's income had increased by 81 percent between 1949 and 1952.[13]

Once the peasants had a stake in their land, some surplus income with which to make improvements in irrigation, and other needed inputs, rice production began to increase. Between 1948 and 1952, the increase was 47 percent.[14]

As production grew and the country's wealth increased, employment rose, construction of new houses increased, and schools were built. The IMR declined from around 155 in the 1930s to 9.1 today.[15] Health care, education, and family planning all improved, and birth rates declined substantially—from 42.1 per 1,000 in 1954 to 26 per 1,000 in the early 1970s.[16] As this developmental process took hold, industrial capacity increased. Taiwan also opened up new markets, especially with Western countries.

China

During the Chinese revolution, Mao Tse-tung and the Communist Party emphasized measures designed to end hunger.

While one approach was bringing hunger to an end in Taiwan, a very different program was ending hunger in China. Even during the three decades of revolution (1920–1949), Mao Tse-tung and the Chinese Communist Party emphasized measures designed to eliminate hunger.[17]

During World War II, China's communists instituted a variety of programs in the areas they controlled. They carried out land reform, set up grain-rationing systems, and extended agricultural credit to peasants. The Chinese formed compulsory primary schools, and formally legislated equality for women.

In the initial years after the 1949 revolution, the Chinese confiscated land from the landowners and gave it to the peasants for their individual plots. However, after a few years, China's farms were collectivized, and their productivity improved considerably.[18]

Along with collectivization, the Chinese government launched many other projects that contributed to the end of hunger. These included:

Simple health care, in the form of "barefoot doctors";

388

Rates per 1,000 Population

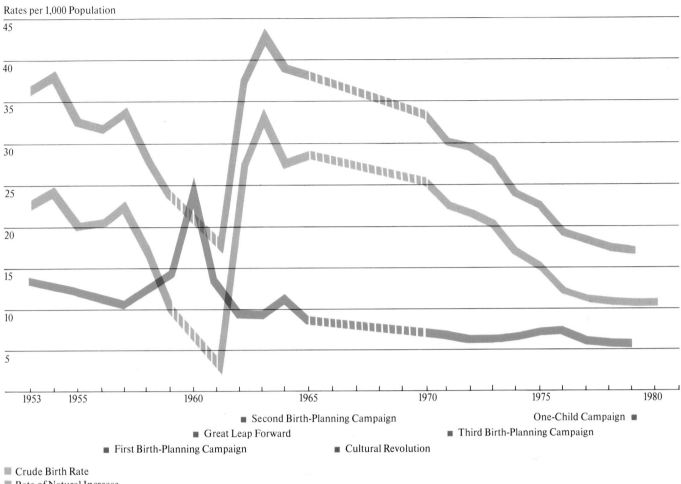

■ Second Birth-Planning Campaign   One-Child Campaign ■
■ Great Leap Forward   ■ Third Birth-Planning Campaign
■ First Birth-Planning Campaign   ■ Cultural Revolution

■ Crude Birth Rate
■ Rate of Natural Increase
■ Crude Death Rate

Note: No official figures are available for the Great Leap Forward and the Cultural Revolution.

Source: Population Information Program, Johns Hopkins University, "Population and Birth Planning in the People's Republic of China," *Population Reports,* Series J, no. 25 (January–February 1982): J–579.

During the 1950s and 1960s in China, birth rates fluctuated in response to birth-planning efforts, political upheavals, and economic disruptions. The steady decline in birth rates during the 1970s is attributed to a government population-planning campaign.

Massive literacy campaigns;

Organization of peasants so that they could set up flood-control projects;

Eradication of major diseases, such as cholera and smallpox;

Establishment of small factories in the countryside, and emphasis on local self-sufficiency; and

Family planning.[19]

In 1950, just after the revolution, the IMR was at least 125. Today it is 44.[20] China has created an economic and social miracle that, in the 1930s, was thought unimaginable. People are being fed; full employment exists; the country has a remarkable health-care system for a nation that still has a per capita income of just $304.[21] Literacy is widespread, abject poverty is almost unknown.[22] *And this was done for a population of over one billion people.*[23]

Sri Lanka

Sri Lanka is a third country that has ended hunger as a basic issue. It is a success story of development. Sri Lanka, which gained its independence in 1948, had an IMR of 141 in 1946; by 1983, the IMR was 37.[24] This remarkable drop in IMR occurred despite the fact that the country has remained very poor—its per capita income is just $302, or about $25 a month.[25]

Sri Lanka's democratic government has committed itself to meeting the basic needs of its people, and has instituted a program to achieve adequate nutrition through a food-subsidy program. Each person receives one to two pounds of rice per week at no charge.[26]

To achieve food self-sufficiency, Sri Lanka successfully introduced a land-reform policy to provide landless laborers with land for subsistence farming. In addition, between 1953 and 1972 Sri Lanka increased its actively farmed land by 15 percent through irrigation—that is, by almost an additional 5 million acres.[27]

Sri Lanka also improved its health-care system. Of Sri Lanka's expectant mothers, 98 percent receive prenatal care, compared with 10 to 15 percent in India. There is 1 hospital bed for approximately every 350 people, compared with 1 for every 1,500 in India and 1 for every 8,000 in Bangladesh.[28] The life expectancy of sixty-six years is six years above the Asian average.[29]

More than 80 percent of Sri Lanka's population is literate; 71 percent of the women can read and write (a fact that is particularly unusual for a developing country).[30] Moreover, Sri Lanka is home to one of the most remarkable self-help movements in the world, Sarvodaya Shramadana, which has made the development process an integral part of Sri Lankan village life.[31]

Ending World Hunger: The Opportunity

The achievement of Taiwan, China, Sri Lanka, and the seventy-two other countries that have ended hunger as a basic issue points the way and provides a foundation for the end of hunger everywhere.

Not long ago, the question was not "Is the world progressing toward ending hunger?" but "Can hunger be ended at all?" Today, there is wide recognition that humanity can, in fact, end hunger. There is a growing consensus among experts that we already have the necessary resources, technology, and know-how to end hunger on our planet in this century.

In 1977, the National Academy of Sciences issued the *World Food and Nutrition Study*, on which 1,500 scientists had consulted. The study concludes:

If there is the political will in this country and abroad ... it should be possible to overcome the worst aspects of widespread hunger and malnutrition within one generation.[32]

In 1980, the Presidential Commission on World Hunger—a panel of twenty Americans, including scientists, business people, and nutritionists—issued a report. It found that:

Each major cause of hunger could be averted or overcome if the human community were to act cooperatively and decisively. Conversely, the persistence of hunger reflects a lack of sufficient political will to eliminate its causes....

If decisions and actions well within the capability of nations and people working together were implemented, it would be possible to eliminate the worst aspects of hunger and malnutrition by the year 2000.[33]

In 1980 the Brandt Commission, composed of representatives of seventeen rich and poor countries, issued a report of its two-year study. The study concludes:

Mankind has never before had such ample technical and financial resources for coping with hunger and poverty. The immense task can be tackled if the necessary collective will is mobilized. What is necessary can be done, and must be done.[34]

UNICEF's 1980 *State of the World's Children* report states that, by the year 2000, the number of infant deaths in low-income countries could be reduced to 50 or fewer per 1,000 live births:

Although idealistic in the context of past experience, [this goal is] realistic in the sense that the principal obstacle standing in the way of [its] realisation is the will and the commitment to achieve [it].[35]

The Food and Agriculture Organization (FAO), the largest organization in the world dealing with global food issues, has undertaken a thorough examination of "what needs to be done to achieve the entirely feasible result of abolishing widespread hunger during the two decades ahead." FAO reports that its study, *Agriculture: Toward 2000,*

leads to the conclusion that hunger could be abolished. The requirements for doing so are demanding but they are feasible.... It is not the purpose of this report to propose another target but rather to point out what needs to be done to achieve the entirely feasible result of abolishing widespread hunger during the two decades ahead.[36]

These prestigious studies mark a turning point in the global fight to eradicate hunger. They are a recognition of the fact that for the first time in history the world now possesses the agricultural, technological, and financial resources to eradicate the persistence of hunger forever.

391

FIGURE E.5. RICE PRODUCTION IN SRI LANKA (1965–1981)

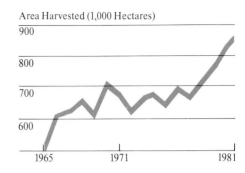

Area Harvested (1,000 Hectares)

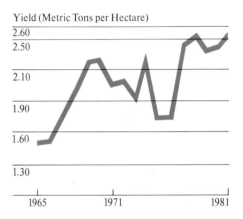

Yield (Metric Tons per Hectare)

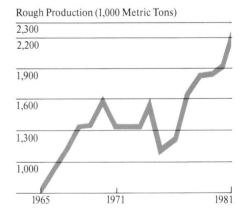

Rough Production (1,000 Metric Tons)

Source: U.S., Department of Agriculture, *Foreign Agriculture Circular* (FG-22-82), 30 September 1982, 117.

Land-reform policies, an irrigation program, and the village-level Sarvodaya Shramadana movement have all contributed to increased productivity in Sri Lanka.

FIGURE E.6. ENDING HUNGER—IT CAN BE DONE

In 1900, not a single nation on earth had an infant mortality rate of less than 50.

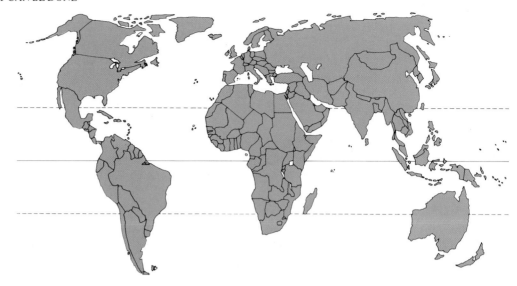

By 1984, the people of 73 nations, half the world's population, had lowered their IMRs to less than 50, essentially ending hunger as a basic issue in those countries.

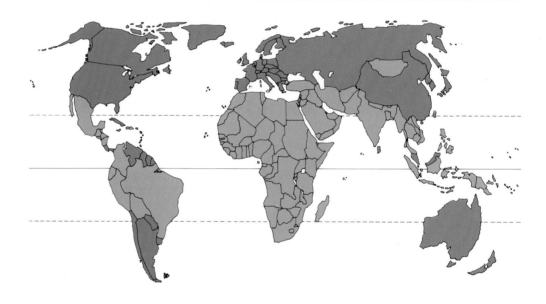

By the year 2000, it is possible that the IMR of every nation on earth will have been lowered to less than 50. This can be achieved only with the combined will and commitment of all peoples, acting in a global effort on behalf of humankind.

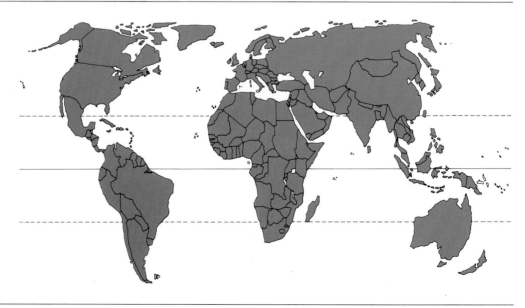

Source: *A Shift in the Wind*, no. 18 (May 1984): 11.

The end of the persistence of hunger by the end of this century is now achievable.

We have the resources to end it; we have proven solutions for ending it; we have test cases for the end of hunger in those countries that have already ended it.

Hunger, given the facts and figures about it, turns out to be one of those fundamental problems that we have proven we can resolve.

Hunger is one of those fundamental problems that we have proven we can resolve.

The end of hunger is now a possibility, but it is not a promise. It is not something that will happen inevitably, regardless of what we do or don't do. Hunger *can* end—but that is not the same as saying it *will* end.

Recent progress notwithstanding, we cannot wait for the end of hunger. If we simply kept on doing what we have done in the past, hunger would still persist in the year 2000. Merely redoubling our existing efforts, or quickening our pace, or intensifying already existing programs will not fulfill the need and the opportunity before us.

We now have the opportunity to see what is missing in the global effort to end hunger. Our world possesses sufficient resources, technology, and proven solutions to achieve the end of the persistence of hunger and starvation by the end of the century. What is missing is the commitment.

Those of us who are interested in the end of hunger, committed to the end of hunger, or working to create the end of hunger now have the opportunity to bring forth this new kind of commitment—a commitment to actually ensure that what can be done shall be done.

We have the opportunity to bring forth a new commitment to actually ensure that what can be done shall be done.

This breakthrough in our individual and global commitment can produce the gathering force throughout the planet that every major study has identified as the missing ingredient.

This breakthrough in our individual and global commitment can make the idea of ending hunger by the year 2000 an idea whose time has come.

NOTES

1 Derived from Population Reference Bureau, *1984 World Population Data Sheet* (Washington, DC: Population Reference Bureau, 1984). As this book neared completion, the Population Reference Bureau released the *1984 World Population Data Sheet.* The 1984 data sheet was used to update this figure in the text. Information from the *1983 World Population Data Sheet* used elsewhere in this book is still timely and relevant.

2 United Nations, Department of International Economic and Social Affairs, *Population Bulletin of the United Nations,* no. 14-1982 (ST/ESA/SER. N/14), 1983, 36–40; and Mary Kent, Population Reference Bureau, Washington, DC, telephone communication with The Hunger Project, San Francisco, 1984.

3 Population Reference Bureau, *1983 World Population Data Sheet.*

4 Ibid.

5 Ibid.

6 Ibid.

7 United Nations, Department of International Economic and Social Affairs, *Population Bulletin of the United Nations,* no. 14-1982, 38.

8 Population Reference Bureau, *1983 World Population Data Sheet.*

9 Ibid.

10 United Nations, UNICEF, *The State of the World's Children 1981–82,* by James P. Grant, 7.

11 Chen Cheng, *Land Reform in Taiwan* (Taiwan, Republic of China: Ching Publishing Co., 1961), 9.

12 For more information about landlord response to land reform, see Martin M. C. Yang, *Socio-Economic Results of Land Reform in Taiwan* (Honolulu: East-West Center Press, University of Hawaii, n.d.), 154–59.

13 Shirley W. Y. Kuo, Gustav Ranis, and John C. H. Frei, *The Taiwan Success Story: Rapid Growth with Improved Distribution in the Republic of China, 1952–1979* (Boulder, CO: Westview Press, 1981), 50.

14 Cheng, *Land Reform,* 42.

15 James P. Grant, *Disparity Reduction Rates in Social Indicators,* Monograph no. 11 (Washington, DC: Overseas Development Council, September 1978): 70; and Population Reference Bureau, *1983 Population Data Sheet.*

16 Simon Kuznets, "Growth and Structural Shifts," *Economic Growth and Structural Change in Taiwan,* ed. Walter Galenson (Ithaca, NY: Cornell University Press, 1979), 38.

17 Sartaj Aziz, *Rural Development: Learning from China* (New York: Holmes & Meier Publishers, 1978), 9.

18 Ding Chen, "The Economic Development of China," *Scientific American* 243, no. 3 (September 1980): 152.

19 Carol L. Thompson, Mary M. Anderberg, and Joan B. Antell, eds., *The Current History Encyclopedia of Developing Nations,* s.v. "China" (New York: McGraw-Hill, 1982), 225, 227; A. Doak Barnett, *China and the World Food System,* Monograph no. 12 (Washington, DC: Overseas Development Council, April 1979): 29; and H. Yuan Tien, "China: Demographic Billionaire," *Population Bulletin* 38, no. 2 (Washington, DC: Population Reference Bureau, April 1983): 5.

20 United Nations, Department of International Economic and Social Affairs, *Population Bulletin of the United Nations,* no. 14-1982, 38; and *1983 Population Data Sheet.*

21 *1983 Population Data Sheet.*

22 H. Yuan Tien, "China: Demographic Billionaire," 23; and Michael P. Todaro, *Economic Development in the Third World,* 2nd ed. (New York: Longman, 1981), 281.

23 *1983 Population Data Sheet.*

24 Grant, *Disparity Reduction Rates,* 19; and *1983 Population Data Sheet.*

25 *1983 Population Data Sheet.*

26 K. M. de Silva, ed., *Sri Lanka: A Survey* (Honolulu: University of Hawaii Press, 1977), 307, 308.

27 American Friends Service Committee, *Development Case Study: Sri Lanka* (New York: American Friends Service Committee, n.d.), 2; and *The Current History Encyclopedia of Developing Nations,* s.v. "Sri Lanka," 215.

28 American Friends Service Committee, *Development Case Study: Sri Lanka,* 5, 6.

29 *1983 Population Data Sheet.*

30 United Nations, Fund for Population Activities, *Sri Lanka,* Population Profiles, no. 13 (April 1980): 5.

31 Denis Goulet, *Survival with Integrity: Sarvodaya at the Crossroads* (Colombo, Sri Lanka: Marga Institute, 1981), 1.

32 National Research Council, Commission on International Relations, *World Food and Nutrition Study: The Potential Contributions of Research* (Washington, DC: National Academy of Sciences, 1977), 54.

33 U.S. Presidential Commission on World Hunger, *Overcoming World Hunger: The Challenge Ahead* (Washington, DC: U.S. Government Printing Office, 1980), 28, x (respectively).

34 Independent Commission on International Development Issues, *North-South: A Program for Survival* (Cambridge, MA: MIT Press, 1980), 16.

35 United Nations, UNICEF, *The State of the World's Children 1980,* by James P. Grant, 18.

36 United Nations, Food and Agriculture Organization, "Agriculture: Toward 2000," prepared for the Twentieth Session, Rome, 10–29 November 1979 (C 79/24), July 1979, 223.

The end of hunger

our planet by the e

An idea whose tim

and starvation on

nd of the century.

e has come.

Appendix

About The Hunger Project

Established in 1977, The Hunger Project has as its purpose to generate a global context of individual will and commitment for ending hunger on our planet by the end of the century. As of February 1985, more than 3,300,000 individuals living in 152 countries had publicly declared their commitment to the end of hunger by enrolling themselves in The Hunger Project.

The international office of The Hunger Project is located in New York City. Joan Holmes serves as the executive director.

The Hunger Project is currently active in twenty-four countries: Australia, Austria, Belgium, Belize, Brazil, the British Isles, Canada, Denmark, Finland, France, India, Ireland, Israel, Jamaica, Japan, Mexico, the Netherlands, New Zealand, Norway, Peru, Sweden, Switzerland, the United States, and West Germany.

The Hunger Project informs and educates people throughout the world about the persistence of hunger and starvation in a way that supports them in participating effectively in its solution.

One of The Hunger Project's educational programs is the Ending Hunger Briefing. Created by a team of experts in the field of development, the Briefing presents a comprehensive overview of the facts of world hunger. More than 600 highly trained volunteers in ten countries have been certified to lead this four-hour educational presentation. Since its inception in January 1982, the Briefing has been presented to more than 220,000 individuals in North America and Western Europe.

The Hunger Project also publishes a range of educational materials about the persistence of hunger and the work to eradicate it that has already been done.

The Hunger Project newspaper, *A Shift in the Wind,* is the world's largest-circulation publication on the subject of hunger. Each issue is distributed to more than 1.5 million households throughout the world, as well as to more than 20,000 key individuals in the media and in the diplomatic, business, and academic communities.

World Development Forum, a twice-monthly newsletter of facts, trends, and opinion in international development, is distributed to more than 10,000 policy and opinion leaders in many countries of the world.

The newest Hunger Project publication— *The Hunger Project Papers*—was inaugurated in May 1984. These occasional papers present technical/professional analyses of subjects related to ending hunger and are circulated to more than 20,000 people.

For more information about The Hunger Project or how you can participate in the work of The Hunger Project in your area, write or call:

Australia
The Hunger Project
Suite 6, Third Floor
154 Elizabeth Street
Sydney 2000
2-267-1055

The British Isles
The Hunger Project
77 Cromwell Road
London SW7 5BN
01-373-9003

Canada
The Hunger Project
1652 West 8th Avenue
Vancouver, BC V6J 1V4
604-734-4233

Le Projet Faim
360 St-François-Xavier, 3e étage
Montréal, PQ H2Y 258
514-287-1997

India
The Hunger Project
Bajaj Bhawan, Second Floor
Jamnalal Bajaj Marg
226 Nariman Point
Bombay 400 021
22-202-6804

Sweden
Hunger Projektet
Box 16249
S-103 25 Stockholm
08-11-30-40

United States
The Hunger Project
2015 Steiner Street
San Francisco, CA 94115
415-346-6100

West Germany
Das Hunger Projekt
Georgenstrasse 61
D-8000 München 40
89-271-5367

The Hunger Project

Joan Holmes Executive Director

Board of Directors

The global activities of The Hunger Project are directed by a Board of Directors. This body of individuals is responsible for The Hunger Project worldwide. The Hunger Project's directors are:

Ian Watson Chairman of the Board; chairman and director of Tellson Holdings, Ltd., an investment company; international financier; cofounder and director of Oak Resources, Ltd.; former finance chairman of the Progressive Conservative Party in Canada.

Joan Holmes Executive director of The Hunger Project; member of the Executive Committee of InterAction; member of the Board of Directors of the Overseas Development Council.

Ramkrishna Bajaj Leading Indian industrialist; head of the Bajaj Group of Industries; chairman and managing director of Hindustan Sugar Mills, Ltd.; president of the Federation of Indian Chambers of Commerce and Industry.

Peter G. Bourne, M.D. President of Global Water, Inc., in Washington, DC; physician; anthropologist; former assistant secretary general with the United Nations Development Program, coordinating the UN Water Decade; White House special assistant for health issues to U.S. President Carter.

John Denver* Composer; musician; entertainer; commissioner on the U.S. Presidential Commission on World Hunger (1978-1980); founder and president of the Windstar Foundation in Snowmass, Colorado.

Ellis M. Deull, J.D.* Attorney and consultant; member of the Panel of Arbitrators of the American Arbitration Association; member of the Section on International Law of the American Bar Association.

Paul Dietrich Publisher and editor in chief, *Saturday Review* magazine; president, John Davis Lodge Institute for International Study; president, National Center for Legislative Research; head, Knights of Malta Foundation; state representative, Missouri General Assembly, 1976-1980; former president, Citizens for Reagan.

Werner Erhard Originator of a technology of transformation; founder of an international network of individuals, organizations, and foundations carrying out the work of individual and social transformation.

John J. Gilligan** Professor of law and public policy at the White Center for Law and Government, Notre Dame University; authority on international economic development; former U.S. congressman; former governor of the state of Ohio; former administrator of the U.S. Agency for International Development (AID).

David L. Guyer* President of Save the Children Federation, Inc., U.S.; former vice president of the Institute of International Education in New York; former advisor for International Organization Affairs at the United States Mission to the United Nations; a leader in private U.S. relief and development.

Donella H. Meadows, Ph.D.* Adjunct professor of environmental and policy studies at Dartmouth College; educator; authority on environmental issues; co-author of the Club of Rome study, *Limits to Growth;* consultant to numerous governmental and nongovernmental bodies, including the United Nations University.

Roy Prosterman, J.D. Professor of law at the University of Washington; expert on land reform and rural development; director of the World Without War Council, U.S.; advisor and consultant to numerous governmental bodies on issues affecting hunger, development, and land reform.

Arturo Tanco President of Transagri International; former minister of agriculture for the Republic of the Philippines; internationally recognized expert on global food problems and their elimination; former president of the United Nations World Food Council (1977-1981).

 *Emeritus
**Honorary

401

Acknowledgments

This book has no author in the traditional sense. Rather, it is the product of many individuals who participated at various stages of the manuscript's development over a four-year period.

The Hunger Project wishes to acknowledge deeply the magnificent contribution that scores of men and women made to this project. Without their vision, creativity, commitment, and perseverance, *Ending Hunger: An Idea Whose Time Has Come* never would have been published.

We particularly wish to thank the experts and specialists in the international-development and hunger-response community—including various United Nations agencies, nongovernmental and private voluntary organizations, academia, and government—who made themselves available to guide us in our research, critique the text's numerous drafts, and generally ensure that we stayed on course. They gave generously of themselves and of the experience and expertise they had gained in many years on the front lines of ending hunger worldwide.

It is our intention that this book be a tribute to the difference they have made, and continue to make, in the global effort to eradicate hunger and starvation. Any merit and value to be found in this book belongs rightfully to them. The Hunger Project, of course, is solely responsible for any errors or inaccuracies that might exist.

We wish to acknowledge especially several individuals who assumed major responsibility for the successful completion of this project. Our heartfelt thanks to Dr. Donella Meadows, who played a critical role in formulating this book and bringing it into existence; and to Dr. John Richardson, who contributed his inspiration, his enthusiasm, and literally thousands of hours of his time in the preparation, research, and conceptualizing of the manuscript.

We wish also to thank Peter J. Rosenwald for his continuing guidance and support in many areas of this endeavor; Massimo Vignelli for creating a design that makes the information on the end of hunger accessible and graspable; and Jim Stockton for executing the design and advising us on the book's production.

Finally, it is appropriate to acknowledge the contribution of three Hunger Project staff members: Dr. Elizabeth Neeld, who played a decisive role in the completion of the manuscript and in the overall management of the book; Jean Goldman, who headed up the production team that turned a manuscript into a finished work; and Ted Howard, in whom the vision of this book has been as a living spirit since the day it was conceived, and who ensured that through the countless drafts and iterations of the manuscript this book emerged true to its original intention and vision.

On the following pages we acknowledge by name many of the men and women whose work has made this book possible. There is no way that our gratitude for their contributions could be expressed adequately in words. Their true acknowledgment will be a planet at last free from the persistence of hunger and starvation.

Joan Holmes
Executive Director
The Hunger Project

Research and Research Support
Sherry Barto
Leo Belohlav
Sylvia Block
Helen Borgan
Toni Bryan
Diane Campbell
Katie Cantwell
John Coonrod
R. J. DeCristoforo
Bapu Deolalikar
Brian Dvorak
Catherine Edelman
John Field
Chris Gilbert
Gloria Goldberg
Nathan Gray
Barbara Hartford
Kathleen Kook
Eliot Lippman
Lynne Locatell
Jon Love
Elliot Marseille
Norman Marshall
Ambassador Edwin
  Martin
James McCawley
Donella Meadows
Tom Ogden
Debra Rein
Terry Rogers
Bob Saxon
Gloria Simon
Diana Soule
Jim Strong
Beverly Tangri
Jack Thomas
Hollis Wagstaff
Wendy Wheat
David Whitman
Mary Wolff
Chuck Woolery

Writing
Sherry Barto
Valerie Brooks
Larry Flynn
Deirdre Frontczak
Allan Henderson
Ted Howard
Elizabeth Neeld
John Richardson

Editorial Services
Andrew L. Alden
Mu'frida Bell
Teresa Castle
Zipporah W. Collins
Sean Cotter
Barbara Ferenstein
Katherine L. Kaiser
Elinor Lindheimer
Diana Lorentz
Naomi Steinfeld
David L. Sweet
Lisa Young

Project Management
Deirdre Frontczak
Linda Goldstone
Judith Lesser
Elliot Marseille
Doug May
Candice Miller
Elizabeth Neeld
Catherine Parrish
Sherry Urner Pettus
John Richardson
Peter Rosenwald
Lynne Twist
Chuck Woolery

Word Processing
Joan Anderson
Pam Fine
Larry Fuller
Michael Vanni
Laura Woolery

Design and Production
Doug Akagi
Byron Callas
Shawn Donnelley
Jean Goldman
Tom Ingalls
Mort Kohn
Jim Miho
Rik Olson
Dorothy Remington
Jim Stockton
Tee Thomas
Karen Tucker
Massimo Vignelli

Manuscript Review and Comment*
Earl Babbie
Caroline Beatty
Marjorie Benton
David Berenson
Peter Bourne
Roger Brooks
Richard Buchheim
Pran Chopra
Victoria Colella
Peter Davies
Charles Deull
Paul Dietrich
Delmar Dooley
Mark Dowie
Walter Falcon
Marilyn Ferguson
Nancy Foushée
Dick Fulton
The Honorable
  Benjamin Gilman
Vic Gioscia
James P. Grant
Brian Green
Herb Hamsher
Shirley Hartley
Father Theodore
  Hesburgh
John Hotson
Alan Hovey

Brian Hull
Tom Jackson
Ashok Jaitly
Clay Jones
George Kent
Mary King
David Kinley
Uwe Kracht
Martin Leaf
Peter Lenn
Barry Levy
Jon Love
C. Payne Lucas
Charles MacCormack
Duart Maclean
George Marotta
Lynn Marshall
Abby Mason
Joan McKinney
Martin McLaughlin
Charles McNeill
Dan Miller
Judith Oringer
Ann Overton
Fred Pinkham
John Poppy
Mario Postiglione
Roy Prosterman
Eva Reycraft
Jeremy Rifkin
Robert Rodale
Martin Rogol
Nathan Rosenberg
Elizabeth Russell
Catherine Sands
Howard Schneider
Loretta Schwartz-
  Nobel
Diane Silverman
Lawrence Simon
Ellen Sokoloff
John Steiner
Eugene Stockwell
Peggy Streit
Jim Strong
Beverly Tangri
Lee Traband
Les Traband
Greg Votaw

General Support
Barbara Ailes
Michael Baker
Noreen Banks
Amy Bittinger
Mary Claire Blakeman
Paul Borrillo
John Bostrom
Ann Brent
Linda Buchheim
Mark Burgess
Elly Cantor
Mary Earle Chase
Cary Clark
Ronald Clark
David Clausnitzer
Ron Coon
Steve Costenbader
Kay Curtis
R. J. DeCristoforo

Al deFillippi
Pamela DeSio
Ellis M. Deull
William Durrell
Barbara English
Elliott Espana
Judith Evans
Tunde Fafunwa
Kim Fleishell
Larry Flynn
Joe Goddu
Jim Goeke
Joan Goldsmith
Jay Greenspan
Heidi Guber
Paul Gutfreund
Jerald Harris
Mark Hellman
Cheryl Hendrickson
John Heney
Kerry Hillier
Tracy Howard
Alison Huff
The Hunger Project
  Board of Directors
The Hunger Project
  U.S. Staff
John Ingleby
Charles Ingrasci
Michael Johnston
Martha Jones
Bob Kazanjian
Dolores Kazanjian
George Kent
Lisa Kimbrough
Mary King
Kathleen Kook
Janina Lamb
Ron Landsman
Carole Litowsky
Chris Lytle
Carol MacIntosh
John Margulis
Lauri McCool
Regina McGrath
Jeanne McKie
John McMillen
Rosie McMurray
Margo Meadows
Sue Michalson
Mark Moldover
Pierrette Montroy
Moellen Moy
Tahrir Neman
Lisa Oglesby
Ami Olstein
Bill Parrish
Joel Pashkin
Asit Phakran
John Poppy
Anne Prescott
Zev Putterman
Alan Raynor
Heather Richardson
Neal Rogin
Susi Salgado
Gloria Simon
Paul Singleton
Iain Somerville
Sean Spies
Arlene Stanisi

John Stone
Jack Thomas
Bill Twist
Lynne Twist
Thomas Tyburski
Brian Van der Horst
Della van Heyst
Lady Olivia Waldron
Wendy Walsh
Virginia Weiss
Dave Wharton
Jim Whitton
Helaine Witt
Laura Woolery
Danielle Yariv

Photo Research and Editing
Antonia D. Bryan

Fundraising
Alan Andreini
Peaches Andreini
Pat Dillan
David Peterson
Kay Peterson
Nathan Rosenberg
Les Traband
Mike Wick

*The manuscript went through three separate phases of review and comment beginning in the spring of 1981. Most reviewers did not participate in all phases of the review. Many participated in only one.

Donor Acknowledgment

The work of The Hunger Project is funded through the voluntary financial contributions of tens of thousands of individuals. These men, women, and children choose to express their commitment to the end of hunger by directing their personal resources to the resolution of this global problem.

The following individuals, families, foundations, and corporations each made a special donation to The Hunger Project in support of the creation and production of *Ending Hunger: An Idea Whose Time Has Come.* Their substantial financial contributions enabled us to carry out the research, writing, and design of this book, and, ultimately, to make it available to the world.

The Hunger Project wishes to acknowledge gratefully these individuals, families, foundations, and corporations for the difference they chose to make with their money.

Alan and Peaches Andreini, Hathaway, John, and Alan, Jr.

Gus Sessions Arnold

Virginia Wolf Briscoe, Mark Briscoe, and Alexander Briscoe

Louis A. Carta

CFS Foundation

Marguerite Chandler and Richmond Shreve, Mark, Laura, and Adam

Robert and Annetta Chester

Tom Driscoll and Nancy Nicholson

Cameron Duncan

Edmar Corporation/Central Jersey Industrial Park

End World Hunger, Inc.

Werner Erhard and Associates Forum Leader Body and their Families

The est Foundation

David G. Gamble, Jr., Foster and Dania Gamble and Family

Tyler and Nancy Glenn

Irene Emery Goodale, Nathaniel, Martha, and Anna, Peter, Kate, and Rene

Doug and Deborah Gouge

Paul Gutfreund and Kitty Gutfreund

Valerie Harper

Nick and Jane Heyl

James C. Hormel

Paul and Lydia Hughes and Family

Raul, Merel, and Raul Sigmund Julia

David and Tres Klein

Lance Lavenstein

The Charles Luchessa Family

Higgins Maddigan, Margaret McLaughlin, and The Lahaina Market Place Corporation

The Mastery of Empowerment Course #2

Dr. Richard Mazurek

Jonathan and Pat Meyers

Bob Nakagawa

Donn and Julianne Peden and Family

Sunny Peltier, Jim Britain, and Jay Allgood

David and Kay Peterson and Family

Ronald A. Petty

Courtney, Cynthia, and Noah Price

Ronnie, Gail, Lisa, and Cori Raben

The Sarah and Matthew Rosenhaus Peace Foundation Inc.

Peter and Lee Ross, Healy, Emily, and J. P.

Julian and Joanna Ryder and Family

Arnold Siegel

Alan Silverstein

Leonard, Roz, Harold, Jan, Rachal, Mark, and Shelly Solomon and Barbara, Jeffrey, and Amy Beth Liss

Gerald, Joan, Stephen, and Sharon Starika

Faith Fayman Strong, Barry, Margaret, Linda, Hope, Bill, David, Mickey, Christopher, Marietta, and Deborah

Mary Tiscornia and Jennifer Tiscornia

Ron and Fran Travisano

Bill and Lynne Twist and Family

Ian and Vicky Watson

Mike and Sharon Wick and Family

404

Directories of Organizations

In this section you will find a listing of directories of thousands of governmental and nongovernmental organizations whose work contributes to ending hunger. Published in eleven countries, including three in the Third World, the directories indicate the scope and variety of these organizations. Supported by both voluntary contributions and government funds, these organizations are engaged in development assistance, development education, relief, refugee assistance, agricultural research, tropical medicine, and a myriad of other activities in virtually every country of the world.

International

1. Development Centre of the Organisation for Economic Co-operation and Development. *Directory of Non-Governmental Organisations in OECD Member Countries Active in Development Co-operation/Répertoire des Organisations Non-Gouvernementales des Pays Membres de l'OCDE Actives dans le Domaine de la Coopération pour le Développement.* 2 vols. Paris: 1981.

Lists 1,702 organizations engaged in development education and development aid. Organizations are based in Australia, Austria, Belgium, Canada, Denmark, the Federal Republic of Germany (West Germany), Finland, France, Iceland, Ireland, Italy, Japan, Luxembourg, the Netherlands, New Zealand, Norway, Portugal, Spain, Sweden, Switzerland, the United Kingdom, and the United States.

Volume I: Profiles. Gives brief profiles of organizations. Organization names in the national language, French, and English; descriptions in French or English. 741 pages.

Volume II: Index. Indexes include: French-Spanish-English equivalents of standardized descriptors of development activity, and organizations listed by type of activity and location of overseas operations. 773 pages.

Available from:

Bureau des Publications de l'Organisation de Coopération et de Développement Économiques
2 rue André-Pascal
75775 Paris Cedex 16
France

Also available from sales offices in 36 countries. Some of those are:

Australia
Australia and New Zealand Book Company Pty, Ltd.
P.O. Box 459
Brookvale, N.S.W. 2100
Australia

Canada
Renouf Publishing Company Limited
2182 St. Catherine Street West
Montréal, Que. H3H 1M7
Canada

The Federal Republic of Germany (West Germany)
OECD Publications and Information Center
4 Simrockstrasse
5300 Bonn
West Germany

India
Oxford Book and Stationery Co.
New Delhi-1, Scindia House
India

Japan
OECD Publications and Information Center
Landic Akasaka Bldg., 2-3-4 Akasaka
Minato-ku, Tokyo 107
Japan

New Zealand
Publications Section
Government Printing Office Bookshop
Retail: Mulgrave Street
Cubacade World Trade Centre, Wellington
Mail Orders: Private Bag
New Zealand

United Kingdom
H.M. Stationery Office, P.O.B. 569
London SE1 9NH
England

United States
OECD Publications and Information Center, Suite 1207
1750 Pennsylvania Ave., NW
Washington, DC 20006-4582
United States

Australia

1. Australian Council for Overseas Aid. *1984 Directory of Member Organisations.* Canberra City: 1984.

Lists 58 Australian nongovernmental organizations engaged in overseas assistance and international relations. Agencies listed include those that provide development assistance, relief, education, and health care. Gives brief profile and information on how to contact each organization. 39 pages.

Available from:

Australian Council for Overseas Aid
G.P.O. Box 1562
Canberra City ACT 2601
Australia

Canada

1. Canadian Council for International Co-operation. *Directory 82: Directory of Canadian Non-governmental Organizations Engaged in International Development/ Répertoire 82: Répertoire des Organismes Non Gouvernementaux Canadiens Engagés dans le Développement International.* Ottawa: 1982.

Lists, in English and French, 169 organizations involved in all aspects of international development. Gives staff names, objectives, fields, countries of activity, and other basic program information. 261 pages.

Available from:

Canadian Council for International Co-operation
450 rue Rideau
Ottawa, Ontario KIN 5Z4
Canada

2. Canadian Council for International Co-operation. *Development Education Survey.* Ottawa: 1984.

Lists over 104 Canadian organizations engaged in development education. Describes information and activities; lists organizations by province. Available in English or French. 112 pages.

Available from:

Canadian Council for International Co-operation
450 rue Rideau
Ottawa, Ontario KIN 5Z4
Canada

3. Association Québécoise des Organismes de Coopération Internationale. *Répertoire des Organismes de Coopération Internationale du Québec (Directory of International Cooperation Organizations of Québec)*. Montréal: 1982.

Lists 21 nongovernmental Québec-based organizations involved in international cooperation, including overseas development assistance, education, health, and agriculture. Gives objectives and national and international activities. Tables show organizations by activities and countries in which they work. Supplementary list of names and addresses of related international organizations grouped under main activity. In French. 78 pages.

Available from:

Association Québécoise des Organismes de Coopération Internationale
1115 boul. Gouin est
Montréal, Québec H2C 1B3
Canada

The Federal Republic of Germany (West Germany)
1. Deutsche Stiftung für internationale Entwicklung. *Medizinische Zusammenarbeit mit Entwicklungsländern (Medical Cooperation with Developing Countries)*. Bonn: 1983.

Lists 51 West German organizations, including those involved in tropical medicine, tropical hygiene, refugee assistance, aid to catastrophe victims, gynecology, and child care in developing countries. In German. 35 pages.

2. Deutsche Stiftung für internationale Entwicklung. *Landwirtschaftliche Zusammenarbeit mit Entwicklungsländern (Agricultural Cooperation with Developing Countries)*. Bonn: 1982.

Lists 201 West German organizations. Indexed by topic, country of activity, and people involved. In German. 163 pages.

Available from:

Deutsche Stiftung für internationale Entwicklung
Zentralstelle für Erziehung, Wissenschaft und Dokumentation
Hans-Böckler Str. 5
5300 Bonn 3
West Germany

India
1. Academy of Development Sciences. *Information Base on Voluntary Sector, Part One*. Taluka Karjat: 1980.

Lists 1,135 Indian agencies by state, district, and type of activity. Activities include agriculture, community health, cooperatives, ecology, irrigation, inland fisheries, and technology. Gives address for each agency. 105 pages.

Available from:

Academy of Development Sciences
At & Post Kashele, Taluka Karjat—410 201
District Kolaba, Maharashtra
India

Mexico
1. Consejo del Sistema Nacional de Educación Tecnológica. *La Investigación en Tecnología de Alimentos: Catalogo, 1983 (Research into Food Technology)*. Mexico, DF: 1983.

Includes a directory of over 75 institutions with departments in food technology, and descriptions of research topics in food science and technology. In Spanish. 327 pages.

This volume is part of a series designed to bring together researchers in the area of food science. Other titles from the same source are: *Perfil de la Investigación en Tecnología de Alimentos, 1983 (Profile of the Research into Food Technology, 1983)* and *La Investigación en Tecnología de Alimentos: Vinculacion, Directorio, 1983 (Research of Food Technology: Connections, Directory 1983)*.

Available from:

Consejo del Sistema Nacional de Educación Tecnológia
Apartado postal 25–311
Mexico, DF
C.P. 03400
Mexico

New Zealand
1. Clark, Kevin, ed. *Overseas Aid and Development: A Directory of NZ Organisations*. Wellington: Overseas Development Committee, 1980.

Lists 47 organizations located in New Zealand and involved in international aid and development. Gives address and brief description of each organization, including educational resources. 80 pages.

Available from:

United Nations Association of New Zealand (Incorporated)
P.O. Box 1011
Wellington
New Zealand

Nigeria
1. Federal Department of Agricultural Planning. *Directory of Nigerian Agricultural Organisations*. Lagos: 1982.

Lists 73 federal agencies, 65 state agencies, and 100 miscellaneous organizations (including consultants, farms, research centers, and cooperatives). Gives address for each organization. 65 pages.

Available from:

Federal Department of Agricultural Planning
59, Awolowo Road
Ikoyi
Lagos
Nigeria

Sweden
1. Swedish International Development Authority and Swedish United Nations Association. *U-Katalogen 80: Materialförteckningens Uppgifter Från Klanenderåret (Foreign Catalogue '80: Lesser Developed Countries)*. Stockholm: 1983.

Lists Swedish organizations involved in development work, as well as selected organizations from other Nordic countries. Also catalogued are periodicals, audio-visual rentals, libraries with resources on foreign countries, opportunities to work abroad, and general information on foreign aid.

Available from:

Svenska FN-förbundet
Box 15115
104 65 Stockholm
Sweden

United Kingdom

1. Overseas Development Administration. *Overseas Development and Aid: A Guide to Sources of Information and Material.* London: 1982.

Lists 118 organizations in the United Kingdom that publish material and supply information (primarily for educational use) on overseas development and aid. Gives brief description of organizations, including address, telephone number, and types of information they can supply. Index lists organizations by both country and subject for which they can supply materials or information. 56 pages.

Available from:

Information Department
Overseas Development Administration
Eland House
Stag Place
London SW1E 5DH
England

United States

1. Boynes, Wynta, ed. *U.S. Nonprofit Organizations in Development Assistance Abroad,* 8th ed. New York: Technical Assistance Information Clearing House of the American Council of Voluntary Agencies for Foreign Service, Inc., 1983.

Lists 497 U.S. nonprofit organizations. Gives address, names of executive and overseas program directors, objectives, assistance programs, and countries of activity. Indexed by type of assistance, including community development, cooperatives, education, food production and agriculture, medicine, nutrition, population, and family. Also indexed by country

of activity and states where offices are located. 584 pages.

Available from:

UNIPUB
P.O. Box 433
Murray Hill Station
New York, NY 10157
United States

2. Knowles, Louis L. *A Guide to World Hunger Organizations: Who They Are and What You Should Know About Them.* Decatur, Georgia: Seeds/Alternatives, 1984.

Gives in-depth analyses of 5 Protestant and 7 other organizations working to end world hunger. Also gives brief descriptions of 8 other organizations engaged in relief and development. 104 pages.

Available from:

Seeds
222 East Lake Drive
Decatur, GA 30030
United States

3. Lowenstein, Florence M., ed. *Development Education Programs of U.S. Nonprofit Organizations.* New York: Technical Assistance Information Clearing House of the American Council of Voluntary Agencies for Foreign Service, Inc., 1983.

Lists 108 organizations located in the United States. Gives address, contact person, program activities, target audience, and geographic area served for each organization. Indexed by area of program focus, including: community development, disaster relief, family planning/population, global interdependence, hunger/food production, medicine, nutrition, poverty, refugees, and water. Also indexed by target audience, region served, and location of offices. 140 pages.

Available from:

Technical Assistance Information Clearing House
American Council of Voluntary Agencies for Foreign Service
200 Park Avenue South
New York, NY 10003
United States

4. Worthington, Linda, ed. *Who's Involved With Hunger: An Organization Guide,* 3rd ed. Washington, DC: World Hunger Education Service, 1982.

Lists more than 400 private voluntary organizations that serve as major sources of materials on education and development. Gives executive director and main activities for each organization. Table of contents lists programs by area of focus (national/international) and type of activity. Also has a section on regional agencies, government agencies, and religious organizations. 50 pages.

Available from:

World Hunger Education Service
1317 G Street, NW
Washington, DC 20005
United States

5. U.S., Agency for International Development. *Voluntary Foreign Aid Programs: Reports of American Voluntary Agencies Engaged in Overseas Relief and Development Registered with the Agency for International Development.* Washington, DC: 1983.

Lists the 167 nongovernmental organizations registered with the U.S. Agency for International Development (AID) as eligible for AID funding. Gives brief description of activities for each agency. Tables summarize agencies' income and expenditures. Also gives percentage of funds for international programs received from non-U.S.-government sources. 35 pages.

Available from:

Bureau for Food for Peace and Voluntary Assistance
Agency for International Development
Washington, DC 20523
United States

Glossary

In this glossary you will find brief definitions of some of the words and phrases that are used in the book. For the most part, we exclude terms that are defined in the text, as well as terms whose meaning may be inferred from the context in which they appear.

Many of the words in this glossary have no single, simple, objective definition. Nearly every word can be defined in several different ways, depending on the point of view. (To confirm this, try consulting three or four good dictionaries on any subject—say, economics.) Further, even if the definition is not affected by a political point of view, it may be affected by values or areas of expertise. Indeed, some glossaries are actually written from particular, identified positions.[1]

Even the decision to include certain terms instead of others in the glossary may reflect a particular point of view—for example, "developing countries" but not "South," or "free market economies" instead of "demand economies."

We invite you to use this glossary carefully and judiciously. After reading a definition, check the index and read the various points of view on that term. Consult other dictionaries, as well.

Language is a powerful tool. We hope you will not be content with most of the definitions we have provided. This glossary is intended to broaden your search and encourage you to explore these terms further.

Acre An acre of land equals 43,560 square feet, or approximately 200 feet by 220 feet. One acre equals 0.4047 hectares.

Appropriate Technology A technology that utilizes locally abundant resources in preference to locally scarce resources. Developing countries usually have a large labor force and relatively little capital; thus, appropriate technology, here, would be labor-intensive. The term is often used to refer to small-scale, decentralized development approaches.

Balance of Payments A summary statement of all the economic transactions between one country and the rest of the world in a given period, usually a year. In an accounting sense, the receipts are always equal to the payments; hence the balance of payments always balances.

The term is sometimes used to refer to the difference between a country's receipts and payments—for example, there can be a balance-of-payments deficit (payments exceed receipts) or a balance-of-payments surplus (receipts exceed payments).

Basic-Human-Needs Approach A strategy for focusing development assistance on programs that most directly benefit the poorest people. Priorities are: the provision of food, clothing, and shelter; and access to basic services, including primary health care, education, and clean water.

Bilateral Aid The transfer of funds, goods, and/or services directly from one country to another.

Birth Rate, Crude The number of live births each year per thousand population. A "crude" rate is the rate computed for an entire population.

Brandt Commission The Independent Commission on International Development Issues, established in 1977 and chaired by Willy Brandt, former chancellor of the Federal Republic of Germany.

Its members served in a private capacity. The Commission studied the global issues arising from the economic and social disparities in the world community. Its 1980 report, *North-South: A Program for Survival*, provides a framework for discussions of the New International Economic Order.

Calorie A unit of measure of the energy value of food. When used as a measure of the energy produced by the oxidation of food in the body, a calorie is the amount of heat needed to raise the temperature of one kilogram of water one degree centigrade at one atmosphere pressure. This is also known as a "kilocalorie" or "large calorie."

Capital Goods that are used in production and have themselves been produced—for example, factories and machinery. "Capital" can also mean financial capital.

Carrying Capacity The maximum size of a resident population that can be sustained in a given ecosystem.

Cash Cropping Growing crops for sale in the market rather than for family consumption, as in subsistence farming.

Centrally Planned Economies Economies (sometimes called "command economies") in which some or all of the decisions about allocation of resources, production, investment, and distribution are made by the government. Usually the government is the owner of the means of production.

Chronic Undernutrition The long-term consumption of fewer calories and less protein than the body needs.

Collective Agriculture An agricultural system that is organized into farms owned by the state or a collective. The farms are managed by the workers and/or the state. Countries with collective agriculture include China, the USSR, and Israel.

Concessional Terms The conditions of loans that have lower interest rates and/or longer payback periods than do commercial loans.

Constant Prices Prices that have been adjusted for changes in the purchasing power of money. The comparison is made with prices in a given or base year.

For example, measuring GNP in constant prices (or "real" terms) enables one to make more meaningful comparisons of economic growth in times of inflation or deflation.

Death Rate, Crude The number of deaths each year per thousand population. A "crude" rate is the rate computed for an entire population.

Demographic Transition The transition of population growth rates from a slow-growth stage (with high birth and death rates), through a rapid-growth stage (in which birth rates are high and death rates are low), to a low-growth stage (with low birth and death rates).

Developed Countries See *Footnote 2.*

Developing Countries See *Footnote 2.*

Development The process of improving the quality of human lives in many areas, including: income and consumption levels; social, political, and economic institutions; and freedom of choice. The term is sometimes used to mean economic growth. However, "economic growth" refers solely to changes in per capita income, whereas "development" usually connotes institutional and structural change. (Some writers would include changes in individuals, as well.) See also *Footnote 2*.

Development Assistance Committee (DAC) DAC, established in 1961, is a committee of seventeen members of the Organization for Economic Cooperation and Development (OECD). Member nations are: Australia, Austria, Belgium, Canada, Denmark, Federal Republic of Germany (West Germany), Finland, France, Italy, Japan, the Netherlands, New Zealand, Norway, Sweden, Switzerland, the United Kingdom, and the United States. DAC provides a forum for these nations to consult and coordinate with each other on their development-assistance policies. Its purpose is to improve, harmonize, and coordinate aid policies and programs of its members.

Dwarf Varieties High-yielding varieties of grains—including corn, wheat, and rice—that have been bred for their short stalks capable of supporting large heads of grain.

Exponential Growth Growth in which a constant percentage of an expanding whole is added each time period. Also known as a "geometric ratio of growth." Exponential growth may be compared with "linear growth," in which a constant amount is added to the base each time period. Linear growth is also known as an "arithmetic ratio of growth."

Extension Services Educational and technical services provided to farmers, usually by government, including: advice and training on agricultural innovations; marketing practices and use of fertilizer and irrigation; and accounting and nutrition education.

Family Planning Planning by individuals to achieve a desired number and spacing of births. While the term usually implies efforts to limit births, it also includes attempts to induce pregnancy.

Family planning is not necessarily related to national or international goals. However, the family-planning movement often mentions a reduced birth rate as a goal.

Family-Planning Programs Program activities include sex education, promoting lower birth rates, and making means of contraception available.

Famine A widespread lack of access to food, caused when drought, flood, or war disrupts the availability of food in a society of chronically undernourished people.

Fertility Rate, General The number of live births per thousand women of childbearing age (generally 15–49 years old).

Fertility Rate, Replacement Level The fertility rate at which women of childbearing age have just enough daughters to replace themselves in the population.

First World See *Footnote 2*.

Food and Agriculture Organization (FAO) Founded in 1945 as a specialized agency of the United Nations, the FAO is a cooperative group that includes almost every nation in the world.

The aims of the FAO are to raise levels of nutrition and standards of living; to improve the production and distribution of all food and agricultural products; and to promote rural development.

Foreign Aid The gift or loan of funds, goods, and/or services from one government to another, either directly (bilateral) or through an intermediary organization (multilateral). This includes such categories as: emergency food aid; military hardware; funding for public-works projects; and consulting by experts on development projects.

Foreign Exchange All monetary instruments whereby residents of one country hold claims on another. This includes the currency of that country, interest-bearing bonds, and gold. "Foreign exchange earnings" refers to income earned by countries from their exports.

Fourth World See *Footnote 2*.

General Agreement on Tariffs and Trade (GATT) GATT, in force since 1948, is a multilateral agreement.

GATT's principles include: promotion of equal treatment for all trading nations; negotiated tariff reductions; and elimination of import quotas. GATT is both a code of rules and also a forum in which countries discuss world trade problems and opportunities.

Grain Reserves Stocks of grain held by governments to supplement supplies of food when harvests are poor, and to moderate price fluctuations.

Green Revolution The development and widespread adoption of high-yielding strains of wheat, corn, and rice in the Third World. The term has been used to describe the increase in agricultural production in India in the 1960s and 1970s, particularly in the Punjab. Recently, "Green Revolution" has become popularized and now refers to almost any package of modern agricultural technologies introduced into the Third World.

Gross National Product (GNP) The total value of all final goods and services produced by a nation in a given year, expressed in monetary terms. It includes both foreign and domestic output claimed by residents. (An example of a "final" good is a loaf of bread purchased by a consumer, but not the wheat or flour used to produce the bread.)

"Per capita GNP" is the gross national product of a nation, divided by its population.

Group of 77 Originally the seventy-seven developing countries that formed a coalition at the United Nations Conference of Trade and Development in 1964. The group sponsored the "Declaration and Programme of Action on the Establishment of the New International Economic Order" in 1974. Now the term is applied to the caucus of all developing nations in the United Nations.

Hectare (Ha.) A hectare equals 10,000 square meters of land, or an area 100 meters by 100 meters. One hectare equals 2.471 acres.

High-Yielding Varieties (HYV) Recently developed varieties of grains that, when grown under the required conditions, produce higher yields per unit of land.

Hunger An urgent need or desire for food. Hunger manifests itself as chronic undernutrition, malnutrition, malabsorptive hunger, seasonal hunger, and famine.

Hungry Countries Nations where hunger persists as a basic issue, as indicated by an infant mortality rate above 50.

Import-Substitution Government policies to encourage the domestic production of goods that are currently imported, often to improve a country's balance of payments or increase its self-sufficiency.

Industrialized Economies See *Footnote 2*.

Infant Mortality Rate The number of deaths among children under age one per thousand live births.

International Bank for Reconstruction and Development (IBRD) An agency of the United Nations that was established in 1945 to help finance the reconstruction of postwar Europe. Shortly thereafter, its purpose was broadened to include promotion of economic development of developing countries. In 1982, 141 countries were members of the IBRD.

The IBRD channels private funds and provides loans from its resources for development projects and technical assistance to developing nations. It is often called the World Bank. (See also *World Bank*.)

International Development Association (IDA) IDA was established in 1960 as an affiliate of the International Bank for Reconstruction and Development.

It provides loans to low-income developing countries on more favorable terms than those offered by private lenders or the IBRD.

International Fund for Agricultural Development (IFAD) Established in 1977 as a major outcome of the Rome World Food Conference of 1974, IFAD is the only international institution in which member nations of the Organization for Economic Cooperation and Development (OECD) and the Organization of Petroleum Exporting Countries (OPEC) are major contributors.

IFAD supports agricultural projects for the poorest of the poor farmers in developing countries.

International Monetary Fund (IMF) Established in 1945 to promote stability in the international monetary system, the IMF is a fund from which member governments can borrow foreign currency to meet balance-of-payments deficits.

Loans are granted provided the receiving country adopts a plan that embodies measures designed to correct the deficit.

Land Reform Reorganization of the existing system of land ownership and management to bring about a more equitable division of agricultural land.

Less Developed Countries See *Footnote 2*.

Life Expectancy at Birth The number of years an infant born in a particular year can be expected to live, given current conditions of mortality.

Literacy Rate, Adult The percentage of the population age fifteen and over who can read and write.

Malabsorptive Hunger Hunger caused by an inability of the body to absorb the nutritional value of food consumed. Also known as "secondary malnutrition."

Malnutrition Any faulty or insufficient dietary condition. Specifically, a condition resulting when an individual's diet has a relative deficiency or relative excess of specific nutrients vital to good health.

Market Economies Economies (sometimes called "demand economies") in which decisions on allocation of resources, production, investment, and distribution are made by demand and supply (the price system). In practice, most market economies have elements that are nonmarket directed.

Market economies are usually based on a system of private ownership.

See also *Centrally Planned Economies*.

Marshall Plan Also called the "European Recovery Program." Instituted in 1947 by U.S. Secretary of State George C. Marshall, the plan was a joint effort of the United States and Europe to support Europe's recovery after World War II.

More Developed Countries See *Footnote 2*.

Multilateral Aid Contributions from several countries to an intermediary institution, such as the World Bank, which then allocates the assistance to the recipient.

Multinational Corporation (MNC) A company with subsidiaries, investments, or operations in more than one country. Also called a "transnational corporation."

Natural Rate of Increase of Population The rate at which a population grows over a given period, say a year, due to an excess of births over deaths. The rate is expressed as a percentage of the base population. It may be found by subtracting the crude death rate from the crude birth rate.

The "natural" rate of increase of population differs from the rate of increase of population (population growth rate) in that the former excludes increases that result from changes in immigration and emigration.

New International Economic Order (NIEO) A set of proposals for structural change in the international economy that were made by developing countries in the UN and were adopted by the United Nations General Assembly in 1974. These proposals are designed to redress the international economic imbalance felt by the developing nations.

Nongovernmental Organization (NGO) A nongovernmental, not-for-profit, voluntary organization established by private initiative. "NGO" is used as an official designation for such organizations affiliated with the United Nations Non-Governmental Liaison Service. See also *Private Voluntary Organization*.

Nonhungry Countries Nations where hunger no longer persists as a basic issue, as indicated by an infant mortality rate of 50 or below. Using this measure, there are seventy-five nonhungry countries in the world. Although hunger no longer persists as a basic issue in these countries, there are still individuals in these countries who are hungry.

North A grouping of the "rich," more developed countries, based on the recognition that all these countries, except for Australia and New Zealand, are geographically north of the "poor," less developed countries (the South). See also *Footnote 2; South; North-South Dialogue;* and the *New International Economic Order.*

North Atlantic Treaty Organization (NATO) A mutual-security organization established in 1949. Its original members were Belgium, Canada, Denmark, France, Iceland, Italy, Luxembourg, the Netherlands, Norway, Portugal, the United Kingdom, and the United States. These countries were joined in the first half of the 1950s by Greece, Turkey, and the Federal Republic of Germany (West Germany).

NATO is the Western counterpart of the Warsaw Treaty Organization.

North-South Dialogue Discussion of global economic change between the developed countries and the developing countries, usually in the framework of the New International Economic Order.

Official Development Assistance (ODA) Funds provided to developing countries and multilateral agencies. These funds must be concessional in character, contain a grant element of at least 25 percent, and be administered with the prime objective of promoting the economic development and welfare of developing countries.

In 1970, the UN General Assembly called upon Western countries to contribute a minimum net amount of 0.7 percent of their GNP as ODA to Third World nations. The Brandt Report has called for a level of 1 percent of GNP from Western and Eastern nations.

Organization for Economic Cooperation and Development (OECD) In 1961, the fourteen-year-old Organization for European Economic Cooperation (OEEC) changed its name to the Organization for Economic Cooperation and Development. The name change reflected a broader membership base, which now includes: Australia, Austria, Belgium, Canada, Denmark, the Federal Republic of Germany (West Germany), Finland, France, Greece, Iceland, Ireland, Italy, Japan, Luxembourg, the Netherlands, New Zealand, Norway, Portugal, Spain,

Sweden, Switzerland, Turkey, the United Kingdom, and the United States. Yugoslavia has special membership status.

The OECD's purpose is to further economic growth and to contribute to the development of the world economy by encouraging cooperation among its members and promoting technical analysis of economic trends.

Organization of Petroleum Exporting Countries (OPEC) Established by major oil-exporting countries in 1961. Current members are: Algeria, Ecuador, Gabon, Indonesia, Iran, Iraq, Kuwait, Libya, Nigeria, Qatar, Saudi Arabia, United Arab Emirates, and Venezuela.

OPEC acts as a cartel, promoting members' joint economic interests. From 1973 to 1975, its price-setting policy essentially quadrupled world oil prices.

Paddy Rice, especially before the husk has been removed. Also refers to the irrigated or flooded field in which rice is grown.

Per Capita GNP (GNP Per Person) The gross national product of a nation, divided by its population.

Physical Quality of Life Index (PQLI) A composite measure of human well-being that combines the infant mortality rate, life expectancy at age one, and the literacy rate. Individual countries are ranked on a relative scale of 0 (low) to 100 (high). The measure was devised by the Overseas Development Council and provides a nonincome measure of well being.

Population Age Structure The composition, by age, of a given population, expressed as a percentage of the population for each age category. The population age/sex structure is the percentage of population of each sex in different age categories.

Population Density The number of inhabitants per unit area of land; for example, six persons per square mile.

Population Growth Rate The rate at which a population grows in a given year. Includes increases resulting from change in immigration and emigration. See also *Natural Rate of Increase of Population.*

Population Planning The development and implementation of policies by government, designed to influence the size, rate of growth, distribution, or composition of the population.

Primary Products Products and materials taken directly from nature, such as food crops, fish, timber, and minerals.

Private Voluntary Organization (PVO) A nongovernmental, not-for-profit organization. The term commonly used in the U.S. to refer to a nongovernmental organization. See also *Nongovernmental Organization.*

Seasonal Hunger Hunger that occurs when food from the last harvest runs out before the next crop is harvested.

Second World See *Footnote 2.*

South A grouping of the "poor," less developed countries, based on the recognition that these countries are generally located south of the more developed countries.

See also *Footnote 2; North; North-South Dialogue;* and the *New International Economic Order.*

Special Drawing Rights (SDRs) A currency-equivalent created in 1969 by the International Monetary Fund, for use by countries to make international payments.

Starvation The act of becoming weak, suffering, or dying from lack of food.

Subsidy A payment by government to producers or distributors to: ensure the economic viability of an industry; prevent an increase in prices; or increase incomes. Examples include subsidies on some foodstuffs to keep prices down in urban areas, and farm subsidies to expand production.

Terms of Trade The relationship between export prices and import prices.

If export prices rise more rapidly than do import prices or fall more slowly than do import prices, the terms of trade are said to improve.

The terms of trade are usually expressed for countries, but are also used for producers and regions.

Third World See *Footnote 2.*

Transnational Corporation (TNC) See *Multinational Corporation.*

Underdeveloped Countries See *Footnote 2.*

United Nations Children's Fund (UNICEF) Established in 1946 by the General Assembly of the United Nations, UNICEF (originally called the United Nations International Children's Emergency Fund) provided emergency supplies of food, clothing, and medicine to children in war-torn countries. UNICEF is financed entirely by voluntary contributions from governments, organizations, and individuals.

UNICEF's broadly based, integrated approach focuses on health, water, education, nutrition, and emergency famine relief to solve the problems of the most disadvantaged children and their mothers.

United Nations Conference on Trade and Development (UNCTAD) Founded in 1964 to establish world-trade policies, UNCTAD is a part of the United Nations Secretariat. One of its principal functions is to negotiate multilateral legal instruments in the field of international trade.

UNCTAD convenes every three or four years to discuss trade, development, and balance-of-payment problems of developing countries.

United Nations Development Program (UNDP) Established in 1965 as a part of the United Nations Secretariat, UNDP is funded by United Nations members.

UNDP works with governments, United Nations-related agencies, and international agencies to plan, manage, and implement technical cooperation on a global basis. Projects include: nutrition; health and education programs; and building up agricultural, industrial, and transport infrastructures.

Warsaw Treaty Organization (Warsaw Pact) A mutual-security alliance established in 1955. The Warsaw Pact includes Bulgaria, Czechoslovakia, the German Democratic Republic (East Germany), Hungary, Poland,

Romania, and the Union of Soviet Socialist Republics.

The Warsaw Pact is the Eastern counterpart of NATO.

World Bank This term sometimes refers to the World Bank group—three separately funded but closely related agencies: the International Bank for Reconstruction and Development; the International Development Association; and the International Finance Corporation (IFC), which makes loans to private companies in poor countries.

"The World Bank" sometimes refers only to the IBRD.

World Food Council (WFC) Founded in 1974 to implement the resolutions of the Rome World Food Conference.

The WFC's stated goal is the eradication of hunger. The council generates awareness and political support for agencies and programs working directly to eliminate hunger.

World Food Program (WFP) The WFP was established in 1963 and is administered by the Food and Agriculture Organization.

The WFP uses contributions of food and funds to provide emergency relief during famines and other disasters and to stimulate economic development.

World Health Organization (WHO) Established in 1948 by the United Nations General Assembly, WHO is funded by member states of the United Nations and by voluntary contributions.

WHO plans and coordinates health action on a global basis. Its stated purpose is for all peoples to attain the highest possible level of health. Since 1977, its first priority has been "health for all by the year 2000."

Footnote 1

Two such glossaries are:

GJW Government Relations. *Handbook of World Development: The Guide to the Brandt Report.* Compiled by Peter Stephenson. Essex, England: Longman Group Limited, 1981.

Starrels, John M. *The U.S.—Third World Conflict.* Washington, DC: The Heritage Foundation, 1983.

Footnote 2

"Developed countries" is a term that has been used to describe nations with relatively high per capita incomes. "Developing countries" refers to those nations with relatively low per capita incomes.

Other criteria besides the level of per capita income often are used to distinguish between the developed and the developing countries. For example, developing nations have been characterized as having: low productivity; high illiteracy rates; high birth rates; a dependence on subsistence-level agriculture; limited educational facilities; and rudimentary communication and transportation facilities.

Prior to 1960, developed/developing countries were described in several ways, including: "rich/poor"; "advanced/backward"; "developed/undeveloped"; and "developed/underdeveloped." A gradual recognition that some of these terms are offensive led to the use of "developed/developing" and "more developed/less developed." All these terms, however, characterize the developing countries in terms of the standard of developed countries.

The UN currently uses the term "more developed countries" to refer to Japan, the USSR, and all countries in Europe, North America, and Australasia. All others are classified as "less developed countries."

The general assembly of UNCTAD introduced a further distinction in 1971, when it applied the term "least developed countries" to those countries with: a per capita gross domestic product (GDP) of $100 or less; 10 percent or less of GDP in manufactures; and a literacy rate of 20 percent or less.

Another way of delineating nations in this area is by the terms "First World," "Second World," "Third World," and "Fourth World." "First World" refers to the developed market economy nations (Western Europe, North America, Australia, New Zealand, and Japan).

"Second World" refers to developed nations with centrally planned economies (Eastern Europe and the USSR). "Third World" is used for the developing countries. (In this book, we use "Third World" to mean the 141 African, Asian, and Latin American member countries of the United Nations.) "Fourth World" refers to the poorest of the Third World countries.

Use of "First," "Second," "Third," and "Fourth World" generally adds a political dimension to the economic characterizations.

Other terms by which countries are categorized include "North/South" and "industrialized/nonindustrialized."

"Industrialized countries" (often used as a synonym for developed countries) is used to refer to those countries whose gross national product comes primarily from industrial activity.

Bibliography

Agency for International Development. *War on Hunger* 11, no. 6 (June 1977).

——. *World Development Letter* 3, no. 10 (May 1980).

——. *World Development Letter* 4, no. 13 (June 1981).

Almeida, Silvio, et al. "Analysis of Traditional Strategies to Combat World Hunger and Their Results." *International Journal of Health Services* 5, no. 1 (1975).

Ambroggi, Robert P. "Water." *Scientific American* 243, no. 3 (September 1980).

Ariyaratne, A. T. "A People's Movement for Self-Reliance in Sri Lanka." In *Collected Works: Volume I*. Edited by Nandasena Ratnapala. Dehiwala, Sri Lanka: Sarvodaya Research Institute, n.d.

——. *In Search of Development*. Moratuwa, Sri Lanka: Sarvodaya Shramadana, 1982.

Aziz, Sartaj, ed. *Hunger, Politics and Markets*. New York: New York University Press, 1975.

——. *Rural Development: Learning from China*. New York: Holmes & Meier, 1978.

——. "We Need Development for Sheer Survival." Interviewed in *Ceres* 8, no. 1 (January–February 1975).

——. "The World Food Situation—Today and in the Year 2000." *Proceedings: The World Food Conference of 1976*. Ames, IA: Iowa State University Press, 1977.

Barnet, Richard J. "The Profits of Hunger." *Nation,* 9 February 1980.

Barnett, A. Doak. *China and the World Food System*. Monograph no. 12. Washington, DC: Overseas Development Council, April 1979.

Barr, Terry N. "The World Food Situation and Global Grain Prospects." *Science* 214 (4 December 1981).

Barraclough, Solon L. "Politics First." *Ceres* 7, no. 5 (September–October 1974).

Batie, Sandra S., and Robert G. Healy, eds. *The Future of American Agriculture as a Strategic Resource*. Washington, DC: The Conservation Foundation, 1980.

Bauer, Peter T. *Dissent on Development: Studies and Debates in Development Economics*. Cambridge, MA: Harvard University Press, 1972.

Bauer, Peter T., and John O'Sullivan. "Foreign Aid for What?" *Commentary,* December 1978.

Bauer, Peter T., and Basil S. Yamey. "Foreign Aid: What Is at Stake?" *Public Interest,* no. 68 (Summer 1982).

——. "The Third World and the West: An Economic Perspective." *The Third World: Premises of U.S. Policy*. Edited by W. Scott Thompson. San Francisco: Institute for Contemporary Studies, 1978.

Bednar, James. "Foreign Aid: Generosity Returned." *Agenda* 3, no. 10 (December 1980).

Bekele, Maaza. "False Prophets of Doom." *Unesco Courier,* July–August 1974.

Benoit, Emile. *Defense and Economic Growth in Developing Countries*. Lexington, MA: D. C. Heath & Company/ Lexington Books, 1973.

Benor, Daniel, and James Q. Harrison. *Agricultural Extension: The Training and Visit System*. Washington, DC: World Bank, May 1977.

Biswas, Asit K. "Agricultural Development and Environment." *Mazingira,* no. 11 (1979).

Borlaug, Norman E. "Using Plants to Meet World Food Needs." In *Future Dimensions of World Food and Population*. Edited by Richard G. Woods. Boulder, CO: Westview Press, 1981.

——. "Without Pesticides, 'The World Population Will Starve.'" *U.S. News & World Report,* 1 November 1971.

Brackett, James W.; R. T. Ravenholt; and John C. Chao. "The Role of Family Planning in Recent Rapid Fertility Declines in Developing Countries." *Studies in Family Planning* 9, no. 12 (December 1978).

Brooks, Roger A. "Multinationals: First Victim of the U.N. War on Free Enterprise." *Heritage Foundation Backgrounder,* no. 227, 16 November 1982.

Brown, Lester R. *By Bread Alone*. New York: Praeger, 1974.

——. *State of the World 1984*. New York: W. W. Norton, 1984.

Bunch, Roland; Mary McKay; and Paul McKay. "Problems with Food Distribution Programs: A Case in Point." Occasional paper. Oklahoma City, OK: World Neighbors, 1978.

Caliendo, Mary Alice. *Nutrition and the World Food Crisis*. New York: Macmillan, 1979.

Campbell, Keith O. *Food for the Future*. Lincoln, NB: University of Nebraska Press, 1979.

Canada. House of Commons. "Proceedings and Evidence of the Special

Committee on North-South Relations." *Parliamentary Papers,* no. 25, 32nd Parliament, 1st sess., 18 November 1980, 25.

Chen Cheng. *Land Reform in Taiwan.* Taiwan, Republic of China: Ching Publishing Co., 1961.

"A Choice of Securities," *Ceres* 14, no. 3 (May–June 1981).

Chopra, Pran. "The Poor Are Not a Burden." *A Shift in the Wind,* no. 11 (October 1981).

Commission on International Development. *Partners in Development.* New York: Praeger, 1969.

Committee on Poverty and the Arms Trade. "Magweta or How Does the Arms Trade Affect Development?" *Development: Seeds of Change* 1 (1982).

Critchfield, Richard. "It's Time to Give Foreign Aid a Good Name." *The Christian Science Monitor,* 13 July 1979.

Cutler, M. Rupert. "The Peril of Vanishing Farmlands." *New York Times,* 1 July 1980.

de Cautin, Mario. "Native Americans' Struggle for Survival." *IFDA Dossier,* no. 28 (March–April 1982).

DeHoogh, Jerrie, et al. "Food for a Growing World Population." *Technological Forecasting and Social Change* 10, no. 1 (1977).

de Silva, K. M., ed. *Sri Lanka: A Survey.* Honolulu: University of Hawaii Press, 1977.

Development Case Study: Sri Lanka. New York: American Friends Service Committee, n.d.

Dietrich, Paul, ed. *Congressional Policy: A Guide to American Foreign Policy and National Defense.* Washington, DC: National Center for Legislative Research, 1982.

Ding Chen. "The Economic Development of China." *Scientific American* 243, no. 3 (September 1980).

Dumont, René. *Utopia or Else....* Translated by Vivienne Menkes. New York: Universe Books, 1975.

Edwards, R. Dudley, and T. Desmond Williams, eds. *The Great Famine: Studies in Irish History, 1845–52.* New York: New York University Press, 1957.

Ehrlich, Paul R. *The Population Bomb.* Rev. New York: Ballantine, 1968.

Ehrlich, Paul R.; Anne H. Ehrlich; and John P. Holdren. *Human Ecology.* San Francisco: W. H. Freeman, 1973.

"Family Size and the Black American." *Population Bulletin* 30, no. 4 (1975).

"Food Aid: For Peace or Patronage?" *Reading Rural Development Communications,* Bulletin 10, July 1980.

"Foreign Aid: Debating the Uses and Abuses." *New York Times,* 1 March 1981.

Frank, Isaiah. "Big Business in the Third World: Gains on All Sides." *The Christian Science Monitor,* 10 July 1981.

Frankel, Francine R. *India's Green Revolution: Economic Gains and Political Costs.* Princeton, NJ: Princeton University Press, 1971.

Freeman, Orville L., and William Persen. "Multinational Corporations: Hope for the Poorest Nations." *Futurist* 14, no. 6 (December 1980).

Fuller, R. Buckminster. *Critical Path.* New York: St. Martin's Press, 1981.

Fulton, Tom, and Peter Braestrup. "The New Issues: Land, Water, Energy." *Wilson Quarterly* 5, no. 3 (Summer 1981).

Gabel, Medard. *Ho-Ping: Food for Everyone.* Garden City, NY: Doubleday/ Anchor Press, 1979.

Galenson, Walter, ed. *Economic Growth and Structural Change in Taiwan.* Ithaca, NY: Cornell University Press, 1979.

George, Susan. "Dear Friends and Colleagues of the North-South Food Roundtable." *Development: Seeds of Change* 1 (1982).

———. *Feeding the Few: Corporate Control of Food.* Washington, DC: Institute for Policy Studies, n.d.

———. *How the Other Half Dies.* Montclair, NJ: Allanheld, Osmun & Co., 1977.

Glick, Edward Bernard. *Peaceful Conflict: The Non-Military Use of the Military.* Harrisburg, PA: Stackpole Books, 1967.

Global Negotiations Information Project. *Global Negotiations Action Notes,* no. 3 (19 January 1981).

Goodsell, James Nelson. "A Continent Resists Birth Curbs." *The Christian Science Monitor,* 29 December 1970.

Goulet, Denis. *Survival with Integrity: Sarvodaya at the Crossroads.* Colombo, Sri Lanka: Marga Institute, 1981.

Goulet, Denis, and Michael Hudson. *The Myth of Aid.* New York: IDOC North America, 1971.

Grant, James P. *Disparity Reduction Rates in Social Indicators.* Monograph no. 11. Washington, DC: Overseas Development Council, September 1978.

Green, Cynthia P. *People: An Endangered Species?* Rev. Washington, DC: National Wildlife Federation, 1980.

Hardin, Garrett. "Lifeboat Ethics: The Case Against Helping the Poor." *Psychology Today,* September 1974.

———. "The Toughlove Solution." *Newsweek,* 26 October 1981.

Hartley, Shirley Foster. *Population: Quantity vs. Quality.* Englewood Cliffs, NJ: Prentice-Hall, 1972.

Hartmann, Betsy, and James Boyce. *Needless Hunger: Voices from a Bangladesh Village.* San Francisco: Institute for Food and Development Policy, 1979.

Haverstock, Mike. "Cali: City on the Move." *Americas* 34, no. 2 (March–April 1982).

Hayami, Yujiro, and Vernon W. Ruttan. *Agricultural Development: An International Perspective.* Baltimore, MD: Johns Hopkins University Press, 1971.

Honsa, Carol. "Nonaligned Want a $300 Billion Slice of Pie." *The Christian Science Monitor,* 13 February 1981.

Huntington, Samuel P. *American Politics: The Promise of Disharmony.* Cambridge, MA: Harvard University Press, 1981.

Huq, Muzammel. "The Structure of Hunger." *Unesco Courier,* September 1980.

Huston, Perdita. *Third World Women Speak Out.* New York: Praeger, 1979.

Independent Commission on International Development Issues. *North-South: A Program for Survival.* Cambridge, MA: MIT Press, 1980.

Irwin, Wallace, Jr. *America in the World: A Guide to U.S. Foreign Policy.* New York: Praeger, 1983.

Janowitz, Morris. *Military Institutions and Coercion in the Developing Nations.* Chicago: University of Chicago Press, 1977.

Johnson, Stanley. *The Green Revolution.* New York: Harper & Row, 1972.

Kahn, Herman; William Brown; and Leon Martel. *The Next 200 Years: A Scenario for America and the World.* New York: William Morrow, 1976.

Katz, Robert. *A Giant in the Earth.* New York: Stein and Day, 1973.

Kirk, Dudley, and Ellen K. Eliason, eds. *Food and People.* San Francisco: Boyd & Fraser, 1982.

Kissinger, Henry. *For the Record: Selected Statements, 1977–1980.* Boston: Little, Brown & Company, 1981.

Krauthammer, Charles. "Rich Nations, Poor Nations." *New Republic,* 11 April 1981.

Kuo, Shirley W. Y.; Gustav Ranis; and John C. H. Frei. *The Taiwan Success Story: Rapid Growth with Improved Distribution in the Republic of China, 1952–1979.* Boulder, CO: Westview Press, 1981.

Lappé, Frances Moore, and Nick Allen. "Central American Victims." *New York Times,* 28 May 1982.

Lappé, Frances Moore, and Joseph Collins. *Food First.* New York: Ballantine, 1982.

Lappé, Frances Moore; Joseph Collins; and David Kinley. *Aid as Obstacle: Twenty Questions about Our Foreign Aid and the Hungry.* San Francisco: Institute for Food and Development Policy, 1980.

Letiche, John M., ed. *International Economic Policies and Their Theoretical Foundations: A Source Book.* New York: Academic Press, 1982.

Lewis, John P. *1981 Review: Development Co-operation.* Paris: Organisation for Economic Co-operation and Development, November 1981.

Lincoln, Robert A. "In Turkey: Preserving Democracy by Coup." *Army* 31, no. 8 (August 1981).

Lipton, Michael. "Salting Grain Away." *Guardian,* 30 July 1979.

Lofchie, Michael F., and Stephen K. Commins. "Food Deficits and Agricultural Policies in Tropical Africa." *Journal of Modern African Studies* 20, no. 1 (1982).

Maddox, John. *The Doomsday Syndrome.* New York: McGraw-Hill, 1972.

Malthus, Thomas Robert. *An Essay on the Principle of Population.* Edited by Philip Appleman. New York: W. W. Norton, 1976.

Mamdani, Mahmood. *The Myth of Population Control: Family, Caste, and Class in an Indian Village.* New York: Monthly Review Press, 1972.

Mao Tse-tung. *Quotations from Chairman Mao Tse-tung.* Edited by Stuart R. Schram. New York: Bantam, 1972.

Mark, Jeremy. "Cambodia: Hope for a Future." *1981 World Refugee Survey.* New York: United States Committee for Refugees, 1981.

Markandaya, Kamala. *Nectar in a Sieve.* 2nd American ed. New York: John Day Company, 1955.

Marshall, George C. "European Unity." *Vital Speeches of the Day* 13, no. 18 (1 July 1947).

M'Bow, Amadou-Mahtar. "The Will for Peace." *Unesco Courier,* April 1979.

McCleary, Paul F., and J. Philip Wogaman. *Quality of Life in a Global Society.* New York: Friendship Press, 1978.

McCormack, Fr. Arthur. "Plenary IV— Population, Social Change and Development." *Since Bucharest—and the Future.* Washington, DC: World Population Society, 1976.

McDowell, Jim. "The Month When the Children Wait for Food." *UNICEF News* 85, no. 3 (1975).

McNamara, Robert S. *The Essence of Security.* New York: Harper & Row, 1968.

———. *The McNamara Years at the World Bank: Major Policy Addresses of Robert S. McNamara, 1968–1981.* Baltimore, MD: Johns Hopkins University Press, 1981.

Mills, Donald O. "Cry from Third World: 'Listen to Us!'" *U.S. News & World Report,* 31 July 1978.

Millwood, David. *Help or Hindrance? Aid, Trade and the Rich Nations' Responsibility to the Third World.* Geneva, Switzerland: SODEPAX, 1971.

Mitterand, François. "France in the World." Address at New York University, 8 December 1980.

Moraes, Dom. *A Matter of People.* New York: Praeger, 1974.

Murdoch, William W. *The Poverty of Nations.* Baltimore, MD: Johns Hopkins University Press, 1980.

Muskie, Edmund S. "The Secretary of State on Foreign Aid." *World Development Letter* 3, no. 19 (29 September 1980).

National Research Council. Commission on International Relations. *World Food and Nutrition Study: The Potential Contributions of Research.* Washington, DC: National Academy of Sciences, 1977.

Newman, Barry. "World Hunger: Graft and Inefficiency in Bangladesh Subvert Food-for-Work Plans." *The Wall Street Journal,* 20 April 1981.

Nobile, Philip, and John Deedy, eds. *The Complete Ecology Fact Book.* Garden City, NY: Doubleday/Anchor Books, 1972.

Nyerere, Julius K. "One Party Government." *Spearhead: The Pan-African Review* 1, no. 1 (November 1961).

———. "A Trade Union for the Poor." *Bulletin of the Atomic Scientists* 35, no. 6 (June 1979).

Overseas Development Council. *U.S. Foreign Policy and the Third World: Agenda 1983.* Edited by John P. Lewis and Valeriana Kallab. New York: Praeger, 1983.

———. *U.S. Foreign Policy and the Third World: Agenda 1982.* Edited by Roger D. Hansen et al. New York: Praeger, 1982.

———. *The United States and World Development: Agenda 1980.* Edited by John W. Sewell et al. New York: Praeger, 1980.

———. *The United States and World Development: Agenda 1979.* Edited by Martin M. McLaughlin et al. New York: Praeger, 1979.

Paxton, John, ed. *The Statesman's Year-Book.* London: Macmillan Press, 1981.

Petersen, William. *Population.* 2nd ed. New York: Macmillan, 1970.

Pimentel, David, and Marcia Pimentel. *Food, Energy and Society.* London: Edward Arnold, 1979.

Pimentel, David, et al. "Food Production and the Energy Crisis." *Science* 182 (2 November 1973).

Pine, Art. "Trade Threat: Third World's Gains in the Basic Industries Stir a Sharp Backlash." *The Wall Street Journal.* Western ed. 13 April 1984.

Pope Paul VI. "The Encyclical Letter 'Humanae Vitae.'" *The Pope Speaks* 13, no. 4 (Winter 1969).

Population Reference Bureau. *1984 World Population Data Sheet.* Washington, DC: Population Reference Bureau, 1984.

———. *1983 World Population Data Sheet.* Washington, DC: Population Reference Bureau, 1983.

———. *1982 World Population Data Sheet.* Washington, DC: Population Reference Bureau, 1982.

———. *1981 World Population Data Sheet.* Washington, DC: Population Reference Bureau, 1981.

Pradervand, Pierre. "The Malthusian Man." *New Internationalist,* no. 15 (May 1974).

Prosterman, Roy L. *The Decline in Hunger-Related Deaths.* The Hunger Project Papers, no. 1. Edited by Beverly Tangri. San Francisco: The Hunger Project, May 1984.

———. "More Food, Fewer Children." *A Shift in the Wind,* no. 3 (November 1978).

Revel, Jean-François. "How Well Is the Third World Governed?" *The Wall Street Journal,* 5 November 1981.

"Review & Outlook." *The Wall Street Journal.* Western ed. 13 April 1984.

Rodale, Robert, and Thomas Dybdahl. "The Coming Food Crunch." *Cry California* (Summer 1981).

415

Rodney, Walter. *How Europe Underdeveloped Africa*. London: Bogle-L'Ouverture Publications, 1972.

Samuelson, Paul A. *Economics*. 11th ed. New York: McGraw-Hill, 1980.

Schneider, Laurel. "Thai Refugee Report." *Tucker* 5, no. 1 (Fall 1981).

Schumacher, E. F. *Small Is Beautiful*. New York: Harper & Row, Perennial Library, 1975.

Schwartz-Nobel, Loretta. *Starving in the Shadow of Plenty*. New York: G. P. Putnam's Sons, 1981.

Scully, William L. "The Brandt Commission: Deluding the Third World." In *Heritage Foundation Backgrounder,* no. 182 (30 April 1982).

Semmel, Andrew K. "Helping Others Help Us." *Defense 82* (November 1982).

Shihata, Ibrahim. "OPEC and the Third World." *IFDA Dossier* 24 (July–August 1981).

Shuler, Alexanderina. "Making a Difference," *Agenda* 3, no. 8 (October 1980).

Simon, Julian L. "The Case for More People." *American Demographics* 1, no. 10 (November–December 1979).

——. *The Ultimate Resource*. Princeton, NJ: Princeton University Press, 1981.

——. "World Food Supplies." *Atlantic Monthly,* July 1981.

Sivard, Ruth Leger. *World Military and Social Expenditures 1983*. Washington, DC: World Priorities, 1983.

——. *World Military and Social Expenditures 1982*. Leesburg, VA: World Priorities, 1982.

——. *World Military and Social Expenditures 1981*. Leesburg, VA: World Priorities, 1981.

Snow, C. P. *The State of Siege*. New York: Charles Scribner's Sons, 1969.

Soedjatmoko. *Development and Freedom*. Ishizaka Lectures 2. Tokyo: Simul Press, 1980.

"The Somber Waves of Grain." *Newsweek,* 17 January 1983.

Sommer, John G. "Does Foreign Aid Really Help the Poor?" *Agenda* 4, no. 3 (April 1981).

Spanier, John. *Games Nations Play*. New York: Holt, Rinehart & Winston, 1981.

Spitz, Pierre. "Silent Violence: Famine and Inequality." *International Social Science Journal* 30, no. 4 (1978).

Stockholm International Peace Research Institute. *World Armaments: The Nuclear Threat*. Stockholm: SIPRI, 1977.

Stout, B. A. *Energy Use and Management in Agriculture*. Belmont, CA: Wadsworth, Breton Publishers, 1984.

"Summary of Kissinger Commission Report." *Congressional Quarterly,* 14 January 1984.

Taylor, Maxwell D. *Precarious Security*. New York: W. W. Norton, 1976.

Technical Assistance Information Clearing House. *U.S. Nonprofit Organizations in Development Assistance Abroad: TAICH Directory 1983*. Edited by Wynta Boynes et al. New York: American Council of Voluntary Agencies for Foreign Service, 1983.

Thomas, Hugh. *A History of the World*. New York: Harper & Row, 1979.

Thompson, Carol L.; Mary M. Anderberg; and Joan B. Antell. *The Current History Encyclopedia of Developing Nations*. New York: McGraw-Hill, 1982.

Thorsson, Inga. "The Arms Race and Development: A Competitive Relationship." *Development: Seeds of Change* 1 (1982).

Tien, H. Yuan. "China: Demographic Billionaire." *Population Bulletin* 38, no. 2 (April 1983).

Timmer, C. Peter; Walter P. Falcon; and Scott R. Pearson. *Food Policy Analysis*. Baltimore, MD: Johns Hopkins University Press, 1983.

Tinbergen, Jan, et al. *Reshaping the International Order: A Report to the Club of Rome*. New York: E. P. Dutton, 1976.

Todaro, Michael P. *Economic Development in the Third World*. 2nd ed. New York: Longman, 1981.

Trezise, Philip H. *Rebuilding Grain Reserves: Toward an International System*. Washington, DC: Brookings Institution, 1976.

Truitt, George A., ed. *Multinationals: New Approaches to Agricultural and Rural Development*. New York: Fund for Multinational Management Education, 1981.

Truman, Harry S. "The Faith By Which We Live." Inaugural Address. Washington, DC, 20 January 1949. *Vital Speeches of the Day* 15, no. 8 (1 February 1949).

United Nations. Department of International Economic and Social Affairs. *Population Bulletin of the United Nations,* no. 14-1982 (ST/ESA/SER.N/14), 1983.

——. Department of International Economic and Social Affairs, Population Division. *Report on the Fifth Population Inquiry among Governments*. ESA/P/WP/83, 11 January 1984.

——. Department of International Economic and Social Affairs. *World Population Prospects as Assessed in 1980*. ST/ESA/SER.A/78, 1981.

——. Department of Public Information. *Everyone's United Nations*. E.79.I.5, December 1979.

——. Department of Public Information. *Towards a World Economy That Works*. DPI/666-80-40759, 1980.

——. Development Program. *The United States' Stake in a New International Economic Order*. By Bradford Morse, n.d.

——. Food and Agriculture Organization. "Agriculture: Toward 2000." Conference report on the Twentieth Session. C 79/24, July 1979.

——. Food and Agriculture Organization. *Agriculture: Toward 2000*. Rome: Food and Agriculture Organization, 1981.

——. Food and Agriculture Organization. *Energy for World Agriculture*. FAO Agriculture Series, no. 7 (1979).

——. Food and Agriculture Organization. *The Fourth World Food Survey*. FAO Statistics Series, no. 11 (1977).

——. Food and Agriculture Organization. *Monthly Bulletin of Statistics* 5, no. 11 (November 1982).

——. Food and Agriculture Organization. *Proposals for a World Food Board,* 1 October 1946.

——. Food and Agriculture Organization. *The State of Food and Agriculture 1982*. FAO Agriculture Series, no. 15 (1983).

——. Food and Agriculture Organization. *The State of Food and Agriculture 1980*. FAO Agriculture Series, no. 12 (1981).

——. Fund for Population Activities. *Sri Lanka*. Population Profiles, no. 13 (April 1980).

——. Fund for Population Activities. *The State of the World Population 1982*. By Rafael M. Salas.

——. General Assembly. *Declaration on the Establishment of a New International Economic Order*. A/AC.166/L.47, 30 April 1974.

——. General Assembly. *Report of the United Nations Conference on Desertification*. A/CONF. 74/36, 1977.

——. General Assembly. *Resolutions*. Supplement no. 28. A/8028, 15 September–17 December 1970.

——. Secretariat. *Text of Statement by Secretary-General, U Thant, at Opening of Orientation Course for Population Programme Officers,* Press Release SG/SM/1055, SOC/3624, 14 January 1969.

——. UNICEF. *The State of the World's Children 1981–82.* By James P. Grant.

——. UNICEF. *The State of the World's Children 1980.* By James P. Grant.

——. World Food Council. *Food Strategies: Overcoming Hunger Country by Country.* DESI.E76, May 1980.

——. World Health Organization. *Strategies for the Prevention of Blindness in National Programmes: A Primary Health Care Approach.* 1984.

U.S. Arms Control and Disarmament Agency. *World Military Expenditures and Arms Transfers, 1971–1980.* ACDA Publication 115, March 1983.

——. *World Military Expenditures and Arms Transfers, 1969–1978.* ACDA Publication 108, December 1980.

U.S. Congress. House Committee on Agriculture. *World Hunger Situation.* 97th Cong., 1st sess., 21, 22, 23 July 1981.

——. House Committee on International Relations and the Committee on Agriculture. *International Emergency Wheat Reserve.* 95th Cong., 2nd sess., 13, 21 June 1978.

——. Senate. *Congressional Record.* Statement of the Honorable William E. Simon. 94th Cong., 1st sess., 1975, 121, pt. 27: 35129–31.

——. Senate. *Congressional Record.* Statement of Senator Paul Tsongas. 96th Cong., 1st sess., 1979–1980, 125, pt. 28: 37330–32.

——. *World Population and Fertility Planning Technologies: The Next 20 Years.* Washington, DC: Office of Technology Assessment, February 1982.

U.S. Department of Agriculture. *Composition of Foods.* Agricultural Handbook, no. 8. By Bernice K. Watt and Annabel L. Merrill. Washington, DC: U.S. Government Printing Office, 1963.

——. *Foreign Agriculture Circular.* FG-29-82, 15 September 1982.

——. *USSR: Review of Agriculture in 1981 and Outlook for 1982.* Washington, DC: U.S. Government Printing Office, May 1982.

U.S. Department of State. *North-South Dialogue.* Current Policy, no. 182, 15 May 1980.

——. *Opening Statement at Confirmation Hearings.* Delivered by Secretary of State Alexander Haig. Current Policy, no. 257, 9 January 1981.

——. *Tasks for U.S. Policy in the Hemisphere.* Address by Thomas O. Enders. Current Policy, no. 282, 3 June 1981.

——. "World Population: Silent Explosion." *Department of State Bulletin.* Department of State Publication 8956, October 1978.

U.S. Presidential Commission on World Hunger. *Overcoming World Hunger: The Challenge Ahead.* Washington, DC: U.S. Government Printing Office, March 1980.

Vanderslice, Lane. "Real Security in an Insecure World." *Background Paper,* no. 69. Washington, DC: Bread for the World, October 1983.

van der Tak, Jean; Carl Haub; and Elaine Murphy. "Our Population Predicament: A New Look." *Population Bulletin* 34, no. 5 (December 1979).

van Teutem, Onno. "Grain Stock Policies in Developing Countries." *Science and Public Policy: Journal of the Science Policy Foundation* 3, no. 3 (June 1976).

Varma, S. P. "Gandhi and Contemporary Thinking on Development." *IFDA Dossier,* no. 37 (September–October 1983).

Waterlow, Charlotte. *Superpowers and Victims: The Outlook for World Community.* Englewood Cliffs, NJ: Prentice-Hall, 1974.

Weidenbaum, Murray L. *The Economics of Peacetime Defense.* New York: Praeger, 1974.

"What It Will Take to End Worldwide Recession." Interview with A. W. Clausen in *U.S. News & World Report,* 15 November 1982.

Wittwer, S. H. "Food Production: Technology and the Resource Base." *Science* 188 (9 May 1975).

World Bank. *World Development Report 1983.* New York: Oxford University Press, 1983.

——. *World Development Report 1982.* New York: Oxford University Press, 1982.

——. *World Development Report 1981.* New York: Oxford University Press, 1981.

——. *World Development Report 1980.* New York: Oxford University Press, 1980.

Wortman, Sterling, and Ralph W. Cummings, Jr. *To Feed This World: The Challenge and the Strategy.* Baltimore, MD: Johns Hopkins University Press, 1978.

Yang, Martin M. C. *Socio-Economic Results of Land Reform in Taiwan.* Honolulu: East-West Center Press, University of Hawaii, n.d.

Permissions

Agency for International Development, *AID's Challenge in an Interdependent World* (Washington, D.C.: Agency for International Development, January 1977), pp. 13–14. (Updated by AID, December 1984.)

Agency for International Development, "The Marshall Plan: The Plan," *War on Hunger* vol. 11, no. 6, June 1977, p. 22.

Silvio Almeida et al., "Analysis of Traditional Strategies to Combat World Hunger and Their Results," *International Journal of Health Services* vol. 5, no. 1, 1975, p. 128. Copyright © 1975, Baywood Publishing Company, Inc.

The American Heritage Dictionary of the English Language, s.v. "hunger." Copyright © 1981 by Houghton Mifflin Company. Reprinted by permission from *The American Heritage Dictionary of the English Language.*

A.T. Ariyaratne, *In Search of Development* (Moratuwa, Sri Lanka: Sarvodaya Shramadana, 1982), pp. 32, 45–46.

A.T. Ariyaratne, "A People's Movement for Self-Reliance in Sri Lanka," *Collected Works: Volume I,* ed. Nandasena Ratnapala (Dehiwala, Sri Lanka: Sarvodaya Research Institute, n.d.), p. 26.

Sartaj Aziz, "The World Food Situation— Today and in the Year 2000," *Proceedings: The World Food Conference of 1976* (Ames, Iowa: The Iowa State University Press, 1977), p. 23.

Sartaj Aziz in "We Need Development for Sheer Survival," *Ceres* vol. 8, no. 1, January–February 1975, p. 24. Reprinted from *Ceres,* the FAO Review on Development.

Richard J. Barnet, "The Profits of Hunger," *The Nation,* 9 February 1980, pp. 129, 146.

Solon L. Barraclough, "Politics First," *Ceres* vol. 7, no. 5, September–October 1974, p. 28. Reprinted from *Ceres,* the FAO Review on Development.

Peter T. Bauer, *Dissent on Development: Studies and Debates in Development Economics* (Cambridge, Mass.: Harvard University Press, 1972), pp. 97–98, 100, 101. Reprinted by permission. Copyright 1972 by P.T. Bauer.

Peter T. Bauer and John O'Sullivan, "Foreign Aid for What?" *Commentary,* December 1978, p. 47.

Peter T. Bauer and Basil S. Yamey, "Foreign Aid: What Is at Stake?" *The Public Interest* no. 68, Summer 1982, pp. 53–54, 57, 61. Reprinted with permission. © 1982 by National Affairs, Inc.

Peter T. Bauer and Basil S. Yamey, "The Third World and the West: An Economic Perspective," *The Third World: Premises of U.S. Policy,* ed. W. Scott Thompson (San Francisco: Institute for Contemporary Studies, 1978), pp. 107, 116–117.

James Bednar, "Foreign Aid: Generosity Returned," *Agenda* vol. 3, no. 10, December 1980, pp. 3, 4, 5.

Maaza Bekele, "False Prophets of Doom." Reproduced from the *Unesco Courier,* July–August 1974, pp. 43, 44, 45.

Emile Benoit, *Defense and Economic Growth in Developing Countries* (Lexington, Mass.: D.C. Heath & Co., Lexington Books, 1973), p. 17.

Daniel Benor and James Q. Harrison, *Agricultural Extension: The Training and Visit System* (Washington, D.C.: World Bank, 1977), pp. 51–52.

Asit K. Biswas, "Agricultural Development and Environment," *Mazingira* no. 11, 1979, pp. 11–12. Reprinted by permission of the author.

Norman E. Borlaug, "Using Plants to Meet New Food Needs," *Future Dimensions of World Food and Population,* ed. Richard G. Woods (Boulder, Colo.: Westview Press, 1981), pp. 175, 181. Reprinted by permission of Westview Press.

Norman E. Borlaug, "Without Pesticides, 'The World Population Will Starve.'" Excerpted from *U.S. News & World Report,* issue of 1 November 1971, p. 93. Copyright, 1971, U.S. News & World Report, Inc.

Norman E. Borlaug, Memorandum to Pakistan's Agricultural Secretary (as quoted in Robert Katz, *A Giant in the Earth,* New York: Stein and Day, 1973, pp. 40, 41).

James W. Brackett et al., "The Role of Family Planning in Recent Rapid Fertility Declines in Developing Countries," *Studies in Family Planning* vol. 9, no. 12, December 1978, The Population Council, pp. 315, 322.

Roger A. Brooks, "Multinationals: First Victim of the U.N. War on Free Enterprise," *The Heritage Foundation Backgrounder* no. 227, 16 November 1982, p. 7.

Lester R. Brown et al., *State of the World 1984* (New York: W.W. Norton, 1984), pp. 17, 187. Sources for p. 17: Morgan Guaranty Trust Company and International Monetary Fund.

Roland Bunch, Mary McKay, and Paul McKay, "Problems with Food Distribution Programs: A Case in Point," occasional paper (Oklahoma City: World Neighbors, 1978), pp. 1–2.

Mary Alice Caliendo, *Nutrition and the World Food Crisis* (New York: Macmillan, 1979), pp. 198, 199–200.

Canada, House of Commons, "Proceedings and Evidence of the Special Committee on North-South Relations" (statement by James Grant), *Parliamentary Papers,* no. 25, 32nd Parliament, 1st Session, 18 November 1980, p. 25:6.

Hollis B. Chenery in "Foreign Aid: Debating the Uses and Abuses," *The New York Times,* 1 March 1981, p. E–5. Copyright © 1981, by The New York Times Company. Reprinted by permission.

Pran Chopra, "The Poor Are Not a Burden," *A Shift in the Wind* no. 11, October 1981, p. 4.

Commission on International Development, *Partners in Development,* chaired by Lester Pearson (New York: Praeger Publishers, 1969), p. 55.

Committee on Poverty and the Arms Trade, "Magweta or How Does the Arms Trade Affect Development?" *Development: Seeds of Change* vol. 1, 1982, pp. 34–35. Reprinted by permission of Campaign Against Arms Trade.

Congressional Quarterly, "Summary of Kissinger Commission Report," 14 January 1984, pp. 64, 65.

David Crabbe and Simon Lawson, *The World Food Book* (London: Kogan Page, Ltd., 1981), p. 94.

Richard Critchfield, "It's Time to Give Foreign Aid a Good Name," *The Christian Science Monitor,* 13 July 1979, p. 13.

M. Rupert Cutler, "The Peril of Vanishing Farmlands," *The New York Times,* 1 July 1980, p. A–19. Copyright © 1980, by The New York Times Company. Reprinted by permission.

Mario de Cautin, "Native Americans' Struggle for Survival," *IFDA Dossier* 28 March–April 1982, p. 83.

Jerrie DeHoogh et al., "Food for a Growing World Population," *Technological Forecasting and Social Change* vol. 10, no.1, 1977, p. 31.

J.P. Dickenson et al., *A Geography of the Third World* (London and New York: Methuen & Co., 1983), pp. xx, 2.

Paul Dietrich, "Central America: El Salvador," *Congressional Policy: A Guide to American Foreign Policy and National Defense,* ed. Paul Dietrich (Washington, D.C.: National Center for Legislative Research, 1982), pp. 199–200, 202–203.

René Dumont, *Utopia or Else...,* trans. Vivienne Menkes (New York: Universe Books, 1975), p. 51.

Paul R. Ehrlich, *The Population Bomb* (New York: Ballantine Books, a Division of Random House, Inc., 1968), p. 1. Copyright © 1969 by Paul R. Ehrlich.

Paul R. Ehrlich, Anne H. Ehrlich, and John P. Holdren, *Human Ecology* (W.H. Freeman and Company, 1973), pp. 10, 11, 12. Copyright © 1973.

Thomas O. Enders, *Tasks for U.S. Policy in the Hemisphere,* U.S. Department of State, Current Policy no. 282, 3 June 1981, p. 2.

Edward J. Feulner in "Foreign Aid: Debating the Uses and Abuses," *The New York Times,* 1 March 1981, p. E-5. Copyright © 1981, by The New York Times Company. Reprinted by permission.

Dr. John Field, School of Nutrition, Tufts University, Medford, Mass., telephone communication, 30 April 1984.

Isaiah Frank, "Big Business in the Third World: Gains on All Sides," *The Christian Science Monitor,* 10 July 1981, p. 23.

Francine R. Frankel, *India's Green Revolution: Economic Gains and Political Costs.* Copyright © 1971 by Princeton University Press. Excerpts pp. 12–13, 39 reprinted with permission of Princeton University Press.

Orville Freeman and William Persen, "Multinational Corporations: Hope for the Poorest Nations," *The Futurist* vol. 14, no. 6, December 1980, pp. 3, 4, 10.

R. Buckminster Fuller, *Critical Path* (New York: St. Martin's Press, 1981), pp. 199, 200.

Medard Gabel, *Ho-Ping: Food for Everyone* (Garden City, N.Y.: Doubleday/Anchor Books, 1979), pp. 32, map; 221, text. Copyright © 1979 by Medard Gabel. Reprinted by permission of Doubleday & Company, Inc.

Jim Geier, Burlington, Vt., 1981. Reproduced courtesy of the artist.

Susan George, "Dear Friends and Colleagues of the North-South Food Roundtable," *Development: Seeds of Change* vol. 1, 1982, pp. 79, 80.

Susan George, *Feeding the Few: Corporate Control of Food* (Washington, D.C.: Institute for Policy Studies, n.d.), pp. 1, 2–3, 5, 7, 20, 61–62.

Susan George, *How the Other Half Dies* (Montclair, N.J.: Allanheld, Osmun, 1977), pp. 251, 261.

Edward Bernard Glick, *Peaceful Conflict: The Non-Military Use of the Military,* quoting Indian Army Educational Corps., (Harrisburg, Pa.: Stackpole Books, 1967), p. 154.

Global Negotiations Information Project, *Global Negotiations Action Notes* no. 3, 19 January 1981, p. 3.

James Nelson Goodsell, "A Continent Resists Birth Curbs," *The Christian Science Monitor,* 29 December 1970, p. 1.

Denis Goulet and Michael Hudson, *The Myth of Aid* (New York: IDOC North America, 1971), pp. 78–79, 129.

Cynthia P. Green, *People: An Endangered Species?* (Washington, D.C.: National Wildlife Federation, 1980), pp. 6, 7.

Alexander Haig, *Opening Statement at Confirmation Hearings,* U.S. Department of State, Current Policy no. 257, 9 January 1981, p. 2.

Roger D. Hansen and Contributors, *U.S. Foreign Policy and the Third World.* Copyright © 1982 Overseas Development Council. Reprinted and adapted by permission of Praeger Publishers.

Mahbub ul Haq, "A View from the South: The Second Phase of the North-South Dialogue," *The United States and World Development: Agenda 1979,* ed. Martin M. McLaughlin and the Staff of the Overseas Development Council. Copyright © 1979 Overseas Development Council. Reprinted and adapted by permission of Praeger Publishers.

Garrett Hardin, "Lifeboat Ethics: The Case Against Helping the Poor," *Psychology Today,* September 1974, pp. 38–40, 41, 126. Reprinted from *Psychology Today* Magazine. Copyright © 1974 American Psychological Association.

Garrett Hardin, "The Toughlove Solution," *Newsweek,* 26 October 1981, p. 45. Copyright © 1981 by Newsweek Inc. All rights reserved. Reprinted by permission.

Betsy Hartmann and James Boyce, *Needless Hunger: Voices from a Bangladesh Village* (San Francisco: Institute for Food and Development Policy, 1979), pp. 48–49, 50.

Arthur Haupt and Thomas T. Kane, *The Population Reference Bureau's Population Handbook* (Washington, D.C.: Population Reference Bureau, 1978), p. 12.

Mike Haverstock, "Cali: City on the Move," *Americas* 34, no. 2, March–April 1982, pp. 3, 5, 7. Reprinted from *Americas,* bimonthly magazine published by the General Secretariat of the Organization of American States in English and Spanish.

Carol Honsa, "Nonaligned Want a $300 Billion Slice of Pie," *The Christian Science Monitor,* 13 February 1981, p. 6.

The Hunger Project, *The Ending Hunger Briefing Workbook* (San Francisco, 1984), p. 17.

Samuel P. Huntington, *American Politics: The Promise of Disharmony* (Cambridge, Mass.: Harvard University Press, 1981), pp. 248–249, 251. Reprinted by permission.

Muzammel Huq, "The Structure of Hunger." Reproduced from the *Unesco Courier,* September 1980, p. 16.

Perdita Huston, *Third World Women Speak Out* (New York: Praeger Publishers, 1979), pp. 60, 61, 67–68, 74, 83.

Independent Commission on International Development Issues, *North-South: A Program for Survival,* Willy Brandt et al. (Cambridge, Mass.: MIT Press, 1980), pp. 14, 16, 49–50, 100, 124–125. © The Independent Commission on International Development Issues 1980.

International Monetary Fund Staff, *World Economic Outlook* (Washington, D.C.: International Monetary Fund, Occasional Paper no. 27), p. 62.

International Planned Parenthood Federation, correspondence to The Hunger Project (London, 21 January 1983).

Morris Janowitz, *Military Institutions and Coercion in the Developing Nations* (Chicago: University of Chicago Press, 1977), pp. 152–153. Copyright © 1964, 1977 by The University of Chicago. All rights reserved.

Stanley Johnson, *The Green Revolution* (New York: Harper & Row, 1972), pp. 178–179. Reprinted by permission of Stanley Johnson. © Stanley Johnson 1972.

Philip Johnston, Executive Director of CARE, unpublished paper, 29 November 1984.

Herman Kahn, William Brown, and Leon Martel, *The Next 200 Years: A Scenario for America and the World* (New York: William Morrow & Co., 1976), pp. 106, 111, 112.

Robert Katz, *A Giant in the Earth* (New York: Stein and Day, 1973), pp. 40–41, 109, 111–112, and 197–198. Copyright © 1973 by Robert Katz. Reprinted by permission of Literistic, Ltd.

Adapted from Charles E. Kellogg, *Agricultural Development: Soil, Food, People, Work* (Madison, Wis.: SSSA, 1975), p. 4. By permission of Soil Science Society of America.

Michael Kidron and Ronald Segal, *The State of the World Atlas* (New York: Simon & Schuster, 1981), Map 3.

Henry Kissinger, *For the Record: Selected Statements, 1977–1980* (Boston: Little, Brown & Company, 1981), pp. 191–193.

Uwe Kracht, World Food Council, Rome, correspondence with The Hunger Project, 15 September 1981.

Charles Krauthammer, "Rich Nations, Poor Nations," *The New Republic,* 11 April 1981, p. 21. Reprinted by permission of *The New Republic,* copyright © 1981, The New Republic, Inc.

Daniel N. Lapedes, ed., *McGraw-Hill Encyclopedia of Food, Agriculture and Nutrition* (New York: McGraw-Hill, 1977), p. 7.

Frances Moore Lappé and Nick Allen, "Central American Victims," *The New York Times,* 28 May 1982, p. A–27. Copyright © 1982, by The New York Times Company. Reprinted by permission.

Frances Moore Lappé and Joseph Collins, *Food First* (New York: Ballantine Books, a Division of Random House, Inc., 1982), p. 128. Copyright © 1977 by Institute for Food and Development Policy.

Frances Moore Lappé, Joseph Collins, and David Kinley, *Aid as Obstacle: Twenty Questions about Our Foreign Aid and the Hungry* (San Francisco: Institute for Food and Development Policy, 1980), pp. 10–11, 15, 17, 24, 94–95, 97–98, 123–124.

John P. Lewis and Valeriana Kallab, eds., *U.S. Foreign Policy and the Third World.* Copyright © 1983 Overseas Development Council. Reprinted and adapted by permission of Praeger Publishers.

Robert A. Lincoln, "In Turkey: Preserving Democracy by Coup," *Army* vol. 31, no. 8, August 1981, pp. 22, 23–24.

Michael Lipton, "Salting Grain Away," *The Guardian,* 30 July 1979, p. 13.

John Maddox, *The Doomsday Syndrome* (New York: McGraw-Hill, 1972), pp. 82, 83.

Halfdan Mahler, "People," *Scientific American* vol. 243, no. 3, September 1980, pp. 72–73. Copyright © 1980 by Scientific American, Inc. All rights reserved.

Thomas Robert Malthus, *An Essay on the Principle of Population,* ed. Philip Appleman (New York: W.W. Norton, 1976), pp. 19, 20, 59–60.

Mahmood Mamdani, *The Myth of Population Control: Family, Caste, and Class in an Indian Village* (New York: Monthly Review Press, 1972), pp. 76, 78, 99.

Jeremy Mark, "Cambodia: Hope for a Future," *1981 World Refugee Survey* (New York: United States Committee for Refugees, 1981), pp. 21–23.

Kamala Markandaya, *Nectar in a Sieve,* 2nd American Edition (New York: John Day, 1955), pp. 121–122.

George C. Marshall, "European Unity," *Vital Speeches of the Day* vol. XIII, no. 18, 1 July 1947, pp. 553–554.

Jean Mayer, U.S. Congress, House, Committee on Agriculture, *World Hunger Situation,* 97th Congress, 1st Session, 23 July 1981, p. 386.

Amadou-Mahtar M'Bow, "The Will for Peace." Reproduced from the *Unesco Courier,* April 1979, pp. 4, 5.

Roger J. McHugh, "The Famine in Irish Oral Tradition," *The Great Famine,* eds. R. Dudley Edwards and T. Desmond Williams. (New York: New York University Press, 1957), pp. 434–435.

Martin M. McLaughlin, *The United States and World Development: Agenda 1979.* Copyright © 1979 Overseas Development Council. Reprinted and adapted by permission of Praeger Publishers.

Robert S. McNamara, *The Essence of Security,* pp. 146, 149. Copyright © 1968 by Robert S. McNamara. Reprinted by permission of Harper & Row, Publishers, Inc.

Robert S. McNamara, *The McNamara Years at the World Bank: Major Policy Addresses of Robert S. McNamara, 1968–1981* (Baltimore, Md.: Johns Hopkins University Press, 1981), pp. 242, 244–245, 246, 248. Published for The World Bank.

Donald O. Mills, "Cry from Third World: 'Listen to Us!'" Excerpted from *U.S. News & World Report* issue of 31 July 1978, p. 61. Copyright, 1978, U.S. News & World Report, Inc.

David Millwood, *Help or Hindrance? Aid, Trade and the Rich Nations' Responsibility to the Third World* (Geneva: 1971) SODEPAX.

François Mitterand, "France in the World" (address at New York University, 8 December 1980), pp. 6, 7.

Dom Moraes, *A Matter of People* (New York: Praeger Publishers, 1974), pp. 41, 43, 127–128, 191. Reprinted by permission of UNFDA.

William W. Murdoch, *The Poverty of Nations* (Baltimore, Md.: Johns Hopkins University Press, 1980), pp. 257–258.

Edmund S. Muskie, *World Development Letter* 3, no. 19, 29 September 1980, p. 76.

National Research Council, Commission on International Relations, *World Food and Nutrition Study: The Potential Contributions of Research* (Washington, D.C.: National Academy of Sciences, 1977), p. 54.

New Internationalist, June 1980, p. 14; April 1981, pp. 12, 13; August 1983, pp. 10–11. Reprinted by permission of *New Internationalist,* 175 Carlton Street, Toronto, Ontario M58 2K3, Canada.

Barry Newman, "World Hunger: Graft and Inefficiency in Bangladesh Subvert Food-for-Work Plans," *The Wall Street Journal,* 20 April 1981, p. 1. Reprinted by permission of *The Wall Street Journal,* © Dow Jones & Company, Inc., 1981. All rights reserved.

Richard M. Nixon, "Radio Address on Defense Policy," 29 October 1972, *Public Papers of the Presidents of the United States, 1972* (Washington, D.C.: U.S. Government Printing Office, 1974), pp. 1066, 1067.

Julius K. Nyerere, "A Trade Union for the Poor," *Bulletin of the Atomic Scientists* vol. 35, no. 6, June 1979, pp. 38, 39. Copyright © 1979 by President Julius K. Nyerere.

Julius K. Nyerere, "One Party Government," *Spearhead: The Pan-African Review* vol. 1, no. 1, November 1961, p. 8.

Robert Paarlberg, "A Food Security Approach for the 1980s: Righting the Balance," *U.S. Foreign Policy and the Third World: Agenda 1982,* eds. Roger D. Hansen and Contributors. Copyright © 1982 Overseas Development Council. Reprinted and adapted by permission of Praeger Publishers.

David and Marcia Pimentel, *Food, Energy and Society* (London: Edward Arnold, 1979), pp. 142–143.

David Pimentel et al., "Food Production and the Energy Crisis," *Science* vol. 182, 2 November 1973, p. 448. Copyright 1973 by the AAAS.

Art Pine, "Trade Threat, Third World's Gains in the Basic Industries Stir a Sharp Backlash," *The Wall Street Journal,* 13 April 1984, p. 1. Reprinted by permission of *The Wall Street Journal,* © Dow Jones & Company, Inc., 1984. All rights reserved.

Rutherford M. Poats, *1982 Review: Development Co-operation* (Paris: Organisation for Economic Co-operation and Development, November 1982), pp. 183, 194.

Norman Podhoretz, "An Overview of American Foreign Policy: The Present and Future Danger," *Congressional Policy: A Guide to American Foreign Policy and National Defense,* ed. Paul Dietrich (Washington, D.C.: National Center for Legislative Research, 1982), p. 17.

Pope Paul VI, "The Encyclical Letter 'Humanae Vitae,'" *The Pope Speaks* vol. 13, no. 4, Winter 1969, pp. 341–342.

Population Information Program, "Population and Birth Planning in the People's Republic of China," *Population Reports,* J–25, January–February 1982 (Population Information Program, Johns Hopkins University), p. J–579.

Population Reference Bureau, "Family Size and the Black American," *Population Bulletin* vol. 30, no.4 (Washington, D.C.: Population Reference Bureau, 1975), p. 11.

Population Reference Bureau, *1982 World Population Data Sheet* and *1983 World Population Data Sheet* (Washington, D.C.: Population Reference Bureau, 1983).

Pierre Pradervand, "The Malthusian Man," *New Internationalist* no. 15, May 1974, p. 13. Reprinted by permission of *New Internationalist,* 175 Carlton Street, Toronto, Ontario M58 2K3, Canada.

Roy L. Prosterman, "More Food, Fewer Children," *A Shift in the Wind* no. 3, November 1978, p. 10.

Roy L. Prosterman, interview with Ted Howard of The Hunger Project, May 1982.

Reading Rural Development Communication Bulletin, "Food Aid: For Peace or Patronage?" Bulletin 10, July 1980, p. 10.

Ronald Reagan, "Address Before a Joint Session of the Congress on the Program for Economic Recovery," 18 February 1981, *Public Papers of the Presidents of the United States, 1981* (Washington, D.C.: U.S. Government Printing Office, 1982), p. 112.

Jean-François Revel, "How Well Is the Third World Governed?" *The Wall Street Journal,* 5 November 1981, p. 22. Reprinted by permission of *The Wall Street Journal,* © Dow Jones & Company, Inc., 1981. All rights reserved.

Robert Rodale and Thomas Dybdahl, "The Coming Food Crunch," *Cry California,* Summer 1981, pp. 7, 9, 10.

Walter Rodney, *How Europe Underdeveloped Africa* (London: Bogle-L'Ouverture Publications, 1972), pp. 258–259; first published in the United States, 1974, by Howard University Press, Washington, D.C.

Vernon W. Ruttan, "Agricultural Research and the Future of American Agriculture," *The Future of American Agriculture as a Strategic Resource,* eds. Sandra S. Batie and Robert G. Healy (Washington, D.C.: The Conservation Foundation, 1980), p. 145.

Paul Samuelson, *Economics,* 11th Edition (New York: McGraw-Hill, 1980), p. 27.

Laurel Schneider, "Thai Refugee Report," *Tucker* vol. 5, no. 1, Fall 1981, pp. 2, 3.

E. F. Schumacher, *Small Is Beautiful* (New York: Harper & Row, Perennial Library, 1975), pp. 193–194. First published by Blond & Briggs Ltd., London.

Loretta Schwartz-Nobel, *Starving in the Shadow of Plenty* (New York: G.P. Putnam's Sons, 1981), pp. 35–36.

Andrew K. Semmel, "Helping Others Help Us," *Defense 82,* November 1982, pp. 12, 20.

John W. Sewell and the Staff of the Overseas Development Council, *The United States and World Development: Agenda 1977 and 1980.* Copyright © 1977 Overseas Development Council. Reprinted by permission of Praeger Publishers.

A Shift in the Wind no. 18, May 1984, p. 11.

Ibrahim Shihata, "OPEC and the Third World," *IFDA Dossier* 24, July–August 1981, pp. 68, 69.

Alexanderina Shuler, "Making a Difference," *Agenda* vol. 3, no. 8, October 1980, p. 4.

Julian L. Simon, *The Ultimate Resource.* Copyright © 1981 by Princeton University Press. Excerpts pp. 9, 55–69, 221–222, 338, 339, 340 reprinted with permission of Princeton University Press. (Excerpts on pp. 55–69 appeared in *Atlantic Monthly,* July 1981 and were revised from *The Ultimate Resource.*)

Julian L. Simon, "The Case for More People," *American Demographics* vol. 1, no. 10, November–December 1979, pp. 26, 28, 29.

William E. Simon, *Congressional Record,* 94th Congress, 1st Session, 1975, 87, pt. 27, p. 35131.

Ruth Leger Sivard, *World Military and Social Expenditures,* 1981 (p. 15) and 1983 (p. 25). Copyright © World Priorities, Leesburg, Va. 22075.

C. P. Snow, *The State of Siege* (New York: Charles Scribner's Sons, 1969), pp. 25, 30, 39–40.

Soedjatmoko, *Development and Freedom,* Ishizaka Lectures 2 (Tokyo: Simul Press, 1980), pp. 17, 18.

John G. Sommer, "Does Foreign Aid Really Help the Poor?" *Agenda* vol. 4, no. 3, April 1981, p. 3.

South no. 32, June 1983, p. 55.

John Spanier, *Games Nations Play* (New York: Holt, Rinehart & Winston, 1981), p. 381.

Stockholm International Peace Research Institute, "World Military Expenditures— 1908–1976," *World Armaments: The Nuclear Threat* (Stockholm: SIPRI, 1977), p. 6.

Pierre Spitz, "Silent Violence: Famine and Inequality," *International Social Science Journal* vol. 30, no. 4, 1978, pp. 884–885, 889, 890.

M. S. Swaminathan, "The Green Revolution Can Reach the Small Farmer," *Hunger, Politics and Markets,* ed. Sartaj Aziz (New York: New York University Press, 1975), pp. 83–84.

Maxwell D. Taylor, *Precarious Security* (New York: W.W. Norton, 1976), p. 64.

U Thant, Press Release by the Secretary General of the United Nations, 14 January 1969.

The Third World Foundation, *Third World Diary 1981* (London: Radnor House, 1980).

Inga Thorsson, "The Arms Race and Development: A Competitive Relationship," *Development: Seeds of Change* vol. 1, 1982, pp. 12, 15.

C. Peter Timmer, Walter P. Falcon, and Scott R. Pearson, *Food Policy Analysis* (Baltimore, Md.: Johns Hopkins University Press, 1983), p. 13. Published for The World Bank.

From *Reshaping the International Order* by Jan Tinbergen et al., pp. 15–16. Copyright © 1976 by B. V. Uitgeversmaat Schappij Agon Elsevier. Reprinted by permission of the publisher, E. P. Dutton, Inc.

From *Economic Development in the Third World,* Second Edition, by Michael P. Todaro, xxxii, xxxiii. Copyright © 1977 & 1981 by Michael P. Todaro. Reprinted by permission of Longman Inc., New York and Longman Group Limited, London.

Philip H. Trezise, *Rebuilding Grain Reserves: Toward an International System* (Washington, D.C.: Brookings Institution, 1976), p. 3.

George A. Truitt, ed., *Multinationals: New Approaches to Agricultural and Rural Development* (New York: The Fund for Multinational Management Education, 1981), pp. 21–22, 32–33.

Harry S. Truman, "The Faith By Which We Live," Inaugural Address, Washington, D.C., 20 January 1949, in *Vital Speeches of the Day* vol. XV, no. 8, 1 February 1949, pp. 227, 228.

Mao Tse-tung (Zedong), *Quotations from Chairman Mao Tse-tung,* ed. Stuart R. Schram (New York: Bantam, 1972), pp. 99, 110.

Paul Tsongas, U.S. Congress, Senate, *Congressional Record,* 96th Congress, 1st Session, 1979–1980, 125, pt. 28, p. 37331.

United Nations, "Declaration on the Establishment of a New International Economic Order," General Assembly Resolution 3201 (S–VI), 30 April 1974, pp. 3, 4.

United Nations Development Program, *The United States' Stake in a New International Economic Order,* statement by Bradford Morse, p. 1.

United Nations, Food and Agriculture Organization, Conference Report on the Twentieth Session, *Agriculture: Toward 2000,* July 1979, pp. vii, xv, xvi, 223.

United Nations, Food and Agriculture Organization, *Energy for World Agriculture,* FAO Agriculture Series no. 7, 1979, pp. 42, 75.

United Nations, Food and Agriculture Organization, *1981 FAO Production Yearbook 35,* FAO Statistics Series no. 40, 1982.

United Nations, Food and Agriculture Organization, *Proposals for a World Food Board,* 1 October 1946, pp. 1, 3, 5.

United Nations, Food and Agriculture Organization, *World Food Report 1983* (Rome: FAO, 1983), p. 54.

United Nations, General Assembly, *Report of the United Nations Conference on Desertification,* 1977, p. 2.

United Nations, *Population Bulletin of the United Nations* no. 14, 1982 (New York: United Nations, 1983), p. 49.

United Nations, UNICEF, "The Month When the Children Wait for Food," by Jim McDowell, *UNICEF News,* Issue 85, no. 3, 1975, pp. 27–28.

United Nations, UNICEF, *UNICEF News,* Issue 113, 1982, pp. 8, 9.

United Nations, UNICEF, *The State of the World's Children 1980,* by James P. Grant, p. 18.

United Nations, UNICEF, *The State of the World's Children 1981–82,* by James P. Grant, p. 7.

United Nations, UNICEF, *The State of the World's Children 1984,* p. 6.

United Nations, *World Population Prospects as Assessed in 1980,* Population Studies no. 78, 1981, p. 5.

U.S. Arms Control and Disarmament Agency, *World Military Expenditures and Arms Transfers, 1972–1982* (Washington, D.C.: Arms Control and Disarmament Agency, Publication 117, April 1984), pp. 2, 6.

U.S. Congress, House, Committee on International Relations and Committee on Agriculture, *International Emergency Wheat Reserve,* statements by Brennon Jones and Hon. John J. LaFalce, 95th Congress, 2nd Session, 13 and 21 June 1978, pp. 9, 11, 143.

U.S. Congress, House, Committee on Agriculture, *World Hunger Situation,* testimony of M. Peter McPherson and John R. Block, 97th Congress, 1st Session, 21, 22, and 23 July 1981 (Serial 97-Q), pp. 278, 281–282, 300–302.

U.S. Department of Agriculture, *1983 Handbook of Agricultural Charts,* Agriculture Handbook no. 619 (Washington, D.C.: U.S. Department of Agriculture, 1983), pp. 65, 66.

U.S. Department of Agriculture, *World Agriculture: Outlook and Situation Report* (Washington, D.C.: U.S. Government Printing Office, June 1984), p. 26.

U.S. Department of Commerce, Bureau of the Census, *World Population 1983: Recent Demographic Estimates for the Countries and Regions of the World* (Washington, D.C.: U.S. Government Printing Office, 1983), p. 35.

U.S. Department of State, *International Security and Development Cooperation Program,* Special Report no. 116, April 1984, p. 11.

U.S. Department of State, *North-South Dialogue,* Current Policy no. 182, 15 May 1980, p. 3.

U.S. Department of State, "World Population: The Silent Explosion," *Department of State Bulletin,* October 1978, pp. 5, 6.

Excerpted from *U.S. News & World Report,* issue of 2 August 1982. Copyright © 1982, U.S. News & World Report, Inc., p. 48.

U.S. Presidential Commission on World Hunger, *Overcoming World Hunger: The Challenge Ahead* (Washington, D.C.: U.S. Government Printing Office, 1980), pp. x, 4, 28, 76, 89, 90, 208.

Lane Vanderslice, "Real Security in an Insecure World," Background Paper no. 69 (Washington, D.C.: Bread for the World, October 1983), p. 1.

Jean van der Tak, Carl Haub, and Elaine Murphy, "Our Population Predicament: A New Look," *Population Bulletin* vol. 34, no. 5, December 1979, pp. 2, 4, 11.

Onno van Teutem, "Grain Stock Policies in Developing Countries," *Science and Public Policy: Journal of the Science Policy Foundation* vol. 3, no. 3, June 1976, pp. 208, 209.

S.P. Varma, "Ghandi and Contemporary Thinking on Development," *IFDA Dossier* no. 37, September–October 1983, p. 30.

The Wall Street Journal, "Review & Outlook—Asides," 13 April 1984, p. 26. Reprinted by permission of *The Wall Street Journal,* © Dow Jones & Company, Inc., 1984. All rights reserved.

Barbara Ward, "Foreword," *Hunger, Politics and Markets,* ed. Sartaj Aziz (New York: New York University Press, 1975), pp. xi, xii.

By permission. From *Webster's Ninth New Collegiate Dictionary.* Copyright © 1984 by Merriam-Webster Inc., publisher of the Merriam-Webster® Dictionaries.

Murray L. Weidenbaum, *The Economics of Peacetime Defense,* pp. 28–29. Copyright © 1974 Praeger Publishers, Inc. Reprinted by permission of Praeger Publishers.

Thomas W. Wilson, Jr., "Hunger, Politics, and Security," *Food and People,* eds. Dudley Kirk and Ellen K. Eliason (San Francisco: Boyd & Fraser, 1982), pp. 390, 395. Reprinted by permission of the author.

S. H. Wittwer, "Food Production: Technology and the Resource Base," *Science* vol. 188, 9 May 1975, p. 583. Copyright 1975 by the AAAS.

The World Bank, *World Development Report 1980,* pp. 35, 42, 60; *World Development Report 1981,* pp. 12, 105; *World Development Report 1982,* p. 109; *World Development Report 1983,* pp. 142–143; *World Developmeni Report 1984,* pp. 68, 76, 149 (New York: Oxford University Press).

World Development Letter vol. 3, no. 10, 12 May 1980, p. 39.

World Development Letter vol. 4, no. 13, 24 June 1981, pp. 49–50.

Sterling Wortman and Ralph W. Cummings, Jr., *To Feed This World: The Challenge and the Strategy* (Baltimore, Md.: Johns Hopkins University Press, 1978), pp. 64, 271, 366–367, 391.

Harry F. Young, *Atlas of United States Foreign Relations* (Washington, D.C.: Bureau of Public Affairs, U.S. Department of State, June 1983), p. 31.

Index

Brundin, Hjalmar, on food-for-work failures, 238
Bulgaria
foreign aid by, 214
infant mortality rate, 385
as Warsaw Pact nation, 412
Bunch, Roland, on Guatemalan food aid failures, 236–37
Burkina Faso (Upper Volta)
famine in, 10–11
foreign aid abuses, 233
infant mortality rate, 384, 385
Burma, positive role of military in, 286
Burundi
famine in, 10–11
infant mortality rate, 385

Cali, Colombia, foreign aid success, 219–20
Caliendo, Mary Alice, on population problem, 48–49
California
foreign aid benefits to, 222
land use conversions, 104
Calorie, defined, 408
Calorie consumption, rich vs. poor nations, 323
Camaroon, infant mortality rate, 385
Cambodia (Kampuchea)
CARE food aid to, 227–28
famine in, 10–11, 13
human rights issues, 278
U.S. military aid to, 277
Canada
See also North America
as DAC member, 213, 409
hunger aid directories, 406
Hunger Project in, 400, 401
as NATO member, 411
as OECD member, 411
Cape Verde, infant mortality rate, 385
Capital
defined, 408
methods of creating, 323–27
role of, 323–24
Capital development, benefits of, 217
Capital investment
military spending as inhibitor of, 272
sources, 323–27
CARE
programs and successes, 224, 226–28
size of, 215
Caribbean
child mortality from malnutrition, 12
U.S. moral role in, 280
Carrying capacity, defined, 408
Carter, President Jimmy. See Carter Commission on World Hunger
Carter Commission on World Hunger
on grain market problems, 156–57
on grain reserves, 95, 159–60, 162–63
national security report to, 272, 274
on possibility of success, 391
report on multinationals, 337
Cash cropping, defined, 408
Cassava, as African food source, 13

Catfood consumption, 47
Catholic Relief Services, size of, 215
Central African Republic
famine in, 10–11
infant mortality rate, 385
Central America
foreign aid failures in, 234–35
terrorism vulnerability, 283
U.S. role in, 280–82
Central Intelligence Agency (CIA), ITT and, 337
Centrally planned economies
defined, 408
foreign aid by, 214
Chad
famine in, 10–11
infant mortality rate, 385
Chao, John C., on desire for children, 42
Chemical fertilizers, 108, 110
controversy, 116–19
Chenery, Hollis B., on foreign aid benefits, 217
Children
anemia statistics, 12
hunger death statistics, 9
hunger statistics, 14
infant mortality rates, 8
iodine deficiency statistics, 12
malnutrition effects, 12
in population age structure, 27, 30
seasonal hunger effects, 13
undernutrition effects, 12
Chile
famine in, 10
indebtedness, 324, 325
nutrition project's benefits to U.S., 221–22
China
birth and death rates, 389
collective agriculture in, 408
famine in, 10–11
famine mortality in, 17
GNP per capita, 26, 386, 390
as government aid model, 210
grain production increases, 387
hunger ended in, 386, 387, 388–90
population growth rate, 26, 33
population planning, 30, 389
population projections, 34
as success story, 172, 229, 387, 388–90
Chopra, Pran, on poor as productive asset, 16
Chronic undernutrition, 12
defined, 9, 408
malabsorptive hunger and, 12
as normal hunger, 14
CIA. See Central Intelligence Agency
Cities, growth of, 35, 104
Collective agriculture, defined, 408
Collins, Joseph
food distribution views, 96
on food and power structures, 172
on foreign aid failures, 210, 232, 233–34
Colombia
foreign aid successes, 218, 219–20
women's desire for children, 42

Colonialism
economic dependence as legacy of, 332
map, 1914, 336
by multinationals, 335
obligations of postcolonial powers, 314, 338
Commercial banks
as private investment source, 327
as Third World borrowing source, 324
Committee for Economic Development, report on multinationals to, 342–43
Committee on Poverty and the Arms Trade, on military aid, 275–77
Communism
human rights issues, 278
viewed as threat, 265, 278–88
Comoros, infant mortality rate, 385
Concessional terms, defined, 408
Congo, infant mortality rate, 385
Connecticut, land use conversions, 104
Constant prices, defined, 408
Construction aid. See Foreign aid
Contraception, as immoral, 52–53
Cooper, Richard, as NIEO critic, 340
Cornucopia Project, 118
Cretinism, from iodine deficiency, 12
Crippling, from iodine deficiency, 12
Critchfield, Richard, on Java success story, 220
Cuba
human rights issues, 278
viewed as threat, 281, 282
Cummings, Ralph, Jr.
on agricultural technology, 117
on free market food system, 167–68
as land reform advocate, 96, 169–70
Cutler, M. Rupert, on land use, 104
Czechoslovakia
foreign aid by, 214
as Warsaw Pact nation, 412

DAC. See Development Assistance Committee
Dadzie, Kenneth, on need for NIEO, 332
Dahomey. See Benin
DDT, 116
Deaf-mutes, from iodine deficiency, 12
Death rates. See Mortality
Deb Goswami, Shri K. N., Green Revolution effects on, 112–13
Defense. See Military establishment; Military spending; National security
Defense, on foreign military training, 266
Deficiency diseases, from malnutrition, 9, 12
DeHoogh, Jerrie, on food production adequacy, 45
Democracy, liberty and, 279
Demographic transition theory, 27, 33, 408

Denman, Sir Roy, on Third World success, 341
Denmark
amount of aid by, 214
as DAC member, 213, 409
Hunger Project in, 400
as NATO member, 411
as OECD member, 411
Denver, John, on Hunger Project Board, 401
Depo-Provera, 50–51
Desertification, 104, 117
Design revolution, 287
Deull, Ellis M., J.D., on Hunger Project Board, 401
Developed nations
defined, 412–13
gap between Third World nations and, 15, 323
population growth rate, 33
Developing nations, defined, 412–13. See also Third World nations
Development
defined, 409
military role in, 284–86
as national security prerequisite, 274
Development Assistance Committee (DAC)
amount of aid by, 214–16, 324
described, 213, 409
private investor resources, 327
Diarrhea, 12
Dietrich, Paul
on Hunger Project Board, 401
on revolution and disorder, 283
on U.S. Central America role, 280
Dignity, food aid and, 235–38
Diphtheria, 12
Dissent, Third World view of, 282
Djibouti, infant mortality rate, 385
Doctor availability, developed vs. less developed nations, 15. See also Health-care delivery
Dogfood consumption, 47
Dole, Senator Robert, food storage views, 95, 162–63
Dominican Republic
foreign aid successes, 218
U.S. military aid to, 277
Dumont René, on food consumption, 47
Dwarf varieties, defined, 409
Dybdahl, Thomas, on agricultural technology, 118–19

East Africa, foreign aid failures, 232
East Asia, population distribution, 23
Eastern Europe, as Second World, 412. See also Europe
East Germany. See German Democratic Republic
Ecological perspectives
agricultural technology, 118–19
Green Revolution, 116–17
Economic aid. See Foreign aid
Economic development
basic needs and, 346–47
ending hunger and, 386
human development and, 346–47
military role in, 284–86

Economic Development in the Third World (Todaro), 27
Economic structure. See Socioeconomic problems
Economic Support Fund, foreign aid role, 232
Economic systems, population planning vs., 22
Ecuador
famine in, 10
indebtedness, 325
as OPEC member, 411
Education
ending hunger requires, 386
expenditures, rich vs. poor nations, 323
food aid and, 226–27
foreign aid success stories, 220–21
military's role in, 284, 286
progress in, 220–21, 339
Egypt
dynastic period population, 23
Economic Support Fund aid to, 232
famine in, 10–11
indebtedness, 324
infant mortality rate, 385
military's economic role in, 286
Ehrlich, Paul, 22, 37–38, 39–40
Elite
foreign aid recipients, 232–35
NIEO problems, 345
El Salvador
famine in, 10
terrorism vulnerability in, 283
U.S. role in, 280, 281–82
Enders, Thomas O., on U.S. Central America role, 280–81
Ending Hunger Briefing, 400
Energy crisis, population growth and, 44
Energy loss, from nutrient deficiency, 12
Energy use, for food production, 106–10, 118
England. See United Kingdom
Equatorial Guinea, infant mortality rate, 385
Erhard, Werner, on Hunger Project Board, 401
Erosion, 102, 104
in United States, 118
Essay on the Principle of Population, An (Malthus), 37
Essence of Security, The (McNamara), 274
Ethiopia
famine in, 10–11
infant mortality rate, 385
Peace Corps volunteer experience in, 223
Europe
See also Eastern Europe; Western Europe
famine in, 10–11
food production, 100
infant mortality rates, 386
land use changes, 102
Marshall Plan successes, 211
as "more developed," 412
population density, 23, 24–25
population distribution, 23
population growth rate, 33
population projections, 34
Exponential growth, defined, 409

425